THE NEW SOCIETIES OF
TROPICAL AFRICA

A SELECTIVE STUDY

THE
NEW SOCIETIES OF
TROPICAL AFRICA

A SELECTIVE STUDY

GUY HUNTER

Issued under the auspices of the
Institute of Race Relations, London
OXFORD UNIVERSITY PRESS
LONDON   NEW YORK   IBADAN

Oxford University Press, Amen House, London, E.C.4

GLASGOW NEW YORK TORONTO MELBOURNE WELLINGTON
BOMBAY CALCUTTA MADRAS KARACHI LAHORE DACCA
CAPE TOWN SALISBURY NAIROBI IBADAN
KUALA LUMPUR HONG KONG

First edition 1962
Reprinted 1963 *and* 1966

SET IN GREAT BRITAIN BY
HAZEL WATSON AND VINEY LTD.
AND REPRINTED LITHOGRAPHICALLY BY
JARROLD AND SONS LTD
NORWICH

TO
MY WIFE

CONTENTS

LIST OF PLATES

LIST OF TABLES

LIST OF MAPS

FOREWORD

by Philip Mason

Director of the Institute of Race Relations

Some three years ago, a director of a firm with widespread interests in Africa came back from a tour convinced that his general managers were faced by a situation entirely different from that in which they had grown up. They had now to live and do business in a nationalist instead of a colonial world. This was not just a change of government; it meant a new kind of society and a new set of values. How could they be helped to make a re-assessment of nearly all their old assumptions?

So important did he think this that he suggested employing several teams of research workers under centralized direction to produce a series of studies of the new African states. But it soon became clear that, quite apart from the practical difficulty of finding enough workers of the right calibre and apart from the speed with which events were likely to overtake them, their labours would not really produce the solution he wanted. The results would be far too massive; the general managers would certainly not have time to digest them and the work of co-ordination would still have to be done. There is no point in recalling all the discussions that then took place; it is enough to say that eventually the Institute of Race Relations was asked to tackle the problem, that a number of other firms agreed to join the first as financial sponsors, and that in the summer of 1959 Mr. Guy Hunter was appointed to be Director of the project. He had unusual qualifications and qualities for the task. He had been Co-ordinator of Studies to the Duke of Edinburgh's Conference and had some previous experience of Tropical Africa; what was almost more important, he had an ability to understand the language of many different specialists, and a sense of the practical. It was obvious that he would need advice from many different worlds, and we were fortunate in securing the help of a guiding committee whose members were:

Sir Jeremy Raisman : Deputy Chairman, Lloyds Bank (Chairman)
Sir Jock Campbell : Chairman of Booker Brothers McConnell

Professor Daryll Forde : Director, International African Institute
Professor Herbert Frankel : Nuffield College, Oxford
Dr. Audrey Richards : President, Royal Anthropological Institute
David Williams : Editor of *West Africa.*

and on which I also served.

At an early stage of the consultations, Mr. Hunter had the courage to tell the men who were finding the money that what they would get would be a matter more of art than of science. They had the vision to accept this in the sense in which it was meant, and it has proved true. But that is not to say that this book is merely an individual's impression; it is far more. It is based on the work of many writers, on interviews with over a thousand people, on work done specially for this purpose by study groups in Africa. It has drawn on the experience of government officials, of commercial and industrial leaders, of nationalist politicians, of teachers in universities and schools, of missionaries and many others. The amount of information absorbed and digested is prodigious. But it is essentially an interpretation and an evaluation rather than an assembly of facts, and an interpretation can never claim finality.

None the less, what it seeks to do is something immensely ambitious—to catch, at a moment of acute crisis and transition, not one but a series of national societies, to draw them as they are in the round, and to attempt to forecast how they are likely to change and develop. Lord Hailey's majestic *Survey* may be regarded as describing the anatomy of a continent but it leaves the way open to successors to attempt the still more difficult task of adding breath and life to the bones and muscles. To be comprehensive without being superficial; to be impartial and yet be committed to positive values; to draw together without misrepresenting them the contributions of the specialists—anthropologists and dieticians; economists and divines; historians and psychologists—and of those who are immersed in the day-to-day life of the country as farmers and traders—this is a target ambitious enough. But the task becomes even more difficult when the societies to be described have changed at so bewildering a speed, have absorbed so much from our own culture and have so decisively rejected so much more.

It may be argued that Mr. Hunter's book is likely to be more valuable to Dr. Nkrumah or to Mr. Nyerere than to the industrialists to meet whose needs it was undertaken. In a sense, this is true; it is with the dilemmas in which the new States are likely to find themselves, with the solutions they are likely to adopt and with those which would be wise, that Mr. Hunter is concerned. But surely this is just what the industrialist needs to understand; indeed, it has always been recognized that this book would be of value to far wider circles than those whose initiative and generosity made it possible. Our own statesmen and civil servants—and possibly those of our allies—our bankers, writers, churchmen : there can be hardly anyone among them, however well he knows Africa, who will not find here some moment of insight, some formulation in words of a phenomenon with which he has been perhaps familiar without having analysed it. Let me give one instance only. I have nowhere seen so explicitly stated a situation which I saw in India, which has repeated itself at lightning speed in Ghana and Nigeria. A group of the ablest and most determined young men in a changing society see Western education as the key to success, not only for themselves but for their country; painfully they perfect themselves in alien habits of thought, often achieving real distinction as lawyers, as civil servants, as professors—and in India as soldiers—only to find at the crown of their maturity that they are supplanted by a generation who approach Western values with far greater independence of outlook and who definitely reject much which they accept. Of course this is obvious as soon as it is stated, but this is one of many manifestations which need to be formulated if we are to reach a full understanding.

And surely a full understanding has never been more needed and more difficult to reach. Can we really look at these new societies with a consciousness of all that we have ourselves inherited from Athens, Rome and Jerusalem, of all we owe to St. Augustine, Newton, Voltaire and Michelangelo, and at the same time recognize in them a vigour and an independence which are hardly ever to be found in combination with long tradition? Can we put a just estimate on what they are trying to save from their past? In Asia, there have been ancient civilizations, in Africa balanced tribal societies and some beginnings of wider civilizations, all of which have lost much of spiritual value as they have grown, or as they begin to grow, into industrial nations. It is one of the first of their problems to save as much of the old as can still be saved, and that just because it is their own. This is as true of India as of Africa. In the past, it was our blindness to scorn many values of theirs which we now see more clearly; today it is sometimes a temptation to overestimate them. We have surely to try to see these and all the other problems of the new nations with balance and in perspective; we must, if we are to understand them and be friends with them. This book is the most courageous and I believe successful attempt I have yet seen to provide such understanding. I say an attempt, because of its nature it cannot be final; it seeks rather to stimulate thought than to define. It will be a dull mind that is not stimulated and a cold heart that does not find fresh understanding from these pages.

AUTHOR'S PREFACE AND
ACKNOWLEDGEMENTS

As Philip Mason implies, this is not a work of research in a strict sense. There is some new-made information in it, such as the analysis of African members of Parliaments and Legislative Councils, an 'opinion survey' among some African managers, and a great number of facts scattered through the book, obtained by personal contacts or the kindness of various organizations in preparing special figures. But in essence it relies on existing information and published work.

The difficulty of intensive research in a confined field is that local events are not intelligible without reference to the surrounding society; and that society is not intelligible save in terms of its history and of the economic, social, political, and spiritual factors which helped to form it. These difficulties are, of course, accepted by the research worker, who at least helps to bring to light the facts of certain situations, within assumptions about the wider environment which can be stated though not fully explored. Unfortunately these assumptions may differ in the different disciplines. The pure economist may take economic growth as his *summum bonum*; the administrator, justice and good order; the missionary, spiritual excellence. To some extent, specialist studies bear the stamp of these inclinations, and there may be apparent conflict between them. These conflicts reflect not only differing standpoints among the observers, but also the rough-and-tumble of human societies, in which now one aim seems most important, now another. Only superhuman wisdom could stand so far away from all these conflicts as to see them as one clear whole. What I have tried to do throughout this book is at least to remain aware of the wider issues, as each specialized subject is discussed, in the hope that each reader may be able to form for himself a shadowy picture of the whole.

In accepting the obligation to produce a more rounded picture, and therefore to cover many different fields, I am acutely aware of the risks taken. I have been greatly comforted by reference to a distinguished Committee, who have, I hope, steered me away from the worst pitfalls and errors. But in traversing so quickly the work of many scholars I am bound to have stated crudely what they had carefully defined and refined, and to have distorted here and there simply by shortening—and I must at once make it clear that I alone am responsible for the contents of this book. I can only therefore ask for the indulgence both of scholars and of practical men, in the hope that this effort to see Tropical Africa in perspective will make some bridge between them. This may atone in some measure for the omission or distortion of detail which such perspective must involve.

The countries mainly covered by this book are Uganda, Kenya, Tanganyika, Northern Rhodesia, the Belgian Congo before Independence, Nigeria, Ghana and Senegal. We also visited Brazzaville and Abidjan. In general, the French-speaking territories are far less thoroughly covered, and information about them is used more for contrast than as a solid whole. In particular, I am conscious that the Muslim cultures of the savannah countries in West Africa are inadequately described. They will no doubt be far more thoroughly dealt with by scholars much better equipped than I am. I also much regret that it was impossible in the time to visit more French-speaking countries or Sierra Leone, Gambia, Liberia. In consequence, the title of this book implies a critique of the types of society emerging in Tropical Africa rather than a survey of each in turn.

Finally, I can turn to the pleasant task of thanking all those who have made this work possible and who have contributed so much to it. In a world full of tensions and competition, and a very busy world, it has been a most heartening experience to meet, both in the academic and practical fields, so much generosity in time and trouble from busy men, so much ungrudging help from scholars far more learned in African affairs than I, so much help and hospitality from Africans, Asians, Europeans, Americans here and in Africa.

This book has been in many ways a co-operative venture, and it is impossible in any reasonable space to thank every individual and all the organizations who have given help. On the side of hospitality alone my wife and I are indebted to scores of people in Africa who have entertained and helped us in so many ways. I hope that they will individually accept our very sincere thanks and appreciation of so much generous kindness; without it, intensive travel in Africa would have become a heavy labour.

On the official side I would like to acknowledge the generous help of the Governments of all the countries we visited in putting facilities at our disposal so freely, and to thank the great number of senior civil servants and members of the provincial administrations who have helped us. In particular we are indebted to the Governments and administrative staff of Uganda, Kenya, Tanganyika, Northern Rhodesia, the Congo Republic (Léopoldville), the République du Congo (Brazzaville), the three Regions of Nigeria and the Federation, Ghana, the Ivory Coast, Senegal and Mali. We are indebted to the Belgian Government and the French Government for assistance in visiting the Congo and other French-speaking territories. We were very greatly assisted by the Foreign Office, Colonial Office and Commonwealth Relations Office and by British Missions in Africa, especially in Addis Ababa, Elisabethville, Léopoldville, Brazzaville, Accra, Abidjan and Dakar. Perhaps we could add here our thanks to the staff of the British Council in many countries; and to Mr. Tom Haighton and M. and Mme de Lusignan of the C.C.T.A. (Brazzaville) for their great assistance.

Secondly, we owe a great debt to a large number of firms, both in England and in Africa. Without their generous help in the field it would have been impossible for us to visit so many factories, mines and plantations and to talk unreservedly with their staff. We were constantly indebted to them for hospitality, transport and facilities and kindness at every turn. We should mention in particular the help and hospitality of the Union Minière du Haut Katanga in Elisabethville.

Thirdly, we have had the greatest assistance from the academic world. We would like to acknowledge a debt of thanks in East Africa to Bernard de Bunsen, Principal of Makerere College, Professor David Walker, Dr. Aidan Southall and almost the entire staff of the Economics and Sociology Departments and of the Institute of Social Research at Makerere; in Northern Rhodesia, to Mr. Henry Fosbrooke, Dr. Raymond Apthorpe, Mrs. Wateridge and the staff of the Rhodes-Livingstone Institute; in the ex-Belgian Congo, to Professors Bibouyck, Bezy, de Visscher, Leclerq and Caprasse at Lovanium and to Rector Hiernaux and Professor J. J. Maquet at Elisabethville; in addition we were much assisted by M. Georges Brausch, of the Institut Solvay in Elisabethville, by the headquarters of the Institut in Brussels and by Professor Clémence of F.U.L.R.E.A.C.; at the same time, we could also acknowledge the help of Professor Malengreau of the University of Louvain, M. Soyer of I.R.S.A.C., M. Daxhelet and M. Grévisse of C.E.P.S.I. In Nigeria we would like to thank Professor Barback of the Nigerian Institute of Social and Economic Research and almost all the members of the Departments of Politics, Sociology and Economics; and again at the University of Accra almost every member of these Departments gave us advice and practical assistance. Finally, we are most grateful to Professor Mauny and Dr. Abdulaye Ly of I.F.A.N. (Dakar) and to the Principal and many members of the staff of Dakar University.

In addition to the universities in Africa, I owe much to the kindness of many individual scholars and to the Directors of African study programmes in many American universities; I should like to thank particularly Professor James Coleman, David Apter, Carl Rosberg, Immanuel Wallerstein and other American scholars; Professor de Vries and others from the Netherlands; M. de Briey from I.N.C.I.D.I. in Brussels; Miss Margery Perham, Thomas Hodgkin and Mrs. E. M. Chilver in Oxford. I need not say how grateful I am to my own Committee for reading the manuscript and suggesting many valuable improvements.

The actual content of the book has been much enriched by the work of several 'Study Groups' which agreed to work on a purely voluntary basis in Africa, and we are most grateful to the Chairmen and members of these groups who gave up spare time from a busy life to serve on them. I should thank particularly Mr. Paul Howell and members of the group in Uganda (unfortunately it did not prove possible to collect a group in Kenya); Mr. J. A. K. Leslie and the Tanganyika group which produced a most valuable report; Mr. C. Nightingale and Mr. A. H. St. John Wood in Ndola and Lusaka, who also produced an excellent report from a large group; the Chairman and members of the Town and Gown study group in Ibadan who allowed me to see their minutes; and Mr. Snodin in Enugu, who brought together a group for discussion on our visit there. All these groups included African and sometimes Asian members.

Apart from these groups, a large number of individuals provided special papers on their own subjects, and these are listed below. In many cases, only a sentence or two in this book may

AUTHOR'S PREFACE AND ACKNOWLEDGEMENTS xix

refer to this group and individual work; but in some ways it has
been the most useful of all sources in helping to make clear the
background of opinion and events upon which the whole book is
based.

Uganda

Dr. C. Ehrlich—Paper on Uganda Economics.
Dr. and Mrs. W. Elkan—Annotated Bibliography and Statistical
Tables and collection of documents.
Dr. C. Kumalo—Research on African Managers.
Dr. P. Whitaker—Research on African Members of Legislative
Council.
Mr. J. Whyte—Paper on Uganda Political Parties.

Kenya

Mr. G. Delf—Brief Biographies of some Kenya African Leaders.
Mr. F. P. B. Derrick—Paper on Political Opinion in Kiambu
District.
Mr. C. Hayes—Details of African Members of Legislative
Council.
Dr. A. Jacobs—Paper on the Masai.

Tanganyika

Mr. J. A. K. Leslie and Mr. A. Nihill—Details of African
Members of Legislative Council.

Congo (Léopoldville)

M. Georges Brausch—Paper on Belgian Social Policy.

Congo (Brazzaville)

Mme de Lusignan—Details of African Members of Parliament.

Nigeria

Mr. M. Crowder—Three months' work in Senegal and Mali and
a number of special papers.

Ghana

Mr. P. Garlick—Papers on 'The African Trader'.
Mrs. Niculescu—Papers on Domestic and Social Life in Ghana.

Mr. E. Twumasi—Details of Members of Parliament in Ghana, and in the four Nigerian Houses of Assembly.
Mr. K. A. B. Jones-Quartey—Paper on Public Opinion in Ghana.

In addition, Mr. Tom Soper of Queen Elizabeth House, Oxford, not only provided most of the economic tables, but has checked the more technical economic material in the book and made most helpful comments; and Miss Merran McCulloch provided a most useful annotated bibliography on labour and industrial relations in Africa.

In London, I have had the advantage of help from the Librarian and staff of the International African Institute and especially that of the Institute of Race Relations, where the Director and the whole staff have helped in every possible way, and particularly in the detailed work of preparing this book for publication. The two maps of Africa were drawn by Dr. Michael Morgan.

Finally, this book should really have my wife's name on it in addition to my own, since she not only took part in almost every interview and visit in Africa and the full rigours of travel, but brought back some 80,000 words of notes taken and written up *en route*. She has throughout contributed enormously to the ideas and balance of the book by suggestion and comment; typed the first manuscript; and sustained the author through two years of intensive work.

G. H.

1 *September*, 1961.

PART I
HISTORICAL INTRODUCTION

CHAPTER I

THE MEETING OF TWO WORLDS

It is less than a century since the powerful influences of Europe reached inwards from the coastlines to the central mass of Tropical Africa. It was then little known. There were the fables, the scholars' manuscripts of Muslim empires South West of the Sahara; there was the history of slavery on the Guinea Coast or from Zanzibar; and there were the new reports from missionaries and geographers, of plains and forests, great herds of game, villages and tribes and kingdoms with strange customs—tiny inset pictures on the empty map. If we look again, now in the 1960s, we see, as though emerging from the moving shadow of eclipse, new States, ancient kingdoms changed, great rivers dammed, new crops, new cities, peoples with new life, revealed in the broad light of the twentieth century world. It is only as the shadow of foreign rule moves on that we can see clearly, without the distortions of power and the responses to power, the real quality of these societies, the depth of change which has taken place in these years of encounter between the developed genius of the West and the self-taught societies of Africa.

This book deals with that encounter—with the entry of Africa into the scientific and industrial civilization which now dominates the whole world. It is a sequence of history with a unique excitement, since it has been compressed into so short a time, the contrast of cultures has been so great, and it has come when trained observation could be directed to it.

Save for China, Tropical Africa was the last great land area which, in the mid-nineteenth century, had not been penetrated by Western civilization. The outward surge of men and ideas from Europe had covered North and South America, had swept past the Middle East to reconquer India, broken on the coasts of China, entered the mind of Japan, and was covering Australia and New Zealand. It is important—and the story of South America would illustrate this—that it was not the older, Catholic Europe which finally took hold of the heart of Africa, but the self-assured, Protestant, capitalist, industrial, scientific spirit, bred particularly in

Europe's West and North—in France, Germany, the Netherlands, England. There had been, indeed, many earlier contacts from the time of Phoenicians and Greeks: the great Muslim conquerors and traders from North Africa who came across the desert; the Arabs and Indians and Portuguese on the East Coast; the Dutch in the Cape; European traders and missionaries from the fifteenth century along the West Coast. Fascinating as it is to study the local and often lasting effects of all these incomers, none save perhaps the Muslims in their area really grasped and changed the inner core of Africa. Partly, there were the physical difficulties, though Arab and Muslim journeys across the Sahara and from the East Coast to the Congo were remarkable. Partly, there were not the techniques of movement and communication: Napoleon could not have held down Europe as Hitler might have done. But above all, although there was the will to conquer, or to use, there was not the will to change. It needed the spirit of the missionary journeys of St. Paul, the expansive spirit of Protestant capitalism, the imperial spirit of the nineteenth century European states and the growing power of their economies to give both the moral impetus and the physical strength to grasp, to hold and to change. It was not the trader alone, nor the missionary alone, nor the government alone, but the three together, and the settler in their train, who were strong enough; and these four, with their different yet interwoven interests, will figure again and again in the story.

It is worth looking for a moment at some early and unabashed statements of the expansionist motive; for, although such ideals would not be so expressed today, they have left traces in the mind of both Europeans and Africans and still play a part in their attitudes. For example, to Defoe in the early eighteenth century there seemed no need to mince words about the expansion of commerce:

It is the most unaccountable mistake of its kind that can be imagined, that one should suppose civilising Nations do not increase Commerce; the contrary is evident in all our Colonies. What then have the people of England to do but to increase the Colonies of their own Nation, in all the remote parts where it is proper and practicable, and to civilise and instruct the Nations of those Countries, so as to bring them, by the softest and gentlest methods, to fall into the Customs and Usage of our own Country, and incorporate among our people as one Nation.

I say nothing of Christianising the Savages, 'tis remote from my present purpose, and I doubt much more remote from our Practice, at least in some Places; but I speak of an incorporation of Customs and Usages as may in time bring them to live like Christians whether they may turn Christians or not.[1]

Living like Christians implied to Defoe 'clothing with Decency, not shameless and naked; feeding with Humanity and not in a Manner brutal; dwelling in Towns and Cities, with Œconomy and Civil Government, and not like Savages'.

If this has a slightly naïve and mercantilist ring, it does combine several themes which, to this day, have a place in European attitudes in Africa—not merely the idea of trade, but of softer manners, of civilized government, of industrialization. A more capitalist and less attractive speech comes from- the Earl of Carnarvon in 1854 :

In China, which already employs beneficially between thirty and forty millions of our commercial capital, a gigantic Empire is crumbling away to give fuller and freer scope to Anglo-Saxon energy and enterprise.[2]

The element of force must not be forgotten. A century before Lobengula's struggle to save the Matabele from South African concession-hunters, the Emperor Chien Lung was replying to the Macartney Mission (1793) :

As to your entreaty to send one of your nationals to be accredited to my Celestial Court, this is contrary to all usage of my dynasty and cannot possibly be entertained . . . As your ambassador can see for himself, we possess all things. I set no value on objects strange or ingenious, and have no use of your country's manufactures.[3]

Such replies, later to be repeated in Africa, had little deterrent effect. By 1840 Palmerston is sending, in classical form, the fatal Despatch to China :

Now as the distance is great which separates England from China, and as the matter is of urgent importance, the British Government cannot wait to know the answer which the Chinese Government may make to these demands . . . The British Government has therefore

[1] Daniel Defoe, *A Plan of the English Commerce* (1728) (London and Edinburgh, Blackwood, 1927).
[2] Quoted by Sir Frederick Whyte in *China and Foreign Powers* (London, Royal Institute of International Affairs, 1937). [3] Ibid.

determined to send a Naval and Military Force to the coast of China to act in support of these demands.[4]

But it would be wrong to weight too heavily the motives of commerce or imperial expansion. The passion of evangelism was as strong or stronger, and needs no illustration here—the graves of missionaries all over Africa speak for it. But the religious motive was mixed with a merely moral urge to spread 'good government' or liberty. Carlyle was capable of saying :

Surely of all 'rights of man', this right of the ignorant man to be guided by the wiser, to be, gently or forcibly, held in the true course by him, is the indisputablest. . . . If Freedom have any meaning, it means enjoyment of this right, wherein all other rights are enjoyed.[5]

We find a missionary in the nineteenth-century Belgian Congo saying to the Congolese :

I told them plainly that God had permitted the State authorities to take over possession of their country because they could not rule themselves. They were always fighting and killing one another . . . This they were unable to deny.[6]

These quotations from an earlier age are not given to reopen old wounds but to revive more vividly the mixed outlook of the civilizing mission. While for long enough such speeches have been discarded from the conversation of nations, yet they have lingered much longer in Mission stations and schools. Many an African heard them in his youth; and the deep sense of inferiority and aggrievement they left in African minds remains a lively influence in attitudes today. Form must be distinguished from content. No moral action between individuals or nations can be planned without a standard of the better and the worse. District Commissioners, African Governments, the United Nations in the Congo are honourably and rightly concerned to bring 'Œconomy and Civil Government', more gentle ways and truer knowledge to the peoples of Africa. There was sometimes self-interest or self-righteousness, which grates in earlier statements of these aims. There was above all the ignorance of men entering a society

---

[4] Quoted by Sir Frederick Whyte in *China and Foreign Powers* (London, Royal Institute of International Affairs, 1937).

[5] T. Carlyle, *Chartism* (London, 1839).

[6] V. L. Cameron, *Across Africa* (London, 1877), quoted by Ruth Slade in *King Leopold's Congo* (London, Oxford University Press for Institute of Race Relations, 1962).

whose real nature and true values they had in their day no means of understanding.[7] Yet in the long view, some of their objects were achieved, some of their ideals are still as greatly needed in the Africa of today.

The history of European penetration into the heart of Tropical Africa has been often told and only the barest reminder is needed here, partly to underline the lateness of effective occupation of the inland areas, not only in the East and in the Centre, but in the West; for perhaps the knowledge of long European contacts on the Guinea Coast has led to an exaggerated belief in the length of European influence inland of the coastal strip.

Some of the earliest contacts read strangely today. The Portuguese in 1480–90 treated the King of the Congo, who was at once converted to Christianity, as a Christian kingly colleague; they accepted Congolese notables for education and as ambassadors to the Court at Lisbon and instructed their own ambassadors to treat the Congo Court with conventional respect.[8] Later European contacts on the West Coast were not so courteous, and were indeed different in quality and purpose. The whole period from 1500 up to the abolition of the slave trade in 1807 is a story of coastal contact by the traders; and although from 1807 trade changed from slaves to palm-oil, relations were still basically the same until Lander discovered the mouths of the Niger in 1830. During this long period of the slave trade, in which perhaps six million Africans were shipped across the Atlantic,[9] the traders were firmly kept to the coastline by the African peoples of the coastal belt; their goods were 'entrusted' [10] to Africans, who in due course brought back slaves, or later palm-oil. The traders might live in their ships, and perhaps build barracoons on land in which to hold slaves awaiting shipment; but they were well aware of danger to their lives if they sought to break through into the interior.

[7] Cf. M. Sékou Touré: 'C'est une très lourde responsabilité des civilisations de conquête que d'avoir orienté leurs forces vers la destruction de sociétés humaines dont ils n'avaient ni la capacité ni le pouvoir d'apprécier objectivement les valeurs.' (*Présence Africaine*, 2nd Congress, Rome, 1959.)

[8] Slade, op. cit.

[9] K. O. Dike, *Trade and Politics in the Niger Delta* (Oxford, 1956). Professor Dike prefers this figure to the higher estimates of ten million which have sometimes been given.

[10] It was estimated that in 1848 between £500,000 and £600,000 worth of European goods were 'entrusted' to African middlemen on this system. Dike, op. cit.

Muskets and cloth and other trade goods might pass inland; the Europeans did not. They treated the African rulers with enforced respect.

The real change began with the 1832 expedition up the Niger when Laird and Lander reached Lokoja at the confluence of the Niger and the Benue, the 1841 expedition,[11] which suffered such heavy European losses, and the expeditions of 1854 and 1857 under William Balfour Baikie. Missions were established up the Niger, past Lokoja to Jebba, and up the Benue, and goods went up the river as well as missionaries. Nevertheless, the traders were still mainly pinned to the coast, and as late as 1867–73 King Jaja, having moved his headquarters from Bonny to Opobo, was effectively barring the way inland. It was British public opinion which forced the British Government to protect the Mission stations, and from 1860 onwards gun boats were making more frequent appearances, until between 1871 and 1880 their arrival was an annual event; in 1879 H.M.S. *Pioneer* bombarded Onitsha for three days and the town and walls were burnt to the ground. In the same year Goldie welded many of the traders into the United Africa Company and in 1885 the Niger Coast Protectorate was proclaimed, running up to Lokoja and the Benue river. Thus the period of the forceful penetration of inner Nigeria dates from 1860 at the earliest and it was 1900 before Lugard completed his conquest of Kontagora and Sokoto.

Similar developments took place later, but not greatly later, in the East. The Arab slavers had already opened up the long routes inland by their expeditions. Burton and Speke reached Lake Tanganyika in 1858, Speke and Grant were at the Ripon Falls in 1862, Bishop McKenzie was at the mouth of the Zambezi in 1861 to follow up Livingstone's exploration, the Bakers were at Lake Albert in 1864–5. But trade had been going on long before. By 1856 three American firms had a trade with the Arabs worth £250,000 per annum in Zanzibar, and German, French and Indian traders were there.[12] The spread of Missions across to Lake Tanganyika and to the North East corner of Northern

---

[11] 'Of the 162 white men who entered the river in August, 54 died of malaria before the surviving ship reached Fernando Po in October of the same year.' K. O. Dike, *Origins of the Niger Mission* (Ibadan University Press for C.M.S. Niger Mission, 1957).

[12] Roland Oliver, *The Missionary Factor in East Africa* (London, Longmans, 1952).

Rhodesia, up to Uganda, and along Lake Nyasa, goes ahead in the second half of the century, and here too it is in the 1890s and up to 1900 that the political occupation finally takes place. In Northern Rhodesia and Katanga we reach the same dates, despite Livingstone's earlier penetration of Barotseland.

Thus between 1890–1900 there are critical dates all over the continent. In the Gold Coast, the Ashanti Wars; in Nigeria, the conquest of the North; in Katanga, the shooting of King Msiri and the raising of the Belgian flag in 1891; in the North West of Rhodesia the Order-in-Council establishing a Protectorate in 1899, and in the North East in 1901; in East Africa the final declaration of the Protectorate in 1894, after Sir Gerald Portal's mission to Uganda.

It was almost entirely the coastal towns—Dakar, Freetown Accra, Lagos—which provided the long start of the West Coast in European education : the first doctor was trained from Sierra Leone before the turn of the century; Samuel Crowther, the first African Bishop of the Niger, was a slave landed at Freetown and accompanied the 1841 expedition to Onitsha and Lokoja as a young catechist. It was the existence of these centres of education, the long familiarity with trade, and the influence of the large Yoruba towns in Western Nigeria which together account very largely for the faster development of the West. It is an illusion to think of the Western 'hinterland' as subject to much longer European influence than in the East : the influence which counted was that of Islam, right down the savannah belt from Senegal to Lake Chad.

It has been the fashion of administrators and missionaries to describe in bloodcurdling terms the horrors of the old African life. 'Bloodstained misery, hopeless poverty, brutish pagan life' is a description by one East African Governor.[13] Anthropologists and sociologists on the other hand have emphasized more the close texture of family and village relationships, the courtesies and human warmth which supported personality with a deep and comforting sense of tradition. Both are true. Disease above all, war and slave raiding and the dangers of horrible punishment for supposed witchcraft were indeed scourges of the tropical countries. But if we take the microscope to individual lives and villages, a balance

[13] Sir Philip Mitchell, quoted in Grove Haines (Ed.) *Africa Today* (Johns Hopkins Press, 1959).

begins to appear. We can hear an old woman of Northern Nigeria tell of her long life, her marriages, the rescue of her aunt from slavery, the wars and the coming of the British;[14] we can see the Ibo village women pelting down the forest path to hurl mud at the house of a transgressor;[15] we can read the story of Rashid Bin Hassani, captured as a boy in an Ngoni raid on his village in Central Africa, carried to slavery in Zanzibar and converted to Islam;[16] or recall the accounts by Mary Kingsley of West Coast villages; or study the Lovedu,[17] so distressed by an unseemly conjugal quarrel that a village purification is needed. It begins to emerge that the misery is sustained by the culture; that it is the amazingly strong support which the evolved network of human relationships gave to the individual which made the miseries bearable and occasionally irradiated life with deep contentment.

It was perhaps the cruelty and the witchcraft which horrified the early Europeans most, because they seemed to be part of character while war and slave raiding were more external. Mary Kingsley, quoting De Cardi, mentions some of the penalties for household slaves in the Bonny kingdom:

Ear cutting in its various stages from clipping to total dismemberment; crucifixion round a large cask; chilli peppers pounded and stuffed up the nostrils and forced into the eyes and ears; fastening the victim to a post driven into the beach at low water and leaving him there to be drowned by the rising tide or eaten by the sharks and crocodiles piecemeal...[18]

Bishop Crowther, in his Report of 1877, records of a funeral:

A living slave was dressed up and ordered down the grave; at the bottom of which he was commanded to lie on his back with his face upwards with both arms stretched open; in this position the corpse of his master was let down and placed on his breast, which he embraced with both arms, when the grave was covered up with earth.[19]

Yet horror is a bad guide to understanding; it is only in the

[14] Mary Smith, *Baba of Karo* (London, Faber and Faber, 1954).
[15] M. M. Green, *Ibo Village Affairs* (London, Sidgwick and Jackson, 1947).
[16] M. Perham, *Ten Africans* (London, Faber and Faber, 1936).
[17] E. J. and J. D. Kriege, 'The Lovedu', in *African Worlds,* edited by Daryll Forde (London, Oxford University Press for International African Institute, 1934).
[18] Quoted by Dike in *Trade and Politics in the Niger Delta.*
[19] Quoted by Dike in *Origins of the Niger Mission.*

light of later knowledge that the structure and motives of African life, including its horrors, have slowly been established.

These societies were extremely varied in their social and political structure. Nothing could be politically less alike than the hierarchical kingdoms in some areas and the villages scarcely linked by any political structure in others. The greater our knowledge, the more differences of detail appear in every cultural field. Yet certain factors were widely found which make the sharpest distinction between the principles and values informing the whole life in Tropical Africa and the engrained assumptions of the Europeans.

In the first place, techniques were in the handicraft stage, often extremely simple, but sometimes including the working of iron, tin, copper or bronze for tools, weapons and ornaments. Though sometimes of high artistic value, they were almost wholly empirical. Even to the nineteenth-century European, with his limited scientific knowledge and equipment (but with a background of simple theory, mathematics, chemistry), they seemed grossly backward. But quite false conclusions were often drawn as to African skill and intelligence. It is true that Africans, whether in high forest, in swamps, in open bush, savannah or near-desert, lived much more in partnership with their environment of plants and animals than as a dominant controlling it. But as partners they showed high skill, observation and intelligence. Dr. Audrey Richards has pointed out how intimately the Bemba of Northern Rhodesia knew the trees and plants and animals of the bush; any one of them could name fifty varieties of tree and know their qualities and uses. A walk through the bush, so monotonous to most Europeans in Northern Rhodesia, was to the African an experience of constant and animated interest.

I once stumbled on a bush path, turning to look at a strip of sunset against a black cloud. The native who helped me up said sympathetically, looking at the bough which he believed had received my attention, 'Yes, I saw that swarm of caterpillars, too, but the grubs are not big enough to eat yet. I shall tell my wife to get them later on. I shall say, "Look for the *umotonda* tree, to the east of where the path forks." ' [20]

The same author notes the skill and daring shown by the Bemba

[20] A. I. Richards, *Land, Labour and Diet in Northern Rhodesia* (London, Oxford University Press, 1951).

in climbing and pollarding high trees, and many others have been struck by the dexterity, the economy of means and the knowledge of materials which Africans show in relation to their traditional occupations and needs.

In the second place, African social and often political organization was built up almost invariably on units of the extended family, lineage or clan, sometimes cross-cut horizontally by organizations of age-grades and further complicated by individuals, groups or associations with a particular religious status or function. This veritable cat's-cradle of relationships, stretching far back into the past, sometimes covering a wide area with many villages, embracing a host of rights and obligations, taboos and status rules, was intimately connected with religious observance through its link with ancestors. It combined both a rigid framework of support, certain built-in flexibilities (through exogamy and other rules) and often a system of checks and balances to avoid an undue concentration of power.[21]

This exact and complex network *was* society (and widely still is) to the African mind. There might indeed be a chief or even a king with councillors and officials, though in many African societies there was not. But the existence of a chief did not necessarily imply, as the European was so apt to think, a single all-embracing power. The fact that the life-force and well-being of a tribe might be symbolized and immanent in the chief did not imply an autocracy. But many Europeans, partly because it was convenient to find some chief from whom to ask hospitality, with whom to make treaties, through whom to rule, in total ignorance of the real social entity they were meeting, treated all Africans as 'tribes' with 'chiefs', and accordingly supposed their political organization to be as simple and undeveloped as their techniques. They had no means of appreciating the complexity, the subtle political texture, the elements of grass-roots democracy, the balance between communal, family and individual rights which have since been disclosed by patient and sympathetic study.

[21] See, for example, arrangements among the Nupe for alternation of power between three ruling families, discussed by S. F. Nadel (*A Black Byzantium*, Oxford University Press for International African Institute, 1942) and the somewhat similar alternation of dynasties in the Emirate of Zaria described by M. G. Smith (*Government in Zazzau*, Oxford University Press for International African Institute, 1959), or the complicated systems of relationships, duties and prohibitions among Nilotic tribes which made intertribal quarrels or wars less easy to start or sustain.

In the third place, African societies were dominated by an intense and pervasive belief in the Spirit. Many studies [22] have shown that there was often a belief in a supreme and all-powerful Creator, often conceived in very lofty terms. But there were lesser and more capricious spirits, needing observance and propitiation; there were spirits of ancestors, and there was a man's own spirit, or 'force' as Father Tempels has described it. [23] It is difficult to over-emphasize how powerful and effective spirit was felt to be. Scientific knowledge secularizes a great area of the world, creating a restful neutral zone in which events are due to 'natural causes' and not to powerful spirits; without such knowledge, Africans, like other pre-scientific people, could only fall back on magical or spiritual forces to control or at least influence the course of daily life in almost all its minutiae. Well aware of proximate causes—the arrow through the heart or the fallen bough on a crushed body—they still asked : 'Why this man rather than that in the arrow's path?' and found no answer in chance or the laws of probability. [24] Living with minds wide open to spiritual influence—and thereby dangerously vulnerable—Africans were constantly preoccupied, not only with the right observances and sacrifices, but with right conduct, since a breach might bring danger or disaster to themselves and indeed to the whole community, requiring communal atonement and purification. The tribesman was sensitive not only to superhuman spirits but to the quality and force of organic things, whether plant or animal, and particularly to human ill-will which might be directed against him by the strength of an enemy among his neighbours or even by the wife of his bed. It was therefore no wonder that to the Europeans these seemed to be people obsessed by imaginary terrors, worshippers of idols or devils, practising a witchcraft which had only quite recently been stamped out of rural practice in Europe. Accustomed to the classical forms of Greek and Christian art, Europeans were at first profoundly shocked by the grotesque power of African imagination in ritual and carving. There was little chance that the severe outlook of a Scottish missionary would see African belief in more sympathetic terms—for example, accept the relation with ancestors as

---

[22] See in particular Forde, *African Worlds*.

[23] Fr. Tempels, *La philosophie bantoue* (Paris, Editions Africaines, 1949).

[24] Where life itself is at stake, and it was so much more often for Africans than for us, even the Western airman is not comforted much by 'chance'.

a Virgilian piety, which has often been counted a virtue in human societies. Nor were Europeans (and perhaps particularly the Protestants of the nineteenth century) always very mindful of the doctrine of Immanence in their own religion ('The Holy Ghost is the sustaining vigour of all things whatsoever'; 'Every creature hath a beam of God's Glory in it')—a doctrine which might have given them more sympathy with the Africans' belief in the essentially spiritual force inhering in nature and sustaining it. Here then was another field of little understanding and of instinctive condemnation.

Finally, the underlying basis of the economies of Tropical Africa was the rural subsistence economy. Many writers have pointed out the profound psychological effects of this situation. In the first place, it inclines to a fatalist philosophy, interpreted often by Europeans as fecklessness or laziness. If the future is both uncertain and uncontrollable, it is better not to think about it—it might be intolerably painful or daunting to do so. It is well enough known in Western societies that there is a certain threshold of security above which forethought and effort is possible and below which resignation and fecklessness set in. The uncertainty of subsistence economies is characteristic—sometimes an alternation between plenty and starvation, occasionally complete disaster. Africans in a subsistence economy (and without the techniques or facilities for storage) eat immensely when food is plentiful and will eat almost nothing, without great surprise or complaint, when it fails. The same situation causes the intense lifelong passion for land; for land is the only security, poor as it may be—perhaps at least it will produce a few roots, a few grubs, a few edible leaves when every crop has failed. For this reason, land means not only the patch actually under cultivation, but the surrounding 'bush', which seems unoccupied to the Europeans but is in fact the reservoir of wild foods, of game, perhaps of fish. It is also a recreation ground, it often contains the sites of old villages and the graves of ancestors; it is as much a part of life as the village clearing and its huts. Again, the subsistence economy produces an intense cohesion of the community; for the individual is even more helpless than the group, if the flood or the elephants or the enemy or the blight falls on his plot. Land and the community are inseparables in these conditions.

This psychology of the subsistence economy (combined, too,

with malnutrition and debilitating disease) was at the root of many European judgements on African mentality—on lack of forethought, lack of effort, lack of persistence, lack of individual ambition, the obstinate refusal to alter land tenure, the elevation of communal loyalty to a shibboleth beyond all sense and reason.

Thus, from the beginning, there were to be deep misunderstandings between white men and Africans, due to mutual ignorance. It would be wrong to accuse Europeans generally of ill-will. Not only the missionaries but many administrators and, as Mary Kingsley so strongly believed, many traders were entirely sincere in the will to help and often to understand. Over-confident in their own rightness they may have been; yet without this conviction Africa might never have been explored, let alone brought into the modern world. Later history shows how these confusions came to light.

There is, too, a more deep-seated result of the conditions of contact. Mannoni, in his most interesting study of the Malagasies,[25] has shown the effects of the relationship both on European colonizer and on the subjects of colonization. On the European side there is apt to appear the paternal attitude, an exaggerated superiority, perhaps springing from the original decision to leave the competition and frustration of the metropolitan country for a place where the ego can be constantly flattered by an evident superiority of race. There is, too, a tendency to project on to the subject group both the weaknesses and temptations of the colonizer; the constant accusations of sexual licence and the irrational emotions surrounding 'apartheid' seem quite clearly related to a suppression of guilty desire. Mannoni too remarks—and this will be of great importance in considering 'settler' territories—that the second generation of colony-born Europeans, now more assured of their superiority, react with an intensity amounting to hatred towards the metropolitan country when their attitudes or privileges are called in question.

But the effect on a subject people matters more. As a child does not feel a need to thank parents for their daily care, so the Africans expected to receive from the paternal figure of the white man daily protection and benefits; the expression of gratitude is a way of paying for a benefit and thereby asserting independence. Euro-

[25] O. Mannoni, *Psychologie de la colonisation*, English edition: *Prospero and Caliban* (London, Methuen, 1956).

peans have constantly remarked (characteristically attributing a quality to a race rather than a situation) that 'Africans' have no sense of gratitude, and that the more is given the more is asked. 'The essential qualities of honesty, truthfulness, industry and sobriety are absent from his character, and, what is the greatest obstacle of all, the Bantu tongues hold no word for gratitude.' [26] While dependence may not bring crisis as long as the paternal situation continues, signs that the European 'parent' may be abandoning his 'children' may well give rise to furious and hysterical reactions. Ruth Slade records the passionate reproaches addressed by a Congo tribe in the nineteenth century to a departing missionary : 'You know our language and can teach us, and now you are going to leave us in the dark again. You are bad ! You are bad !' [27] The gradual growth of these attitudes of superiority and dependence was to bedevil relationships in Africa perhaps more deeply than the more obvious occasions of direct conflict. Events in the Congo will bear this out.

[26] Statement of a Rhodesian farmer in 1928, quoted by R. Gray in *The Two Nations* (London, Oxford University Press for Institute of Race Relations, 1960). Europeans in India were apt to say that there was no word for 'Thank you' in Hindustani, though there are in fact at least four ways of expressing thanks, all in common use.   [27] Slade, op. cit.

CHAPTER II

THE EUROPEANS AND THEIR PROBLEMS

The period, long in men's lives and memories but short in the scale of History, between the settling in of the Europeans and the final years of political conflict and independence cannot be character- ized by a single set of attitudes on either side. For the Europeans this was a period of adjusting their first sweeping hopes and pur- poses to the puzzling, stubborn realities of Africa. For the Africans it was a period of transformation : as among them new kinds of men and new attitudes appeared, they evoked a different Euro- pean response, to be met in turn by fresh alignments and chal- lenges from the African side. As time moves on, the camera must be turned from one group to the other to follow the exchange. Since the Europeans forced the pace, we may look first at the issues as they first saw them.

In the process of growing contact and control, four very differ- ent modes of European action have an importance which is almost equally significant today—the style of the trader, the missionary, the settler and the government. To the trader (later to be the 'expatriate company', 'foreign capital') life is as you find it. You may trade with all sorts and conditions of people, from the naked Terra del Fuegian to the Parisian millionaire, provided that he has something to sell or money to buy. There is no immediate reason to try to change his way of life, still less to assume responsibilities towards him. The trader's call on government is to maintain or extend law and order, and to leave him alone. The missionary, by contrast, is deeply and wholly concerned to change, and in African societies he found so much to change—not only idolatry, but polygamy, initiation, sexual behaviour, cruelty, magic, the treatment of children, almost every aspect of life. His call on government was for protection and if necessary support in sup- pressing unchristian customs or the revolts which excessive mis- sionary pressure occasionally set off. Both in attitude and inter- ests the settler is again wholly different. He saw in Africa not only land which could be developed (to the benefit not only of himself but of Africans), but also the possibility of creating a true 'colony'—that is, a daughter-cell of a metropolitan society, but one which escaped some of the restraints, the physical and spiritual constriction of the home country. So it was in the American colonies, in South Africa, in Kenya. His demand on the government, once granted land, is for labour and for a framework within which the little European society, the daughter-cell, can be built. It is this second demand which can only be really satisfied by exclusive possession of an area or by a political and social domination which can keep the indigenous society (which is of a different culture and *ipso facto* not a daughter-cell) at arm's length or in 'reservations'. If this demand is dropped, the settler becomes no longer a colonist but a man who has adopted a foreign country for his home.

Finally, government has its own, and different, interests. It is concerned, like the others, to maintain law and order. It will be under pressure from parts of the home electorate to favour trader, missionary and settler, whose needs and policies may conflict. And it has, to a greater or less degree, a policy of its own, a long-term policy which statesmen may conceive as best fitted to the interests, to the honour, and to the self-imposed moral image of their country. In a sense government is saddled with the obligation to make good the original moral promises of the civilizing mission, and to prove that these promises were sincere and practicable and not an excuse for plunder; it may have other promises, to settlers, which will be difficult to fulfil. The history of Tropical Africa since 1850 can be partly written in terms of these four aspects of European influence in contact with the growing self-consciousness of African peoples.

At first, the deeper nature of future difficulties was slow to appear. After the treaty-makings and the first establishment of effective rule, whether direct or through major chiefs or kingdoms; after the first terrible loss of life by missionaries struck down by disease; after the conquest of the Arab slave traders, and the end of major tribal fighting, the country grew quiet. In rural areas, where small chiefs were ruled by Europeans, the District Officer began his patient, paternalist rule, matched very often by a willing dependence of tribal Africans. A considerable degree of mutual trust and even affection grew up at this level and white men became proverbially possessive about 'their' District and 'their' Africans. In time, as some have told me, some D.O.s began to resent or avoid the visits even of other Europeans—traders who might exploit ignorance, emissaries of the central government who would not understand. So also the Mission stations grew, the converts multiplied, the simple schools and clean uniforms made their appearance. On some settlers' farms, after initial difficulties, trusted headmen and old retainers formed pockets of contentment and progress.

In this analytical age, which sees, as the subject does not, the subconscious motive behind the conscious, and which can bring later history to support its criticism of judgements far harder to make in their time and place, it is difficult to do justice to the administrators and missionaries of Africa. Both in their age found a vocation worthy of their ideals and devoted their lives to it. Over large areas of Africa and for many simple people they brought security, justice and hope. The effort to understand the past must be generous to those who worked their way through it with honesty and courage and often with a vision which we should find hard to match as we peer ahead into our own future. Slowly the underlying misunderstandings, the intrinsic problems of contact between two so widely different cultures, began to show, in a series of profound difficulties. First, there was the difficulty of making piecemeal change. A culture has a certain unity. It is a religious, economic, social and political system in which the parts are related to each other, with a set of values informing all these parts. Together they enable a community to pursue its varied ends, its way of life, and to meet the contingencies which it can expect. It is seldom static, but well able to absorb minor modifications and borrowings of its choice which, given time, become part of the whole complex and may in all amount to great change. Indeed, Daryll Forde has remarked that: 'The cultural capital of any given community is almost entirely borrowed.'[1] A society in transition will always show some tensions, more marked if the pace of change is fast; but, if it moves at its own rate, balance can be retained and vitality may even be increased. This is very different from the attempt to make from outside a sudden and radical

[1] D. Forde, *Habitat, Economy and Society* (London, Methuen, 1934).

change in a major institution, or even, as Malinowski has shown, an unassimilable minor change : [2]

> While it may seem easy to change a custom here and there, or transform a technical device, such a change of detail very often upsets an institution without reforming it, because, as we have seen, beliefs, ideas and practices are welded into bigger systems.

Moreover, what seem to Europeans 'mere' customs have far greater significance to those who live them.

> In archaic societies beliefs are modes of being; they are customs, that is to say, but customs which are ultimately bound up with personality, or even part of it. It is unthinkable, therefore, to change them in the way opinions are changed. They can be changed only through a crisis during which the old structure crumbles to make way for something new.[3]

Thus, when the administrator, the agricultural officer, or the missionary set himself to alter some African custom on grounds of health, or efficiency, or morality, he was sure to find emotional resistance. Worse still, he might well find this one custom so intimately woven into the whole African way of life, and particularly its religious sanctions, that to pull at one thread seemed to tear at the whole garment. Often enough these implications were neither seen nor guessed and the change was enforced with varying results—a sulky compliance, a secret persistence in the old ways, a violent revolt, or sometimes a consequential effect worse than the original custom.[4] Again and again this cultural unity disarmed European attempts to introduce improvements by facing the reformer with major institutions or beliefs behind a minor practice.

On the other hand, direct attempts at radical change were equally embarrassing. Missionaries who went too far in condemning or subverting local customs got themselves into trouble and had to be rescued by the Provincial Administration, sometimes

[2] B. Malinowski, *Dynamics of Culture Change* (London, Oxford University Press, 1945).
[3] Mannoni, op. cit.
[4] Cf. the attempt to induce earlier weaning of children, resulting in more frequent and debilitating pregnancies, since the old spacing of children depended on a taboo of intercourse while a child was still unweaned. See E. H. Spicer (Ed.), *Human Problems in Technological Change: A Case Book* (Russell Sage Foundation, 1952).

with a bad grace, since relations with a tribe on whose co-operation other reforms depended were upset. Indeed, colonial governments were constantly attempting to change vital elements of
African life without subverting authority, withering initiative or
breaking moral fibre.

Year by year, and cumulatively, the societies found by the first
white men were being eroded away. At the very base, tribal education and initiation, the prime means of cultural continuity, began
to yield to the missionaries. Agricultural reform hit almost equally
hard at the fundamental relationships of the tribe. The abolition
of war, the prohibitions of dancing by missionaries or government,
in some cases altered techniques, took away many of the emotional
outlets, often without substitute. Dr. Richards has described the
test of manhood and the outlet for daring and pride which the tree-
lopping gave to the Bemba cultivators : [5]

The young men seize their axes and run whooping up the trees,
squabbling as to who shall take the highest trunk. They dare each
other to incredible feats and fling each other taunts as they climb.
Each falling branch is greeted with a special triumph cry.

The same young men, asked to admire a particularly good bit of
cultivation achieved by a woman in a single day's work 'shrugged
their shoulders with the kind of pity we usually reserve for obses-
sional cases : "Yes ! Poor woman. Grubbing away all day like a
dog !" '

Elspeth Huxley [6] comments on the special festivity, the ox roast-
ing and beer drinking and dancing when the young men in the
Kerio Valley of North Kenya had completed the difficult work
of repairing the props of the water furrows on the steep slippery
rocks—'but today the Government will do it quicker with cement,
and there is no feast'. In the Sudan Gezira, all efficiently marked
out in squares, some of the tenants commented : 'We hate these
straight lines, we would rather be hungry once every few years,
with freedom to range with our cattle unconfined, than have full
bellies and be fined if we stray outside these horrid little squares.' [7]
Behind the propaganda of Kenyatta's *Facing Mount Kenya* [8] was

[5] Richards, *Land, Labour and Diet.*
[6] E. Huxley, *A New Earth* (London, Chatto and Windus, 1960).
[7] A. Gaitskell, *Gezira* (London, Faber and Faber, 1960).
[8] Jomo Kenyatta, *Facing Mount Kenya* (London, Secker and Warburg, 1938).

the same regret for an emotional life stifled by the new European ways. It was not always the direct challenge or the brutal change but the slow degradation of village life in its human satisfactions which was later to send the young men drifting to the towns and mines.

A similar difficulty arose in the system of administration. Without the chiefs, a handful of Europeans could not rule enormous tracts of Africa; so the chiefs must be used and their authority preserved. But the more the chief became the mouthpiece of the alien government rather than of his own people, the less his authority was respected and the less valuable he was to Africans and to Europeans alike. If, on the other hand, the chief retained real power, a great deal of the purpose and justification of the colonial government was defeated; as late as 1950 some parts of Northern Nigeria were described as 'an autocracy ineffectively supervised by the British' [9] and the same could have been said of many very large parts of Africa at various times. In either case, African authority was waning in the general erosion of cultural life. For it was not a simple civil power but one buttressed by status in war, in religion, and in economic and family life. As each prop, save the political one, was in turn undercut by government, by missionaries, by education, by the exchange economy, there was little left on the African side to hold it, save the ultimate reliance on their own society for social security. Later, as the schools improved, there were to emerge young Africans who had learned there something of the concepts of liberty, of responsible government, of free speech, of free personal development, of monogamy, of science. They were faced not only by the older chiefs but by a European government which supported them politically, which seemed to be in league with the old conservative and autocratic world. Indeed, government support was often to make the African system itself less rather than more democratic, since it removed the safety valves by which chiefs could be removed or dynasties changed by a dissatisfied people. [10] Indirect rule was always balanced on a razor edge.

[9] M. G. Smith, op. cit.
[10] See Lloyd Fallers, *Bantu Bureaucracy* (Cambridge, Heffer for East African Institute of Social Research, 1955); A. I. Richards (Ed.), *East African Chiefs* (London, Faber and Faber for East African Institute of Social Research, 1960); L. Gray Cowan, *Local Government in West Africa* (Columbia University Press, 1958). This point is further developed in Chapter XI.

A third group of problems, perhaps the most intellectually difficult, lay in the reconciliation of social paternalism with economic
growth. European governments—and this includes the Southern
Rhodesians [11]—felt a genuine obligation to the societies which
they had conquered, alongside their own more selfish interests.
They were at least dimly aware of the danger of complete disruption, and were perhaps more sharply aware of their own experiences in Europe. If the industrial revolution, allowed to run on
laissez faire philosophy, had in its first impact degraded and
brutalized a rural population, had created the nightmare towns
of the nineteenth century, how much more surely would African
societies, so much less able to protect themselves, so much more
abruptly attacked, fall a victim to uncensored economic pressures?
Governments in any case are unsympathetic to the unplanned,
apparently haphazard turmoil of the free market, marred by the
failures which are the price of its progress and by the hardships
of individuals through which the toughest survive. They are particularly hostile when this process affects a subject population
which is both easily exploited and liable to revolt. Throughout the
colonial period there has been a brake on maximum economic
growth through paternalist concern to sustain the older social
system or to protect particular groups. Unquestionably, this has
often been misguided. The Royal Commission on East Africa
remarked that

. . . these tribal units cannot . . . go forward, or even stand still,
under their present customary, legal and economic organization of
land, labour and capital. To . . . stand still in the dawn between old
institutions which are dying and the new which are struggling to be
born could be to court economic disaster.[12]

Yet although it was an illusion to suppose that a step into the
new economy could be made without hardship; although possibly
greater hardship was sometimes caused by paternalist hesitation;
yet the European governments could perhaps be more justly
blamed for occasional failure to exercise social control when
powerful European interests were involved than for their protec-

[11] For some emphasis on the sense of responsibility of the Southern
Rhodesians in framing the Land Apportionment Act between 1925–30, see
chapter by P. Mason in R. Gray, *The Two Nations*, supra.
[12] *Report of East Africa Royal Commission, 1953–5* (Dow Report)
(H.M.S.O., 1955), Cmd. 9475.

tive caution at other times. There are also deeper issues involved here, which will emerge.

The issue of labour supply was from the first the most difficult test. Mines and plantations, both needing large amounts of unskilled labour, were naturally the easiest way of starting the economic development of the tropical belt. They demanded the immigration of labour. For governments to have prevented this would have held up economic advance indefinitely. Unfortunately, the supposed interests of employers and the government's own conviction that Africans must not become permanently detached from their tribal system allowed a fatal compromise—the temporary migration of adult male labour to labour-lines at the point of employment. Within a short time, the forest paths, the tracks, the roads of Tropical Africa began to carry the streams of migrants, at once weakening the village life (sometimes to an appalling degree —the 1937 Census found 60 per cent. of adult males absent from the villages in West Nyasaland) and 'detribalizing' the men themselves in certain important ways.[13] Indeed, detribalization was an essentially negative concept, implying prevention or palliatives;[14] it lacked the positive corollary of creating a new institutional system which would meet the needs of Africans attracted or pressed into a new economic world. It would have horrified the European to state the bald fact that without at least some detribalization progress in certain major fields was barred.

The labour problem was naturally sharpest in areas of major European settlement and enterprise, such as the Kenya farms or, on a far larger scale, the mines of the Copperbelt—areas, be it noted, of maximum new economic development. Philip Mason[15] has recorded the early tussles between farmers and a government unwilling to sanction forced labour levies in Southern Rhodesia, and the similar battle in Kenya laid foundations for the long guerrilla war between settlers and civil servants there. Farmers and

[13] Malinowski, op. cit, p. 63. 'The drafting of the African into world economics in a special role as a cheap laborer, with all that it implies in mulcting his autonomous economics, is one of the big problems of culture change.' But there are modifications of this view, discussed more fully in Chapter IX.

[14] For another administrator's view of this, see the *Report on Detribalisation* by M. J. B. Molohan, Senior Provincial Commissioner (Tanganyika Government Printer, 1957).

[15] P. Mason, *The Birth of a Dilemma* (London, Oxford University Press for Institute of Race Relations, 1959).

mining companies, convinced that their efforts and their risked capital provided both government revenue and the only long-term basis for the enrichment of Africa, could also borrow arguments from the missionaries; it was essential to teach the African 'habits of industry'. Moreover, in the settler countries, this issue went far deeper. The extraordinary confusion in economic thinking goes back to the European dream of political and social segregation within a single economy;[16] because apartheid has focused world attention on these contradictions in South Africa it is sometimes forgotten how deeply this vision affected both Rhodesia and Kenya. Its effect was ever to re-emphasize that the proper social home for the African was his 'tribal village' and thus to frustrate or delay his full partnership in the new economic system which the Europeans were striving to establish.

In the same field of confusion lay the problems of commerce and the growth of towns. Here among all the Europeans the British attitude is the most strikingly confused. The dominant vision of African development in British eyes was of an agricultural society, based on the village, technically improved, wisely guided by more educated chiefs, and later by democratic counsellors. This would least disturb the cultural pattern of Africa which they found. Perhaps, too, it sprang from a reaction against the growing industrialization at home, a typical nostalgia for village life and the open country which was the spiritual home of the administrative classes.[17] Equally, they had little sympathy for commerce, a fact of which even British merchants and traders have bitterly complained. While they accepted with some amazement the existence of the Yoruba towns and trading habits in West Africa, they gave way to alarm at the growth of new administrative and economic towns in other areas. These were indeed slums, shack-towns, a focus of unemployment, detribalization, indiscipline, prostitution, drunkenness and political agitation. As, at any given time, the existing towns were necessary, government policy

[16] See particularly S. H. Frankel, 'The Tyranny of Economic Paternalism in Africa', *Optima* (Supplement), October 1960, and the same author's *The Economic Impact on Underdeveloped Societies* (Oxford, Blackwell, 1952), pp. 135–6.
[17] Cf. in 1961, Victor Bonham-Carter: 'The village, as the *small* community, serves the deepest needs of human personality.' (*The Listener*, April 6, 1961)—a view which neither an ancient Greek nor a modern Frenchman would accept.

too often issued as a half-hearted attempt to prevent them from growing and to discipline them—a continuous minor harrying of the urban African by permits and passes, hygienic regulations, licensing, ineffective efforts to control room densities, and, as a concession to positive action, the establishment of 'community centres' for communities which did not exist. If one of the happier pictures of colonial Africa is that of a District Officer and local chief proudly surveying a cotton crop or a new village well, the most gloomy is that of the police in East Africa harrying the vegetable sellers, usually women, on a periodic round-up of unauthorized markets in an urban estate.

It was much the same with commerce. The rich agricultural community which was the aim was bound in the end to involve an exchange economy—money, traders, middlemen, credit, contracts (even lawyers to enforce them), distribution and consumer industries and services. Yet those who provided these services—Asians and Arabs in East Africa, mainly Africans in the West—had little sympathy or help from the administration. The dangers were always more considered than the opportunities. It was felt to be the duty of the Government to protect the Africans both from the merchants and moneylenders (there was an echo of Indian experience here) and from themselves. Systems of licensing, regulations, statutory boards, Marketing Organizations, government enterprise and reliance on the large, easily handled expatriate companies sprang up on every hand. It was a later and minor modification of this attitude which started training courses for African traders and carefully regulated revolving loans to train them in the use of credit.

The economic implications of this attitude are not relevant here; it is enough to record the frustration, suspicion and often hardship which this attitude caused to the literate or semi-literate African trying to find in the town a use for his abilities and an escape from the constriction of village tribal life.

While these embarrassments began to be felt in cultural change, in administration, and in economic policy, the greatest achievement and the most profound problem for the Europeans lay in education. The original missionary commitment to give to Africans a Western education in a Western language is the key historical event of this whole time. However slowly, it unrolled before African eyes a great unknown world of thought and power, and

gave them access to all its secrets. Yet strangely few among the
Europeans foresaw and accepted, in all their reality, the consequences of this act. There were indeed many, particularly among
the settlers, who felt the underlying threat and made their protest.
But the whole enterprise from metropolitan Europe was the
prisoner of its own ideals : the Europeans had indeed come not
merely to conquer but to civilize and develop. Without education
neither missionary, farmer, nor government could make a start.
The reasons were at first so simple—the missionary must have a
reader, a simple teacher; government, a clerk to keep its records;
the farmer, a headman who could handle new methods and new
tools. Yet none foresaw that as new light began to break in on
fresh and active minds all over Africa, there could be no way of
limiting to such simple tasks the dreams and visions which would
come. In due course, the educated townsman was to appear, fluent
in a Western language, contemptuous of agricultural life. He
found the European unprepared to accept him, suspicious, too
often hostile. Here many of the seeds of bitterness were sown.

All unwittingly, too, in the gift of education the European had
admitted the African to his own ideals. He taught—he could not
avoid it—a religion of humility and poverty, a politics of democracy; and he seemed, as a colonial ruler, to practise neither. It
was not for him to point out the inevitable gap in Europe between
the kingdom of this world and the kingdom of heaven.[18] He came,
dowered with immense technical power, labelled as Christian, a
self-confessed reformer, before a most observant African audience,
and he showed them the secrets of his beliefs—the struggle for
freedom and the equality and brotherhood of man. By these he
was to be judged.

If these problems affected every European group, there were
differences in national character and style which have their interest for the future. Perhaps the British in non-settler territories
were most firm in their conception of trusteeship, an intention, at
however distant a time, to hand over an African society to Africans. Hence in part the effort to maintain African local rule, the
emphasis on rural life, the difficulties of both. In education the
British aim would be to train the rural craftsmen, the teacher, and
then the impartial civil servant, the local counsellor, the forester,

[18] A C.S.M. teacher once described to us her shock and misgivings when
an African pupil told of his longing to see 'your great Christian London'.

the doctor, perhaps the scientist. For lawyers, tradesmen and townsmen they had little time—here were to be the opponents of the future. French policy, though modified, was aimed far more at the creation of a French society in Africa. It was logical, then, to sweep away unsuitable forms of African government and substitute a French administration, and this simpler policy avoided much of the juggling which the British had to do, and was perhaps easier for Africans to grasp. It was to leave a later problem of reviving African initiative and an African style in rural areas so long used to centralizing methods. More sympathetic to the town (where civilization grows), with more emphasis on intellect and less on character, the French could more easily conceive the *évolué*—a trained lawyer perhaps, speaking good French, fit to be a *député* in Paris.[19] Perhaps at this very general level, Portugal should come with France, as an even more extreme version of incorporating overseas 'Provinces' with Portugal herself [20] and of turning Africans, however slowly, and at a more humble level, into Portuguese citizens, traders and peasants.[21]

Belgian policy again strikes a different chord. Its dominant note was to turn the Congo [22] into a great industrial and commercial enterprise in partnership with Belgium. It was primarily to this end (with a parallel and powerful missionary effort) that the massive Belgian educational programme was directed, creating an extension of primary education and industrial training to artisan levels unrivalled in any part of Tropical Africa and accompanied by a far-reaching programme of industrial insurance and social regulation. The aim of education was the good workman or the Catholic priest.[23] If there had to be *évolués,* Belgium, like Portugal, would apply Defoe's test of manners—'clothing with decency,

[19] The first *député* from Senegal was elected to Paris in 1870.

[20] 'The Overseas Provinces of Portugal are an integral part of the unitary Portuguese Republic.' . . . 'We face here only one fact : Portugal is entitled to declare that she does not administer territories which fall into the category of non-selfgoverning territories.' (Representative of Brazil before the 4th Committee of the 11th General Assembly (U.N.), January, 1957.)

[21] About 1 per cent of 11 million Africans in Portuguese territories were 'assimilado' in 1961.

[22] When 'Congo' is used, it refers to the Congo under Belgian administration or to the succeeding independent Congo Republic. République du Congo is invariably used for the ex-French country with its capital at Brazzaville.

[23] Nine out of the first twelve graduates of Lovanium University at Leopoldville entered the Catholic Ministry.

I. Traders on the West African coast.   From an eighteenth-century print

[By courtesy of the United Africa Company Ltd

28]

II. Seismic drillers of Shell-B.P. in the Niger delta. The column of mud and water is from a seismic shot [*A Shell photograph*

eating with humanity'—before awarding a *Carte* to admit them, if grudgingly, to European life.

National style is reflected in the monuments which each European power was to leave in Africa. Perhaps the best of British achievement will be the Gezira cotton, the lovely cultivations of the Kikuyu below Mount Kenya, the coffee on Kilimanjaro or the quiet palm plantations, largely African-managed, above Calabar. The French, with a certain Roman feeling, leave cities and buildings—Dakar and Abidjan; the Belgians, industry and a massive group of artisans. Both British and French were to leave rulers trained in their different ways; only the British would leave, in North Nigeria, the old régime transformed but still in power.

It may be worth while to put into broad perspective this account of the formation of attitudes during the main impact of Europe on Tropical Africa.

The lateness of effective European penetration greatly widened the gap between Western and African cultures. It was not medieval Europe but a Europe which had passed through the scientific revolution of the seventeenth century and much of the industrial revolution of the nineteenth century which broke in upon an Africa which had suffered neither. Each system had a certain unity in which technical, social, religious and economic systems were interrelated and held together by the relevant motives and values—and they were utterly different. Here is the origin of misunderstanding.

On the African side, techniques were at the level of empirical crafts; the social system was based on intricate extensions of the family; religion and magic pervaded great areas of life already neutralized in the scientific West : a subsistence economy held the great majority in its psychological grip—the passion for land, the negation of forethought and creative energy by an overwhelming insecurity. Judgements of this system by Europeans ignorant of its real working and contemptuous of its results led to the 'myths' of African character and society which have lasted long in European thinking. Further, these myths were in part created and in part reinforced by the profound psychological relationship between rulers and ruled—assertiveness and projection on the European side, 'dependence' with its possibility of furious reaction on the African.

On the European side, four different and in part conflicting modes of approach—of the trader, missionary, settler and government—led to cultural tensions and contradictions. While there could be a fairly easy compromise between trader, missionary and government, the settler-colonist ideal, based on the creation of a daughter-cell of European society, was almost completely irreconcilable. The different approaches of major European Powers in handling the problems of cultural clash reflected the underlying philosophy and eventual aims of the Power concerned.

It was not long before the inherent difficulties of the relationship in Africa came to light, despite many areas of peaceful patriarchal rule in the rural sector. The difficulties of making either piecemeal or radical change; the conflict between efforts to sustain a native system of authority and efforts to destroy its basis; the conflict between paternal social care and economic growth; the unlimitable liability of education; the underlying contrast between Christian and democratic preaching and the necessities of colonial rule—these were among the prime origins of struggles which were to come.

Finally, it may seem that this account has emphasized only the misunderstandings, the difficulties and the failures. This is natural since it is designed to trace the origins of conflict. What must be stressed, as in the opening paragraph of this book, is the transformation of Africa in less than 100 years—not merely the technical advance but the assimilation of two such different cultures, the emergence of new societies. In a struggle with manifold difficulties and misunderstandings this could only have been achieved by the creation of trust and good faith between individuals, by the fact that here and there, in ten thousand instances all over Africa and all through the long years, men devoted themselves with a personal sincerity and humility to the gigantic tasks which faced them.

CHAPTER III

THE AFRICANS—DEPENDENCE, CONFLICT, INDEPENDENCE

I

Africans were not always so greatly alarmed, or even so impressed as is sometimes supposed, by the first Europeans whom they saw. Some came as lowly missionaries or explorers, often in need of help and hospitality, which they constantly received even among people of infinite poverty. Some came to deal with kings self-confident in their power. By the nineteenth century the rulers of the West African Coast had long experience of the Europeans' ways and were well aware of their internal quarrels. In Central and East Africa perhaps the missionaries made the greatest impact, because they came, not as slave raiders, which all other foreigners had been, but preaching a religion and healing the sick. Certainly the white men could do most remarkable things, with fire-arms and medicines; sometimes they were a useful protection against slave raiders, or a trump card of prestige against a rival tribe. Sometimes, indeed, they were regarded as gods or great magicians; but the more advanced peoples—for example, the Muslim Fulani kingdoms of Northern Nigeria—were certainly not impressed in such ways, and the statuettes of Portuguese soldiers and officials produced in bronze by West Coast craftsmen are naturalistic and not invested with religious or cultural awe. In the early days, while many African rulers allowed missionaries to teach, though perhaps on sufferance, it was frequently only a small proportion of their people, often outcasts,[1] who were converted; while many admired European techniques, they were often surprised and contemptuous of their strange social and political ideas relating to work or women or war or religion. Even when in full co-operation, and after signing one of the thousands of treaties which the Europeans pressed upon African chiefs, they had little idea (save where direct conquest was involved) that their association with Europeans was to imply not merely subjection but a radical change of

[1] Cf. Oliver, op. cit., and also C. Achebe, *Things Fall Apart* (London, Heinemann, 1958).

their whole social and political way of life. Many chiefs who made
an allocation of land to Europeans supposed that this, like any
other allocation, simply gave user, not freehold (which was unknown), and that the land remained part of the tribal inheritance.
The discovery of such mistakes helped to create the belief that
Europeans had swindled the African people out of their land. In
the long sequence between the first European appearance, the
Chartered Company, and finally the government, many African
peoples and rulers drifted almost imperceptibly from hosts to
treaty partners to subjects of the Crown. It was the Niger Company which conquered the Nupe kingdom of Nigeria and sacked
its capital, Bida; but it was Captain Lugard, acting for the British
Government, who in the next decade defeated first Kontagora and
then Sokoto.

These differences in early history remain lively influences today.
The Africans of Nyasaland look back to treaty relationships with
the British Crown, as do the kingdom of Buganda,[2] the Lozi, the
Masai. In Southern Rhodesia, on the other hand, and in some
French West African territories, there is the direct memory of
conquest. Nor do these memories work only on the African side;
I was strongly reminded by a senior European in Salisbury in
1961 that the Mashona and Matabele were conquered peoples,
with the implication that Colonial Office methods towards Protectorates were not for export to the South.

Away from the main centres, white influence spread out from
small, scattered points, the District headquarters and above all the
Mission stations and their schools. It was in the rural areas that
dependence became strongest. It has some affinity with the moods
of adolescence—the alternation between willing acceptance and
sudden sulky revolt. The European [3] was powerful, to be respected
(also to be irreverently nicknamed), best accepted and loved when
nearest to his godlike image. But there remained a deep element of
suspicion and its companion, secretiveness, especially at a touch
on the quivering sensitivity concerning land. 'I am not such a fool

[2] Uganda, the whole Protectorate, Buganda, the area of the Baganda, or
Ganda people. The Lozi are the ruling group of Barotseland. I have used
Matabele, as the well-known form, though Ndebele is more correct. I do not
claim consistency!

[3] For some detailed description of the image of the European in African
eyes (Ghana), see G. Jahoda, *White Man* (London, Oxford University Press
for Institute of Race Relations, 1961).

that I cannot see that his methods are better than mine; but if we followed his methods, the whites would see that our land is good and take it away from us as they have done before.'[4] So said a Zulu chief, looking at a demonstration plot of maize. This deep suspicion persists to this day; it may even reappear, directed against an African government—it is the peasant's world-wide passion for his land.

Dependence, too, implies a hesitation to take responsibility. Many Europeans have had great trouble in stepping down from their paternal role. In the Sudan Gezira scheme,[5] 'The local villagers' first reaction to promptings towards responsibility had been : "You decide for us : we will only quarrel among ourselves." Later they were apt to go to the opposite extreme and resent any interference or advice from the field staff.' This sequence of violent reaction if responsibility is thrust upon a dependent group has been repeated again and again, both in the growth of Co-operatives and in the political field. Even in Trade Unions, the first tendency might be to choose the white supervisor as leader, followed by reversion to the wildest extremist.[6]

Finally, as an outcome of these contacts at rural level, if change was pressed too fast, if the missionaries denounced polygamy too fiercely, if the dances were stopped, the digging of terraces was too laborious, goats were prohibited, chiefs removed, there might be a purely regressive and violent rebellion. The African Messianic movements, flat refusal to co-operate, armed revolt, many elements in the Mau Mau rebellion, much of the nostalgia in *Facing Mount Kenya*, all testify to this danger.

2

But it was the exact reverse of the nostalgia which was to count for the future. From education, from ideas moving from mouth to mouth, from direct contact with Europeans, there came to be a growing number of Africans who were to make European ways their model. In the villages, as one system changed, another was growing in its place. Even in a remote area, among the Mekhadma

[4] Quoted by Max Gluckman, *Custom and Conflict in Africa* (Oxford, Blackwell, 1959).

[5] Gaitskell, op. cit.

[6] See W. A. Warmington, *A West African Trade Union* (London, Oxford University Press, 1960).

far out in the French Sahara,[7] exactly the same tendencies are found—

a tendency for the patriarchal family to weaken and to transform itself into a series of conjugal families . . . numerous young people, seeking to escape from paternal authority . . . the tribal system is in full decay . . . in place of tribal organization there will be substituted a new structure of social organization. Officials and public employees and traders are forming little by little a kind of 'middle class' which is perhaps the embryo of the Saharan social system of tomorrow.

Here was a general pattern. It was a still faster change for those who went to the towns into employment—in commerce or industry or mining or in the European government offices. It represents a change of perspective of fundamental importance. The European system, previously regarded as a kind of arbitrary and often incomprehensible interference, suddenly becomes attractive. Its amazing power to create wealth, to control disease, to liberate from fear, begins to impress. In contrast, traditional society, previously accepted simply as life with its ups and downs, is suddenly seen as unnecessary poverty, avoidable ill-health, irksome and unprogressive tribal disciplines, the futile worship of impotent gods. It was not a group who made this decision, but a host of scattered individuals, some seeing much of the new vision, some only a hazy glimpse of a single part. But together they are to be the revolution—they have become themselves part of the corroding influence on their own society, a widespread reinforcement of the agencies of change. Henceforth, European education, language, dress, the tin roof, the bicycle, the brick house, the radio set and, one day, the motor-car were the aims of progress and the symbols of status.

It is important that this is far from a complete break with African tradition. In the towns, life would have been insupportable without some form of substitute for the traditional social life. In fact, various institutions were adopted or adapted from the rural background to give support to the lonely individual. There is an immense growth of associations of all sorts, partly new, partly tribally modelled. Dr. Banton, in his study of Freetown,[8] records the mushroom growth of social clubs, with their array of officers

[7] 'Les Mekhadma', *Prohuza* (Paris, 1960) (Trans.).
[8] M. Banton, *West African City* (London, Oxford University Press for International African Institute, 1957).

carrying European titles. Claud Tarditz [9] records how, in Porto Novo, Christian and animist traditions are carried on simultaneously—of eighteen 'middle-class' families who were polygamous, sixteen also described themselves as Christian. Balandier,[10] in his classical study of Brazzaville, notes the urgent need for the African townsman to establish his identity, to find a social niche and a substitute for the participation in traditional life which formed and protected his personality.

Much has been written about the emergence of an African 'middle class'.[11] But in the 1920s and 1930s this would have been a false analogy. There were, mainly, on the West Coast, a certain number of well-educated men, entering the Civil Service, the professions and journalism; and there were men of ruling families, still both rich and influential under indirect rule. These were leading men, mainly concentrated in the cities. Often much westernized in outlook, they entered into the problems of power and politics at a level far above that of the general African life around them. But at a simpler level, among those with primary schooling, the far larger mass of 'new' Africans began to grow up. They were new because they accepted new ideas; but they held neither power nor wealth. Working in subordinate posts, perhaps wearing some European clothes, they lived at home in the full context of African life, subject to its family laws, weighing the Christianity of the Mission school against traditional observance and perhaps witchcraft. They were able to see, though dimly, the new horizons, and able to read books, strangely assorted, to open still wider the door of new thoughts. They worked in offices, mines, garages, as messengers and clerks under the European, or found means to trade, to build African housing, to open a carpenter's shop or a bar. They were at least in mind 'detribalized', because they no longer saw the tribal community as the final horizon though they still relied upon it for social security; and they were anxious to enter the European type of world. In social position they would run from the

[9] Tarditz, *Porto Novo* (Paris, Mouton et Cie., 1958).

[10] G. Balandier, *Sociologie des Brazzavilles Noirs* (Paris, Armand Colin, 1955). 'Dans cette société nouvelle, mediocrement structurée, le citadin noir cherche à se situer; il le fait en multipliant les distinctions, qu'il s'agisse de la profession, de la foi adoptée ou de tous autres engagements ou conditions particuliers . . . il s'efforce de trouver des substituts aux anciennes participations qui déterminaient et protégeaient sa personalité.'

[11] For the development of the African 'middle class', see collection of papers for the XXIXth Session of INCIDI (Brussels, Compte Rendu, 1956).

primary teacher, and the senior clerk, with brief-case and well-pressed suit, to much humbler levels, men from village schools clinging sometimes with difficulty to town life in a constant change of temporary work. They saw little of the European save his authority as employer or ruler; they watched and talked and explored the possibility of a different way of life.

This emerging group of Africans often met the coldest reception from the Europeans themselves. Certainly, those who had risen high enough in the schools were accepted and encouraged in taking work as teachers, government or commercial clerks, agricultural demonstrators, medical assistants and the like, and they often had a life-long friend in their old European headmaster. But they were socially still far outside the European circle. Indeed, from their emergence dates an increasing hostility between European and African. To the white men, they seemed neither fish nor fowl, without the virtues of the African peasant or the European himself. Industry in particular liked to take and train raw labour from the bush rather than employ the African with schooling; in the Copperbelt I was repeatedly assured of this as late as 1958.

Moreover, the Europeans were drawing apart. There were more of them, with families, enough to form a club and a private social life. They saw less of the African outside working hours. *'Nous avons perdu nos blancs'*, said the Congolese villagers when the Belgians began to bring their families to the Congo—a phrase which the unemployed of Leopoldville were to use again in the dark days of 1960. Those in the bush seldom if ever saw the best-educated Africans, soon to include graduates. They saw the older chiefs and headmen and the half- or quarter-educated, and compared them to the detriment of the latter. Those in the towns never saw the rural African at his best.

There was family life and more Europeans on the station. They saw less of the Africans in the setting where they were superb, as watermen or hunters. They saw more of them as misfits in urban and industrial life. They travelled less in the African way and among Africans and more by motor car . . .[12]

Too often the wives generalized on 'African' character from

[12] An ex-Provincial Commissioner in Nyasaland, quoted by Colin Leys and Cranford Pratt (Ed.) in *A New Deal in Central Africa* (London, Heinemann, 1960). He is referring to the 1930s.

their knowledge of inexperienced servants stumbling blindly through the routines of a European household.

Certainly, these European attitudes were more marked in the 'settler' countries, and above all in the Rhodesias, where a class of white artisans and clerks was potentially threatened by African advance. The attitude of many Rhodesians and of much of the Rhodesian press towards Africans has been described by many writers; it is only necessary to record here the deep sense of in-dignity and bitterness and the appalling damage to race relations which the worst examples of it have caused. The employment of European women as secretaries and clerks, giving orders to Afri-cans, was often especially unfortunate. But even elsewhere, as more Europeans appeared who were neither missionaries nor administrators (both in their way dedicated men), sourness and hostility began to grow. The colour bar only becomes painful or important when there are real possibilities of contact. While the white man is a god, he can and should be aloof; but when an African can speak his language, drive his car, wear his clothes, and worship his god, it is different. Moreover, the Europeans per-sisted in their view that Africans must continue to live in a tribal society. Even on the Copperbelt, in a melting-pot where more than 70 different tribes might be represented on a single mine, the first thought of employers was that the African workers should be represented, not by a Trade Union, but by tribal elders.[13] It was not long before this emphasis on traditional needs and structures, even the attempt to adapt a too academic European education to African needs, was taken by the modernist Africans as a deliberate attempt to delay African advance.

All through these developments a genuine goodwill was seeking to reach down from the European administration, multiplying the schools and training courses, planning agricultural reform, con-cerned for social welfare, fostering local self-government. The very best of the African graduates and civil servants, now more europeanized, moved towards the position of favourite sons. But much of this goodwill was lost or destroyed a little lower down, among 'the insulted and injured', the clerks and small traders, the employees of firms and factories and mines, with all the ineffici-

[13] See particularly papers for the Rhodes-Livingstone Institute by C. Mitchell and A. L. Epstein, *Politics in an Urban African Community* (Man-chester University Press for Rhodes-Livingstone Institute, 1958).

ency of a first generation in new circumstances, with all the raw
sensitivity to the impatient patience of European supervision.
Here was created the material for the mass anti-colonial parties
of the future.

To move from dependence to maturity is hard enough, even
with the best blend of sympathy and firmness by the dominant
group. The most probable step is to furious rejection and revolt.
For Africans in a half-world, at odds with their own traditions,
rejected and seemingly overpowered by the European, the straight
transition was almost impossible. It was usually to need several
years of experience in the metropolitan countries of Europe or in
America before there were leaders toughened in fibre and reinforced in confidence to meet the European eye to eye.

3

The last phase of the colonial period can be divided ideally into
two—the period of compromise with the first generation of usually
well-educated African leaders; and the rise of the younger un-
compromising mass parties. But this is a sequence of attitudes or
situations rather than of time. It is seen clearly in the British and
some French territories on the West Coast. But it is telescoped or
distorted in different ways in the Congo and in Central and East
Africa. For, while the first phase was developing between 1918
and 1939 in the West, it had barely started in East Africa, the
Rhodesias or the Congo. When, after the war, the West Coast
sprang forward to the second phase, the younger leaders elsewhere
were not content to follow through each slow, painful step. Indian
independence in 1947 echoed through Africa; the race was on.
The independence of Ghana was the final spur. From that
moment, not only was it proved that Africans could win; there
was a voice, and then a dozen voices, to cheer on the later runners.
In consequence the Centre and East of Africa tuned their tactics
to those of the last phase, but without the experience or the support of a substantial educated group. This telescoping was to have
important results.

The older leaders in West Africa, often lawyers or journalists,
or from other employment outside government patronage, were
usually well-educated and sophisticated men, from families of
three or more generations of Western culture. They came often
enough from the leading schools and colleges—Katsina, Achi-

mota, Fourah Bay. They were fierce enough in political opposition. But as they joined the Legislative Councils, became Judges,
became Ministers, they were accepted by the Europeans. A number of their equals were civil servants, slowly building a small but
tough corps of Africans able to convince Europe of their ability
and balance. Here was a moment which had elements of satisfaction for both sides—growing responsibility and growing rewards
for the Africans; a vision among Europeans that their policy of
measured advance would succeed. But the pace was too slow for
the forces which were gathering underneath. In some cases the
first leaders of intellectual-aristocratic type managed to hold on to
power; in some cases they retired into quiet professional posts; in
some cases they carried on a losing rivalry with the rising forces of
revolution—'nationalist *prima donnas* without effective popular
support',[14] in some cases they joined the new mass parties.

There are many special cases. While Ghana and Southern
Nigeria and Guinea followed the full pattern, the Emirs of
Northern Nigeria were differently placed, anxious to avoid the
social radicalism of the South which could destroy their régime.
The kingdom of Buganda had no wish to find its individuality
swamped in a directly elected Uganda government. In the Congo
there was, in 1945, no African political leadership at all. In Central and East Africa the European governments were still leaning
on the chiefs; an occasional moderate African was to be hesitantly
invited towards a representative post; neither in East Africa nor
in the Rhodesias was there any serious expectation of an African
elected majority within a lifetime.

It may be useful to note the earliest dates at which African
notables began to serve in the Legislative Councils which were
slowly established in British territories. Sierra Leone must come
first; there were 'black settlers' in both legislative chambers in
1798–1800, before the transfer to the Crown. In 1811 one Creole
unofficial member was appointed to the Governor's Advisory
Council, replaced in 1863 by a Legislative Council with nominated members. The first Africans were *elected* in 1924.[15] In

[14] David Apter, *The Gold Coast in Transition* (Princeton University Press, 1955).
[15] See Lord Hailey, *An African Survey* (revised 1956) (London, Oxford University Press, 1957), from which most of these dates are drawn.

Senegal the French, treating the colony as part of the *métropole*, gave citizenship and a franchise to some Senegalese in 1848, and the first deputies were sent to Paris in 1870. Territorial assemblies were established only in 1946. In the Gold Coast it was 1888 before the first African was nominated to the Legislative Council (established in 1850), and the first elected members appeared in 1925. In Nigeria a nominated Legislative Council established, without Africans, for Lagos colony only soon after its annexation in 1862, expanded in 1913 to a 'Nigerian Council' which included six nominated unofficial Africans; in 1922 a Legislative Council was established with four elected unofficial Africans—the first elected Africans in a British African Legislature.

In East Africa the whole sequence is, of course, later. Kenya had a European elected Legislative Council in 1919, but the first African nominated member did not appear until 1944, although Asian elected members had sat since 1927. In Tanganyika provision was made in 1926 for a nominated African, but none were in fact nominated until 1945, when two took their seats. In Uganda three Africans were nominated in 1944.

Finally, in Central Africa the first two Africans were nominated to Legislative Council in Northern Rhodesia in 1948, in Nyasaland in 1950; in 1961 there were no Africans in the Southern Rhodesian Parliament, though there are to be fifteen under the Constitution approved by Referendum in July 1961. In the first Federal Parliament of 1953 two Africans from each of the three Territories were included, by special election in the Protectorates and on a common roll in Southern Rhodesia.

These dates do not, of course, give a full picture of African participation in the processes of government, on the West Coast particularly. There were the existing chiefs and other rulers, operating under the supervision of British Residents or Provincial Commissioners; and in the West Coast towns there was extensive African participation, in a variety of forms, in local government. In East Africa there were not only the kingdoms in Uganda but a gradually developing network of local councils; and in Central Africa there were the chiefs and the kingdom of Barotseland. But the growth of election to a Legislative Council does give an idea of the beginnings of *politics*, and it is easy to see how late a growth this is. There was plenty of strong political talk by the notables and early political journalists in West Africa before the 1939–45 War; but the mass of African people had not then been drawn in.

The younger African leaders of the second phase, in the ten years from 1950 to 1960, swept this whole situation into the pages of history. Western-trained, in contact with international movements, modern in the political techniques of press and radio and loudspeaker, the party cell and the capture of key posts, they were to leap ahead. They represented not merely an opposition to the Europeans but the simultaneous political and social revolution within African society—the emancipation of a new class not only from the rural tribal society but from the central traditional leadership. They gathered in the discontented literates, the progressives in rural areas, the insulted and injured, the young professionals, the unemployed of the towns and sometimes, as in southern Nigeria, a considerable section of the traditional notables as well. Knowing their own, they were ruthless with waverers, and they played consistently on every grievance, real or imagined, both of the country and the town. Against settler governments, ammunition was ample—land, wages, colour bar, minority rule; the main difficulty was to break the attitude of dependence. Against the administration in non-settler territories, still experimenting with chiefs and Native Authorities, with tentative County Councils and complex franchises, their impact was as simple and direct as a hammer blow—modern elected government by universal suffrage, neither more nor less. On such a simple programme, TANU in Tanganyika, typical of such a modern party, swept over that huge area in a flash of time, presenting an astonished government with its national force and ubiquity where before there had been scattered and contradictory grumbles.

The reaction of Europeans to these last two phases must be mentioned, for it still plays a part, not only in the dwindling number of territories under European rule, but as residuary thinking towards the new African States. It was partly characterized by an underestimate of the power behind the younger nationalist leaders, in all countries; and by the most acute crisis in settler countries not only between Europeans and Africans on the spot but between the colonists and the metropolitan government.

Europeans have been apt to classify African leaders into three classes—chiefs, who were gentlemen; intellectuals, who could make good civil servants; and agitators, to be put in gaol.[16] Their long-term plans relied on the first two—the chiefs to form a stable local society and gradually, perhaps, join a central government; the intellectuals not only for the central Civil Service but to provide the doctors and agricultural officers to service the growing economy. Moreover, in the decade 1950–60 great successes were being achieved. At last new agricultural schemes were working; Community Development and Co-operatives seemed to have found a key to release African energy; even land tenure and grazing control showed signs of hope. Dams and irrigation, new cash crops and a new outlook on capital development, with world financial assistance, were all pointing to a growing future of prosperity and co-operation. Moreover, an African group of sturdy individual farmers, Co-operative secretaries, local councillors and treasurers, even a few fully qualified District Officers, was growing up, all with a vested interest in the continuance of the régime.

In this picture, the 'agitator' appeared as an unnecessary and purely destructive force. He alarmed and harried the chiefs, he traduced the sincerity of sincere reformers, he advised the peasants to sabotage schemes palpably in their own interest, and he challenged every aspect of the European presence and power. Moreover, he was to be suspected of influence or aid from Communism, he might well be intemperate in speech, playing on the very prejudices of race and ideals of democracy which the Europeans were hoping to bury under advancing prosperity and a more liberal paternalism. Governments were slow to realize that he led a revolution against the very African traditionalism which they had weakened and in favour of the very economic revolution which parts of their policy had been preparing for a generation. They misjudged also the link between the African *élite* and the common man. The studies of Tarditz,[17] in Porto Novo and Caprasse in Elisabethville[18] emphasize the great part which the extended

[16] I am indebted to Thomas Hodgkin for this observation, as for his classic book *Nationalism in Colonial Africa* (London, Muller, 1957), and for much personal help and inspiration.   [17] op. cit.

[18] 'Les membres d'une même famille, le clan, tout comme ceux de la tribu, se situent à tous les niveaux socio-économiques. Si des membres sont instruits, d'autres sont illettrés . . . Ce qui renforce encore le poid de ces liens de parenté et empêche les differenciations de jouer, c'est que les femmes ne sont en général instruites et qu'elles gardent les contacts étroites avec le milieu coutumier.' P. Caprasse, 'Leaders africains en milieu urbain', *CEPSI*, Vol. 5, 1959.

family and the tribe play in this connexion, since every literate has an illiterate cousin and since the women in particular keep in the closest touch with the old traditional society. The observer in Africa during this decade could be constantly struck by confident European predictions that a strike or boycott led by an 'agitator' would find no support, often to be taken aback by its highly organized and massive following.

As soon as the government made the first major concession to the younger leaders, the situation was in danger of becoming wholly out of hand. The government would find itself negotiating in London or Paris with the leader in person while the Provincial Officers and the chiefs were still following the old policy of harrying local party meetings, treating their organizers as agitators and layabouts while security men laboriously and ostentatiously recorded the proceedings.[19] The first concession led to a second, for 'the hatred of authorities is most marked just when they seem most full of goodwill',[20] and soon government was mainly concerned to conduct at least a dignified retreat without having to swallow its own words and Constitutions too often. In the melancholy case of the Belgian Congo, the emergence of political ambitions among the Congolese found the Belgian Government not only unprepared but dumbfounded by a situation which its policy was supposed to have excluded. Rather than face a long period of difficult, expensive and unrewarding political training, with all its dangers, it attempted a short cut. It now seems clear that this was a classic case of abandonment which, as Mannoni so prophetically said, would lead to 'a hysterical outburst of fury and violence'. The Congolese, left in a situation for which they were unprepared and which they could not control, turned in fury on the absconding parent—a fury (as so many stories confirm) directed as often at those who left as at those who risked life to stay. In French West Africa the struggle never reached so far down into society. The African leaders, well used to Paris and often *députés* of long standing, were able to use French political divisions to further their cause and gain their independence diplomatically, with only an occasional call on the mass support of Trade Unions and the

[19] This situation was very noticeable in Northern Rhodesia during 1960— whole Provinces were harrying UNIP as Mr. Kaunda prepared to meet the Colonial Secretary in London. It is no accident that Nationalist leaders are apt to emerge from detention to assume their final power.

[20] Mannoni, op. cit.

massive *Rassemblement Démocratique Africaine* which at one time spanned virtually the whole of the French dependencies.

While in West Africa and in Tanganyika the British were able to pursue their retreat with reasonable dignity, as did the French in Equatorial and West Africa, the settler countries faced far greater difficulties. The original divergence between the government vision of trusteeship and the settlers' intention of founding a true colony or daughter-cell could now no longer be papered over; the much earlier decision of the metropolitan government to give representative institutions to the settlers returned to plague the inventor. The young but strong patriotism of the daughter community, focused in a central assembly, comes into play at this point, charged with surprising venom not so much at the African nationalist as at their own home government, its weakness and its treachery. The belief to which the settler community clings—that, left alone, it could handle the situation—is supported by the Provincial Administration, who feel able to control their local 'hotheads'. At this stage there is apt to be vigorous political manoeuvring with multi-racial parties and 'moderate' Africans or with tribal or other rivals of the main nationalist leader. In this situation there is a razor edge between major catastrophes—a hesitant metropolitan government overawed by settlers (Algeria) or a headlong flight (Belgian Congo). Where the metropolitan government reads rightly the signs of the times, there are bound to be periods of compromise, unsatisfactory in itself. But these interim Constitutions serve a double purpose, both to give African leaders an experience of responsibility and to give time for a slowly changing European opinion in the territory to adjust to a new situation and new prospects. Even the complex franchises may be justified on these two grounds.

Kenya has already exhibited almost every phase of this drama, and Northern Rhodesia is likely to follow a similar course. The issue in Southern Rhodesia is not likely to be settled so soon; the catastrophe which would follow failure is no less grim. The fact that the Africans of Southern Rhodesia are, perhaps, more deeply dependent and the Europeans more numerous is not an advantage but a greatly added danger. It will need skill and determination almost beyond human power to achieve a transition from dependence not to hysterical revolt but to maturity, and to prevent the

III. A party of seismic drillers of Shell-B.P. with heavy equipment in a delta creek, Eastern Nigeria   [*A Shell photograph*

IV. A seismic driller checks with the control before firing a shot. Shell-B.P.,
Eastern Nigeria   [*A Shell photograph*

suicidal resistance of the French 'colons' of Algeria from repeating itself South of the Zambezi.

The detailed tactics, constitutions, conferences and crises of the final years and months before Independence are not for this book ; some indeed are not yet completed. It remains to suggest some general criterion by which to judge the political situation of the new African societies as they assume their own power. The criterion is, I believe, the stage which social revolution, in its widest sense, has reached in a given country at its hour of Independence. For the struggle for international freedom and the social, economic, moral and religious revolution within African societies have been parallel and interacting but not identical.

The international object may be achieved at very different stages of internal change. Between Senegal and Mali, between the Kabaka of Buganda and the Uganda Parliament, between the Federal Government of Nigeria and the Northern dynasties lie differences and difficulties which only internal social analysis will disclose.

There is, too, one startling change which is more general. As an independent African government emerges to stretch its wings, it is indeed unlike the chrysalis from which it sprang. Many of the attitudes of the battle against European rule suddenly disappear. New problems form. There is a power vacuum, which must be filled. Tribal rivalries become menacing. Effort, work, enthusiasm replace boycott and strikes. Trade Unions, a powerful anti-colonial tool, may be a threat to national production. Opposition is near-traitorous; taxation must be raised; foreign enterprise is needed; the primitive, backward, customary ways must be more speedily reformed than ever a colonial government would have dared. Again, there is a swing in outward style back to the African tradition, a search for dress and art and institutions and history which will give personality to the new nation. Federations and Unions, often bitterly opposed, become desirable. Personal relationships between African and European suddenly become easier and more natural. The whole colour of life has changed. Europeans, regarding with anxiety and foreboding the attitudes of conflict, have found it hard to foresee this transformation. Yet it is important for the future, both of Europe and of Africa, that they should switch their attention and their sympathy to an entirely new world, yet made from the materials of the old. It is the world in which African societies, after the first joy of liberation, begin to face the real problem of their economy, the real social ferment, the real task of local government, the age-old problems of power and freedom and democracy, the hard facts of their relations with neighbouring African states, the place which they must win by their efforts and their wisdom in a world economy and a world society of nations.

PART II

CHAPTER IV

THE AFRICAN ECONOMIES AND
THEIR GROWTH

As each year passes it is harder to remember how quickly Africa
has changed. It is always worth while to go back just a little—to
the deer grazing unfrightened by the ox-wagons as Livingstone
pressed on into Barotseland, less than 100 years ago; to Lord Delamere among the Masai and the lions in Kenya, 60 years ago; or to
Williamson finding an emerald as he rested in the shade in Tanganyika 20 years ago. For long enough, after the first European
entries and discoveries, changes seemed slow. The patient process
of administration, education, road building, the trial of new crops,
learning the language of Africa's soil and people, went quietly
along. Here and there, as in the Copperbelt, a startling change
might take place; here and there a new crop (such as cotton in
Uganda in 1905) might make a large difference. But in the main,
foundations were being laid. The transformation of the two
decades 1940–1960 sprang from many causes, including the
higher prices for raw materials and the new policies of developing the colonial territories. But it also rested upon the long record
of administration, on many daily duties and local achievements
—small surveys, the schools in the bush, bridges, soil sampling,
the training of police, the dipping of cattle, malaria control.
Even the existence of statistics, on which economic policy can be
based, is a by-product of the patient effort to bring Africa within
a modern system of administration.

In economists' terms, the societies of Tropical Africa are extremely poor. Table I (opposite) gives a rough comparison of
nine countries, with India, Pakistan and the United Kingdom for
contrast. But poverty is a complex term. It is not altogether to be
measured by cash. Hundreds of thousands of Africans who have
left their villages for the towns are indeed earning more than
any possible *monetary* estimate of their standards in the subsistence economy of the bush. Their earnings raise the statistical
average; but they may be in many senses poorer, paying rent for a
bed-space in Lagos or Nairobi, eating little but paying cash for it,

working harder, landless, in Western rags. In terms of well-being
—nutrition, housing, health in particular—many sections of the
subsistence way of life provided better for the African than employment at the lowest levels of the modern economy. Thus a figure
of £18 or £20 per head per annum in some ways conceals the fact
that on this income people have a house, food, clothing as far as
it is necessary, all of which would cost very much more in the cash
economy. In the forest areas of West Africa, where food is easy to
get and the climate is warm, it is not poverty in the sense of hunger
and misery which is striking, but the extreme simplicity of the
essential basis of life, and the toll of infant mortality and disease
which has kept population within the limit of its resources.

Table II (see page 51) shows the growth of government
revenues (expenditure roughly corresponds except in the very
early years). Even allowing for change in the value of money, the
increase in the twenty years from 1938 to 1958 in all territories is
startling—almost every budget is multiplied by ten and some, in
West Africa, by twenty. Further, these figures show only *current*
revenue, excluding the capital development programmes which
barely existed before the war and are now so impressive.[1]

For a few years even after 1945 it was still usual for experts to
emphasize the poverty of Africa and the limited hope of advance.
Soils were poor, eroded, leached; distances enormous and transportation sparse; climate exacting and inimical to effort and
enterprise; deposits of basic minerals, such as coal and iron ore,
few and badly placed. African peoples, debilitated by disease,
were also widely regarded as congenitally indolent and incapable
of modern economic effort.[2]

There was some truth in these views, in terms of the actual situation as it was then known. Much additional potential has since
been discovered. As late as the 1920s Sierra Leone was said to have
no mineral resources of importance; it now exports £16 million
of diamonds and over £4 million of iron ore annually. Moreover,
many of the difficulties of climate and distance applied with equal

[1] See Chapter VIII.
[2] Cf. Sir John Hall, Governor of Uganda: 'Speaking generally, and judging
by European standards, the people of Uganda are ignorant, indolent, irresponsible and not infrequently suspicious of foreign intervention.' (Quoted by
E. B. Worthington in *A Development Plan for Uganda* (Entibbe, Government
Printer, 1947). There are a multitude of similar observations for all countries
in Tropical Africa. But see Chapter IX.

Table II

CURRENT REVENUE IN SELECTED BRITISH TERRITORIES, 1900–1960

	1	2	3	4	5	6	7	8	9
	Kenya	*Tanganyika*	*Uganda*	*Nyasaland*	*N. Rhodesia*	*S. Rhodesia*	*Central African Federation*	*Nigeria*	*Ghana*
1. 1900 (a)	£64,000		£82,000	£49,000	£3,000	£406,000		£639,000	£333,000
2. 1907 (a)	£475,000	£395,000	£112,000	£75,000	£82,000	£554,000		£1,673,000	£704,000
3. 1913 (a)	£1,124,000	£688,000	£257,000	£125,000	£138,000	£777,000		£3,327,000	£1,302,000
4. 1938	£3,776,000	£2,113,000	£1,864,000	£664,000	£1,594,000 (e)	£4,371,000 (e)		£5,741,000	£3,683,000 (d)
5. 1947	£9,877,000	£5,777,000	£5,331,000	£1,505,000	£4,439,000 (c)			£7,342,000	£7,567,000 (c)
6. 1950	£13,224,000	£10,397,000	£11,037,000	£3,462,000	£10,957,000	£16,621,000		£32,794,000	£18,120,000
7. 1956/57	£32,793,000	£17,492,000	£19,047,000	£5,263,000	£18,264,000	£17,286,000	£52,402,000	£70,567,000	£52,456,000
8. 1957/58	£33,429,000	£18,834,000	£18,788,000	£5,017,000	£18,179,000	£19,723,000	£55,387,000	£70,945,000	£48,036,000
9. 1958/59	£33,468,000	£19,412,000	£20,248,000	£4,951,000	£15,745,000	£19,638,000	£50,137,000	£77,316,000	£52,779,000
10. 1959/60	£33,394,000 (b)	£22,066,000	£19,534,000 (b)	£5,002,000 (b)	£15,218,000 (b)	£19,517,000 (b)	£54,511,000	£83,924,000 (b)	£65,600,000 (f)

Sources:

S. H. Frankel, *Capital Investment in Africa*, London, 1938.

An Economic Survey of the Colonial Territories, 1951, Colonial No. 281–3. H.M.S.O.

East African Statistical Department, *Quarterly Economic and Statistical Bulletin*.

Monckton Report, Appendix VI, *Survey of Developments Since 1953*. Cmnd. 1149, H.M.S.O., 1960.

Federation of Nigeria, *Digest of Statistics*.

Official Year Book of Southern Rhodesia.

Notes:
(a) Gross revenue and expenditure excluding Imperial Grants and Grants from the Colonial Development Fund.
(b) Estimates.
(c) Including development and welfare revenue expenditure.
(d) 1938/39.
(e) 1940.
(f) 1960–1.

General Note:
The statistics in the above table relate as far as possible to *current* revenue and expenditure. Development expenditure, grants in aid from the United Kingdom Government C.D. & W. Funds, &c. have been excluded.

force to the two dominant economies of the world, the U.S.A. and Russia. They are disadvantages, not an absolute bar to development. Today, it is the potential of Africa which is more remarked. In minerals there is not only the Copperbelt but the gold of Ashanti and Tanganyika, the diamonds of Tanganyika, Ghana, the Congo and Sierra Leone, and above all the belt of aluminium ore running for 1,700 miles from Guinea to Angola. Many more mineral deposits are known though not yet exploited.[3] There are the new oil fields of the Niger Delta and of the French Sahara, as well as in Angola and perhaps elsewhere. In hydro-electric power Africa is reckoned to hold 40 per cent of the world's reserves. Even the soils, rightly treated, in many places have shown a surprising power of yield and of recovery. There are, indeed, large areas of fragile or degraded soils, such as many in the central plateau.[4] Yet others, apparently stripped bare by erosion and wrong use, have recovered almost miraculously under quite simple care.[5] Moreover, there is not the long winter waiting of Northern climates; in parts of Africa, where rainfall or irrigation is adequate, growth and regeneration go on throughout the year.

It is often said that colonial governments, at least before the last war, failed to develop their African territories. It is true that finance and budgeting were, to say the least, strait-laced. Colonial civil servants were bound to see their work as administration and the minor improvement of the rural economy, while on the West Coast the trading companies were concerned mainly with buying produce. The mineral enterprises, plantations and white farmer-settlers were the main developers, though here and there government, or enterprising District Commissioners, made an important contribution.[6] Moreover, in the whole period from 1928 to 1936 the metropolitan countries were passing through a crisis of 'over-production' (as they saw it, for Keynesian economics had not yet prevailed). The idea of large investment in Africa, whether in

---

[3] See Chapter VIII.

[4] Cf. F. Fraser Darling: 'The plateau soils of Africa bear the stamp of senility . . . Under cultivation their weakness is apparent in that they lose structure, organic matter and the power to conduct water through them.' *Wild Life in an African Territory* (London, Oxford University Press, 1960).

[5] Cf. descriptions by Mrs. Huxley (*A New Earth*) of regeneration in two years, by fencing and controlled grazing, of badly eroded soils in West Suk, Baringo and in the Machakos country (Kenya).

[6] For example, the introduction of coffee growing by Mr. Dundas, when District Commissioner, to the Chagga on Mount Kilimanjaro.

agriculture or industry, was hardly likely to have taken hold when Brazilian coffee was being dumped in the sea and the factory workers of Europe were anxiously spinning out work or queueing for relief. In British territories it was Treasury policy that colonies must balance their own budgets; and this rule worked very restrictively in the days of conservative finance. It is interesting that, in the last two years, the unsubsidized English-speaking territories have thereby found it easier to stand on their own feet in independence, while the French-speaking areas, long dependent on generous investment and subsidy from metropolitan France, are finding it much harder to establish economic independence.

Whatever the causes of delay, this period of laying down a minimum basis of education, communications and administrative services provided a foundation without which attempted development might well have sunk in the sands. Even since the war, European ignorance of African soils and of the social systems of Africa and African unpreparedness for the new future brought many hopeful projects to a sad end. But at least by 1939 Tropical Africa had not only a structure more capable of supporting development, but a considerable hold on world markets, and this was to prove a vital asset after the war.

The figures of growth since the war are striking. The figures in Table II (see page 51) were certainly beyond the imagination of administrators in 1939. There are, naturally, differences in scale and period of growth between countries. For example, the Belgian Congo and the Rhodesias, with a considerable industrial base under European management, and Kenya with its white agricultural settlement,[7] were inclined to outstrip Uganda and Tanganyika. Between 1952–4 and 1957–9 Kenya's national income rose by 56 per cent, Tanganyika's by 28 per cent, Uganda's by 15 per cent; taking population growth into account, real standards may have risen by as much as 40 per cent in Kenya, under 20 per cent in Tanganyika and perhaps only marginally in Uganda.[8] On the West Coast high cocoa prices brought Ghana forward with a rush. An immense programme of French government aid and

[7] Lord Hailey estimates that £40 million was invested by European farmers in Kenya by 1956.
[8] *East Africa—Economic and Fiscal Commission Report* (H.M.S.O. Cmd. 1279, 1961), paras. 65–67.

investment was poured into the large but sparsely populated French territories.[9]

Table III (opposite), showing domestic exports, gives a different indication of growth, even allowing for the falling value of money. Not a single country in the Table has experienced less than a tenfold increase in value of domestic exports since 1935. Certainly, prosperity is unevenly spread. Although, for example, Northern Rhodesia, thanks to the Copperbelt, is high in the table of incomes and Uganda very low, many of the rural districts of Uganda would show a level of moderate prosperity and well-being far ahead of most of Northern Rhodesia once away from the line of rail. The extent of reliance on mineral exports is one index of the spread or concentration of wealth. The figures (Table III) for Ghana have fallen from 41 per cent in 1935 to 24 per cent; for Southern Rhodesia from 80 per cent to 29 per cent; but the figure of 96 per cent for Northern Rhodesia has remained unchanged. While therefore the simple figures of growth in national income conceal differences in human welfare, and differences in the distribution of wealth both geographically and as between Africans and Europeans, they are nevertheless important as a gross indication of increasing economic strength. They also represent, although in differing degrees, a movement from the subsistence into the money economy, one index of which lies in the percentage of Africans in wage-earning employment (Table IV, page 56). In view of the 1960 catastrophe in the Belgian Congo, it is perhaps worth quoting separately a series of figures showing the startling economic growth achieved there in the last ten years of Belgian rule.[10] These are an indication of what may yet be achieved if political stability can be re-established.

The task now facing African societies may be divided into four elements : first, to develop the skills, energy and initiative without which capital cannot be made productive ; second, to find capital, from both at home and abroad ; third, to decide rightly on

[9]	Area (sq. miles)	Population	Density (per sq. miles)
British W. Africa	496,485	39,178,000	76
French W. Africa	1,799,159	16,735,000	9

(Source: R. W. Steel and C. A. Fisher, *Geographical Essays on British Tropical Lands* (London, Philip, 1956).

[10] *L'économie congolaise à la veille de l'indépendance* (Brussels, Fédération des Entreprises Congolaises, April 1960).

Gross National Income, 1950–8 = Increase of 53·3% against a 19·5% rise in population.

Investment per head, 1947–57 = 148 dollars, against an African average of 30, excepting the Rhodesias (200) and the Union (139).

Gross Investment as % of Revenue (Average of 1950, 1953, 1956, 1957) = 34% compared with 12% in Ghana and 10% in Nigeria. Only the Rhodesias, at 39%, exceeded this figure.

Index of African Money Earnings (1958) = 272 (1950 = 100).

Infant Mortality (0–1 yr) per 1,000

		1950	1957
	= Léopoldville	197	75
	= Elisabethville	205	54

priorities, both as between industry and agriculture and as between infrastructure and productive investment; fourth, to maintain a rate of social adaptation within a stable political framework which will allow development to take place. The question of skills and initiative and the question of social adaptation will be considered in later chapters. But, without entering too deeply into the controversies of professional economists, it is necessary to say something on the formation and use of capital. For it is on this issue that the future of the new African societies greatly depends.

Capital for investment involves saving from consumption. Either these savings must be squeezed out of the existing standard of living in Africa, or they must be borrowed from abroad or invested directly by foreign business.[11] If capital is to be raised internally, means must be found to raise it from the mainly agricultural economies of Tropical Africa. Even if it is borrowed or invested from abroad, there is an element of saving in the payment of interest and the maintenance of the capital asset. The prospects for borrowing are in one sense good, in that there are strong political motives for rival investment by the East and West as part of the 'cold war', and a world-wide feeling that the gap between rich and poor countries must be narrowed. Nevertheless, capital is scarce in the world—the Royal Commission on East Africa remarked that East Africa needed capital more than capital needed East Africa. In the long run and on the large scale, investment

[11] Cf. W. A. Lewis, 'The central problem in the theory of economic growth is to understand the process by which a community is converted from being a 5 per cent to a 12 per cent saver, with all the changes in attitudes, institutions and techniques which accompany this conversion.' *The Theory of Economic Growth* (London, Allen and Unwin, 1955).

Table IV
AFRICAN POPULATION AND LABOUR

	Kenya 1959	Tanganyika 1959	Uganda 1959	Nyasaland 1956	Northern Rhodesia 1958	Southern Rhodesia 1958	Nigeria 1958	Ghana 1959	Congo 1959	Senegal	Mali
TOTAL AFRICAN POPULATION (a)	6,171,000	8,942,000	6,429,000	2,580,000	2,220,000 (f)	2,700,000	35,000,000 (f)	6,700,000 (g)	13,800,000		
AFRICANS IN WAGE EMPLOYMENT (b)	537,000	433,000	224,000	164,000	267,000	617,000	478,000	302,000	961,000		
AFRICAN EMPLOYEES IN AGRICULTURE	249,000	224,000	49,500	69,000	47,000	230,000	45,000	54,000	280,000		
AFRICAN EMPLOYEES IN MINING (c)	5,000	9,600	5,000	530	39,000	53,000	49,000	30,000	79,000		
AFRICAN EMPLOYEES IN SECONDARY, TERTIARY AND OTHER INDUSTRIES INCLUDING DOMESTIC SERVICE	283,000	203,400	169,500	94,470	181,000	334,000	384,000	218,000	602,000		
NUMBER OF NON-INDIGENOUS AFRICANS EMPLOYED	20,000 (e)	58,000	50,000 (e)	9,000	46,000 (d)	310,000 (d)			50,000 (h)		

Notes:
(a) Men, women and children.
(b) Including forestry.
(c) A residual item.
(d) 1956.
(e) Rough estimate.
(f) 1959.
(g) 1960.
(h) Including 18,000 from Ruanda Urundi.

Sources:
Tanganyika, *Annual Report of the Labour Department 1959*.
East African Statistical Department, *Quarterly Economic and Statistical Bulletin*.
Advisory Commission on the Review of the Constitution of the Federation of Rhodesia and Nyasaland, Appendix VI, Cmd. 1149, of 1960.
Federation of Nigeria. *Digest of Statistics*.
La Situation Economique du Congo Belge et du Ruanda-Urundi, 1959, Brussels, 1960.

from abroad will have to show a profit if it is to continue—indeed, if it did not it would be a sign that Africa was misusing it.

Very broadly, the prospects for investment in Africa must depend on low labour and social costs in production. It is not without reason that economists have emphasized [12] that this is the one weapon by which Africa can find a niche in the competitive economic system of the world. Low labour costs—the combination of wage level and efficiency of labour—do not imply the lowest wage for which labour can be found. Employers in Southern Rhodesia who had bitterly opposed the virtual doubling of African wages by Mr. Garfield Todd in 1957 were admitting a year later, with some surprise, that their labour costs were reduced by lower labour-turnover and better work. But they do involve a level of wages and salaries well below that of the highly developed countries. Although Africa still has this advantage, it is somewhat endangered by the inheritance, in some fields, of expatriate levels of pay.

In a country where the mass of the people receive a cash income of less than £20 per annum, an indigenous professional *élite* is being trained to expect salaries, based originally on expatriate scales, which compare favourably with those earned in the richest countries in the world.[13]

There is a social as well as an economic risk here; such resentment as there was at the differential between Europeans and Africans was part of anti-colonial feeling; when the differential is between Africans, it becomes part of internal politics. The economic risk is that these standards will continue to spread, setting salary levels for Africans in industry and administration far above the strength of their economy.

As yet these salary levels affect only the fairly small number of Africans in the higher grades of industry (though they weigh down the large governments of small countries). Perhaps more important are the social and environmental costs which have been associated with the employment of Europeans. It was natural enough for companies to establish very high standards for employees who had to be tempted overseas; the pleasantness of their

[12] E.g. P. Bauer, *West African Trade* (Cambridge University Press, 1954).
[13] C. Ehrlich, 'Some Social and Economic Consequences of Paternalism in Uganda' (East African Institute of Social Research Conference, 1959).

life as seen from England was offset by difficulties in educating children, in limited social life and contact with their home culture. But the extensive housing estates with large gardens, with miles of roads and main services, the air-conditioned offices, the lifts and cars and telephones, all carry a heavy load of maintenance and set standards which cannot easily be lowered. The huge boulevards and skyscrapers of Léopoldville, in one sense a capital asset, are a heavy liability to the Africans who inherit them; and they contrast altogether too sharply with the life of the Congo forests.

Thus, even if foreign governments and investors are sympathetic, African governments have still to decide how best to find internal savings to create capital and to pay for their borrowings, and how best to employ the capital they can find; and they are somewhat handicapped in using their chief advantage of low labour costs by the spreading legacy of European standards.

It was natural, but unfortunate, that first thoughts should move towards 'industrialization'.[14] Psychological pressures in this direction have been exceptionally strong. European power and wealth appeared to rest on industry. Africans are anxious to have a modern, scientific, technological society, most obviously exemplified by the machinery of the modern factory; and they suspect that colonial powers deliberately endeavour to retard industrial growth in order to keep Africa as a source of cheap food and raw materials and as a market for European manufactures. The overwhelming dependence of some countries on agricultural exports (Kenya, 90 per cent; Uganda, 93 per cent; Nyasaland, 99 per cent; Nigeria, 88 per cent; see Table III, page 54) appears also to give good reason for 'diversification'. There is pressure to find employment for newly educated groups in the African community no longer willing to stay on the land. On the more strict economic level, there appears to be a possible gain to national income and to the balance of payments if much that was exported as raw material can be processed in Africa. Finally, industry is often quoted as the most likely method of starting a snowball of capital accumulation.

These arguments have had a strong appeal. But they require

[14] I have used 'industrialization' in the loose sense in which it is commonly used, to imply a contrast with agricultural development and conjure up a vision of factory chimneys. In fact, what is meant is the creation of secondary industry, whether using indigenous or imported raw materials.

much more careful analysis. One of the clearest brief statements—
and one which was not popular—was the Report of Professor
Arthur Lewis on 'Industrialization in the Gold Coast'.[15] Some of
the opening paragraphs lay down simple but key principles. In
the world competition in processing for export,

The undeveloped country relies usually on two advantages : (a) low
labour cost, based on low wages, and (b) an advantage in transport
cost, if the material loses weight in the course of processing. (Para. 4.)
The likelihood of low labour cost offsetting the disadvantages of
operating in a non-industrial environment is greatest where labour
cost is a substantial element in total cost. . . . If an operation is performed mainly by machinery, with only a small element of labour, it
is almost certain to cost more in the Gold Coast than in the United
Kingdom because the cost of buying, erecting and maintaining
machinery is higher in the Gold Coast than it is in an industrialized
country. (Para. 6.)

In manufacture for the home market in Africa, local production is favoured in terms of transport costs—

(a) if the industry uses a heavy raw material which is available on
the spot;
(b) if the manufactured commodity is more bulky than the materials
of which it is made . . . (e.g. furniture, most assembly work, hollow-
ware). (Para. 12.) [16]

Finally,

. . . the prospect of manufacturing for the home market is dominated
by one other consideration, namely, the size of the home market in
relation to the minimum size at which production can be done
economically. (Para. 15.)

This consideration leads Professor Lewis to his main conclusion,
and one which should be inscribed above the door of every
Planning Department in Tropical Africa :

The most certain way to promote industrialization in the Gold
Coast is to lay the foundation it requires by taking vigorous measures
to raise food production per person engaged in agriculture. This is

[15] Government Printer, Accra, 1953.
[16] It was this factor which made reasonable the manufacture of plastic
piping and other hollow-ware in a factory in Ibadan which at first sight had
every argument against it—high capital, low employment of labour, imported
raw material. See U.A.C. *Statistical and Economic Review*, September 1959,
which contains some interesting 'case-studies' of industrialization in West
Africa.

the surest way of producing the large and ever-increasing demand
for manufactures without which there can be little industrialization.

These basic factors of labour cost and capital intensity, transport cost,[17] and size of demand may clearly be combined in different ways, so that judgement concerning a particular industry
needs an exact calculation. It is clear that the establishment of an
industry is by no means automatically an advance; and every
commitment of capital means that some possibly better alternative
use of it has been lost. A good deal of such wastage has happened
in Africa, both from African and European initiatives.

In fact, many of the tempting arguments for industrialization
are shaky. Diversification by installing secondary industry does not
add stability if there is still only one primary source of purchasing
power; for if cocoa or copper collapses, so will the secondary industries and tertiary services which depend on the earnings of the
cocoa farmer or the miner. Nor is it vitally important to diversify
as between organic and mineral exports. Groundnuts, palm-oil,
sugar, tea, coffee, rubber, fibres, cotton, give a pretty wide range
of attack on markets without necessarily adding minerals or manufactured products. It is the single-product economy which is
vulnerable.   Equally, the strong pressure to find employment for
the mounting flood of school-leavers cannot necessarily be met by
industrialization. There is a constant rise in the amount of fixed
capital investment needed to employ one workman in industry, as
machinery becomes more complex, automatic, and costly.

For about three-quarters of British industry the range appears to
be between £1,000 and £3,000 with china and earthenware (£620)
and oil refining (£13,350) at the two extremes. Given below are a
few examples of the initial amounts of working and fixed capital
required per worker to establish selected West African industries :

Cement Works A	£13,150
Cement Works B	£6,500
Vehicle Assembly Plant	£3,000
Plastics Factory	£2,800
Textile Mill	£1,375
Canning Factory	£550
Singlet Factory	£100 . . . (excludes working capital) [18]

[17] Fuel cost may be important in certain industries.
[18] U.A.C. *Statistical and Economic Review*, 23 September 1959.

It is unfortunate for countries short of capital and rich in labour that modern industry tends year by year to give less employment at increasing capital cost; but it serves to force their attention towards the development of the dispersed rural economy, and towards the use of simpler methods. It has been observed [19] that the 'shiny-red-tractor mentality' of European businessmen has even led to over-capitalization in countries as poor as East Africa, out of a belief that a complicated machine must do the work better than an unskilled African or that labour can be tied to the pace of the machine. Not only the groundnut catastrophe in Tanganyika but many minor failures attest to this mistake.

Arguments for greater self-sufficiency and the saving of foreign exchange, although they may spring in part from a political wish to reduce dependence on European sources of supply, are more soundly based where there is also a real improvement in the standard of living. On the political side, Tables V and VI (page 62) show the large dependence of certain African areas on 'ex-colonial' countries and the very low levels of inter-African trade. There is good reason to think that inter-African trade can be increased, wherever transport costs do not too greatly exceed the shipping costs from Europe. On the economic side independence is a dangerous slogan—Africa was economically 'independent', that is cut off from the world economy, far too long. [20] Clearly, where a local raw material can be processed and sold locally, there will be a rise in *monetary* national income as labour is attracted from the subsistence into the cash economy. The extent of any rise in real standards will depend on the cost of the product, which unfortunately may be higher than the cost of the imported article. It is only by the most intensive and highly skilled management and a sharp concentration on labour costs that, for example, the Bata Shoe Company have been able to make local manufacture competitive with imports.

This very brief critique of the dangers in an unthinking drive for industrialization does not, of course, imply that there is no room for it. Some account of the real and growing success in this field will come later. But it does sound a note of caution, and per-

[19] H. W. Ord, 'The Employment of Capital in East Africa' (East African Institute of Social Research Conference, 1959).

[20] See S. H. Frankel in *International Affairs*, October 1960: 'In a technically shrinking world there is little room for absolute political or economic independence.'

haps points in particular to the need for more modest schemes which are able to use existing or easily created African skills and which do not demand either immense blocks of scarce capital or

Table V
DISTRIBUTION OF TRADE OF SELECTED AFRICAN TERRITORIES 1950-7
PERCENTAGE OF TOTAL TRADE

		Imports	Exports
FRENCH AFRICAN COMMUNITY (a)	Trade with French Franc Area	74·7%	75·3%
CONGO	Trade with Belgium	37·1%	52·7%
STERLING AREA AFRICA (b)	Trade with Sterling Area	66·7%	63·6%
UNION OF SOUTH AFRICA	Trade with Sterling Area	45·9%	53·5%
STERLING AREA AFRICA (b)	Trade with United Kingdom	46·0%	51·0%

Notes:
(a) French Cameroons, French West Africa, French Equatorial Africa, Guinea, Malagasy.
(b) Federation of Rhodesia and Nyasaland, Kenya, Tanganyika, Uganda, Nigeria, Sierra Leone and Mauritius.

Source:
U.N. *Economic Survey of Africa Since 1950*, pp. 154–7.

Table VI
INTER-AFRICAN TRADE: SELECTED AFRICAN TERRITORIES 1950-7
PERCENTAGES
Aggregate value of trade with other African countries as percentage of aggregate trade with all countries.

	Imports	Exports	Total
CONGO (including Ruanda Urundi)	7·7%	4·6%	6·1%
FRENCH WEST AFRICA	8·7%	12·6%	10·4%
GHANA	6·1%	2·5%	4·2%
KENYA, UGANDA, TANGANYIKA (a)	4·2%	8·0%	6·0%
NIGERIA	0·8%	1·3%	1·0%
FEDERATION OF RHODESIA AND NYASALAND (b)	36·4%	18·1%	26·9%
UNION OF SOUTH AFRICA (c)	8·5%	10·8%	9·5%

Notes:
(a) Including trade between these countries.
(b) Including trade between members of the Federation prior to 1954.
(c) Including South West Africa from 1955.

Source:
United Nations, *Economic Survey of Africa since 1950*.

heavy social investment. Dr. Elkan has remarked on the slightly supercilious attitude towards small African industries, quoting an official's remark about the Kampala industrial area: 'There are no industries there—only a lot of furniture works, bakeries, maize mills and soda-water factories'[21]—a list of industries admirably suited for local development. Secondly, it will underline the prime need to build up prosperity and demand in the agricultural society which is dominant in Tropical Africa. It is not only the academics who have made this point. Lord Netherthorpe, one of the leaders of the Federation of British Industries Mission to Nigeria in 1961, eight years after Professor Lewis and at the height of the industrializing fashion, echoes his words [22]—'As I see it, agriculture is the key to the prospect and rate of Nigerian industrialization.' The Economic Development Committee in Uganda similarly reported in 1958 : 'The Committee conclude therefore that the most effective steps which can be taken to secure development of manufacturing industry in Uganda, paradoxical though it may seem, are steps which will have the effect of increasing agricultural production.' (Para. 24).[23]

Indeed, it is from raising agricultural incomes that the bulk of savings and capital for development must largely come in most African countries. The widespread belief that maximum movement of employment from agriculture to industry and service implies maximum wealth is not in fact true :

Both the United States and New Zealand have a higher *per capita* income than the U.K. but their agricultural sectors are much greater. The proportion of the active male population engaged in agriculture in the U.K. is 6.5 per cent, U.S.A. 16 per cent and New Zealand 22 per cent.[24]

In an analysis of 'Agriculture's Contribution to Economic Development' recently published by the Food Research Institute of Stanford University,[25] the authors point out the enormous importance of increased labour productivity in agriculture and the capital formation derived from it in the development of Japan and Taiwan. Productivity from the land increased about 100 per

[21] W. Elkan, *Criteria for Industrial Development in Uganda* (Uganda Economics Society, March 1958), an extremely valuable short essay on this subject. See also, P. Bauer, *Economics Analysis and Policy in Underdeveloped Countries* (Cambridge University Press, 1958).
[22] *F.B.I. Mission Report,* February 1961.
[23] *Report of the Economic Development Committee (1958)* (Entebbe, 1959). [24] Elkan, op. cit. (Sweden is another example.)
[25] Bruce F. Johnston and John W. Mellor, *Food Research Institute Studies,* vol. 1, no. 3, November 1960, Stanford University. This article reviews some of the most important contributions of economists to this subject over the last few years.

cent in Japan between 1880–90 and 1911–20, and probably
130 per cent to 160 per cent in Taiwan between 1901–10 and
the 1930s. Land Tax in Japan 'accounted for 86 per cent of the
tax revenue in the fiscal year 1875/6'. The authors go on to conclude :

Since agriculture in underdeveloped countries typically contributes
some 40% to 60% of the national income, the presumption is strong
indeed that the transition from a level of saving and investment
spelling stagnation to one permitting a tolerable rate of economic
growth cannot be achieved unless agriculture makes a significant
net contribution to capital formation in the expanding sectors.

Professor Rostow [26] makes the same point repeatedly :

An environment of rising real income in agriculture, rooted in
increased productivity, may be an important stimulus to the new
modern industrial sector, essential to take-off. . . . It is from rising
rural incomes that increased taxes, of one sort or another, can be
drawn to finance the Government's functions in the transition. . . .
In most cases, increased agricultural supplies are needed to help
meet the foreign exchange bill for capital investment.

Thus the pure economic arguments point to an investment in
the agrarian economy designed to achieve a rapid rise in productivity and real incomes. These incomes would provide both capital
for a 'modern' industrial sector and purchasing power for its products. Moreover, the Stanford study suggests that the agricultural
investment should be in simple equipment, extension services, and
direct, non-monetary investment by the cultivator, in order to
make 'only minimal demands on investible funds, foreign exchange and high calibre entrepreneurial talent'. Considering the
extreme poverty of some of the African countryside and the
conspicuous consumption of some of the towns, it is important to
stress that this does not imply niggardly investment and penal
taxation on the countryman in order to provide prestige air lines,
luxury hotels and palaces for premiers in the towns. On the contrary, it implies that agricultural investment should come first, and
on a massive scale, and that the modern sector cannot be properly
expanded until this investment is bearing real fruit in rural prosperity. This is only to repeat the experience of many now indus-

[26] W. W. Rostow, *The Stages of Economic Growth* (Cambridge University
Press, 1960), pp. 22–24.

trialized countries—that an agrarian revolution must both precede and accompany an industrial revolution.

There could be no policy so thoroughly suited to the deepest needs of African societies. In the first place, population growth demands expansion of food supplies. If, with improving medical services and the mysterious influences of renewed energy and optimism, Africa is on the verge of a population explosion parallel with that of other developing countries, this expansion will have to be swift. There is fortunately plenty of evidence that yields can be raised spectacularly in many parts of Africa, possibly giving a higher rise in productivity per head than any type of industrialization. To give only one example from many, the F.B.I. Mission [27] noted that cotton under controlled cultivation at Zaria was yielding 2,000 lb. to the acre, against an average of 250 lb. in older peasant cultivation. In a great many instances these large increases in yield can be achieved with very small capital investment— better varieties of seed, pest control, and so on. The difficulties are more often social than technical or financial.

Secondly, it is only in the rural economy that the problem of employment can be solved. In countries where extensive and highly mechanized agriculture is practised, the common progress is towards higher production but lower direct employment; but there is much evidence that intensive agriculture, not highly mechanized, can in African conditions support a considerably higher population on the same acreage. The administrators of the Swynnerton Plan in Kenya have reckoned that the Nyeri district, of 322 square miles, could support a population of 460,000 (i.e. almost 1,500 to the square mile), on a basis of six-acre and twelve-acre individual holdings, with both cash and subsistence crops, and a net product of about £8 million. This is based on experience of existing Kikuyu holdings and production in part of the district, and on the Meru experience of coffee growing. [28]

These figures come from a favoured soil and climate with skilled cultivators; but the fact of additional employment could be paralleled elsewhere. It is true that the young generation of school-leavers have been averse to returning to a subsistence

[27] Op. cit.
[28] About 21,000 growers have produced an annual crop worth £750,000, with only half the trees in full bearing and with a variation in yield of from 7 to 20 cwt. per acre between the less good and the best growers. See Huxley, op. cit., pp. 224 and 241.

economy, old style. It is somewhat different if they are returning to a modernized, more scientific agriculture, with a good cash reward. Moreover, there are technical, artisan and clerical jobs to be found in these new schemes. In the Victoria League Cotton Co-operative (Sukumaland, Tanganyika), there are 363 primary societies, each needing a literate secretary/accountant, soon to be equipped with Kalamazoo systems—a worth-while job for a Standard VI school-leaver. Professor Rostow mentions, as one of the conditions for 'take-off', 'a class of farmers willing and able to respond to the possibilities opened up for them by new techniques, land-holding arrangements, transport facilities and forms of market and credit organization'.[29]

Thirdly, it is the primary occupations—agriculture, mining, fishing—which really give diversification; the secondary industries will follow, to process the products and in due course to supply equipment.

Fourthly, agricultural development should contribute greatly to the reduction of the massive labour migrations which are so remarkable a feature of Tropical Africa—Chapter IX records some of the main movements which are taking place at the present time. There is, of course, some value, particularly in a period of rapid economic change, in having a highly mobile labour force. It may be useful if labour is prepared to move fairly readily to areas of greater opportunity, provided that the whole family moves. A certain amount of short-distance or quick movement for seasonal harvesting or cultivation may also be valuable. But the pattern in many parts of Africa has been much less desirable. Much of the West African movement consists of long slow journeys on foot, over hundreds of miles, undertaken annually during the dry season from the savannah and desert fringes to areas of higher rainfall, to the forest belt and the coast. In the Rhodesias and Nyasaland the movement of men to the mines, either within the Federation or to South Africa, will be for at least a year and often longer, leaving behind a denuded agricultural society. The movement into South and East Uganda from Rwanda-Burundi, and from the North and West, predominantly annual, has many of the same social evils—it has been calculated that between 40 and 50 per cent of adult men are normally absent

[29] Rostow, op. cit.

from their home area in these North West provinces.[30] The waste
of time and human energy in those long treks—over 200,000 men
leaving Sokoto Province in Northern Nigeria every year to cover
hundreds of miles on foot—and the social drain on the supplying
areas is a wastage which African societies cannot much longer
afford. Quite apart from the movements to the mines, there is
reason to think that the West African migrations developed within
the last 70 years in response to European-stimulated development,[31] and that the same is true in Uganda.[32] This, then, is a
phenomenon not indigenous to Africa but induced by the exchange economy. It is the enrichment of the home rural economy
or permanent settlement in more productive areas which, in combination, can reverse it.

Fifthly, not only should agrarian development largely avoid the
burden of European salary levels and social expenditure, but it
should be far less expensive in direct and indirect social costs. It is
true that on existing plantations of European origin there are
salaried managers and some quite expensive houses. But the pattern of European salary scales is less likely to be copied there; and
in purely African agriculture no such pattern exists, save for the
salaries of extension and advisory staff. Plantations, though growing, represent in any case a tiny fraction of the vast areas of
African rural life. Although in due course the standards of village
life will have to be raised, particularly those of health, the fact that
millions of Africans have in their traditional environment a house
made of the simplest materials which can be satisfactory, and a
diet which, though monotonous, is by no means always inadequate, is a great asset. Improvement of crop yields which would
allow extra protein to be bought in some areas, and simple improvements to the house, using family labour, could maintain a
viable, and indeed improved, standard of rural life for many years.
Communal effort has already done much in improvement of wells,
paths, bridges, water-supply and markets with negligible capital
expenditure by the State. If this possibility is compared with the
social expense needed if development were concentrated in urban

[30] International Labour Office, *An African Labour Survey*, 1958.
[31] See R. M. Prothero, *Migrant Labour from Sokoto Province* (Northern
Nigeria Government Printer, January 1958).
[32] A. I. Richards (Ed.), *Economic Development and Tribal Change* (Cambridge, Heffer for East African Institute of Social Research, 1954).

industry, the gain is unquestionable. Conditions which no government can long tolerate arise very quickly when poor country folk
flood into towns—over-crowding, total lack of sanitation, neglect
of children, gross undernourishment, and frequently a breakdown
of moral and cultural disciplines under the pressures of poverty,
competition, and the absence of the social sanctions of village life.
The result is heavy municipal expenditure, inflated land values,
waste of capital. In 1961 a man able to put up a building in the
centre of Lagos or Accra could ask five years' rent in advance,
equal to the cost of the building. It is true that distances are great
in Africa, and dispersed development involves investment in roads
and transport; but much of the essential network has already been
created wherever the old export crops had to be moved to the
ports.

Not only does agricultural development make use of existing
simple housing and water supplies, but it can rely on a traditional
social structure for sanctions and security, and it can use a great
number of traditional skills at the level of the cultivator. Moreover,
the very large contribution which women make in the village life
is often almost wholly lost in the town where 'the family hand
becomes the family mouth'.[33] A soil scientist or irrigation engineer
is, indeed, just as costly to train as a mechanical engineer for a
factory. But the training of operatives in factory processes is a
great deal more slow and expensive than the revolution which can
take place in farming practice, with little 'training' once the
farmer has accepted new methods. This has been demonstrated in
Italy with outstanding success in the experiment initiated by Shell
Italiana, under the auspices of the Ministry of Agriculture, at
Borgo a Mozzano in the Lucca district. One agricultural extension worker, by persuasion and example, was able to raise the net
annual income of the village by 192 million lire, the total cost of
technical assistance over the whole period being 25 million lire.
The whole story of this concerted attack on crops, methods, transport, forestry and animal husbandry is an object lesson in what a
village can do from its own resources when the analysis of their
problems and the advice given is correct.[34]

[33] K. A. Busia, 'The Impact of Industrialisation on West Africa' (Nigerian
Institute of Social Research Conference, 1960).
[34] *Borgo a Mozzano* (Genoa, Shell Italiana, 1961). See also Chapter VI for
some results of the introduction of a cash crop in a Uganda village.

The raising of rural incomes by productive investment should also help to maintain social stability. There was always a gap, almost too big for imagination to comprehend or policy to face, between the rural African and the European. There is at present a real danger that this gap will remain, and even grow, between the favoured African *élites* and the villagers. Every step which can narrow this dangerous cleft will be valuable. The same, in lesser degree, is true of economic coherence. 'A Western type of enterprise cannot just be an island of high productivity and efficiency in an ocean of poverty and low standards.'[35]

Finally, the development of rural life and production from the land (duly contributing to the modern sector) is likely to harmonize best with the deeper emotional and cultural instincts of Africans.

The problem is not to wipe the slate clean in underdeveloped countries, and to write our technical and economic equations on it, but to recognize that different countries have a different language of social action; and possess, and indeed have long exercised, peculiar aptitudes for solving the problems of their own time and place; aptitudes which must be further developed in the historic setting of their own past to meet the exigencies of the present and the future.[36]

If indeed there is to be an African personality in the modern world, a great part of it must be rooted in the land, round which both cult and community have been built, which is woven into every institution, which lies deep in the texture of language, and moves the heart and energies of every African more surely than any other vision. Co-operative cultivation, common effort in clearing, in harvesting, in house building, in herding cattle all go back to ancient and still lively patterns of African life. If there is a place in the world in which 'human investment' can be harnessed to cut shorter the road into the modern world, it is to be found in the villages of Africa.

These arguments do not in any way imply a neglect of the growth of towns and the industrial occupations which they can offer. Towns play a vital part as a focus of new ideas and initiatives which are brought back to the rural scene; they will do much,

[35] M. J. Herskovitz in *Africa Today,* supra.
[36] Frankel, op. cit.

in the long run, for the emancipation of women and for setting a higher standard of cultural life. Despite the initial dangers of degradation, there is also the asset of new energy and vision which the more sophisticated urban environment may give. It is a question of the gradual growth of urban life as the essential basis for it is created by rural development.

Nor is the improvement of agricultural practice going to be all plain sailing. There are, indeed, formidable difficulties, often quoted, in the systems of land tenure. It may be that the economists are right in saying that the exchange economy cannot develop without full individual ownership and transfer of land. But, in the agricultural areas at least, very much can be done within existing systems, as many co-operative schemes have proved. Moreover, it is not unreasonable to believe that even seemingly immovable opposition to change may quite suddenly melt away. It was interesting to hear from one of the most perceptive and experienced men in Tropical Africa, whose life has been devoted to the understanding of African ways of thought: [37] 'An African will shed the older customary values very easily when once new economic opportunities and values grip him.' Before looking in more detail at the possibilities of economic development, the extent of the transition from these older values to the new must be considered.

[37] Hans Cory, Government Sociologist in Tanganyika.

CHAPTER V

FROM THE OLD CULTURE
TO THE NEW

'Industrialization is a way of life as well as of production and distribution. . . . Each culture emphasizes certain values which determine the way of life of a people.'[1]

This statement by Dr. Busia, who is contrasting the old African way of life and the incoming influences from Europe, could almost have been taken as the text for this book. For by 'industrialization' is really meant not simply a combination of scientific knowledge and applied techniques but the motives and values of a society which has the will to use and develop this knowledge and whose institutions reflect and support their system of values. Starting from a slightly different point, the whole of de Tocqueville's prophetic study of *Democracy in America* is founded upon an analysis of the underlying motives and values of democracy and their manifestation in personal life and in the shape of institutions. Between industrialization, democracy and even, as some would say, Protestantism, there are close links. For the individualist, competitive, egalitarian spirit which has been typical of the industrializing societies is one hostile to old-established status and authority. Combined with universal education it encouraged the individual to brush aside the older rankings of society and rise by his own efforts to economic independence and even power; and it raised the economic sphere of life, and all the institutions which serve it, almost if not quite to the paramount position in society. The European brought to Africa not merely skills and capital, but the personal motives and social forms without which, however great natural resources may be, economic growth will not take place.

I. SOME CONTRASTS

African political leaders have accepted with enthusiasm the aim of economic development. But African societies, shaped by their earlier and quite different necessities, still contain within them, as

[1] Busia, op. cit.

living forces, the personal attitudes and social institutions of the older world. If we are to understand a little better the outlook and behaviour of Africans, of the men who may come as applicants for a job in a factory or a bank, it is necessary to break down this clash of values into the realities of everyday life. What does it feel like to live, not between two worlds, but simultaneously in both of them?

Here generalization is particularly difficult. Both geographically and culturally, the spread of Western influence has been so un-even. Some African societies, not in deepest forest or desert but just off natural communications, remain to this day extraor-dinarily isolated. The aeroplane from Kariba to Livingstone passes over the valley of the Gwembe Tonga, now largely flooded by the rising lake. Elizabeth Colson has described how, after the with-drawal of the Mission stations in the 1930s:

It was almost twenty years before the Valley would again have Europeans resident within it. . . . No roads led into it. Access could only be had by footpaths, and these, as they wound through the rugged escarpments, were of such a nature that a bicycle was a hindrance rather than a help. (page 31.)

Until the coming of the roads in 1950, everything had to be trans-ported on the back or head or occasionally on donkey-back, and the nearest source of trade goods was some two or three days' travel from the Zambesi. . . . Since 1950, imports have increased, and the people are becoming progressively more dependent upon them. But there are still many women who have never struck a match, never held an electric torch or threaded a needle. People yearn for clothing and salt, and will work to obtain them. Other items seldom enter into their immediate calculations. (page 36.)[2]

Some cultures, though not inaccessible, have resisted change far more strongly than others. This is true of the strong Islamic cul-tures of the West African savannah, and of some groups, such as the Pakot (Suk) of East Africa, who have a highly specialized culture centred on a single occupation. Again, some of the strongly structured political systems have been able to absorb change with-in a traditional framework of institutions, while others, less coherent and definite, have tended to disintegrate.[3] The reasons

[2] E. Colson, *The Social Organisation of the Gwembe Tonga* (Kariba Studies, Manchester University Press for Rhodes-Livingstone Institute, 1960).
[3] See studies of Ruanda and Urundi by Ethel M. Albert, 'Socio-Political Organisation and Receptivity to Change', University of New Mexico, *South Western Journal of Anthropology*, vol. 16, no. 1, Spring 1960.

why one local culture rejects change which another will accept, or abandons one custom while clinging to another, are too complex and various for description here. It is enough to say that a similar European impact may have quite different results on two African groups not fifty miles apart.

Again, some African peoples, particularly on the West Coast, not only had longer European contacts but had evolved an urban and commercial life of their own which was perhaps more easily blended with the Western system when it came in full force. By contrast, in much of East and Central Africa, the money economy scarcely existed as late as 1900, save in the Indian and Arab trade of the East Coast ports.

In addition to these differences of geography, culture and intensity of modernizing influences (whether from European or African leadership), there are differences within any single group, mainly between those with some formal education and the rest. But this is by no means the single cause. Men who have migrated to employment, soldiers or traders who have travelled widely may become deeply influenced by new ideas and patterns of behaviour.

Thus the rate and depth of change can only be measured by careful analysis of individual areas and of the life history of special groups within them. But there is a single *direction* of change which is applicable as to some factors all over Tropical Africa and as to others at least over very wide areas. The traveller in East, Central and West Africa cannot fail to be struck by the repetition of certain situations in every one of a dozen countries on his route. Whether the process is far advanced or barely started, and with all the variations of custom and environment and influence, it moves always one way. This chapter will consider some specific aspects of this change, the groups to whom it chiefly applies, and finally some of the social problems which result.

One measure of change lies in the degree to which everyday events are ascribed to rational or scientific causes rather than to spiritual or magical influences. Jacques Maritain once argued that until the Church had conquered animism in Western Europe, the age of science could not begin—the electric telegraph could not come if a powerful spirit was believed to sit on every pole.

The situation in modern Africa is extremely complex. On the one hand there are the traditional African religious beliefs, usually called animism, very widely connected with religious reverence and service to the spirits of ancestors. 'Ancestor worship'—a phrase which is apt to carry wrong implications of idolatry in Western ears—represents a strong belief in the continuing power and influence of the spirits of the dead, and it has had, as in many advanced cultures such as that of China, many beneficial effects in the support of tribal ethics; it is connected, though in widely differing ways, with parallel beliefs in the existence of God and of other superhuman spirits. Alongside religious belief there has also been belief in magic. Magic is usually distinguished from religion in that the religious believer petitions for help, which he may not receive, while the man who uses magic believes that he has a key to certain occult forces which are compelled to act if the right formula is used. Into this situation have come two new and major religions, Christianity and Islam, both very widely propagated and accepted. It is probably safest to say that, for the majority of African people who have come in contact with these new religions, three elements of belief continue to exist simultaneously—the cult of ancestors, magic and either Christianity or Islam. Dr. Mair observed in Buganda : 'As regards the recourse to magic for supernatural aid, my impression is that with the Baganda Christianity has neither discredited nor replaced the traditional methods.' [4] Claude Tarditz [5] observes that in many Christian families of Porto Novo the customary ceremonies of the ancestor cult were observed in addition to a Christian burial service; and in the Cameroons it has been noted that although 74 per cent of African plantation workers gave their religion as Christian, both animist and magical practices were almost universal. [6] In Ghana Dr. Margaret Field [7] observed that many of those who came to consult local priest-oracles at their shrines were Christians.

Probably each of the three elements of belief fulfils a need. The ancestor cult is so deeply interwoven with tribal customs and rituals and rules of family life that to abandon it altogether would mean the most painful severance from the family and community.

---

[4] L. P. Mair, *An African People in the Twentieth Century* (London, Routledge, 1934).

[5] Tarditz, op. cit. Dr. Field also points out that the frequent 'confessions' (self-accusations) to witchcraft which occur in mental disturbance help to confirm popular belief in the existence of witches.

[6] E. and S. Ardener and W. A. Warmington, *Plantation and Village in the Cameroons* (London, Oxford University Press, 1960).

[7] M. J. Field, *Search for Security* (London, Faber and Faber, 1960).

In honouring such observances the highly educated and Christian African would be showing a certain piety towards tradition and towards other, less sophisticated, members of his family; they may arouse in him the same recollections of childhood and the unity of a community which an urban agnostic in Europe would feel at a funeral in his old village church. Islam and Christianity provide for the need of a higher religion, which includes the promise of life after death, and both have a certain prestige value, since in both cases they were associated with conquering civilizations. Finally, magic remains a living reality, never far beneath the surface. Many anthropologists [8] have pointed out that magic tends to be associated with situations of uncertainty, lack of knowledge, lack of security in personal relations. In consequence it is apt to grow, rather than decrease, in urban situations where Africans are cut off from the support of their home community and feel insecurity in most acute form. Indeed, there is a tendency in modern Africa for the best of the traditional religion to be degraded into magical practices; an improvement in the stability and conditions of town life could probably do most to halt this. Many employers in Africa could testify to the fear of magic among employees— we were told of one man in the Copperbelt who had reached one of the highest ranks open to Africans with some education who abandoned his job with its accumulated long-service rights to return to his village because he feared that his life was threatened by witchcraft.

Superstition, as we know in Europe, never dies completely, and is particularly liable to reappear in times of war, or insecurity and anxiety. It is a form of extra insurance. Indeed, those in Europe who have abandoned all living Christian belief will treat Christianity as a superstition—a mother who believes far more firmly in the efficacy of a 'polio' injection than in Baptism will have her child baptized to be on the safe side; and here Christianity is in a similar relation to science as animism to Christianity in Africa. In terms of the entry of African peoples into a modern economy it is not the ancestor cult as such which is likely to be a hindrance; belief in magic, with its inhibiting effects on ambition (for success invites jealousy and ill-will) and its results in irrational behaviour is far more serious.

[8] e.g. Malinowski, Firth, Richards.

A second, and vital, index of change lies in the degree to which obligations inside 'Western' relationships, and outside the family, are felt to have binding force. A factory or County Council or the Civil Service demand special forms (not degrees) of moral behaviour which are sometimes strange to African values and sometimes conflict with them. The primary, overriding, obligation to the family, the custom of bringing a chief a small present or 'dash' when asking assistance, are deeply embedded in African custom. But the factory personnel officer should not, in Western eyes, give all the jobs to his relatives; the Councillor should not expect a 'dash' if he presses a constituent's complaint; confidential information is supposed to be held in trust for the institution and cannot be passed on to relatives. Africans understand well enough that a man may have different roles in society—as head of family, as chief or in a ritual capacity. But the number of roles was small, and each had its morals attached to it. The new circumstances introduce many new roles—manager, District Councillor, civil servant, trade unionist. To Africans who grasp these new opportunities their own tradition does not supply any corresponding set of rules and their behaviour may conflict with what seems to a European to be the elementary demands of the role. In the field of financial honesty, the issue has been clouded by the presence of Europeans. Both white individuals and their institutions were felt to be almost infinitely rich. They would not really miss a few pounds, and indeed, had they been African, they would have been under some obligation to help the poor. Moreover, they were an alien group, to which the rules for internal behaviour in the African community might not apply. There are many signs that where wholly African institutions are involved, a different attitude is shown. It has apparently been no disgrace to defraud a County Council which is felt to be part of 'government', but to steal the funds of a tribal association or a cotton Co-operative primary society is likely to bring the offender into most serious trouble with his own people. The growth of commercial honesty and of the other qualities which are needed in the new social economy will depend both on a much fuller identification of the African with institutions felt to be genuinely his own, and on a gradual training in the moral systems which attach to the new roles.

It is hard to overstate the importance of the family relationship

Va. Dakar, Senegal

[*Photograph by R. J. Harrison Church*

Vb. Ibadan, Western Nigeria

VI. The District Commissioner's car ferried by canoe and raft across the
Benue River, Nigeria   [*Photograph by Pictorial Press*

in African society. Africans invest in personal relationships,[9] because they supply their ultimate security. When the Wankie [10] Coal Mine dismissed 7,000 African workers in a week in the 1931 slump, they 'just disappeared'—in fact, to relatives and people who had obligations to them. Until an alternative system of social security appears, family obligations are likely to remain paramount, even where they conflict with the obligations of the new type of society.

The recognition of authority is another point of difference. Most Tropical African societies recognize authority in age, in traditional office, in high lineage or sometimes in another tribal group felt to be superior. The industrial hierarchy is built upon technical skill, experience and seniority in employment, which have little to do with age and nothing with lineage or tribal history. The African who finds himself within such a hierarchy is in a very strange world.

Closely related—but not identical—with concepts of authority are those of status. The new westernized society introduces new status ranks—to have Cambridge Overseas School Certificate is a high status symbol, particularly in rural society. These new symbols tend to replace the older ones, or at least to coexist with them. Professor Nadel records how a young, educated African in Bida (Northern Nigeria) remarked to him : 'All our native ranks and titles mean nothing today; what has meaning are only offices under the Native Authority, posts which carry real influence and wealth.' [11] This is a deeply significant—and probably exaggerated —remark, since Nupe society, which Professor Nadel studied, was firmly divided by various ranking systems, as well as by slavery and patronage, as were other sections of the Fulani empire.[12] The caste system in Senegal (nobles, freemen, artisans, freed slaves, griots, slaves, in descending order) is another example of a status system which cannot be fitted into a Western pattern of education, free opportunity and technical hierarchies. It is easy for Europeans to forget how complex such systems are, and how far down in the social scale they run. Even the humblest official of the westernized

[9] See particularly Elizabeth Colson in *Africa Today*, supra.
[10] Near Livingstone, Northern Rhodesia.
[11] Nadel, op. cit.
[12] See M. G. Smith, op. cit.

administration may hold a very high ranking in relation to the African villager.[13]

The relative emancipation of women will provide another obvious conflict between the old culture and the new. But it would be easy to read into this a quite false idea of the status of women in a great many traditional African societies. Apart from the strict Muslim groups, there are many peoples in Africa—for example, the Yoruba of Western Nigeria—where women have by tradition a strong element of economic and social independence; nor are these only the matrilineal[14] societies. Perhaps in almost all African societies, the woman has a 'kingdom' of her own, with both its obligations and its recognition. She frequently has responsibility for cultivation of land; for the preparation of food, with all its customary significance; for rituals concerned with fertility; and in settling a host of questions concerned with the marriage of young people and the obligations connected with it. 'It is because she bears a heavy responsibility that her position in the family and with her husband is a secure one.'[15] Emancipation, in the sense of adopting a Western pattern of behaviour, may in fact deprive the African woman, at least temporarily, both of her duties and her honoured place, particularly if she is living in a large mixed town, far from the ritual of the hearthstones and the ceremonies which helped to express and formalize her place in village life. Only a few have broken right through to a full education and a fully westernized 'professional' life.

Attitudes to work may again show a profound difference between the old and the new culture. Professor Biesheuvel[16] has noted the almost compulsive attitude to the virtues of hard work which colours European society. Whether or not this springs, as Max Weber suggested, from the Protestant ethic, it has certainly been deeply imprinted by the further development of our competitive and technical society. Work is seen, not only as the con-

[13] 'Le facteur des postes d'Oran apparait effroyablement privilégié par rapport de la masse de la population, alors qu'à Arras ou ailleurs il se sent au contraire une personnage très modeste.' M. de Schryver, *L'avenir politique du Congo Belge* (Brussels, Institut Belge de Science Politique, 1960).
[14] I.e. tracing descent through the female line. It does not imply a matriarchy.
[15] D. Westerman, *The African Today and Tomorrow* (London, Oxford University Press for International African Institute, 1949).
[16] S. Biesheuvel, *Race, Culture and Personality* (Johannesburg, South African Institute of Race Relations, 1959).

dition of progress, but as a positive moral good, so that missionaries were constantly preaching 'habits of industry' and 'the dignity of labour'. Certainly, such an attitude is far removed from that of the older African way of life. Europeans have constantly declaimed against the 'apathy', the incorrigible laziness of African tribesmen, sometimes with moral condemnation pure and simple, sometimes with excuses of hot climate, malnutrition or debilitating disease. But if African life was leisurely, if there was time to gossip under a shady tree, to have a three-day beer-drink, to go off hunting more for fun than for any real expectation of a bag, it was partly because life did not offer great vistas of possible headway and achievement. Africans were not pursued by the Western devil called 'Time is Money', nor the anxiety to 'go places' when there was no place to go. Even hunger might not be worth the extra effort of forethought and labour needed to avoid it.[17] Work was necessary for subsistence, to fulfil tribal and family obligations, to amass bride-price or perhaps gain a mark of status : it had no personal moral connotation.[18] To avoid its boredom, it might often be done in company, with song and mutual encouragement. 'Probably the greatest shock to the newly educated African in paid employment is that he has to work all day and every day.' [19] This subject, which is clearly of key importance in a modernizing society, is dealt with at some length in Chapter IX.

The African attitude to land, so different from the commercial attitude, has been mentioned already. It is the symbol of a world where access to land, and therefore to food, is the basic security, however poor the land may be. The transition from a society where security is based on land (with its dangers of floods and famines) to one where it rests on social organization (full employment—with its dangers of disorganization or breakdown) is a profound change and one which stirs deep emotion and fears.

Another field of contrast in the early period of contact between the Western and the African traditional culture has been that of

[17] See particularly Richards, *Land, Labour and Diet in Northern Rhodesia*. The last pages have a balanced assessment of this particular situation among the Bemba.

[18] For a detailed analysis of attitudes to work in a primitive community outside Africa (Tikopia, Solomon Islands), see Raymond Firth, 'Work and Community in a Primitive Society' in Report of H.R.H. The Duke of Edinburgh's Study Conference, 1956, vol. II (London, Oxford University Press, 1957).

[19] Field, op. cit.

African attitudes towards economic exchange and the use of money. It has sometimes been said that at least some African peoples altogether lack an economic sense. Cyril Ehrlich [20] quotes a case in Uganda where a cattle owner, who would refuse 600 shillings for a beast, is prepared to exchange it quite happily for a 300 shilling bicycle; or where Baganda peasants would sell trees worth 100 shillings for 10 shillings. Dr. Mair [21] has noticed similar cases in Uganda and Elizabeth Hoyt [22] in Kenya. In fact, the main proposition only makes sense in relation to a particular stage of society. Professor Polyani, [23] in a symposium on the nature of the market in early civilizations, has pointed out that modern conceptions of the economy are entirely strange in societies which redistribute goods through multiple reciprocal obligations based on kinship and other ties.

The disembedded economy of the 19th Century stood apart from the rest of society, more especially from the political and governmental systems. In a market economy the production and distribution of material goods in principle is carried on through a self-regulating system of price-making markets. It is governed by laws of its own, the so-called laws of supply and demand, and motivated by fear of hunger and hope of gain.

In contrast, in societies regulated by status rather than contract, and relying on reciprocity:

The elements of the economy are here embedded in non-economic institutions, the economic process itself being instituted through kinship, marriage, age-groups, secret societies, totemic associations and public solemnities. The term 'economic' life would here have no obvious meaning.

Thus land, or cattle, or goods would pass at betrothal or marriage, marking a change of status, gifts or food would move from person to person according to the rules of the social situation. Nor is there an exact quantitative measurement—'reciprocity demands adequacy of response, not mathematical equality'.

Firth, [24] in a different context, makes the same observation:

[20] Ehrlich, op. cit.   [21] Mair, op. cit.
[22] E. Hoyt, 'Economic Sense and the African', Africa, XXII, 1952.
[23] Karl Polyani, Conrad M. Arensberg and Harry W. Pearson (Ed.), Trade and Market in the Early Empires (Illinois, The Free Press and The Falcon's Wing Press, 1957).
[24] R. Firth, Primitive Economies of the New Zealand Maori (New York, E. P. Dutton and Company, 1929).

In a primitive society, there is no relationship which is of a purely economic character . . . Therein lies the strength of primitive society, in that it enlists the binding forces of one aspect of society to support those of another.

Finally, Dr. Mair [25] illustrates very well the difference in approach :

When one compares the reason why cattle are desired with the reason why barkcloths are desired, it becomes clear that different commodities are valued from points of view so different that the values cannot be reduced to a single common denominator . . . the possession of most goods is prized for its own sake, rather than for the sake of other goods which might be acquired by disposing of them.

These quotations help to explain the exchange of a cow for a bicycle in what seems an 'uneconomic' way. They do, however, represent the pure theory rather than the changing facts of the present situation. Even in status systems, fairly precise numbers of cattle or other goods become recognized as the right quantity for bride price or other transactions; and as soon as some form of currency becomes common, there is a gradual move towards reducing transactions to a single common standard. The naïveté of early (1910) Baganda cotton-growers,[26] who are said to have delivered their cotton at the collecting point and walked off without waiting for payment (presumably regarding it as a form of tax) does not last long in modern circumstances. While it is important to remember that many African societies are still only beginning to separate out 'economic' from other activities, it would be utterly false to assume that in some way 'Africans' lack economic sense. Professor William O. Jones [27] has demonstrated, over a wide field, that where Africans have a real chance of understanding the issues involved, they have a shrewd sense of economic advantage; and indeed from personal observation, it is difficult not to be struck by the amazing, if sometimes misplaced, ingenuity with which many Africans will snatch at the smallest economic opportunity.[28] As

[25] Mair, op. cit.

[26] See P. G. Powesland, *Economic Policy and Labour* (Ed. W. Elkan), East African Studies, no. 10, 1957.

[27] W. O. Jones, 'Economic Man in Africa' *Food Research Institute Studies* (Stanford University, vol. I, no. 2, May 1960).

[28] For instance the man who obtained free from a bank a large packet of folders, with captioned illustrations showing the virtues of a savings account, and sold them at 2*d*. each as a simple English Primer.

will appear later, some well-intentioned agricultural settlement schemes and some incentives used in industry have come to grief for the very reason that the Africans concerned have worked out what will pay them best more accurately than their employers. The transition from single calculations of what pays to the more complex economic sense which involves calculation of capital, depreciation, ton-miles or machine-utilization obviously will take time and formal education, as it does in the West.

Finally, at the level of more personal life and of institutions such as marriage, the transition from old to new ways is often painful and difficult. There is much evidence, particularly among middle-class Africans, of a movement by both men and women towards accepting the Western monogamous pattern, and towards a much more personal relationship between husband and wife—a movement from a contract between families to a companionship between individuals. An enquiry among Ghanaian students showed that 73 per cent of the sample thought polygamy 'definitely backward', and that 87 per cent (80 per cent of males and 94 per cent of females) thought that 'love' was the most important factor in marriage.[29] The same group were predominantly hostile to the traditional matrilineal pattern by which a maternal uncle assumes responsibility for children. In the same way, and for more commercial reasons, matrilineal inheritance (by the wife's lineage, not by the husband's children) is becoming increasingly unpopular, since a man who builds up a business cannot hand it on to his sons.[30]

These changes in personal life are far more important than the somewhat trivial 'proofs' of them which can be given in a few statistics. It is a fundamental quality and attitude to life which is at issue. In the old world, the community comprehended the individuals within it, supported and sanctioned them, surrounded them with a cocoon of fine-spun relationships, related them to the ancestors of the tribe and to its posterity. In return, it exacted certain disciplines and obligations—the choice of marriage partners which would best serve the harmony and propriety of family life, the duty to contribute in work and wealth to the common

[29] T. P. Omari, 'Attitudes in West Africa towards Marriage', *British Journal of Sociology*, vol. XI, no. 3, September 1960.

[30] Peter Garlick, *African Traders in Kumasi* (University College of Ghana, 1959). See also 'The Matrilinear System and Business Enterprise' (N.I.S.E.R. Conference, 1960).

good. Against this world must be set the Western emphasis on the free individual, free to develop capacities and powers, to choose his friends and his wife, to move beyond his home community into a wider society, to insulate himself against demands from less successful relations or neighbours—but free also to fail, and to find little but the impersonal support of State charity if he does. The new opportunities carry with them the new burden of individual freedom to the deepest level of personality. They involve personal moral responsibility. They involve the strength to live without dependence.[31]

2. THE PRESENT MIXTURE

This clash of values over so wide a field—religion, family, status, authority, land, work, economic choice, marriage, personality itself—has been presented as a series of sharp irreconcilable contrasts. This is not at all how it happens or is lived. It is impossible to describe the numberless shades and variations of 'westernization', between countries, classes, individuals and indeed in the growth of a single personality. At one end of the scale is the tribesman still wholly wrapped in his own culture; at the other end the fully westernized graduate, coming from an educated home, having studied in Europe or America, a man of the world in every sense. It is more confusing than useful to speak of an African 'middle class'. In societies changing so fast there has not yet been time for classes to crystallize, nor any sure criteria to distinguish them. In East and Central Africa, where until very recently there has been no group of wealthy African traders, education and some official job will do most to separate a recognizable group, with a common language of thought and common attitudes. But in West Africa there are many ways of being in a privileged group. Perhaps it is worth while to quote in full a picture of the wealthy Yoruba trader:[32]

The traders, whether they are produce-buyers, wholesale or retail shopkeepers, butchers or lorry owners—and most of them combine

[31] Cf. Mannoni, op. cit. 'The occidental has accepted abandonment and has learned to live in a sort of emotional vacuum, where yearnings towards perfection, the absolute and the infinite may take root and flourish. These yearnings have long been the core of an ideal which the civilizations of the West have cherished, whence are derived alike their success and their discontents.'

[32] P. C. Lloyd, 'The Integration of the New Economic Classes into Local Government in Western Nigeria', *African Affairs*, October 1953.

two or more of these occupations—are the wealthiest men in these towns. Some of the bigger traders in a town such as Ado—a commercial centre with a population of 17,000—probably have an annual income exceeding £2,000. It is these men who build the finest houses, own cars and entertain lavishly. Most of these men are from humble origins; those who are now in their fifties have probably not been to school; many are remembered as being poor men in their youth. They have built up their businesses by their own industry. Almost all are working in their own towns and thus have close kinship ties with their neighbours; many continue to live in their family compounds and their elegant two-storey houses rise above the thatch roofs of their relatives. Since they observe the tribal customs of generosity towards their kinsfolk and strangers, these men are highly regarded as assets belonging to the whole town. They have usurped many of the functions of the chiefs, for people will admire their sagacity and wealth and bring to them their disputes for settlement.

Here, then, is a West African 'middle class'; and to it perhaps should be added many of the wealthier cocoa farmers, men earning £1,000 a year or sometimes much more.[33] But there are other middle classes—for example, the middle- and upper-grade civil servants, living in a hire-purchased house in a new suburb of Lagos or Ibadan, with refrigerator and radiogram proudly predominant among the furniture. There is, in one sense, a middle class of chiefs, both in East and West Africa. In Uganda,

The County and sub-County (Civil Service) Chiefs, together with educated persons of other professions, tend to form social cliques. Such persons share an *élite* style of life, based on higher incomes and in general speak each other's language—language of high-level politics and events beyond the ken of peasants.[34]

This is a very different picture from the village chief, often an oldish man, with little education, simply dressed and living in his thatched home alongside his people.

How much of Western values these men have fully adopted can only be known by knowing them and their background. Almost

[33] F. Morton-Williams calculated in 1953 that there were between 10 and 20 such farmers in one medium-sized town (Ibio, Western Nigeria, population 11,000) earning over £1,000 after paying labour, and 4 earning considerably more. ('The Social Consequences of Industrialism among the South West Yoruba' (W.A.I.S.E.R. Conference, Sociology Section, 1953).

[34] Fallers, op. cit., p. 180. See also Richards, *East African Chiefs*, supra. It was calculated that 68 per cent of Class I and II Ganda chiefs had some secondary education.

certainly they will hold at once to both African and European ways and this happens at all levels. In Nairobi's Pumwani estate there was (in 1961) a woman practising witchcraft for money and investing the proceeds in a trading lorry; in Ghana, Professor Apter mentions 'a tough young C.P.P. official' proudly introducing his wife, a baby of some two years of age.[35] In one respect, certainly, even the most westernized will differ from his European counterpart. He will have a far closer contact with his extended family, and thus will see and know quite intimately people from every rank and occupation, sharing out his salary to a wide range of dependants and often housing a relative from the country who is completely unused to Western ways. The 'two worlds', so far apart in content, are never far apart in the reality of modern African life.

It may be worth while moving a little closer to the detail of modern town life in a single country. A large town in modern Ghana[36] is a scene of great vitality, a seething scramble to find a niche, a snapping up of unconsidered trifles of job or opportunity or cash. There are the local townsmen, settled for a generation or more, and there is the constant influx from the country, particularly from the poorer areas of the Ghana North. Competition is intense. The desire for education is intense. Over the whole scene flickers the entrancing light of modernity and emancipation—the shops, cinemas, gramophones, motor-cars, the dancing and the dressing up, and, of course, the advertisements—'You're not a success unless you own a Chevrolet'. Below the outward show there is real poverty, gross overcrowding, a great deal of prostitution and the exploitation of young girls as housemaids, disclosed in detail by the surveys of Dr. Busia and Ione Acquah.[37] The young man who comes to town to earn a living will at first share a room, probably with several others, and may then find, for a modest payment, a 'cateress', concubine or 'friend' who will cook his meals and wash his clothes; and after a time he will marry.

Marriage in the old system was essentially a linking of families, not of individuals; infant betrothal was usual, and still is quite

[35] Apter, op. cit.

[36] Much of what follows concerning Ghana is based upon an unpublished MS. from Mrs. M. Niculescu, provided for this study.

[37] In Sekondi and Accra respectively. See K. A. Busia, *A Social Survey of Sekondi-Takoradi* (London, Crown Agents, 1950) and I. Acquah, *Accra Survey* (London, University of London Press, 1958).

common in Ghana; certainly families will be consulted and involved. While in the old tradition the wife must be faithful, a good deal of sexual licence was allowed to men, and there was provision, without social stigma, for any children who might be born from such affairs. After the first gifts of betrothal had passed, it was not unusual for the engaged couple to live together, and it might be some time before the final marriage was completed. In some groups it was not the custom for the wife to live in her husband's hut, but to bring his meals over from the women's quarters and perhaps to stay the night. Such a tie, loose in the Western sense of the personal bond between the married pair, but fairly tight in the whole complex of family relationships, is loosened still further in the new urban conditions, save where a Christian concept of monogamous and loving partnership is in rivalry with the older pattern. The modern emancipated girl may give her favours, even after betrothal, to more than one young friend. Middle school goes on often till seventeen, long after puberty, and school books or nursing training cost money which many girls earn by casual prostitution. If a child follows, certainly a father is to be found if possible; but the family in the country is there to help. The possession of children is what matters most, and is welcomed most, rather than the marriage ring.

When the young couple are married in the town, there are still difficulties. The man is out working, and the girl may need to earn too. Children, therefore, may have a hard time, and particularly in early adolescence, when they are virtually expected to look after themselves. In the village system, even if there were not two wives, there were three or four generations all around, and at least two women were really needed for a single family, to garden, cook, care for the children, carry the men's meals.[38] But the grandparents probably do not come to town, and the children run loose and perhaps earn some pennies; a young daughter may well be 'pledged' (now illegal, but still covertly practised) and work as a household slave, sleeping in a corner of the kitchen floor in another household and caring for younger children there. Customary marriages are easily broken, and they remain the usual pattern—in Accra, with a population of about 400,000, the yearly total of marriages under the Ordinance varied between 160 and 280

[38] In many groups, the wife could not handle the men's food at certain times, and this alone demanded a substitute.

over the five years from 1956 to 1960. It is a strange situation, between 'the old system which never demanded a high morality but controlled the results of immorality carefully, and the new, which seems to demand an impossibly high and puritanical standard while at the same time condoning quite as great a degree of actual immorality without appearing even to see the inconsistency.[39] There is no doubt that the women, and particularly those with better education, would like to move towards the monogamous, individual marriage, as the studies of Omari and Tarditz have shown;[40] but the final safety net of the extended family is still needed and welcome.

Life is more expensive in towns, and the old family system which could meet its obligations in the subsistence economy with at least food and shelter is overstrained by the cash economy, where food must be bought, a room must be rented, and at some cost, and school fees, an ever-present worry, have to be met. Further, there is the crippling cost of marriages and funerals, which custom demands; figures of from £80 to £180 have been quoted for funerals even among the poor, and far higher sums for the middle classes. In relation to a worker's wage of £10 or £15 a *month*, these are huge sums. Young girls expect more—cheap necklaces, scented soap, pomade for the hair, a new dress at Easter, and will take a lover to get them. Young married women spend money on 'women's vocational classes' to teach them how to be good hostesses to more educated husbands, how to behave in the new Western manner. Malinowski [41] has pointed out how the pressure to reach these half-Western and half-urban standards results in overwork and undernourishment. But whatever the social cost—and most of it falls on the women and children—the

[39] M. Niculescu, ibid. In Ghana the influence of Christian teaching and modern manners has been so strong that until recently no educated person would have liked to argue the case for polygamy. It was assumed to be part of the old, unregenerate attitude. The new White Paper may have altered their attitude.

[40] op. cit.

[41] 'Family budgets show how the expenditure necessary for the maintenance of the new standards very often, almost invariably, exceeds the regular earnings of the father of the family. This means malnutrition, insufficient training for the children and overwork in additional pursuits, often illegal, by the wife.' Malinowski, op. cit. This refers to life in South African towns; but other observations confirm it in Tropical Africa.

pull of modernity, education, the will to succeed is stronger. The borrowings from libraries show it—textbooks and more textbooks, so that the Regional Library in Enugu had actually a rule that a proportion of Fiction must be taken with the texts; the sales of books on the lines of *How to Make Friends and Influence People* are enormous.

For the husband, work may be hard to find. Yet, despite the risks, he will often change his job again and again. There are so many prizes to be won—for have not young men become M.P.s or Company Directors in a very few years?—that each man is afraid of missing opportunities, of being overtaken by the more enterprising in the race for success.

Although much of this detail refers to Ghana, the same kind of change is going on in all the larger towns of Tropical Africa, though most violently in the new cities rather than in the Yoruba towns which were long adapted to a life at once traditional and fully urban. It is impossible to review the comparable changes in the village, since the cultural variation from Muslim villages in the savannah, pastoral groups in East Africa, fishing villages in the Niger Delta is so great. But wherever money, the radio and second-ary education are beginning to get a grip, the movement is in the same direction, and beginning to be especially strong among women, who have lagged behind. Recent studies of, for example, Ibo women show the new spirit :

Nowadays, women do not care if the husband does not give them any food, for they can go to the farm and get cassava. If a woman has money she rents land and plants cassava. The year after she does this, she can have cassava meal which she can sell and have her own money. Then she can say : 'What is man? I have my own money.' [42]

Without questioning principles, straightforward social policy can do much to alleviate strains in the towns, and particularly through low-cost housing. Very encouraging headway has been made, and some housing in Dar-es-Salaam, the Congo Towns, Lagos and elsewhere is remarkably good; the achievement of

[42] Phoebe V. Ottenberg, 'The Position of Women among the Afikpo Ibo', in W. R. Bascom and M. J. Herskovitz, *Continuity and Change in African Cultures* (University of Chicago Press, 1959). Record of a conversation with an Ibo woman. The more 'modern' Ibo women are now beginning to spend their money on education instead of buying 'titles'.

SICAP,[43] the main housing agency in Dakar, in building to almost garden city standards for lower middle-class Africans is outstanding. It is not only a question of low cost, but of housing suited to the traditional pattern; boxes built for the nuclear family only are forcing a choice on Africa which may not be desirable, and in any case they are often forced to house the extended family, or part of it, with appalling room densities. The conscious choice between the old culture and the European has not really been made, but industry, housing authorities, welfare departments and many more public bodies are in fact prejudging the issue without facing it, by cramming African life into European buildings and institutions.

It would be wrong to attribute to Africans an anxious and solemn brooding over social 'problems'. The word itself has a European ring. The stresses of urban life are, on the whole, taken lightly, from day to day. Neither anxious forethought nor thrifty saving characterized African villagers. Even in England, the real working classes were both more extravagant and more generous than the thrifty white-collar group, and they have always thought of the lower middle classes as close-fisted and too serious about life. Ferdinand Zweig's [44] vivid case histories among the English workers bring out again and again that 'you must take life as it comes', 'saving never made a man a millionaire', 'you can't take it with you', 'have a bit of pleasure when you can'. There is a fine line between generosity and fecklessness, and one which only those who have known real poverty and the monotony of scene and diet and work it brings are entitled to draw.

Further, Africans on the West Coast particularly have invented their own institutions for social support. There are, in great numbers, Friendly and Mutual Benefit Societies based on tribe or occupation or place of origin, and they are extremely popular. An Enquiry[45] in the main towns of the Gold Coast in 1954 listed 193

[43] *Société Immobilière de Cap Vert*. It was originally granted capital in the form of ownership of streets in Dakar, on which money was borrowed. The infrastructure of roads, drainage, &c., is paid for by subsidy, and the houses are let on 10-year hire purchase to cover building and maintenance. About 4,000 houses had been built by the end of 1960.
[44] F. Zweig, *Labour, Life and Poverty* (London, Gollancz, 1949).
[45] *Report on Enquiry with regard to Friendly and Mutual Benefit Groups in the Gold Coast, 1954* (Accra, Government Printer, 1955).

such societies. They included Friendly and Mutual Benefit Societies, often attached to religious orders or churches (such as the 'Think about Yourself Society', 'God Fearers' Society'); Tribal Benevolent Societies, Tribal Improvement Societies, Akan Family Clan Societies (one of which included one-sixth of the population of Cape Coast), Trade and Retail Groups (such as 'Herbalists and Fetish Priests and Priestesses'), Employees Unions, Denominational Groups and various Drumming, Temperance and Dramatic Clubs. These, combined with the Western-type associations, give a great range of choice and possible refuge to the urban African for a very small subscription of 3*d*. to 2*s*. a month and an entrance fee of 2*s*. or 3*s*. Most of them pay out benefits for bereavement, sickness and other special occasions. Where these societies flourish, they are of great social importance, not only in protecting the townsman[46] but in bringing some urban wealth back to the villages. Ibo societies in Eastern Nigerian villages collect large sums for schools and bridges and scholarships, partly by writing round to every son of the village, perhaps far away in Lagos, for a subscription. This is an institution with purely African roots which fits perfectly into the modern scene.

The agencies of change are increasingly pervasive. If the schools, the press, radio and soon television are the most obvious, personal contact is no doubt the most effective. Africans are an extremely mobile people. Although, as in England less than 100 years ago, perhaps most villagers have never left their village, there is a willingness, indeed a desire, to travel over long distances and often on foot, which is far stronger than ever it was in Great Britain. There is a constant coming and going, from town to village and village to town, on labour migration, for education, to visit relations, to trade. Towns in themselves, in any part of Africa, force new ideas upon the visitor. Moreover, they contain, not least in East Africa, an amazing range of European-type societies and activities. In the African estates of Nairobi can be listed :[47]

---

[46] To give one example from the East Coast, the Luo Society in Mombasa is said to have stamped out prostitution by Luo girls there by sending any culprits back to their tribal area near Lake Victoria. For societies in Freetown see Michael Banton, *West African City*, supra.

[47] *Annual Report, Social Service and Housing Department* (City Council of Nairobi, 1959).

Cinemas	Radio Rediffusion	Social Service League
Reading Rooms	Choir Festival	Social Clubs
Boxing	Hockey Club	Record Club
Athletics	Football	Badminton
Billiards	Youth Clubs	Table Tennis
Concerts	Adult Literacy	Community Centres
Women's Clubs	Classes	Women's Housecraft
Boy Scout Clubs	Teenager Clubs	Church Centres
Industrial Training	Girl Guides and	Salvation Army
British Red Cross	Brownies	Child Welfare
Discharged Prisoners'	British Legion	League of Mercy
Aid	St. John Ambulance	Evening Classes
Dances and Tea	Society of St. Vincent	Exhibitions
Parties	de Paul	Day Nurseries
Mission Centres	Y.M.C.A. and	Society for Deaf and
Society for the Blind	Y.W.C.A.	Dumb Children

In British West Africa a similar list could be made, but it would be distinguished by an equal or larger number of the purely African societies mentioned above. In French West Africa, also, the list would be more African, since the British zeal for voluntary associations has never been matched in France.

Outside, in the villages, such influences are fewer. Perhaps the strongest throughout the whole of Tropical Africa are the Community Development activities. The Reports of the Departments in each country reel off an ever-lengthening list of projects and activities almost every one of which contains some westernizing or at least educative element; in the Rhodesias perhaps the work of the Information Departments, the Agricultural Development Services and the Radio Homecraft Clubs [48] should be specially mentioned.

A certain change will take place in these activities as, with independence and the slow disappearance of European staff, they come through wholly African sources; but in almost every case they are and will be none the less modernizing and westernizing influences. The face, though not perhaps the heart, of rural Africa is about to change very fast.

Clearly, a number of major social problems are raised by this transition towards a set of Western values in a society not equipped

[48] Short broadcasts on women's subjects to listening clubs, which proved immensely popular.

with either the institutions or the wealth which have in part created and in part reflected and sustained the Western way of life. Some form of new social security will be needed if the security of land and family weakens or breaks down. Some stabilizing ideal will be needed for marriage and morals. In housing and medical services some methods will be needed which are modern yet not one-tenth as costly as those of the rich, developed countries. Above all, new aims of education in Africa for the possible—rather than the imaginary—African societies of the next twenty years will have to be conceived. These issues form part of the task facing African governments; they will be discussed in later chapters. At this point it is enough to emphasize the mixture, indeed fusion, between two cultural systems which is at present at work. It is not, in Africa, a question of obliterating the old in favour of the new, nor of living with two sharply defined and warring value systems, both in full vigour. The culture of England, of France, of China grew in its own environment, shaped by history, literature, climate, the size of land spaces, the slowly identified genius of different peoples. None of the three would be the same in the African land-scape and in the hearts of Africans. Even at the moment when the gap between European knowledge and skill and African life seemed so wide, so immeasurable that the only course would be wholesale rejection of old ways and simple imitation of the new, there has been an African character to the borrowings, a con-tinuing strong pulse of African life below the European clothes and forms. This is most true in West Africa; but it will be true in East and Central Africa within a decade. For even today, beneath the outward forms of change, in marriage or Parliament or trade, there remains a world of contact and understanding between Africans which is almost wholly hidden from European eyes. Where there is intermarriage, the European learns—and perhaps teaches—a little more. But for the most part it would be false to believe that the appearance of westernization, in any field, in-volves a total change. The private messages that pass from man to man, the long branching channels through which social life and action flow, the unspoken assumptions, the ultimate reserves of energy and emotional force upon which an African will rely in a time of testing—these are deep currents in the stream of African life which the outside watcher sees only here and there where they break against a rock.

VII. Cocoa farmers, Ghana

VIII. Terracing and soil conservation, Elgeyo, Kenya

CHAPTER VI

THE VILLAGER AND RURAL DEVELOPMENT

In the last two chapters some account has been given of the general problems of economic development in Africa and of the social and personal stresses involved in the clash of traditional African and modern Western value systems. It is now possible to turn to the actual process of development, first in the rural areas and, in subsequent chapters, in the field of trade and industry. The theme of this chapter is, then, the coming of the cash economy and of modern methods of husbandry [1] into the life of African villages, and the changing motives and responses of Africans. It is divided into four main sections—the starting point for development; the technical approach, with a note on ecology and game; the social approach; and the future pattern of advance.

I. THE STARTING POINT

Most generalized descriptions of African village life start from 'the subsistence economy', the island society meeting all its needs at a low level, without contact with the great world, and isolated even from its neighbours as much by tribal differences as by distance. But such pure subsistence economies are becoming increasingly rare in Tropical Africa. Approximations do, indeed, exist. The exploration teams of Shell-B.P. in the Niger Delta were finding in 1958 and 1959 some very isolated and 'primitive' groups, and there are more. But even the Gwembe Tonga in their isolated valley knew about traders and wanted salt and clothes, and their young men were moving to the Copperbelt and Bulawayo to earn money. The European demand that taxes should be paid in money, however small the amount, was bound to make a breach in the subsistence economy. The money can be gained either by selling produce, which thus becomes a 'cash crop'

---

[1] I have used 'husbandry' rather than agriculture because it can legitimately include both soil and animal husbandry; but I would like it to include arboriculture, fishing and hunting and food gathering—that is, all the ways in which the natural environment is used to gain essential food or materials.

or by selling labour, usually involving a migration, however short in time or distance. There can be four different situations. First, pure subsistence; second, taxed subsistence, with a cash crop or more often a labour export purely to pay tax;[2] third, subsistence with a cash crop, or labour export, for which the major incentive is no longer tax, but a desire for money to buy consumer goods and other purposes; fourth, the full cash economy, in which food may be bought for money and labour employed on the farm.[3] In modern Africa, even among relatively poor and isolated societies, money is wanted for tax and for cotton cloth; a little higher up the scale will come a demand for household utensils—often the cheap Japanese enamel-ware which must occupy hundreds of yards of Onitsha market. Then there will be school fees. There may be a need to buy a little meat or fish because all the game has been 'chopped'. Finally, perhaps a bicycle or a cheap radio.[4] Nor is it only very modern conditions which broke the circle of subsistence far inland from the coasts. It is recorded that the Luvale, a tribe in the heart of Central Africa,[5] were reached by a Brazilian trader in 1795, and certainly by 1867 they were selling wild rubber and beeswax via the Portuguese to European markets.[6] There has always been a tendency, in emphasis on the backwardness of African culture and economies, to imply a certain sloth, or unwillingness to learn, or obstinate isolationism. But in many cases —the Luvale are one—all that was needed was contact with an outsider who knew of a market and was anxious to trade. It is interesting that the Luvale also sold cassava to the Lozi of Barotseland, in exchange for meat on the hoof or cash—anything can be a 'cash crop', even cassava, usually regarded as the subsistence crop or famine reserve *par excellence*.

[2] Elspeth Huxley in *Red Strangers* (London, Chatto and Windus, 1937), gives a good description of the coming of taxes and money to the Kikuyu in Kenya.

[3] This is more fully set out as a sequence in diagrammatic form in *Survey of Problems in the Mechanisation of Native Agriculture in Tropical African Colonies* (Colonial Office, H.M.S.O., 1950). The authors considered that possibly only the pygmies in the Ituri forest and the South African bushmen had a *pure* subsistence economy.

[4] See E. H. Winter, *Bwamba Economy* (East African Studies No. 5, E.A.I.S.R.)

[5] In the North East corner of Northern Rhodesia, towards the Angola border.

[6] C. M. M. White, *A Preliminary Survey of Luvale Rural Economy*, Rhodes-Livingstone Papers No. 29 (Manchester University Press, 1959).

Indeed, it can be the greatest mistake to suppose that 'Africans' are incapable of grasping advantageous change quickly, a mistake partly due to the early experience of administrators, handed down to their successors, of an epoch when change was not only over-whelmingly new but often attempted without great understand-ing, through interpreters, by a strange conquering race. The Baganda in the last fifty years have transformed themselves from migrant labourers into the employers of migrant labour.[7] Many peoples of Kenya as well as the Kikuyu have, after some resist-ance, embraced land consolidation, grazing control, stock im-provement, new crops and new methods in a matter of five or ten years, once the threat of compulsion was removed and the volun-tary principle wholeheartedly accepted. There is behind some of these changes, particularly in Kenya, Tanganyika and the Rhodesias, a long period of education, agricultural training and patient persuasion by District Officers. But when the change comes, it may come very fast indeed.

It is easy, too, to assume that the second stage of development —money earned solely for tax[8] (or perhaps bride-price)—is still in being when in fact a people have moved on into the third stage —of wanting money for all that it will buy.

Certainly experience has demonstrated that all too frequently tropical man (*sic*) is unwilling to exert extra energies solely for finan-cial reward, once his simple needs have been met. Agricultural officers recount experiences by the score of attempts made to increase pro-ductivity by the introduction of demonstrably better planting materials and methods, only to find that output remained the same while land use or labour input declined.[9]

This is a typical description of a society stuck in the second stage, and it is interesting in its detail—the assumption that 'tropical man' has 'simple needs', and the observation that he will —most sensibly and economically by his own standards—reduce land use and working hours if he is given a more efficient process. In a gay but interesting story of Liberia [10] one of Miss Warner's

[7] See Richards, *Economic Development and Tribal Change,* supra.
[8] This in any case was not common in West Africa.
[9] V. D. Wickizer, 'Some Aspects of Agricultural Development in the Tropics', *Tropical Agriculture,* vol. 37, no. 3, July 1960).
[10] E. Warner, *Trial by Sasswood* (London, Gollancz, 1955).

characters remarks that all Europeans suffer from a terrible wasting disease, 'the Wants', which chews up their insides as a termite
chews wood, until they are reduced to sawdust. It seems certain
that within the next ten or even five years the remaining and
dwindling proportion of 'African man' not yet infected will have
caught 'the Wants', and not from Europeans directly but from
fellow Africans.

Certainly, traditional methods of husbandry over huge areas of
Tropical Africa had and have enormous limitations and inefficiencies, by Western standards, even after there has been a partial
entry into the cash economy. But they have virtues too. It is worth
quoting, a single and skilful description by Professor William O.
Jones:[11]

Farming methods in tropical Africa, with certain notable exceptions
. . ., differ little from those pursued centuries ago, and to western
eyes appear primitive in the extreme. Fields are small irregular
patches in the bush or forest, imperfectly cleared before burning
because of the lightness of axes and knives that are the standard implements, cultivated only by hoes and frequently weedy, and containing a mixture of crops planted in what often appears to be
completely random disorder. Irrigation and fertilizer use are rare,
mechanical or even animal draft power is uncommon, and the area
each farm family cultivates is small. After three or four years in
cultivation, the field is usually abandoned to natural growth, and
may not be cultivated again for 15 to 20 years. When perennials
such as cocoa or coffee are grown the same general practices are
engaged in : natural forest trees are left scattered about the clearing
so as to provide shade for the economic trees, and food crops are
planted among the young trees to provide some return from the land
while waiting for cocoa or coffee to come into bearing. Even the
experienced observer cannot always distinguish garden plot from
bush or abandoned clearing. It is a mistake, however, to assume that
African farming is in fact as crude and inefficient as its casual and
unplanned appearance would suggest. African methods are, on the
contrary, well adapted to the geographical and cultural environ-
ments in which they developed, and changes in them are to be undertaken only after most careful consideration of the ways in which the
traditional systems operate. Tropical African soils are generally light
and relatively low in plant nutrient content even when first brought

[11] Professor William O. Jones, 'Food and Agricultural Economies of Tropical
Africa', *Food Research Institute Studies*, Stanford University, vol. 2, no. 1,
February 1961.

into cultivation, and unless they are handled with care will rapidly lose fertility through leaching and rapid oxidation of humus content. Heavy rains, even in regions where annual rainfall is low, carry essential minerals down into the subsoil out of the reach of growing plants when they do not wash topsoil itself away. High solar radiation raises soil temperature to the point where the organic content is rapidly consumed. African agricultural methods are designed to deal with these problems in various ways. The most common sort of planting arrangement is to put in three or four crops that will mature at different times but that will maintain a green canopy over the ground until the last is harvested. Mixed and sequential cropping, by maintaining a constant vegetative cover over the soil, reduces the damage of rain and sun. It also provides protection against total crop failure when the mixture is made up of varieties having different moisture and soil requirements and with differing tolerances of drought, wind and pests. Imperfect clearing of natural cover, and imperfect cultivation of the growing crops, although they may result from the inadequacy of African farm tools, also serve to provide shade and protection to the soil and to assist in re-establishment of bush or forest. The small, isolated fields are more easily recaptured by the natural vegetation than larger ones would be; at the same time spread of plant disease is much slower and more difficult than it is in the vast fields of America and Europe.

There is much food for thought in this description. Other observers have noted the care devoted to some details in traditional systems—for example, the Bemba women plant three or four different kinds of seeds in different levels of their soil-mounds, according to habit of growth and time of maturity, though the result to Western eyes is 'a riot of vegetation—grasses, cassava and maize shoot up together and pumpkin vines trail across the path'.[12] Some peoples show particular skills and observation in using the minor foods—caterpillars, termites and wild fruits— which often add not only a relish but a valuable dietary element; White noted the keenness of the Luvale in this respect, in which they excelled over both the Luapula peoples and the Bemba.[13] There is also a considerable variation in pastoral skills. The Chief Veterinary Officer (Lake Province, Tanganyika), noting the relatively poor animal husbandry of Sukumaland, confessed by contrast that the Masai knew more about the ailments and the

[12] Richards, *Land Labour and Diet in Northern Rhodesia*, supra.
[13] C. M. N. White, op. cit.

management of their cattle than he did (they know what to do, without the scientific reasons), and this judgement is confirmed by others.[14]

Apart from recognition of the empirical knowledge often shown in traditional systems, it is important that the harmful elements should be correctly described. In relation to 'over-grazing', the World Bank Mission to Tanganyika observed that it sprang, not so much from having too many animals on a given area of land, but from having too many for the poor system of pasture-management on it. Compulsory de-stocking, which has caused so much violent opposition in some places, is not the true remedy for this disease, though it may be a necessary start. In many areas with proper management the same number of much better animals, with a higher fertility rate and a larger offtake of beasts for sale, could be maintained.

Nevertheless, when all is said, most of the traditional systems, unaltered, simply will not sustain economic progress, and they are being and will be replaced by new crops and new methods. In this process it will be important to ensure that small but vital elements in diet, particularly those that come from the wild bush, are not lost. As bush and forest are driven back, as game is reduced, if not destroyed, the diet of those who grudge money for buying food[15] may well be imperilled. In eighteenth century England, despite the savage game laws, many a villager could add a trout or a rabbit to his pot, and apprentices in Scotland actually covenanted with their employer not to be given salmon more than three times a week. The later expansion of population and the move to towns often meant a much worse diet. The larger issue of the place of game in Africa will be mentioned more fully later.

In fact, many rural economies in Africa are already some way along the road to a modern shape. Those of Southern Ghana, parts of East and West Nigeria and Buganda are examples. In Buganda, cotton and coffee have created a prosperous group of farmers. Apart from the richest coffee farmers, who may sell from

[14] e.g. Dr. Alan Jacobs (unpublished MS. contributed for this study).
[15] See particularly Warmington, *Plantation and Village in the Cameroons*, for this effect with plantation workers from subsistence economies who grudge spending their small money wages on food.

5 to 40 tons of coffee a year and employ perhaps a good many labourers,[16] there is a large class of well-to-do peasants.

These people have iron or tiled roofs to their houses, pictures on the wall, a table with a cloth; they eat meat and sugar regularly; their wives are well-dressed; they aim to send their children to Junior Secondary Schools. Such standards of consumption cannot be sustained with an output of less than half a ton of coffee, considerably more if hired labour has to be employed or if there are many children of school age. The peasant of this type may in fact sell from half to five tons a year. He generally employs one or two porters fairly regularly and one or two more occasionally, but he nearly always does at least some manual work himself.

The middling peasant has a grass roof to his house. Meat and sugar are rather occasional luxuries to him, nor does he usually aspire to more than primary education for his children. He sells between 200 and 1,000 lbs. of coffee, and rarely employs regular hired labour. Not uncommonly he supplements the cash income derived from his holding by the practice of some semi-skilled craft such as carpentry or barkcloth-making.[17]

The estimated proportion of these groups is very roughly put at

Large Farmers	2%
Well-to-do Peasants	19%
Middling Peasants	27%
Poor Peasants	32%
Landless Labourers	20%

Some of the Kenya African coffee farmers, or those of the Ivory Coast, or some of the market gardeners in the well-watered coastal strip north of Cap Vert (Dakar) might compare with this picture. There is, indeed, a certain danger that these economies will stick at this halfway mark. Buganda cotton-growing is certainly not efficient, but it provides quite a comfortable standard of life, and to make it more efficient might mean a quite unacceptable revolution in land tenure, hard work and size of holdings. While both the Ghanaian and Nigerian economies, and to a lesser degree the Kenyan, have other and major points of growth, the Uganda budget has been lately very unresponsive. It may be more difficult to keep such economies moving than to make the

[16] Some employ as many as 100; from 12 to 20 is more common.
[17] C. C. Wrigley, 'African Farming in Buganda' (E.A.I.S.R. Conference, 1953).

first and spectacular advances from wholly unreformed systems of cultivation.

In this halfway stage many Africans have a foot in both camps —a job in a factory or a trading interest on the one hand and a small farm or garden on the other. The employees of a tannery outside Nairobi, mostly Kikuyu living not very far away, have a garden for vegetables around their company compound, and another in the Reserve, possibly with a cash crop, in many cases with a wife in each. The combination of a money wage and two gardens made a respectable living. Forty-two per cent of married Africans in a sample studied in industrial employment at Jinja had a wife elsewhere looking after land, and 48 per cent were sending money home.[18]

Local doubling of occupation is an extremely common situation in West Africa, for example among the Ibo, the Yoruba and the cocoa farmers of Ghana,[19] quite apart from the large numbers of men on long distance seasonal migration. While long migration seems clearly undesirable, there is something to be said both for and against the local doubling of jobs. On the debit side, both occupations may be poorly done—the land half cared for, no real identification with the industrial job. On the credit side, both husband and wife are economically active, the rural economy gets a certain subsidy from wage employment, the disruption of the spread of the cash economy is cushioned by its combination with traditional life, and the children are brought up in the country. Provided that the employer, as happened so much in Southern Rhodesia, does not treat this situation as one justifying a wholly inadequate wage ('wages are only pocket-money to Africans'),[20] and bleak labour-lines, it is probably a useful transitional system. But, if there is to be substantial economic advance, an increasingly sharp choice will have to be made—between efficient farming, with some capital going into it and a high money yield, and an efficient industrial labour force, stabilized

[18] C. and R. Sofer, *Jinja Transformed* (East African Studies No. 4, 1955).

[19] See particularly studies by Polly Hill, *The Gold Coast Cocoa Farmer* (London, Oxford University Press, 1956).

[20] The Nyasaland Minimum Wage Order, 1957, 'does not take into account a worker's family responsibilities because every African has a foot in the land, which is cultivated either by him in his spare time or by his family'. Quoted in I.L.O. *African Labour Survey, supra.*

both at work and at home, which will justify the cost of training and give opportunities of promotion.

Even as this choice becomes more common, there will still be room for those who fill up the nooks and crannies of the economy, and particularly in an agricultural life sharply divided by wet and dry seasons. Near my own home in North Hampshire, men in fairly recent times worked as forest woodmen in the winter, made besoms in the spring months, went harvesting on farms up to fifty miles away in summer (sometimes walking and living in a bothy on the farm), found odd jobs as beaters or gardeners in the autumn, and were back in the woods when the leaf fell.[21] It will be a quarter of a century or more before the bulk of African villagers are drawn into high-yielding economic life. There is indeed a very real problem of employment in the dry season in the savannah countries; in Senegal, when the groundnuts are harvested, the vegetation is brown and the land hard-baked, what is the villager to do? In some cases, where the water-table is high enough, tree fruits can be grown if small local wells and pumps can be provided; in others the alternative to migration for trading or labouring has yet to be found. It is in such problems that Africa is apt to look for advice to the Israelis, with their reputation for making the desert blossom.

Thus a balanced estimate of African husbandry must first take into account the limitations of tools and knowledge before the Europeans came. Within those limitations, methods were often well adapted to the soils and climates. Moreover, traditional communal land tenure was itself a good adaptation for common security within the given conditions. But let there be no mistake; it is possible to appreciate, even with a certain admiration, the complexity of a culture so intricately adapted to its limitations, but the limitations are preposterous and the culture is desperately poor. Better methods have still to defer to soil and climatic conditions but in many areas will demand a revolution in land tenure. Provided the reformer's approach is one of patient explanation; provided that the desire for consumer goods has got a hold; and provided that the new method shows a real cash benefit for the extra work which it almost always involves, there is reason to think that Africans will grasp the new opportunities. Perhaps a picture

[21] See also the analysis of income of men living by odd jobs in *Brensham Village* by John Moore (London, Collins, 1946).

of a Kenya woman's experience will put this best into human terms, with its emphasis on small, simple changes backed by the major change in land tenure:[22]

> Before we enclosed the land, I used to carry the manure out to the shamba on my head, a little at a time. Later on, I managed to get a wheelbarrow. Then the instructor advised me to build a shed for the cattle at night. I did this, the manure made heavier crops, and from the profit of the crops I bought a cart. Now life is easier, because with the cart I can take out more manure and so grow more crops. From these profits we were able to educate our sons. One of them went to Makerere, and now he is studying in Britain to be a teacher. All this has been done with money that came from enclosing the land.

2. THE TECHNICAL APPROACH

The most obvious and by far the most important innovation in Tropical Africa has been the introduction of new crops. Even cassava, the great fall-back crop in so much of West Africa, was introduced from South America. Wheat, rice, coffee, tea, bananas, tobacco, cotton, sisal, pineapples, pyrethrum are all grown in Kenya, and all were brought in. If cocoa, groundnuts and rubber are added to the list, here are the products on which whole economies in Tropical Africa now depend, all introduced from the outer world.[23] The Portuguese, with their contact with the New World, were responsible for many introductions; and the Arab contribution is often forgotten. Ruth Slade[24] quotes a French author of the nineteenth century:

> In the midst of savage Africa, if you come across fertile rice plantations, the cultivation of wheat, lemons and guavas, and splendid plantations of bananas, it is entirely due to the Arabs. The plain of Tabora is an excellent example; they have cleared this vast area . . . and turned it into a vegetable garden; they have dug wells and you are surprised to see an irrigation system similar to that of the Egyptians; they keep cattle and live in comfortable houses where formerly there was only a desolate plain, the lair of a few savage bandits.

[22] From a farm north of Maseno, Kenya: Huxley, *A New Earth*, p. 43.
[23] Wild coffee is indigenous in Abyssinia and Liberia and cotton in Egypt.
[24] Slade, op. cit., quoting A. Burdo, *Les Arabes dans l'Afrique Centrale* (Paris, 1885).

In some cases the introduction of a cereal, such as rice, into the forest areas where root crops are mainly used may make a big difference to health by adding protein. In several cases, such as sisal, rubber or pyrethrum, these crops depend on a market in the outside world which was wholly unknown to Africans. In most cases they have entirely altered the balance of trade, and could go further : it is often surprising to note the size of food imports to Africa—for example, of rice to Senegal (180,000 tons in 1960). The Ghana figures of food imports are striking : [25]

	1934–8 (tons)	1959 (tons)
Rice	11,760	33,390
Flour (wheaten)	7,046	58,484
Fish (canned and dried)	3,303	17,800
Sugar	5,609	44,863

These increases reflect a higher and more westernized standard of living, and they also show how far Ghana is from self-sufficiency in food (only the biggest items of a long list have been selected), although these imports would be much more than paid for by exports of another agricultural crop, cocoa. Sometimes the introduction of a new crop can be extraordinarily cheap in terms of development expenditure. To take a small group of about 30,000 people—and much of African progress must come from small groups—Winter [26] noted the increase of cash earnings in the Bwamba (Uganda) economy from 87,000 shillings in 1937 to 797,000 shillings in 1951, almost wholly through the introduction of coffee and rice. The main part of this development took place even before a road was built and the cost was simply that of the services of the regular extension staff.[27]

The second major approach to development is through the introduction of new methods. This includes the use of manure and artificial fertilizers; introduction of new varieties; improved methods of planting, cultivation and harvesting, and the control of diseases and pests. Very great improvements in yields are possible. In Ghana, for example, a normal yield of groundnuts has been about 400 lb. an acre; with an improved variety, close spacing, superphosphate and 'Dieldrex A', the yield is 1,580 lb.

[25] Ghana, Ministry of Agriculture, *Miscellaneous Information 1960–61* (Accra, 1960).

[26] Winter, op. cit.

[27] Cf. also the Borgo a Mozzano experiment mentioned in Chapter IV.

per acre.[28] The Agricultural Officer in Mwanza (Tanganyika) reckoned that, with fertilizers and good methods, cotton yields in Sukumaland could be raised eight times, and improvements up to twenty times have been mentioned for parts of the Central Province in Kenya. These increases in productivity far exceed what could be expected from quite large investments in industry. The multiplication and distribution of new varieties are now reaching a large scale. The West African Institute for Oil Palm Research near Benin is distributing new seed very widely—for example, 387,000 seeds to Ghana in 1959 (against 50,000 in 1952) in addition to its supplies to Nigeria.[29] There is still much room for research, especially in the use of artificial fertilizers on tropical soils, and it is interesting that the Institute is one of the few West African regional units which has continued after the balkanizing effect of Independence.

In certain countries, and above all in Kenya, the influence of European farmers has been decisive in the improvement of methods. Not only have they introduced new crops, very often pioneering at great expense the right cultivation or the breeding of disease-resistant varieties,[30] they have also taught their methods to Africans. The whole standard of cultivation, good order and management has, in the case of the best farmers and plantations, set a style which was completely new to East Africa. It has also introduced new elements into African diet, sometimes with important and beneficial results.

Thirdly, technical advance may come through the supply of power and machinery. There are well-known dangers, most of which were elaborated in the Colonial Office Report of 1950.[31] Appallingly difficult problems may face the attempt at tractor-driven cultivation. At the headquarters of the Mokwa (Nigeria) settlement scheme 'an example of one of the great lateral roots [of the bush being cleared] was exhibited on the verandah . . . it was 70 feet long and six inches thick for most of its length'.[32] Pro-

[28] Ghana, Ministry of Agriculture, op. cit.

[29] Ibid.

[30] Lord Delamere spent about £80,000 of his own money in developing agriculture in Kenya. See E. Huxley, *White Man's Country* (London, Macmillan, 1935.

[31] Op. cit.

[32] K. D. S. Baldwin, *The Niger Agricultural Project* (Oxford, Blackwell, 1957).

fessor Frankel [33] has put in general terms the danger of exporting techniques and capital equipment, unmodified, for use in African conditions :

Technical knowledge, the machine and capital goods in general never exist in the abstract but always in the relatively fleeting form suited to the momentary situation and to that complex of unique problems to which they have been adapted . . . That is why they cannot readily be transferred from one situation to another.

Moreover, even if the machine works well, there is a question of adaptation to the local human pattern of work. By the use of tractors at Mokwa it was possible to prepare for sowing more than 20 acres per family. But a family can only keep about four acres hoed and free of weed. The extra effort and inevitable failure to beat the weed was one of the most discouraging elements in the scheme.

There are, indeed, opportunities for the use of tractors and other machines, usually by some co-operative method.[34] There were a few to be seen on the lakeside lands near Mwanza, and these belonged to small contractors, who can get a government loan to purchase one if they can produce contracts for at least 600 hours of ploughing. In Senegal, the French experimented first with small mobile groups of machines (*trains routiers*), and later with demonstration centres (*Centres d'Expansion Rurale*), where there might be two tractors and some other machinery to serve a group of villages, supported at the provincial level with more equipment (*Centres Régionaux d'Assistance au Développement*). The balance of expert opinion appears now to be that there are six main ways in which power and machines can be most effectively used in the rural economy : (1) for infrastructure—roads, bridges, &c. and for levelling or preparing land; (2) as small 'barn' machinery for processing, hulling, &c.; (3) in the supply of small hand or animal-drawn machines; for example, a simple machine for sowing groundnuts with fertilizers; (4) in rural industry; (5) for irrigation; (6) for the transport of crops and supplies. In the actual operations of husbandry the use for mechanization is at present very limited, at least without major social reorganization.

[33] Frankel, *The Economic Impact on Under-Developed Societies,* supra.
[34] A good ox-cart, suitable for use in Africa, with a let-down tailboard, would have a great use, and seems to be lacking.

Fourth, water control can be of decisive importance. This, however, may need high capital investment in dams, and is in any case expensive in survey and contouring. Moreover, certain types of irrigation, such as that used in the Sudan Gezira scheme, need a high discipline and co-operation among cultivators, to prevent waste, the ruin of crops, and much quarrelling. There can be fairly simple schemes, such as that now being developed in the Vallée du Fleuve (Senegal) for gravity-irrigation of rice from the river, and there are places, such as the coffee land on the slopes of Kilimanjaro, where African cultivators know very well how to use the mountain streams, diverted into small channels, through their four-acre holdings. Further, a good deal of work has been done, particularly in East Africa and the Rhodesias, in making small earth-dams for cattle. But the major planning and control of water resources is the point in the agricultural economy where fairly heavy capital investment may be necessary and rewarding.

Finally, the improvement of physical health is certainly of high importance in the villages, and this may be regarded as a technical task, although it lies mainly in the field of health education. The gradual control of debilitating disease and parasite infection, combined with better diet, will no doubt add to the villagers' energy and productivity, but this is a slow task and expensive, not in equipment, but in trained men. It is really distressing to find, even on a modern plantation with an excellent cottage hospital and dispensaries, so much of a doctor's time spent in remedying (if it is not too late) the shocking though well-meant maltreatment of children by their mothers, for example, through the use of purges or enemas which frequently cause death. Adults equally suffer fearful mishandling from some native doctors and from the illegal sale of drugs and injections which are (at least in West Africa) peddled around by enterprising traders.

3. ECOLOGY AND GAME

Specialist knowledge, heavy machinery and enthusiasm for agricultural development can too easily overreach themselves, with results which later generations deplore. There will have to be some real selectivity about African rural development. Not every area can be turned from a poor subsistence economy to a thriving modern community. Here it is the ecologist rather than the pure agricultural expert or the social reformer, who must have his say. Dr. Fraser Darling [35] has pointed out that in certain parts of the Central African plateau the existing climax vegetation represents the richest and most rapid circulation of energy which it is possible to achieve. The maximum number of animal and plant species have found a niche, in delicate balance with each other and with soil and climate. Attempts by man to exploit these areas, either by crops or grazing animals, degrade the habitat. Fire reduces the plant species; hunting and fencing drive out, reduce or exterminate the animals. Shallow-rooting crops fail to recover the leached minerals which the deep-rooted bush brings back to the surface. Cattle, sheep and goats do not replace the widely varied browsing habits of elephant, giraffe and deer which maintain the habitat in balance, and they are far more likely to cause erosion. Africans in small numbers, with spear or bow or net, and with simple tools, could not make a dominating inroad on the size of Africa and its wealth of animals; indeed they were part of the whole ecological balance, which must include man. But in growing numbers, with rifle and flashlamp, with bicycles or even lorries, and sometimes aided by the bulldozers of an ambitious Agricultural Department, they can destroy the natural vegetation and wipe out the animals. The old balance is destroyed, yet the new method may not give a good living; more often, after the first cashing of stored fertility, it is a still precarious subsistence in a grossly degraded habitat. The wholesale destruction of game in which calves and gravid females are shot indiscriminately, is a heartbreaking waste of resources, quite apart from the loss of beauty and variety. Darling noted that in two communal hunts (*chilas*) in Northern Rhodesia 1,993 red lechwe were shot, of which no less than 64 per cent were gravid females.

The anxiety for 'preservation' has, of course, led to the reserving of Game Parks. But these great natural zoos, however valuable, are not the full answer. In many cases, complete protection, in a habitat which is either not large enough or is already changed, may result in over-stocking by certain species. Modern ecologists are now advocating a controlled cropping of wild game, both to maintain balance and to give a far from negligible supply of meat

[35] Op. cit.

—much-needed protein—to the African diet.[36] In some areas—
and they are very large—the natural habitat, with its proper cover
of tree and ground vegetation, restocked with game and properly
controlled, could make a significant contribution in meat, and in
many wild products, to a small population. It may be that, from
such a starting point, means can be found of so managing the
natural ecology of Africa as to make it more productive for man's
needs without destroying its essential balance. For many years to
come it is on the better soils, the more hopeful and resilient country,
that the great new schemes of modern husbandry should be concentrated. Only they will stand the treatment, and only they will
give the sort of income-rise which the modern African will demand in exchange for altering his ways. In the poorer areas it may
well be better to redevelop the wild ecology, to give what may be a
reasonable living and a good life to fewer people.

On the outer fringes of Europe, on the stony hills and rain-
soaked moors of Western Scotland and the Outer Isles, a problem
has come—whether to attempt to improve on a hard and poor life
or whether to abandon the area. Such people and such a life may
have special virtues. But the wireless and television begin to tell
them of another world; the attractions of richer lands call their
young men away. If the tourists from the city or the rocket launch-
ing site do come, they do not restore the old life but hasten its
destruction. It may be that in Africa there is a Highlands and
Islands problem on a far larger scale—that there are tens of thousands of square miles where nature can maintain a rich life in her
own ways, but man a desperately poor one. As Africans, too, hear
the siren voices on the wireless set, and as they visit richer lands
and towns, they too may begin to move. The conservation of
Africa's wilder lands and unique fauna is not only to preserve for

[36] A. M. Harthoorn, writing from the Department of Veterinary Physiology
in Makerere, has pointed out that wild buffalo meat already contributes over
13 per cent of all meat supplies (cattle, sheep and goats) slaughtered in
Uganda (1956) and 60 per cent to 70 per cent of all meat eaten in some districts. It is believed that, by controlled cropping, the yield could be increased
at least five times without depleting the herds. 'Our studies indicate that these
animals thrive and put on weight on grasses which do not support native
cattle and gain weight faster than either indigenous or exotic cattle when the
fodder is poor. They are known to be extremely resistant to most of the cattle
diseases, including trypanosomiasis. . . . It is doubtful if some of the areas in
which buffalo and other game are now being eliminated will ever be of use in
ranching native cattle.' (*The Veterinary Record*, vol. 70, no. 46).

many peoples a greater space for solitude and learning and wonder : this is indeed a value which will grow. It is also a true conservation of energy, a conservation of potential which we may not yet know how to use, a conservation of an African inheritance for the future which we could destroy today but never create again. It can also have practical economic uses in the present day.

4. THE SOCIAL APPROACH

Technical knowledge will not avail unless the social approach to the agrarian revolution in Africa is successful. The World Bank Mission in Tanganyika suggested that most schemes of advance fall into one of two categories—improvement of an existing system, or 'transformation'. This is a useful general approach, but a very rough one, since there is every gradation between the one and the other. Under the heading 'Improvement' may be considered much of the work on Community Development and Extension Services, and also the growth of Co-operatives based on existing systems of land tenure and village organization. A more radical change of land tenure—Land Consolidation in Kenya, Native Land Husbandry in Southern Rhodesia—comes under 'Transformation'; and so do major schemes of plantation and of land settlement.

Pride of place in the steady improvement of African husbandry must go to the District Administration and the Agricultural and Veterinary Extension Services. It is true that in some areas the key to African co-operation was found by Community Development, which has occasionally been able to achieve changes long and vainly advocated by the Administration. This was partly a reflection of the colonial situation; resentment caused by other processes of government might be expressed in a quite illogical opposition to agricultural programmes. But the long slog fell on the Administration and its specialists. Great uncertainty surrounds the future of supervision in rural areas, and the response of African farmers to it. European officers had two advantages. They were not dependent on local votes, nor was the colonial government; although they could not neglect local opinion, they could ride out much initial grumbling if they were convinced that a scheme would finally succeed and be accepted. Secondly, they had a certain prestige as Europeans. Against these advantages must be set both nationalist feeling, in a wide sense of opposition or suspicion of an alien government, and the sometimes great exasperation of African farmers at the constant pressure put upon them to change their ways.[37] In the last few years the agricultural staff in Kenya, as one example, became convinced that compulsion was useless, and their greatest successes have been through gaining voluntary co-operation in the use of new methods and in land consolidation. Where, as is likely in Southern Rhodesia, European government continues for some time, success in rural areas will depend on the intensity of the struggle for an African majority government, which might involve widespread non-co-operation in every field.

Where African government exists or soon becomes established, much will depend on its political form. If there are two rival parties, it may be extremely difficult for local officers, whether African or European, to exert any real pressure, since their political chiefs would be afraid of losing votes. But with one-party government—which seems both the most common and the most likely—where there is a good chance that politicians and administrators will be pulling together, the prospects are better. However, it must not be forgotten that in some places, notably Uganda, African political parties have widely preached that independence will mean the end of the European interference and petty regulations, the culling of cattle, controls over hunting, laborious terracing and so on. These promises may have sunk in more deeply than their authors intended and prove a rod for their backs later on. Finally, it is hard to know what effective power will be given to the District Officers under an African government. In India the period after 1947 saw a decline in their power, as the Departments at the centre entrenched themselves. The future of local administration is discussed in Chapter XI; but it would seem likely that between the locally elected Councils, the local party cells, and the concentration of power in a central government, District Officers and specialists may find their authority heavily curtailed. It may be that an African District Commissioner will inspire confidence and co-operation among his own people where a European could not; Elspeth Huxley [38] suggests that an African who accepts responsibility and refuses bribes is more trusted than a European, partly because European staff are so often transferred before they are personally well known; but it will take time

[37] Cf. Richards, *East African Chiefs*, supra.
[38] Huxley, *A New Earth*, supra.

for young African officers to gain real authority and prestige. A very great ideal hangs on the answer to these questions, and it is as yet too early to see any decisive evidence of what answer will be given.

Community Development combines the appeal both to traditional and to modernizing emotions; it has used the old tribal pattern of communal effort in aid of the new desire for improvement and efficiency. But its reference to old traditions, and the reliance on enthusiasm, despite their present success, may well become weaknesses in future. There is little doubt that, in the long run, traditional communal effort will be more difficult to arouse; it will begin to die with the conditions of tribal life and subsistence agriculture which gave it birth. As early as 1936, Professor Nadel [39] noted that *efako* cultivation—which was communal— was beginning to weaken among the Nupe of Nigeria; the same has been noted of the Hausa *gayya*; as the cash economy and an element of competition between cultivators spread more widely and deeply, this trend will surely continue.

Enthusiasm, too, is a wasting asset. It was relied upon in the early days of the Russian Revolution, and it inspired the Jugoslav railway builders, with shovels in their hands and school books in their pockets. In Europe, it had a life of five or ten years; we have yet to prove that it will last longer in Africa. There are, indeed, groups remarkable for their sense of community, among whom the Ibo of Eastern Nigeria must stand high. In Ibo country it is startling to find villages not only giving free labour and materials for the construction of a bridge or the building of a market, but in addition finding half the cost in cash—£500, even £1,200 from quite small communities—while Government finds the other half. The impetus of independence, and the drive to modernity which a party such as the C.P.P. in Ghana or TANU in Tanganyika can give, will certainly give a lift to village people and evoke energy and 'free' labour. There is, however, a danger that it will be consciously exploited. There were signs in Western Nigeria of a government plan to achieve a centrally conceived development programme very cheaply by using the free labour offered by local enthusiasm. But the essense of local enthusiasm is in achieving something which local people urgently want, which genuinely expresses their need, not in labouring on part of a

[39] Op. cit.

scheme conceived by a distant government.[40] The idea of *investissement humain*, of using abundant labour as a substitute for scarce capital, has a certain value and has been popularized by the Chinese. It is currently much advocated in French-speaking West Africa. But its very attractiveness creates a danger of a slight shift of emphasis, away from local leadership and local needs and towards national planning. At that point sensible technical help to harness local enthusiasm tips over into central exploitation. While the new African governments are right to use the upsurge of energy and enthusiasm which comes with 'freedom', they will need much restraint to avoid the temptation of misusing and therefore killing it.

There is certainly a future for Community Development for some years, and particularly in the more remote and backward areas. To succeed, it must show real benefits; as these benefits grow in terms of cash income, the cash motive will gradually take over; and at that point it is the expert extension services rather than enthusiasm which will be needed. In fact, much of Community Development work has been concerned with social objects —health, schools, wells, housing. It is seen perhaps in its best balance where development and social needs are hand in hand. In Northern Rhodesia, the early development centres came from minor trade schools, fitting village people to do their carpentry, bricklaying, boat-building, school improvement, &c. This work is now linked with the extension services, to make the centres a focus of balanced technical and social development. The scale of this training is not to be despised. Some hundreds of farmers in Northern Rhodesia go every year to courses at the major centres and several thousand to village courses, including a good proportion of women. The scheme offers ninety posts in the senior African Civil Service and another 140 for more junior instructors in local teams.[41] In Kenya about 6,000 farmers a year are passing through the Agricultural Institutes.[42] This underpinning of community

[40] Philip Mason recalls the experience of Community Development projects in India. After two false starts (in 1937 when the staff were ill trained, and in 1947 when a well-trained staff were telling villagers what to do) it finally began to succeed in 1953, when the staff really succeeded in making village leaders feel that the projects were their own.

[41] Commissioner for Rural Development, *Annual Report*, 1959 (Lusaka, Northern Rhodesia Government Printer, 1960).

[42] Government Statement, 3 October, 1960.

enthusiasm with solid technical advance is perhaps the most balanced and hopeful programme in Tropical Africa. There are still wide differences in the effort which governments devote to it —Kenya, for example, is spending three to four times the proportion of national income which Uganda devotes to this purpose. Both Nigeria and more particularly Ghana have had great successes. In Senegal a scheme for training village leaders (*animateurs*) has recently been launched, and there have already been some good results, for example, in road building. The scheme is integrated with the *Centres d'Expansion Rurale*. To a very large extent this is the kind of work which can go on within the traditional social and agricultural pattern, but with new crops and methods, and this possibility of advance without 'transformation' is widespread.

Secondly, the development of producer Co-operatives can lead to great advance without a frontal attack on land tenure, at least in its early stages. It is specially effective in spreading improvement and financing it. Cultivators are sucked into a successful Co-operative faster than they can be pushed by extension services and the small deductions add up to major central funds. As an example of growth, the Bakweri Co-operative Union of Farmers [43] (Victoria Division, South Cameroons) started with 100 individual members and in the first year (1952) shipped 8,000 stems of bananas valued at £2,500. Six years later it shipped 1,350,000 stems valued at over £900,000, and by 1959/60 had over 4,000 members. The net value to the villagers in 1958 was £300,000, or an income of £150 per member in that year. It would be wearisome to record the achievements of Co-operatives all over Africa, but it is worth while to look for a moment at some reasons for their success and at certain special advantages which they have.

Tanganyika illustrates this as well as any country. The cotton Co-operatives in Sukumaland (the Victoria League) sprang in 1952–3 from an outright demand from the growers, who felt that they were getting a poor bargain from Asian buyers and ginners. The Government Co-operative Officer there emphasized that it was above all this expressed wish, and the feeling that the Co-operative was their own, which led to immediate success. In 1961 the Co-operative had 363 Primary Societies with 150,000 members grouped into eighteen Unions with an output of £6,500,000

[43] Ardener and Warmington, op. cit.

worth of cotton; it is building its own new headquarters, owns six ginneries and gives a variety of services to its members. Probably one essential to success in early years is wise advice on management, and here the Chagga coffee growers on Kilimanjaro, the Sukuma cotton and the Bukoba coffee growers were all lucky to have an enthusiastic adviser seconded to help them.[44] A third element which makes for the more startling successes is a cash crop which does well and meets good prices in the opening years —there must be an element of luck here.

There are, therefore, some dangers or difficulties. It is not easy to force co-operation on people who do not themselves wish it, or in ways which they do not want; the schemes for countrywide extension of State-organized consumer Co-operatives in Ghana may run into some trouble on this score. Secondly, advice must be both skilful and discreet; a Co-operative belongs to its members and is run by them, not by an adviser or manager. This caution is necessary, because there could be a trend towards indiscriminate founding of Co-operatives. The Northern Region of Nigeria, in a burst of enthusiasm, lent out about £950,000 to Co-operatives (who were often more like produce-buyers than small growers) and expectation in Kaduna in 1961 was that little of an outstanding debt of £400,000 would ever be seen again. Moreover, there have been a large number of sad failures all over Africa, either through dishonesty of staff or through attempts to force co-operation on people not ready for it. Success depends on a local feeling of ownership and participation just as it does in Community Development.

To give some idea of scale, the following sample figures may be useful:

	No. of Primaries	Members	Value of Produce Sold
Uganda (1959)[45]	1,583	187,860	£11,607,492
Tanganyika (1959)[46]	617	324,994	£11,252,171
Western Nigeria (1960)[47]	1,035	54,525	£5,239,347

[44] The Bakweri Union had the help of three experts seconded from Elders & Fyffe and three African inspectors under the Registrar of Co-operatives.
[45] Report of Department of Co-operative Development, 1959, Uganda.
[46] Ibid, 1959, Tanganyika.   [47] Ibid, 1960, W. Nigeria.

If it is assumed that the population of adult males is about one-fourth of the total population, the membership figures in Uganda and Tanganyika mean that rather more than one out of every ten are members of a Co-operative.

The advantages of the approach through Co-operatives can be quickly stated. Co-operation is, in a sense, the African style. It is easily understood, even in its sophisticated modern form. It offers training in democratic procedures at village level. It offers employment for the moderately educated as officers of Primary Societies and Unions. It offers some training in management and commercial skills—the making of forward estimates and budgets has been immensely educative among East Africans who have had little commercial experience. It establishes 'secondary powers'—that is, authentic organizations of the community as against the State. It immensely eases the way to agricultural credit—the accounting system can easily show the record of each grower over a period of years. It is a great spur to improved grading and quality because sub-standard produce can be rejected in a way which the members themselves control and understand. How important this can be is illustrated by a figure from Ghana—78 per cent of coffee samples offered by farmers and tested in 1954 and 1955 were unfit for export; only 8 per cent could be placed in Grade I.[48] Finally, small cesses on large crops are an easy way of capital formation.

But there may well be a limit to achievement within the traditional pattern of land tenure. As methods improve and more fertilizer, spraying and mechanical aid becomes possible, small, divided or scattered holdings may come to be an impassable obstacle. The Swynnerton Plan in Kenya (submitted to Government in December 1953) and the Land Husbandry Act in Southern Rhodesia (1951) both aimed at a demarcation of land for individual African ownership with virtually full title. In Kenya the compulsory regrouping of the Kikuyu during Mau Mau and the concentration of administrative effort in their country finally broke through the traditional pattern. On good soils, with a profitable crop, with intensive supervision, the scheme has succeeded in strategy, even if there is criticism in detail, and has spread widely over Kenya, now on a voluntary basis. By October 1960 about 2,000,000 acres were enclosed into separate holdings, for 200,000

[48] Ghana, Ministry of Agriculture, op. cit.

farmers, and 137,000 individual titles registered. Between 1954 and 1959 recorded sales of African produce rose from £5,500,000 to £9,000,000.[49] In Southern Rhodesia land and farming rights have been allocated over 15,000,000 acres, and in some areas remarkable improvements have taken place. But the land is poorer, cash earnings more difficult and the political situation perhaps less acute but also more threatening than in Kenya. Certainly these two schemes have given a remarkable lift to African agriculture. The difficult time will come when present farmers die and the temptation to subdivide holdings [50] among the heirs is strong; it is a race with the growth of wage employment both in the country and in the towns.

Despite present conditions in the Congo, the Belgian experiment of establishing *paysannats* should be mentioned. This was an ingenious plan to combine shifting cultivation with modern methods. Village holdings were rearranged into parallel rectangular strips, each farmer advancing down his strip by the same distance as his neighbours each year and planting the same crops, leaving fallow for regeneration. Thus with certain crops mechanical cultivation or harvesting could be done laterally across the line of strips. About 200,000 families had thus been settled in various parts of the Congo in 1959, with a rate of progress of 20,000 per annum.

The Belgian scheme has been criticized on grounds which could apply elsewhere—the very high cost of extension staff needed to supervise such new methods. On the *paysannats* the ratio of staff to farmers was about one to 320, as against figures of one to 1,000 in Western Nigeria and one to 20,000 in Northern Nigeria.[51] The Belgian administrators, while admitting the high cost of staff, argued that the cost was less than that of creating industrial employment.[52] Undoubtedly where, as in Kenya and the Congo, a radical change is being made both in agricultural and social methods, and made by Government (especially a colonial government which may be politically opposed), a high initial effort of specialist staff is needed. But once such schemes are accepted, it does not follow that supervision must be maintained at such

[49] Kenya Government Statement, 3 October, 1960.
[50] This is at present illegal in Southern Rhodesia.
[51] Figures from Extra-Mural Department, Ibadan University College.
[52] The capital investment per worker was reckoned to be about £1,500 in the Congo. See comparative figures on p. 60, Chapter IV.

strength. It may well be that a ten-year investment in extension staff for a major scheme is money spent better than it could be in any other way.[53] There is, indeed, a serious danger that the loss of expatriate staff in the extension services in some countries now reaching Independence, and particularly in East and Central Africa, could deal a far more crippling blow to African agriculture for the same reason. This is surely one field in which foreign technical aid in the shape of trained men, who should know the country and people, could be of critical importance.

The saving of capital investment which can be achieved by a marriage between peasant agriculture and technical aid and credit is well illustrated in two main schemes in Senegal. On the Senegal River rice growing was first developed on a large scale in the Richard Toll plantations, originally run by a Company but now owned by the Senegalese Government, which developed 6,000 hectares with capital investment of nearly £4 million. The scheme has succeeded, partly owing to very high yields of 3,000 kilos of rice per hectare, said to be the highest yield in the Tropics. Full commercial cultivation was achieved in 1955. More recently the Organization for the Development of the Delta has started a scheme for peasant cultivation of rice paddies. The technical team (seven Senegalese and one Frenchman) agree with the villagers on the right site for the paddy and the canal from the river, which in some cases may mean moving and grouping village sites. The canal is dug by village labour assisted by a bulldozer, and a Co-operative is formed which is responsible for repayment of the initial cost and the cost of annual ploughing. In 1960 about 600 hectares were so cultivated and in 1962 the area may increase to 1,500 hectares. The costs of the Organization are reckoned at about 5,000 francs (C.F.A.) per hectare as against 250,000 francs per hectare on the Richard Toll scheme. Yields are about 1,600 kilos per hectare which compare with those of the *Office du Niger* cultivations.[54] Peasant income from the rice Co-operative alone, after repayment of the costs charged against them, has been between £25 and £30 per annum, among a population with an average annual cash income reckoned at only £7 or £8. The

[53] Cf. the increases among the Bwamba, p. 103.

[54] *The Office du Niger* is a State organization in control of the very large irrigation and settlement schemes of the Niger basin, with production concentrated on rice and cotton.

scheme is not free of dangers—exceptionally high or low floods in the river could damage the paddies severely; but it has had a most invigorating effect on the whole area.

The second main development is in Casamance, a fertile area in Southern Senegal previously somewhat neglected. It has been directed mainly by the *Centre Régional pour Assistance au Développement* (*C.R.A.D.*) which has undertaken multiple functions in the provision of credit for seed, agricultural equipment, fertilizers and housing, and has encouraged the establishment of pilot Co-operatives (*Associations d'Intérêt Rural*) through which crops are directly purchased. There is undoubtedly a good deal of default on the monetary advances, but the general effect has been to increase crop production very greatly and at low cost. The exclusion of commercial middlemen has given somewhat higher prices to the growers; but it is interesting to note that the middlemen, who ran the local store, have now withdrawn, since they could only make profits by buying as well as selling, and the villagers have lost their shop. It is always difficult to assess the element of subsidy in French schemes (for example, the salaries of French officials are paid from Paris) and the real costs in Casamance may be fairly high at present; but they will be a cheap investment if the whole area is eventually activated into self-supporting economic energy.

Plantation agriculture is another main form of 'transformation', and one which is increasingly favoured by the Development Corporations in Nigeria and Ghana, although it forms a small part of total production or employment.[55] Plantations, often described as industrial agriculture, are apt to produce the same social effects as a mining industry in an agricultural area.[56] Frequently, labour will be drawn from some distance and housed on the plantation and it will normally be of mixed tribal origin. Much the same

[55] Sisal plantations in Tanganyika now represent only 25 per cent of *exports* as against 60 per cent some years ago. Uganda sugar estates produce about £3¾ million out of the total export crop of £39 million. In West Africa the main peasant-grown crops of groundnuts, palm fruit and cocoa enormously outweigh plantation crops. Plantations are, however, important in special fields such as rubber, bananas, sugar.

[56] For this effect in the Cameroons plantations, see the article by E. Ardener in A. Southall (Ed.), *Social Change in Modern Africa* (London, Oxford University Press for International African Institute, 1961). 'Life in Victoria Division may have more in common with that in a new Copperbelt town than life in an old Yoruba town.'

conditions—though differing in the quality of housing or management—will be found in a walk around the 'villages' of workers on
the Calabar plantations, on a big sawmill camp, at the gold mines
at Tarkwa or the bigger tin mines at Jos. These are not really
villages in the African sense; in the best cases the beautifully clean
rows of houses with an equally clean company-licensed shop give
a thoroughly aseptic and slightly dead feeling. Near one estate
visited was a real village, much swollen by the local growth of
trade and population, with the usual signs of West Africa—
chickens running about, a Hotel and Bar, a carpenter, a market,
three gramophones playing, children everywhere in the dusty
paths, shady shanties of thatch selling everything under the sun, a
photographer, a chiefs' council meeting going on, eight square
yards of maize here and ten square yards of cassava there—some
banana trees, an antique but functioning motor-car and a lot of
pretty girls. Here, in fact, was life with a great number of hazards
and a great deal of satisfaction. Certainly, it is difficult to run an
efficient productive plantation, in which £3 or £4 million may be
invested, with a labour force showing all the absenteeism associated with the family duties and usual diseases of unregenerate
village life. In some ways, nothing could be more pleasant than,
say, a tapper's work on an old-established rubber plantation, with
work in the mornings under the shady trees, a decent house, a good
employer, a hospital and school near by, and leisure in the even-
ings; and a good number of gold watches for long service are being
given away under these conditions. Possibly the absence of traditional social life is not greatly missed in these favourable cases. But
in modern conditions, and especially where the labour employed
is really large, there might well be a case for attempting to build
a more truly African and vital social life, with something like a
small model town-centre where outsiders can come in to set up
shops and garages and bars, where perhaps even small subsidiary
trades and industries can be carried on. The experiments of the
Belgian 'Forminière' Company in the Congo of bringing considerable tribal groups to live near the mines in their own villages might
be worth more study and adaptation. The high-wire-fence mentality of expatriate enterprise in both mines and plantations is
already beginning to look out of date because it relates to an
Africa conceived to be an ocean of primitive bush out of which an
island of productivity is to be excised and carefully protected.

The real problem of plantations is thus the social integration and industrial management of the labour force. Despite some estates with long-service records, many still depend on short-term migratory workers, particularly in East Africa. The Uganda Company found (1960) that less than 10 per cent of their labour stayed longer than two years. The sisal estates of Tanganyika have constantly complained of the short hours and inefficient work of their largely migrant labour.[57] Although in some West African plantations labour is more stable, there was found to be a constant breaking of work spells in the Cameroons; 60·5 per cent of a sample were found to have completed previous spells of work of a duration of under two years, while only 13·6 per cent had completed previous spells of fours years or more.[58] If work requires very little skill or training and the plantation offers employment and a cash earning to men who could find no other productive outlet, this type of labour-use can be justified, though the costs of high labour-turnover are important. But if the areas now exporting labour themselves become more developed and attractive, it will become more and more difficult to rely on casual migrants or even organized recruiting and at that stage a settled labour force in a proper local society ought to be the aim.

The remaining method of major advance is the large settlement scheme—that is, a transfer of individual farmers, or possibly whole groups, to a new area of cultivation, often associated with the opening of new land by irrigation or mechanical cultivation. The risk of disaster is greatest in this type of proposal. Expectations by the new settlers may be high and there are a dozen reasons why they may be disappointed, at least at first. Even after a successful pilot scheme, the main areas may prove in some way not identical with the sample; settlers may prove incompetent; machinery may be disappointing, water control too difficult to manage. In the past there are some sad cautionary tales—not only the Kongwa groundnuts scheme and the Niger settlement at Mokwa, but many grave disappointments on the French *Office du Niger* scheme and a number of smaller ventures. It is easy to be wise after the event,

[57] 'The average working week for the plantation is probably under rather than over 25 hours.' Matheson & Bovill, *East African Agriculture* (London, Oxford University Press, 1950.)

[58] Ardener and Warmington, op. cit.

but it may be worth while to list some of the deficiencies of the Mokwa scheme as revealed by investigation.[59]

There was no contour-ploughing—with the inevitable result of soilwash; no tests of equipment in relation to rooting systems of bush to be cleared; no improvement on African strains of crop grown; no relation of land cleared and allocated to the weeding capacity of the tenant; the size of the 'pilot' scheme—no less than 30,000 acres; no real incentive to the tenant who had to work very hard; no agreed and efficient method of sharing out the proceeds; no real local supply of labour or shortage of land to induce tenants to come.

No doubt some of these mistakes were due to hurry. It is, however, slightly alarming that a number of major settlement schemes are at present contemplated in various parts of Africa, and some are certainly being done in a hurry.

In some cases, undoubtedly, very careful investigation has gone on. The social effects of the Volta River scheme in Ghana have been the subject of large volumes of reports; and no doubt the various proposals for settlement in the Rufiji River Basin in Tanganyika, reported upon by the World Bank Mission, will be socially as well as technically careful. As yet little seems to be published on the social side of the larger Niger Dam proposal (at Kainji, above Jebba) which is designed not only to give navigation as far as Niamey or beyond but also to bring 100,000 acres of the flood-plain between Jebba and Lokoja under irrigation. While 30,000 acres could be fairly readily handed over to traditional agriculture, the remainder would need high value crops and a much increased labour force. Nor is there any record of a social or anthropological study of the Bacita sugar proposal in which 12,000 to 15,000 acres, north of Ilorin and south of Jebba, may be put down to sugar, although the technical trials of the crop have been highly satisfactory.

Perhaps more alarming still are the proposals in Western and Eastern Nigeria for large-scale settlement of young farmers on lands which, it is hoped, chiefs may make available or governments will acquire. The Western scheme is the more ambitious and is already in being. Each settlement of 5,000 to 7,000 acres is to take 200 school-leavers from Standard VI or Secondary Modern schools. About thirty were already starting in 1961 on each of

[59] Baldwin, op. cit.

thirteen different settlements, and ten more areas were due to start in 1963. The young farmers will be given, after an initial period of two years' training, a holding of thirty acres and a house costing about £500. On this farm they will grow food and a cash crop, suited to the soil and area. Three Farm Institutes for their training have been set up and two more allowed for. The scheme is costing about £2 million for the first eighteen months and may cost about £15 million by 1975, after which it is due to be self-supporting. A central machinery depot, financed by government, will do contract work for the farmers at commercial rates. Each young farmer will be debited with £2,400, as the capital cost of installing him, and this he will be expected to repay at $1\frac{1}{2}$ to 2 per cent over fifteen to twenty years. He is expected to earn a clear cash income, after making these payments, of from £200 to £450 per annum from his cash crops. Members are, if possible, to be drawn from a 30-mile radius of the settlements, so that they will remain in touch with their families.[60]

The schemes in Eastern Nigeria are not as yet so detailed. It was announced by Dr. Okpara in January 1961 that a number of farm settlements would be established, each costing at least £500,000, covering 4,000 to 6,000 acres, and carrying 400 young men and families with individual farms, the Government to carry the initial cost, which (as in the Western scheme) would be repayable. Eventually there might be a scheme of this kind in each of the twelve Provinces of the Region.[61]

These are indeed stirring acts of faith. There are enormous unforeseeable contingencies—for example, whether alternative opportunities will look easier or more profitable to the proposed tenants; whether the crop prices will remain at profitable levels; whether the social groupings, which will be entirely new, will work satisfactorily; what attitude the families of the tenants will take to these schemes and how many of them will descend upon their relatives; how effectively the provisions for repayment can be enforced or whether they will be insisted upon. £2,500 is a large monetary debt for a young Nigerian to carry at the start of his adult life.

A different scheme, but also on an ambitious scale, is the settle-

[60] Details mainly from *West Africa*.
[61] Government Press Conference (*E.N.I.S. Bulletin,* Enugu, no. E 2,200, 18 January, 1961).

ment scheme at Mungwi, near Kasama, which is part of a general development scheme for the Northern and Luapula Provinces of Northern Rhodesia. The actual area for settlement consists of about 100,000 acres (with another 100,000 as a possible reserve), of which 20,000 are being developed in the first phase. Farmers will be offered twenty- to forty-acre plots, with the possibility of extension, after a year's intensive training at a Depot Farm, and they will be able to take oxen and implements on to their farm on interest-free repayable loans. A Development Area Training Centre, teaching crafts and also 'white-collar' subjects, is established in the area. The development scheme includes a model market township, with full secondary education and provision for individual trading or small industries. All services are being developed—roads, water, hydro-electric power at Chisinga Falls near by, telephone and piped-water supply. This settlement forms part of a regional development which includes extensive new forestry and sawmills, development of a water route of 250 miles up Lake Bangweolu, hydro-electric power at Abercorn and Fort Rosebery, a cattle-ranching scheme and a co-operative bus service. The objects of the settlement farms are to break through the old pattern of shifting cultivation (*chitemene*) and also to develop an urban centre which will have some of the 'modern' attractions of the Copperbelt towns and will thus hold or retrieve the Bemba men who migrate there.[62] £2 million was voted for the special development in addition to the hydro-electric scheme and other normal development of services and communications.

This is an exciting proposal, in that it recognizes the need for a market town and a proper community; it is to some degree welded into general development, and it is not attached purely to the 'school-leaver' problem, but will welcome all volunteer farmers for training. The extent of indebtedness envisaged is far smaller, and the scheme is well rooted in ideas of proper land utilization and conservation. There is always some danger in development which

[62] There is a very large labour migration from these Northern Provinces. White, op. cit., records that absentee males from Kasama amounted to 60 per cent, Fort Rosebery 52 per cent, Kawamba 47 per cent. The absences, however, are not normally very long. Of a sample of the Luvale (admittedly a different area) 71 per cent made only one journey and of these 40 per cent were for less than two years, or 66 per cent for less than four years. (*Report of the Rural Economic Development Working Party,* Lusaka, Government Printer, 1960). The Provincial Commissioner (Northern Province) estimates that about 60 per cent of males are normally absent from their villages.

has a social problem as its primary rather than secondary motive; in Nigeria, there is a real danger of finding land for settlers rather than settlers for a carefully planned use of land. There are, too, great risks in the Mungwi scheme. Nothing is more difficult than to 'plan' a new town in the middle of nowhere—the town may refuse to grow, the crops or market fail. The greatest flexibility in allowing unplanned activities to grow and favourite plans to fail will be needed if this theoretically admirable scheme is to give birth to a community reflecting that real combination of economic laws and human motivation which is always so much more complex and surprising than any plan.[63] If previous experience is any guide, it will be on the sheer cash profitability of the crops to be grown at Mungwi that success will depend; Bemba farmers are not going to work hard with new methods unless there is a good and quick reward. It is on this point that some doubts have been expressed; neither transport facilities nor the eventual market appear to be very well assured. On the other hand, some Indian experience is encouraging, and notably the settlement schemes, covering hundreds of thousands of acres, in the Punjab, which were established complete with yeoman and peasant holdings and with their own market towns, and are now thriving communities.[64]

5. THE FUTURE PATTERN

The desire for the things which only money will buy, not only the material things, but education and more contact with the wider world, is spreading all over Tropical Africa, far out into the villages of the forest and the open plain. This is the essential fact on which the agrarian revolution can be built. It is a force so powerful that even cherished customs will give way before it. This agrarian revolution must in part precede, though in part it will fertilize, the industrial development to follow. For a few years there may be a honeymoon period, as the old opposition to the colonial power changes to enthusiasm for building a free nation,

[63] The Rural Economic Development Working Party in Northern Rhodesia, reporting in November 1960, mentions the danger of marking 'market-town' on a plan without the assurance that population will in fact concentrate there. The Working Party favoured siting either near an industrial enterprise or 'where there is already a recognizable tendency towards concentration'. (Report, supra, p. 135.)

[64] See Philip Woodruff, *The Men Who Ruled India*, vol. II, *The Guardians* (London, Jonathan Cape, 1954), pp. 112 et seq.

IX. Kenya farmer and his daughters

[*Photograph by Camera Press Ltd*

V. Fishermen on Lake Mweru, Northern Rhodesia

and as foreign help, which may not last so many years, is freely offered. Much experience has been hardly gained, and in many places African agriculture is poised for a real leap forward. The worst danger lies in the possible loss of experienced and sympathetic advisers just at the time of critical decisions.

The greatest and least costly opening for progress lies in the improvement of existing methods, on good soils, and in turning the new production into money earnings. Research, new varieties, fertilizers, pest and disease control, higher quality through co-operative marketing, all assisted by extension services and Community Development and by investment in roads and bridges and water control, are the methods which lie to hand for this advance. It is worth emphasizing the sheer size of benefit which, in the most favourable circumstances of all, can come from this combination, which does not have to face a direct clash with deep cultural habits or a risky transfer of population. Opening Cocoa House in Accra on 19 November 1960, Dr. Nkrumah said :

The accumulated reserves of the Cocoa Marketing Board is public money, held in trust by the Government for the farmers and the people of this country. Many Ghanaian institutions have received grants or endowments from the Government through the Board. For example, we have given £27 million towards cocoa rehabilitation and control of swollen shoot and capsid, an endowment of £2 million has been paid to the faculty of Agriculture at the University College of Ghana; the West African Cocoa Research Institute has received £2 million in aid of research into cocoa diseases and cultivation of high yielding varieties.

Regional organizations have also received grants of about £3 million to finance local development projects. We are financing the construction of a Memorial Hospital to Tetteh Quarsie, the man who is said to have introduced cocoa into our country, and 40-odd secondary schools are being built by the Ghana Educational Trust.

In all, over £74 million has been given to institutions and organizations for the development and improvement of agriculture, health, education and other economic and social services in Ghana.[65]

There are more difficult situations. There are times when a clean break with customary land tenure, as at Mungwi, may be the only course. Nor is land tenure some isolated legal rule ; systems of holding land or cattle are commonly the central symbol of a whole culture :

[65] *Ghana Cocoa Marketing Board News Letter*, no. 16, January 1961.

This transfer of cattle is the key to the whole Nyakyusa system of blood and affinal relationship. . . . Cattle circulate rapidly; few except chiefs have more than ten cows in their herds at any one time; more often each man has paid out, for his own and his sons' marriages, five, ten or twenty times the numbers of cattle that he now possesses. A young man is given cows by his father and sends them to his father-in-law; his father's income in cattle is derived, partly from increase in his own stock, but chiefly from the marriages of his own or his brother's sisters and daughters . . . the young man's father-in-law gives the cows which he receives, some to his brothers, some to his sons, and some he keeps himself. And thus, continually, the cattle are driven down the paths of human relationships.[66]

How is breeding to be improved, how is herd management to be taught, how is any effective change to be made in such a society where social relationships and husbandry are so intertwined? It is not always so difficult—for example, Masai herd management could probably be fully modernized without revolutionary changes.[67] It is in societies where a bride-price is habitually paid in cattle that the difficulty is usually most acute. It is wrong to assume that these difficulties are rare, or that they can always be avoided.[68] There are many situations where they must be faced squarely or not at all. It is hard even for the anthropologist to forecast the degree of likely opposition. In all the difficult cases it is certain that an evident and immediate economic benefit must be assured if a frontal attack on social custom is the only way ahead.

There are, secondly, schemes for major development, perhaps in new areas, which entail a greater risk. To use the industrial-type plantation is perhaps the easiest short cut; but it is apt to shirk the social problem, relying largely on a system of migratory labour which is in essence retrogressive. There may well be compromises, as the banana Co-operative of the Bakweri has shown; extensive monoculture (with all its dangers) is not the only way of growing most crops. The alternative to plantations may be a major scheme of settlement, associated with hydro-electricity and irrigation. The decisions have been taken already for several—the Volta, Niger,

[66] Godfrey Wilson, 'The Nyakyusa of South West Tanganyika', in *Seven Tribes of British Central Africa*, ed. Colson and Gluckman (London, Oxford University Press, 1951).
[67] Jacobs, op. cit.
[68] As one awkward example: the Mashona of Southern Rhodesia dedicate cattle to individual ancestors, which makes culling very embarrassing.

Rufiji and Mungwi schemes. Always in such programmes, it is hard to balance the very long-term, the spectacular, against the smaller, quicker-yielding alternatives on which the same capital might be spent. £60 million on the Volta scheme will take a long time to pay off; could it be that, when some similar choice is faced, ten schemes of £6 million, or thirty schemes of £2 million, would bring back the capital quicker, would in fact have started to create new capital (as cocoa, or Mwanza cotton have) before the multimillion scheme had even started? There is evidence that investment in rural infrastructure is far quicker to show a return than the same investment in industrial facilities.[69]

It is worth emphasizing once more the amount of employment in modern occupations which a thriving rural economy can give. There are jobs for craftsmen—improved housing, fencing, farm buildings and water supply, ox-carts and so on. There is furniture and household equipment to be made and sold. There are servicing jobs—driving delivery vans, running petrol pumps and repair shops. There are jobs in the markets in the whole business of grading, weighing, inspecting crops; there are clerical jobs in the local councils, in Co-operatives, and even in the larger shops and stores, in the country market towns of today and of the future. The moment there is money to spend and the desire for a more 'Western' standard, work multiplies and there is room for men and women with new skills and ambitions.

Finally, whatever the future shape of African provincial administration in independent countries, the continuance of skilled advice and patient persuasion in rural areas is of key importance. It is too easy to assume that because some racial or nationalist tensions are removed at Independence, willing and energetic co-operation will follow. In fact many Europeans were completely trusted in rural areas, and on the average were better qualified and more experienced than the younger African who will succeed them. Moreover, the great unwillingness of many educated Africans to work for any length of time in the bush will have to be overcome. As politics come to play a greater part in local life—

[69] The expenditure both at Lagos and at the port and industrial area of Tema have been extremely slow to attract the industrial development hoped for. By contrast, road expenditure in Northern Nigeria was described to me as showing an immediate and substantial rise in government revenue from licences, &c. In the longer term, the advantages, on a much bigger scale, would come from crop movements from areas opened to development.

and in the long run it is necessary that they should—the African District Officers and extension services (with any Europeans who may still be employed) will have a hard task to maintain the momentum of rural improvement.

Social betterment has to be paid for by economic success. The more widely economic energy can come to spring from the natural ambitions of individuals and small groups, rather than from the all-endowing State, the more lively and the more free will a society be. In Africa, where this new spring of ambition is so needed, the new attitude must above all be accepted without fear or nostalgia and directed to a social end. This is not simply to advocate a wholesale swallowing of the ultra-competitive individualism of some Western societies. On the contrary, the natural style of most African societies has been far more deeply coloured by co-operative motives, and it may be the small group rather than the individual which dominates African economic advance, particularly in the country. The central State and Marketing Boards could, in accordance with the socialist outlook of many new African governments, assist and support such groups without dominating them. The West has brought not only the cash economy but some of the values, both good and bad, associated with it—the breaking of caste, the sense of personal, adult responsibility for vital choices and satisfying achievement in life with all its responsibilities and dangers. There are larger freedoms on the move in African villages than freedom from European rule, and it is from these that new energies will spring.

CHAPTER VII

THE AFRICAN TRADER

1. PHASES IN THE DEVELOPMENT OF TRADE

Before the Europeans, Arabs and Asians began to penetrate inland, and apart from the Saharan caravan trade,[1] it is extremely hard to picture accurately the amount of trading which may have taken place in the interior of Tropical Africa. We must mainly imagine a diffused system of raiding and barter. Here and there, in the more advanced societies, craftsmen were at work—goldsmiths, potters, brass-founders, carvers; here and there a more regular exchange of food and handicrafts. Certainly in the larger centres and at the courts of kings, raiding and trading had developed sizeable markets; around the Muslim Emirs and the larger centres of the Arabs in East and Central Africa, there were tokens of a civilization more of the Middle East than of Negro Africa;[2] and the old civilizations of Ife and Oyo must have included a rich exchange of handicrafts. When the Arabs and Europeans first came, it was to take what could be most readily grasped —slaves, ivory, sometimes gold. They brought in exchange not only fire-arms but textiles, thus carrying the demand for European goods far into the interior. In West Africa, both in the savannah and in a few centres in the forest belt, they found African towns and the fore-runners of the great markets of today.

A second phase, and a critical change from the first plunder of men and women, ivory and gold, came when the European traders began to buy, and then to grow, the products of the soil. At once the difference between East and West Africa began to widen further. For the main West African product, palm fruit, was collected and processed by Africans; and there were the rivers of the West for contact and for bringing produce to the Coast. The long contact of slaving days had opened lines of trade from the interior, so that the produce trade could start quickly. The imported goods given in exchange went into African hands and

[1] For a full description of the trans-Saharan trade, see E. W. Bovill, *The Golden Trade of the Moors* (London, Oxford University Press, 1958).

[2] See Slade, op. cit.

African markets. The produce-buying companies, gradually ex-
tending inland, found Africans to bring the produce in and Africans to distribute the European goods even to the smallest villages.

The situation in East and Central Africa was very different.
There was no African crop for export; trade had to wait for the
slow process of overland penetration, settlement, the trial and
development of crops or minerals, and the building of a railway
to move goods to the coast. There was no major and little minor
trade with Africans after the slave trade ceased—chiefly a demand
for porters and labour, paid for in calico or beads or cash. Neither
Africans nor Asians handled the wheat, pyrethrum, tea, coffee,
tobacco which white farmers in the Rhodesias and Nyasaland and
in Kenya were growing for export, nor the metals from the
Rhodesian and the Congo mines. The Asians became retailers to
both Europeans and Africans, quickly dominating this trade; and
later they became sugar planters and cotton ginners. Thus, although effective European domination of inland areas on the
West Coast was so little earlier than in Central and East Africa,
African-grown export crops, easier transportation and the earlier
trading contacts gave the West Coast a long start in African
participation in the growth of commerce.

The new towns which arose or expanded from European settlement—Dakar, Abidjan, Lagos, Brazzaville, the Belgian Congo
towns, Salisbury, Nairobi—gave a different opportunity to the
trader, and here again there were wide differences in development.
Very broadly, it was the *petits blancs* [3] who served the European
quarters with shops and garages and restaurants in the main West
Coast towns and in Rhodesia; in East Africa, it was the Asians.
But these towns came also to hold large African populations, and
here, on the West Coast, the African trader had his chance. In
the African townships of Léopoldville or Brazzaville there grew up
a considerable class of African *indépendants*—small traders, bar-
keepers, carpenters and the like, often helped or used by the
petits blancs who were quite willing to extend their trade at least
some way into the African world. The same was true in Lagos or

[3] In French towns, the *petits blancs* were mainly French and Levantines; in
East Congo, Greeks and Pakistanis as well as Belgians; in Léopoldville, Belgians and Portuguese; in the Rhodesias, Europeans of English or Afrikaans
descent, with a very few Asians.

Accra,[4] with Levantines mainly taking the place of *petits blancs*. Thousands of Africans thus gained what was for many their first experience of urban business. But in East Africa, Arabs and Asians on the Coast, and Asians inland to the farthest corners of Uganda and Tanganyika, gripped and held the trade of both village and town; although Nairobi and Kampala grew fast, and had their large African townships, few African *indépendants* established themselves in early days. In the Rhodesias, too, there was little room for the African trader. The labour lines and urban locations had their beer halls and some very simple markets; for most imported goods the African got a very second-class service from white traders and from a sprinkling of Asians. To see an African buying, sometimes under humiliating circumstances,[5] from a European shop in Rhodesia goods which his fellow in West Africa could buy in a thousand African stalls, with all the gaiety of bargaining, was one of the most doleful experiences in Africa.

Peace, the ever-growing production and movement of produce, better roads, railways, the growth of towns, the almost universal use of money in place of cowries or textiles or manillas,[6] together ushered in a new phase. In the East, the Asian merchants grew. In the West, from the mass of petty traders and craftsmen, the market women and the wandering Hausamen, there began to appear, particularly during and after the Second World War, a group of more substantial Africans in a more modern way of business. These might be the big traders of Accra, Kumasi, Kano, Lagos, Port Harcourt, and Onitsha, trading both in produce and European goods; the building contractors, the owners of fleets of lorries. These were men concerned with banks and credit, wages and customs dues; in many ways they were seeking to become modern men of business. This was the real start of a transition from the traditional market to the twentieth century sense of commerce.

The next, contemporary, phase comes in East Africa as the Africans, often with official support, begin to challenge Asian dominance in the commercial sphere; and in West Africa as the large European firms begin to let slip into African hands the less

[4] There were some remarkable African businessmen in Freetown, Sierra Leone, in the last century.
[5] Many of the former discriminatory practices have now been abolisned in the Rhodesias.
[6] Metal rings used for currency.

sophisticated types of trade, particularly the produce-buying and the retailing of simple goods, and to concentrate on more technical types of service and production, where their skills can still have an advantage.

This broad picture seems to correspond closely with the usual generalizations about African trade, which speak of the 'natural aptitude for trade in West Africa', the famous Yoruba market women, the backwardness of East and Central Africa and the dominance of the Asian there. But these are dangerous simplifications. For what kind and level of trade are West Africans suited? Is it certain that the Baganda, or the Wakamba in Kenya, or the Bahaia in Tanganyika will not or cannot show an equal ability when the conditions are right? Is the 'native' of the Rhodesias really 'for the most part childishly simple, irresponsible, improvident and unreliable', as the staff of one expatriate bank report?[7] Was the economist right who noticed in West Africans 'exceptional effort, foresight, resourcefulness, thrift, ability to perceive economic opportunity'?[8] How far will Africans, whether in East or West, be able to take over, and run efficiently, the growing modern economy which lies ahead of them? These questions demand a more careful look at the levels and the quality of African traders and businessmen.

2. THE WEST AFRICAN TRADER AND HIS PROBLEMS

How and why some of the peoples of West Africa, and particularly the Yoruba, developed urban life, and how the tradition of women's trading arose are questions beyond the scope of this book. There were certainly some Yoruba towns in the sixteenth century and Bascom[9] estimates that at least four towns had over 20,000 inhabitants in the time of Lander (1830). In the 1952 census there were six Yoruba towns of over 100,000 and three more of over 70,000. It is a given fact that in much of the coastal and forest areas petty trading in the markets is a skill, a pleasure and a necessity, and few people could excel the West African at it. To walk through the night-market at Ibadan, among the flickering lamps, or along the lagoon streets in Lagos is to appreciate that

[7] In a personal communication.
[8] Bauer, op. cit.
[9] W. Bascom 'Yoruba Urbanism: A Summary' (Summary of a Communication to the Royal Anthropological Institute, June 1958 in *Man*, no. 252, December 1958).

trading is of the essence of social life, from childhood upwards. Here are not only bargains to be made, but gossip and banter and a chance to make assignations. Imported goods and produce from the surrounding country will dominate the stalls. Further out, into the savannah and the desert fringes, there will be a little less of the imported wares, save for textiles, and more of the older constituents of trade—hand-made articles of wood and basket-work, produce of all kinds, the gear for farmers and horses and camels, trinkets for women. Where the cheap Japanese enamelware or the trade goods from the Coast appear, it will be a sign that an Ibo trader from Onitsha, or an Ashanti man from Kumasi has been up with a lorry, or perhaps that Holts, or London & Kano, or the United Africa Company have distributed there.

Numerically, the great majority of these market traders will be small and poor, making a few shillings, sometimes a few pence in the day, pin money for women, a little cash from surplus vegetables or a handicraft. Their skill is in selling, in carrying in their head figures of pennies and halfpennies, in finding a bargain from each other and selling to a stranger. Few of them depend on trade alone. But there are bigger men, with a wider range, often centred in one of the great West African markets, such as Onitsha, Port Harcourt or Kumasi. In the 3,000 shops of Onitsha covered market, and the acres of open stalls outside, it is said that anything available in West Africa can be bought. The imported goods come up the Niger from Burutu, or (particularly textiles, haberdashery and fancy goods) by lorry from Lagos or Port Harcourt or Owerri. Some goods come down from as far as Fort Lamy in Chad, some produce from all the surrounding country. Where the importer is a European firm—there are some, but few, direct African importers—the goods are bought, with much fine selection for fashion and price, by African traders. They build up, with the firm of their choice, a credit which can expand greatly at midmonth but must come down to a fixed figure at each month's end; it may be £1,000 mid-month and £400 at the end. Most, of course, are small, but there are big figures—a turnover of £60,000, even £140,000 in a year, with a mid-month credit of £10,000.

Two main kinds of trader work in Onitsha—those selling locally and the big wholesalers buying to sell to distant markets in the North. These Ibo traders will have agents to whom the lorries go in Jos, in Maiduguri, sometimes in Kano. Many of them work extraordinarily hard. If you notice a man half-asleep in the back of his stall, while a boy is serving, it is quite probably because two days ago he set off in a crowded lorry to cross the Niger Ferry in the evening, sat all night in the jolting lorry for 400 miles to Lagos, traded there all day, and was back on the lorry in the evening for the return journey. The boy will be a relative, taken in as an apprentice trader to learn the job. Many of these Ibo men will work like this (sometimes making two journeys in a week) for little reward. Perhaps, when tax is paid and all the expenses, and the small profit is counted, it may not be more than £100 or £150 in the year—less than he might earn by labouring. Somehow, a few manage to raise themselves from the ruck, and these are the rich men, with a fine house near Onitsha where they will go for weekends, and one or two paid clerks and many relatives to help them and live off them. Most of the traders will specialize and some turn into firms with a name known half across Nigeria. Profit rates are small, some traders working on little more than a shilling in the pound discount which the foreign importer gives; everything hangs on quick turnover, an eye for fashion, a knowledge of prices in markets 100 miles around, and the extras to be earned by breaking bulk and selling in small quantities down to a single cigarette.[10]

No one could fail to admire the energy and vitality of these traders, the range of their contacts and interests, their sharp eye for the slightest chance of trade, their hard work for small results. But there comes to the outsider, walking through yet another hundred yards of stalls, the commonsensical feeling that there are far too many.[11] Then there is the recollection of markets and bazaars in other places, not only the Asian bazaars in East Africa but the suks of Morocco, or Damascus, or Baghdad; and finally of back streets in old industrial towns in England where it seemed impossible that so many little shops, with sweets and

[10] I am particularly indebted to Dr. Margaret Katsin of Northwestern University who was making a special study of the Onitsha market when we were there, and also to the local representatives of U.A.C., John Holt, and Barclay's D.C.O. in Calabar, Enugu and Onitsha for much background information on Ibo trading.

[11] 'In Koforidua, I counted in the market nearly 3,000 sellers on a market day. This did not include the numbers of women selling at the various crossroads and in the streets. . . . One could estimate from this that not less than 70 per cent of the adult female population was engaged in selling.' D. McCall, in Southall (Ed.) *Social Change in Modern Africa*.

cigarettes and newspapers, torches and bicycle-clips, could make a living. This is a sign of poverty, of few better and alternative occupations, of families adding to one wage the extras which a little trading, a room over the shop and a lodger will bring. This thought will come back in considering the efforts of government all over Africa to encourage African trading; but first it is necessary to ask how, out of this jostling throng of competition, the few bigger traders emerge, and what is their quality.

The studies by Peter Garlick of African traders in Kumasi and Accra gives an invaluable insight into the successes and difficulties of some of these larger men.[12] Kumasi, with its 8,000 traders, ranks with the biggest markets in West Africa, with contacts running West and North as far as Abidjan and even Dakar, South to the Coast at Sekondi-Takoradi and Accra, and North East into Nigeria and French-speaking Equatorial Africa. Among about 150 traders who are the biggest men in Kumasi, a turnover from £5,000 to £20,000 was fairly common and the really high figures are at the £100,000 level. Stock is turned over quickly—from three to five times in the year most commonly, compared with a turnover of Kingsway Stores of three and a half times. As many as sixty-two of these traders were doing at least some direct importing from overseas, and most were employing up to three or four assistants (often relatives) with a rare case of twelve or eighteen. These, then, are substantial men. What of their quality and their difficulties?

First, they mostly had a fair degree of education—50 per cent in 'middle school', 70 per cent middle school or below; their spoken English was good to very good. It is interesting that in Onitsha too, where the myth of the illiterate African trader with a large roll of hundreds of pounds was so strong, the tendency is now for the better educated to thrive most. The demands for tax returns and the sheer difficulty of trading on a big scale without accounts are gradually imposing a standard, and there are many jobs for the school-leaver who can keep books to help the older traders, and many younger men are making their own way with the aid of a better education. But a closer look at the bigger firms of Kumasi reveals how uneven and precarious is the trader's world. In some ways he is a petty trader grown large. His know-

[12] Garlick, op. cit. Most of the following detail is drawn from this study, studies by the same author in Accra, and much personal help and suggestion.

ledge of business methods, as the West would know them, is very thin—only six had ever been to Europe. He is constantly attempting a scale and risk in trade out of keeping with his real resources of capital or skill or staff, and in consequence is periodically struck by crippling losses. It has often been remarked that many African traders are over-optimistic. They expect business to do well, and if it does not the less worthy of them are apt to default; if there is a fall in price between buying and selling, they have even gone back to their supplier, demanding a reduction. Margaret Field [13] in Ghana remarked on the tremendous amount of small business enterprise (particularly buying lorries) which is embarked upon without any knowledge or experience. The business lasts as long as the lorry—two to three years. Although the bigger man is more experienced and able, he is still liable to fits of over-optimism and over-trading; he has not had the Asian's long experience of the hardships of trade, nor the Asian's more modest expectations. Above all, he feels starved of credit and often resentful against the Banks, whether expatriate or African, which, in his view, have never helped the African trader as they should.

The position of the Banks is of key importance. In the early days they were, of course, almost wholly the financial wing of European enterprise. But as trade and prosperity grew and with the approach of Independence, the Banks became aware both of African criticism and of the future value of their custom. In recent years they have made very considerable efforts to attract Africans within their doors and to play a part in the increasing wealth of the purely African economy. In certain fields this has been highly successful. There are some large African accounts, and an increasing number of small ones, though the African is apt to be an expensive customer, depositing £20 one day and withdrawing the whole amount by a series of small cheques within a week. In consequence, bank charges are high. Nevertheless, the process of education goes on. The financing of African-grown crops is another important field. In the West the Banks have long financed crop purchases in the season. The new development is the financing of Co-operatives in East Africa—for example, the Mwanza cotton crop purchase has recently been financed between Barclays D.C.O. and the Victoria League, and big amounts of money have gone to Co-operatives in Southern Tanganyika. Finally, the Banks

[13] Field, op. cit.

have run large savings campaigns, and both the number and weight of savings accounts have grown in the last few years. In East Africa, one Bank records a rise from £450,000 to £650,000 in African savings accounts between 1958 and 1960, the number of accounts rising from 9,500 to 16,313, and in some West African towns the figures have almost trebled, e.g., from £120,000 to over £300,000 in one Onitsha Branch Bank between 1957 and 1960.

But when it comes to financing individual entrepreneurs and traders, which may involve quite long-term loans, the Banks have fallen back on the strictest orthodoxy—that this is not, in fact, the Banks' business. A period of more daring experiment in Nigeria resulted in so many defaults and malpractices that the Banks had to retreat somewhat hastily. The greatest difficulty has been lack of mortgageable security, mainly due to African land tenure. Save in special areas, or where Land Consolidation has taken place, freehold title to land is rare. Even the trader's own house is often technically in joint ownership with the family. There was up to 1961 no effective money market in Africa, either for securities or share issues, and indeed the Banks found difficulty in placing their funds, most of which were placed back in London; it has been stated that 'the Banks could increase their loans and advances by 50 per cent with liquidity ratios and leakages from the banking system at their present levels'.[14]

Various methods of bridging this gap between the Banks' need to place money and the African's fervent desire for credit have been tried, and these will be described in assessing government policies towards traders. It is not that no loans are granted. Garlick found that Bank loans up to £3,000 had been given in Kumasi on buildings; from £200 to £1,000 by the use of guarantors; and up to £2,000 on unsecured credit-worthiness to established traders. It is mainly the issue of credit-worthiness which is at the root of the problem, and perhaps the most common difficulty is that the African borrower all too frequently uses his loan not for the purpose intended but to build himself a large house. In consequence, the money does not multiply, and a £5,000 house out in the bush (where these traders are apt to build them) is not an easily negotiable asset. There is also a psychological element involved. When a European, Asian or large Levantine trader

[14] Charles V. Brown, 'The Supply of Bank Money in Nigeria', II, *The Bankers' Magazine,* December 1960.

approaches his bank manager for a loan or overdraft, he carries with him a reputation of being well used to commerce, and of knowing how to use money, although particular individuals may be feckless or dishonest. But an African entering by the same door bears the burden of many past defaults and simplicities (or duplicities) by his fellow-countrymen. For he comes at a time when a whole civilization is getting its commercial education, with the natural crop of experiments more hopeful than well-founded.

Most of the Banks have done excellent work, and borne some losses, in an endeavour to train African customers in credit-worthiness; and governments, expatriate firms, and occasionally Development Corporations have contributed to this. Moreover, the constant criticism of African business sense must be taken with a grain of salt. It is absurd to suppose that every European is even potentially a good businessman. If £500 was handed to the first ten Englishmen in a middle-class suburb, to trade with or to start a business, nine of them would have lost it by the end of the year.[15] What makes things difficult in Africa is that the new African middle class is still so undifferentiated, and the men with a real flair for business are not easily distinguishable from school teachers, cocoa farmers, lorry drivers and clerks, all of whom may try to raise a loan or an overdraft.

While the Banks as such have attempted to steer a moderate and educative course, the same cannot be said of some organizations running hire purchase. No doubt they were tempted by the hope of high profits on the wave of expansion and optimism which has accompanied the growth of African expenditure on consumer goods. In East Africa particularly there was in the winter of 1960–1 a sorry trail of defaults, duplicity by car dealers and ingenious manoeuvres by hire purchase customers, particularly in the motor trade. The backyards of some firms were overstocked with cars shorn of wheels and batteries, re-possessed by the hirers; the roadsides in the bush disclosed all too many burnt-out wrecks, which will no doubt help to feed the new steel-scrap mill at Jinja.[16]

---

[15] It would be interesting to know how many ex-servicemen, or even retired colonial civil servants, made a success of starting a business with their gratuity or compensation.

[16] A common practice was to take a car on hire purchase, use it as a taxi eighteen hours a day with two drivers, spending nothing on maintenance. After a few months profits made would exceed the deposit and first instalments, and the owner would cease payments.

Nothing could be more deplorable than this attempt to introduce a sophisticated commercial mechanism, which in fact relies on regular earnings, a high degree of conscience, a strong public opinion against default, and a simple and effective legal control, into the African situation, where few of these necessities may apply. The result has been to teach many Africans undesirable tricks, to spoil the credit market for honest men, and in some cases to build up violent antagonism to the European companies—there has been more than one pitched battle in Uganda over attempts to re-possess, with half a village setting on the company's agent. Credit is of high importance to African economies, which are in a Keynesian sense habitually under-inflated, since great resources of manpower and material have not been pulled into full productive use. But the expansion of credit and the growth of credit-worthiness will not be forwarded by people in a hurry for quick profits and apparently ignorant of African conditions.[17]

In fact, the African trader's best source of credit is probably the large expatriate importer. The United Africa Company, for example, has 5,000 credit customers in Ghana and 30 per cent of its business is done on credit terms. Another firm said that 30 per cent of the credit it gave in Kumasi went to African customers.[18] A similar method of monthly settlement, with a higher credit at mid-month, is used in Kumasi as in Onitsha, the amounts rising above the customer's original cash deposit in proportion to his reliability as a trader. Firms also use a post-dated cheque and occasionally, but to a less extent, a mortgage on property. Figures of hundreds of pounds, up to £3,000 and even more, were given as monthly credits; and, since a trader might have accounts with more than one firm, he could raise several thousand pounds. Some expatriate firms have made a special effort to build up a group of reliable and successful African customers. In turn, most of the big African traders give credit, on a smaller scale, to their own African customers, though occasionally suffering losses.

Thus slowly the credit-worthy African trader is finding it possible to get credit. But there are other reasons why it is hard for Africans to become and remain credit-worthy. In general, far too

[17] One of the operators offering hire-purchase loans complained of the difficulty of control because 'Africans keep changing their names and you can't identify them because they all look alike'.   [18] Garlick, op. cit.

little money is ploughed back into the business. If the African trader was really putting his money back he would soon have liquid assets on which he could get short-term advances even from the Banks. But his social and cultural background is a constant drag on him. Partly, it is his own fault. Many traders in West Africa are half trader and half farmer—particularly the cocoa farmers. They are apt to put some of the business money into the farm, so that the business is starved of working capital. Again, there is the unfortunate fashion for building a large and expensive house in the home village which may be half empty for long periods or filled with relatives. In one small town in Ghana an estimate of the value of concrete houses built mostly in the last decade by African traders working away from their homes amounted to £250,000.[19] This is purely a prestige expenditure, and again it robs the business. Less under his control are the demands of relatives. Of sixty-two traders interviewed, thirty-eight had more than five children dependent on them and nineteen had more than ten.[20] Apart from direct maintenance, there are constant demands for help with school fees; there are family funerals which will certainly cost £100 and possibly several hundreds. If the trader himself dies, inheritance under the matrilinear system will go to his sister's sons, and this usually means that the buiness is broken up, unless the trader has made a special will to prevent it. Out of a sample of fifty-two Kumasi traders in matrilinear families no less than forty-two had in fact made wills altering the customary inheritance, mainly in favour of the trader's own children.[21]

These family reasons are certainly of major importance. The trader is attempting to build up an individual business in a rough sea of social change in which his obligations to an extended family are felt as binding, and in which he must help at many launches and many rescues. The general flux and instability around him also strain his business in other ways. Customers, themselves under strain, default on credit; employees steal; inefficient relatives have to be kept on the staff; customs officials or police may suddenly become difficult or demand bribes. It is not surprising that the

[19] Garlick, 'African and Levantine Firms Trading in Ghana' (N.I.S.E.R. Conference, December 1960).
[20] Garlick, *African Traders in Kumasi.*   [21] Ibid.

XI. African shopkeeper, Nyanza, Kenya

XIIa. Groundnuts awaiting transport, Northern Nigeria

[*Photograph by The Times*

XIIb. Tobacco seller, Nigeria

[*Photograph by courtesy of the Nigerian Tobacco Company L*

long process of steady growth which makes a well-found business is hard to achieve. Nevertheless, quite a number of African traders in, for example, Ghana are well-established men, with a turnover which at least compares with that of most of the Levantines, though not with that of the few really big Levantine firms. The Table below gives a range of turnover for a considerable sample of African and Levantine firms, excluding those few which have a turnover of more than £200,000.[22]

ANNUAL TURNOVER FIGURES
(251 African and 182 Levantine Trading Years)
£'000's

	Under 5	5–10	10–15	15–20	20–25	25–50	50–75	75–100	100–200	Over 200
African %	Not considered	23	18	14	6	19	9	4	6	—
Cumulative %		23	41	55	61	80	90	94	100	—
Levantine %		8	9	5	5	20	15	13	14	9
Cumulative %		8	17	22	28	48	64	76	91	100

Thus a sober estimate of African traders has many factors to balance. Historically, three stages can be distinguished. First, a society in which almost everyone does a little barter. Second, the beginnings of specialization, when a large number of people do a little trading or even shopkeeping as only one of the family's total methods of earning; this was the stage so widely reached when West Africa earned its trading reputation, and a stage quite widely reached now in East Africa too. Third, the emergence of the bigger, fully specialized trader as part of the modern world. Because there are and have long been in West Africa a multitude of small traders who can bargain very keenly, it would be wrong to conclude that West Africans are ready-made businessmen. The transition from the traditional market stall to modern commerce is a major one in these days, and needs education, business knowledge and character not likely to be found in every stallholder. The communal pattern of life makes the necessary individualism of a business career and accumulation of capital very difficult. Again, the very number of part-time traders makes the emergence of bigger businesses more difficult and the establishment of commercial standards and credit slower. While it is certainly absurd to expect more than 10 per cent of Africans to show high commercial

[22] Garlick, 'African and Levantine Firms Trading in Ghana'.

ability, and unfair to judge all by the commercially adolescent failures of some, it would be equally mistaken to be too impressed even by the successes among the larger marketmen. These successes are still precarious, and will remain so until the novelty of the new commercial situation has worn off a little and trade becomes more professionalized, and the need for experience and method is accepted.

3. ATTITUDES TO EXPATRIATE TRADERS

Before turning to the part which government policy has played, in East as well as West Africa, a word must be said about the attitudes of African traders towards expatriate business in Africa. Something more will be said of governmental and political attitudes, which naturally have a nationalist tinge. But among the traders themselves attitudes to European firms, at least in West Africa, are not particularly hostile, and often traders readily confess to the help they have received. There was certainly bitter resentment that Africans were virtually excluded from the import trade at the close of the war, when goods were scarce and profits high.[23] But much of this feeling has now been forgotten. Opposition to Levantines in West Africa and Asians in East Africa is much stiffer. Garlick found that 50 per cent of traders interviewed in Kumasi expressed this hostility. Both groups are more experienced than most Africans, and both are tough traders, with their very foothold and livelihood at stake. They have perhaps less paternal consideration for the African than the larger European firms may show. The Asians in particular are provident men, as one leading Asian in Nairobi emphasized; they accumulate slowly and carefully, accept a very low living standard, and are not so tempted to display and impulsive expenditure as some African peoples.[24] Possibly African hostility—which is by no means universal— springs from the direct competition at a low level of people who are 'foreigners' without the prestige of the colonial power. It would be natural to quote the Uganda boycott of Asians in this connexion; but although in the villages no doubt local jealousy

[23] A system of allocation based on pre-war trading meant that the expatriate firms were virtually monopolists just at this critical period, when the pent-up demand for consumer goods was at its height.

[24] Not all. The Kikuyu, for example, give the impression of a certain secretiveness and hard business sense, and have not been given to conspicuous spending.

encouraged a chance to drive out the Asian shopkeeper and install an African in his place, the origins of the movement are still obscure and its development in Kampala was deeply involved in political tensions between Baganda groups and parties.

It is perhaps more serious that a Committee of the Federal Government of Nigeria [25] should have taken up and emphasized the hostility to Levantines. They were accused of property speculation—'they buy or lease properties at very low prices only to sell or assign at exorbitant rates'. Africans cannot compete because they cannot get the same short-term loan facilities. 'Instead of real properties being available to the African as securities, they are passed on at sing-song prices to expatriate speculators who themselves sometimes use them as securities for overdrafts or loans from the commercial banks.'[26] And, further: 'The African must be protected in the field of textile and road transport in which he has acquired efficiency. It is not only expedient to do so, it is just and equitable. The Syrians were called in to fill a gap and they have served their usefulness.'

It is significant for the future that the main grounds given by the Committee for differentiating between Levantines [27] and Europeans (apart from easier access to bank credit which both have) is that the Europeans bring in capital, technical knowledge, managerial skill, *and are prepared to share it with Africans*. The Lebanese are alleged to bring no capital, to have only retail skill, no higher than the African ('the supremacy of the African in retail trade has been acknowledged for centuries'),[28] and to be unwilling to share with Africans because they form close family partnerships. The Asian, though bringing capital, has the same pattern of family control. The two criteria which the Committee suggested for the continued admission of expatriate business were:

(a) whether the expatriate himself has technical skill and managerial experience to impart to the Africans, and
(b) if he has, whether he is prepared to impart it in the working out of that partnership.

[25] *Report of Advisory Committee on Aids to African Businessmen* (Lagos, Government Printer, 1959), paras. 267, 269 and 272.
[26] Garlick also found in Ghana that Levantines were accused of monopolizing the best properties and trading sites in towns. See 'African and Levantine Firms Trading in Ghana'.
[27] Usually called Syrians, although the majority are Lebanese.
[28] *Report of Advisory Committee on Aids to African Businessmen.*

The forms of partnership suggested were three :

(a) joint enterprise—the pooling of capital resources, joint management and technical co-operation;
(b) African capital, with expatriate management and technological skill, the advantage being that the African has the fullest opportunity of understudying at all levels;
(c) European capital, management and technological skill, with Africans being employed throughout the gamut of business.[29]

These statements represent quite clearly what is likely to be a common attitude of independent African governments, and lead naturally to some consideration of government policy, both under the colonial régime and after it.

It is interesting that where trade is overwhelmingly in the hands of Europeans and Levantines, as in Dakar, Africans may not even attempt to challenge it. Senegal, with a population of only two million, is in any case too small to provide the businessmen for Dakar, which has a larger industrial sector even than Lagos. The more educated Senegalese have all chosen administration or the professions (we could only find one substantial African businessman in Dakar) and even the small shopkeepers are largely Mauritanians, while the larger stores are both owned and staffed by Europeans or Levantines. 'The most ardent critics of this state of affairs are not the Senegalese themselves but visiting Africans. . . . When a Nigerian shops in "Printania" or goes to the local Bank in Dakar, he is shocked by the number of Frenchwomen employed in jobs he is accustomed to seeing held by Africans in Lagos.'[30] Islamic education, the caste system, and the easy relations between French *petits blancs* and Africans all probably contribute to this situation, which makes Dakar appear so much a French town.

4. PATERNALISM AND EAST AFRICAN TRADERS

It is in East Africa that governments have been most deeply concerned to encourage African participation in trade. In Central Africa there has been a consistent policy of keeping Asians out (there are only about 15,000 in Southern Rhodesia, 8,000 in

---

[29] *Report of Advisory Committee on Aids to African Businessmen.*
[30] M. Crowder (personal communication).

Northern Rhodesia, and 11,000 in Nyasaland), partly to avoid yet another racial problem and partly, as it was put to us by an official in Northern Rhodesia, because 'any advancement here is going to the African'. But the exclusion of Asians in Rhodesia has not in fact greatly helped the African, and has almost certainly reduced the general level of commercial activity, which is still largely in the hands of small Europeans who have shown little interest in the purely African market. In West Africa, until recent years, governments no doubt felt that the African trader was doing quite well. But in East Africa virtually the whole 'modern' section of the economy was shared between Europeans and Asians including both commerce and technical and artisan work. The British administration, particularly as the idea of training Africans for self-government grew and took shape, were concerned at the backwardness of Africans in trade and small retailing, and have made various experiments to remedy it. Courses for African traders were started, notably at the Jeanes School in Nairobi, in which simple business methods and skills were taught. Further, the Departments of Commerce and Industry concerned themselves with the encouragement of small businesses, and in Uganda a special African Trade Development Section was established which particularly—and most energetically—concerned itself with aid and advice to African traders; this Section has run a very large number of training courses.

In addition, an effort was made to make credit available to Africans in a satisfactory way. The most notable and successful experiment in this direction was the establishment in 1950 of the Uganda Credit and Savings Bank with a capital of £600,000, appropriated to this purpose by the Protectorate Government. One part of its function was to encourage African savings and by 1960 there were 41,800 accounts (99 per cent African) to the value of £1,362,225[31] in the bank. A particularly successful feature of the Savings Bank is that all counter staff are African, which makes the Bank a much more homely place for Africans opening their first account. The second function was to receive and investigate African applications for small loans and to administer them if granted. The Bank also acts as agent for an African Loans Fund, with a capital appropriation of £300,000. In 1960 outstanding loans from the Bank's funds stood at just over £300,000 and from

[31] Uganda Credit and Savings Bank, Report and Accounts, 1959–60.

the African Loans Fund at just over £200,000.[32] The Bank's issues of loans in 1960 included loans for fishing (£1,000), agriculture (£13,350), ginneries (£30,000), coffee factories (£18,000), residential buildings (£50,000), industry (£11,000), and shopkeeping (£5,000). Thirdly, the Bank acts as agent for two I.C.A. Revolving Funds, totalling £130,000, which are usually employed for larger loans. The outstanding feature of the small loans to Africans (mainly from the African Loans Fund), which average about £150 and carry 6 per cent interest, is the care with which each application is considered. The Bank's own inspectors, all African, visit the applicant, and the application is then considered by an Area Committee in his locality. If the loan is granted, the local authority guarantees it up to 50 per cent. The result has been to reduce the original rate of default, which reached 63 per cent in early days, to 1 per cent in 1959–60.

In Kenya, Tanganyika and Northern Rhodesia similar I.C.A. Revolving Loan Funds have been in operation, though it has been more difficult to get the money out to satisfactory borrowers and the results have been somewhat less successful. Only £40,000 of a Revolving Fund of £200,000 for housing had been issued in 1959 in Northern Rhodesia,[33] but the whole of a £270,000 Peasant Farming Fund was issued, with an average loan of £100. In Tanganyika only £50,000 had gone out from the I.C.A. Fund of £100,000, and only £10,000 from a £100,000 Local Development Fund.[34] Kenya has had the same difficulty in placing loans.

These achievements may seem small, particularly if compared with the richer economies in West Africa where, for example, the Ghana Guarantee Corporation, established by Ordinance in 1954, had £840,000 out in loans by 1959, of which half were in Kumasi alone.[35] But they have been immensely valuable in an educative sense, particularly when combined with the 'courses' for traders. Some of the borrowers in Uganda had reached their third or fourth loan, all satisfactorily repaid, and were therefore ready to

[32] Divided as to £100,000 for agriculture, just over £50,000 for shopkeeping and trade, and just under £50,000 for miscellaneous purposes, including fishing, cattle trading and small industry.

[33] Northern Rhodesia Government, *Report of the Commissioner for Development*, 1959.

[34] Department of Commerce and Industry, Tanganyika Government, as at 30 September 1960.

[35] Garlick, *African Traders in Kumasi*.

become credit-worthy borrowers from the commercial Banks. By 1959 there were 85 [36] African wholesalers in Uganda—mainly in sugar, maize, kerosene, tobacco—and a large number of stockists for expatriate firms such as East African Tobacco, Uganda Breweries, and Shell.

It would be wrong to underestimate the present extent of African trading in East Africa solely because Asians still hold the biggest share of the market. There are substantial and successful men here and there; in the Land Consolidation areas of Kenya more are appearing and of better quality. And there, as in West Africa, though not on the same scale, a large number of men are selling in local markets as a part-time occupation. In sheer numbers, there were found to be no less than 11,600 African traders in Uganda in 1953, as against 4,800 Asians. But the Asians were installed in the main trading centres, and particularly in Kampala, where 97·5 per cent of traders were non-African against 2·5 per cent African. Analysis of the turnover of African traders, the total of which was estimated at £10,000,000 in 1952, showed that 80 per cent were making a net profit of £50 per annum or less.[37] The vast bulk of them were, in fact, the part-time bush traders.

The record of government activity might seem to show a single-minded interest in establishing private retail and wholesale trade and small businesses in East Africa. But government policies have in fact been extremely confused. There are several different fields in which help has been attempted :

(a) small loans for agricultural equipment—instruments, fishing-nets, etc.—to help the farmer to commercialize his crop;
(b) loans to small retailers for stock or buildings, or to transport operators;
(c) aid to Africans in produce-buying and as middlemen;
(d) aid to small enterprises or businesses, such as brickworks.

Policy on agricultural loans is fairly clear. To give one example, funds were being used in Tanganyika Lake Province for tractors, maize-mills, fishing-gear, including outboard engines; for clearing and developing coffee land on the west of the Lake, where owners have virtually a freehold title; for stock (heifers, bulls &c.); for

[36] Department of Commerce and Industry, Kampala.
[37] Figures from Committee on the Advancement of Africans in Trade (The Maybury Committee) (Uganda Government Printer, 1955).

ox-carts or cream-separators. Similarly, there is a fairly defined policy for helping productive enterprises, though it is not wholly clear whether the object is to develop Afrcian entrepreneurs or to develop the most useful and profitable forms of secondary industry; this point will be discussed in the next chapter. It is in the field of retail and wholesale trade that the difficulties and anomalies really arise.

At the retail level there is, of course, acute competition and probably far too many families involved in petty trade. Had these been all of one nationality, it is difficult to believe that governments would have felt bound to interfere. Certainly in East Africa it would be hard to deny that this is a racial policy, designed to help the Africans to get a foot into Asian-dominated retail trade, and the very title of 'African Trade Development Department' confirms this. Whether or no there is justification for this policy, it is clearly not purely economic. In West Africa the motive is also racial, but in slightly different circumstances—it is more a question of enabling Africans to get commercial credit, which is felt to be the main disadvantage which they suffer in relation to Lebanese and Europeans.

But even in this effort to encourage African retailers, and granted a racial policy, a contradiction in government thinking often appears. For the Town Planning, Sanitary, Police and other Departments concerned with order, cleanliness, and proper standards are apt to insist on conditions which make it impossible for the small African with virtually no capital to get started.[38] Particularly in the Copperbelt towns [39] standards of construction have to be so high that Africans are almost excluded—which may have some connexion with the presence of white traders on Town Boards. This is also a feature of many of the large East African towns. But even in country markets, where a more natural jostle and mess might have been tolerated, far too high standards were often set. Dr. Hugh Fearn [40] has pointed out that in the African District Council markets of Nyanza Province (Kenya) an African,

[38] Cf. Ehrlich, op. cit. 'Established traders do not like hawkers, whether in Oxford Street or a Uganda township. Public Health Authorities do not like the dirt which comes with commerce. But in a poor society . . . authority . . . should sometimes choose dirty development in preference to moribund purity.'
[39] This point was particularly stressed by the Ndola Discussion Group.
[40] H. Fearn, *An African Economy* (London, Oxford University Press for E.A.I.S.R., 1961).

as a condition of his trading licence, had to build a shop to Health Ministry specifications, costing £500. Maximum turnover in the best districts of North Nyanza was about £800, giving an annual gross profit of £120; many figures were far lower. As a result, 'having expended £500 capital on permanent construction they have little or no working capital left to trade; most of the *dukas* are at present uneconomic'.

There is a strong contrast here, not only with the old African towns of Nigeria, such as Ibadan or Abeokuta, but with the new townships built by the French in Dakar or Brazzaville, and especially by the Belgians in Léopoldville and Elisabethville. A tour round the *cités indigènes* in the Congo towns gives a great impression of real town life and town business, without undue squalor. There are bars and 'hotels', carpenters' shops, taxi-garages, builders' merchants and small shopkeepers by the hundred.[41] There was in Elisabethville in 1960 at least one African millionaire (in Belgian francs), but the majority were small men, learning to trade the hard way. The presence of *petits blancs* in both Belgian and French ex-colonies, who were prepared to work alongside, and often help, African traders, has probably contributed greatly. The Belgians seem to have found the secret of reasonable planning and sanitation without complete sterilization. In East Africa, Dar-es-Salaam, with a rather more permissive attitude than Nairobi, had progressed most along these lines.

The devotion to tidiness, simple administration and other non-economic aims plays an even more important part in the larger field of marketing and wholesale trade in English-speaking territories. The idea that 'middlemen' are an incubus on producer and consumer alike is deeply engrained, particularly in the British administrative classes. When, in East Africa, to this cast of mind there was added a fairly widespread prejudice against Asians, who were naturally the chief middlemen, it was almost inevitable that policies would appear by which government, or a government agency, would buy as directly as possible from the peasant producer and sell on world markets. Moreover, such a scheme involved many attractive advantages. The country could be divided

[41] There were 7,000 *indépendants* in Léopoldville in 1959 (population 360,000). For a full description of them, see *Activités indépendantes de la cité indigène de Léopoldville*, published by the Belgian Administration (Plan Décennal) in 1959. The work of Balandier in Brazzaville, V. Pons in Stanleyville and P. Leclerq in Léopoldville is also of great interest.

into neat areas with collecting-points, staffed with government inspectors; buying prices could be fixed; price-stabilization funds could be established; government access to world market information could be used; the policies of agricultural departments could be wedded to Marketing Board policy; quality could be properly controlled; the number and location of ginneries or coffee-factories could be economically planned. Moreover, if the producers could be encouraged to form Co-operatives, every trace of wholesalers and middlemen could be abolished. These advantages have been widely quoted both in East and West Africa. They overcome the uncomfortable feeling of powerlessness and confusion which a government feels when a major economic asset is being handled by the free play of economic laws and the free competition of traders, some of whom are more able and some more unscrupulous than others.

These policies have been fiercely attacked by economists, notably by P. T. Bauer [42] in West Africa and W. Elkan [43] and C. Ehrlich [44] in East Africa. The East African Royal Commission devoted a whole chapter to a careful and devastating critique of restrictionism, however well-intentioned. Part of the arguments are the classical objections to monopoly, which need not be rehearsed here. Part relate to efficiency. Bauer points out that 'price-stabilization' has on occasion resulted in greater fluctuations of price to the producer than the free market would have given. Further, the low prices paid by a Board, in order to accumulate reserves, during a period of high world prices, are bound to slow the rate of crop expansion; cotton development teams were being sent round Nigeria when the producers were being paid about half the local equivalent of the real market price. Elkan describes the assumptions of the 1929 Carter Commission on cotton in Uganda:

First, the Commissioners had no doubt that competition was harmful and that the organisation of the industry was inefficient in the measure that it fell short of complete monopoly. Second, monopoly too was harmful if it was to be obtained by driving competitors into bankruptcy. . . . Finally, middlemen perform no useful functions and therefore merely raise costs.

[42] Bauer, *West African Trade*, supra.
[43] Elkan, *Indian Journal of Economics*, vol. xxxviii, no. 151, April 1958.
[44] Ehrlich, op. cit.

In the outcome, government decided to concentrate the ginners
into a buying group and force them to reduce the number of
ginneries. But, as a result of the second assumption, a deduction
was made from the growers' price in order to compensate the now
tidier 'ring' of controlled ginners for reducing excess capacity. 'In
other words', as Elkan says, 'the growers were to contribute to the
cost of perfecting the very monopoly which, they complained, was
already exploiting them.'

The regulation of the ginners and the creation of buying zones
was intensely unpopular with Africans. Ehrlich notes that in 1934

Every Zaza Chief in the Eastern Province signed a letter to the
Provincial Commissioner expressing their dislike of zoning which
'gives an opportunity to cotton buyers to reduce the prices of cotton,
knowing that people cannot remove their cotton and sell it in neighbouring districts which pay a fair price'.

Here we are up against the exceedingly difficult clash between a
government's proper concern to protect simple people from the
hardships of the free play of economic forces and the equally
proper wish to give them training in the commercial world. In
the early stages of the cash economy, among a population unversed
in the ways of commerce, abuses can indeed arise, particularly if
even a few of the middlemen are unscrupulous. If the paternalism
of colonial governments has been over-cautious, it is as well to
remember that the administrator was responsible to world opinion
—which the academic economist is not—and an opinion very
quick to seize on alleged exploitation of colonial people by commercial interests. If the time has now come to let economic growth
take a more natural course, this is not necessarily a condemnation
of the protection, and consequent retardation, which colonial
governments felt bound to give. However this may be, one effect
of the Uganda policies was certain—Africans were effectively protected out of the wholesale and middleman business. 'The Cotton
Zoning legislation and the Produce Marketing Ordnance of 1933
finally consolidated a rigid framework into which it was virtually
impossible for the small-scale African entrepreneur to penetrate.'[45]

And indeed one part of administrative mentality was probably
hostile to the emergence of large middlemen even if they were
African and not Asian or Lebanese. Bauer[46] quotes a Special

[45] Ehrlich, op. cit.   [46] Bauer, op. cit.

Correspondent of *The Times* (July 1951) as saying that Statutory Marketing policy 'has helped to control the rise of a *kulak* class among Nigerian peasant farmers with incomes out of proportion to the rest of the population'.

It is necessary to add that, from about the date of the Royal Commission, there has been a change in some East African policies. The Uganda Government in 1955 accepted specifically one of the main propositions of the Committee on Advancement of Africans in Trade [47] —'to ensure a commercial and not a welfare approach, with the object of stimulating private enterprise'. The Committee went on to say : 'The paternal measures of protection for Africans which were introduced during the early period of their development are, in our view, now likely to handicap their further progress.' With reference to Marketing Board controls, the Committee added : 'Such controls limit opportunities for Africans to gain experience in the management and marketing of their own produce.' This was indeed a sign of new thinking.

5. SOME COMMENTS ON THE FUTURE PATTERN OF TRADE

If this record is contrasted with the efforts of governments to train African businessmen, it throws into relief two or three central problems of commercial development in Africa. There is, first, the racial element—the attempt to favour Africans against Europeans, Lebanese, Asians. This is particularly distorting in East and Central Africa, though some instances in West Africa have been quoted. Secondly, the clash between paternalism and the gaining of economic experience and skill, in which the experience of being cheated is unfortunately a fairly important item. Finally, the tendency to tidiness, order, control, monopoly in the colonial system becomes a ready-made instrument in the hands of socialist-inclined African governments for a complete State-centralized control of the economic system. This is illustrated by the immediate attempt [48] by President Sékou Touré to nationalize distribution in Guinea; by the concentration of power in the Ghana Farmers Union, Co-operatives and T.U.C.; and by the ever-increasing use of Development Corporations and Marketing

---

[47] Supra. Quotations are from the Memorandum preceding the body of the Report, thus placed by the Committee for additional emphasis.
[48] Now much modified.

Boards in West Africa:[49] one of the latest signs is the effort to remove middlemen from the all-important groundnut trade in Senegal. It is clear that there is much to be said for the centralizing policy—for example, the combination of producer Co-operatives and Marketing Board in the Tanganyika cotton industry has many admirable points, and its effect in democratic education has been noted. These arguments will be considered later in connexion with the wider political and social aims of African governments. At this point it is enough to record that centralized marketing is not conducive to the emergence of a group of competent African entrepreneurs and modern men of business, and that, in old-fashioned language, it almost always ends up as 'a combination in restraint of trade'.

Finally, there are a few comments on the developing commercial life of Tropical Africa which may help to throw some light on the future. First, the period for development of modern, specialized trading, with its need for some capital, for accounts, for mechanical transport and so on, has been very short. Important as early European contacts in West Africa were in developing import-export trade, they did little to modernize it, as the accounts of Mary Kingsley's adventures with traders, very late in the nineteenth century, are enough to show. It is 1900 before Northern Nigeria is even nominally under European control, at which time there were thirty-seven Europeans in the whole of North Western Rhodesia[50] and very few in Nyasaland or East Africa. This first penetration does not imply the spread of modern commercial practices among Africans, which came a generation later—at least after the First World War. Today, with what historians will call the lightning growth of the cash economy (however long it seems to those who lived through it), trade for Africans is in that seething state of amateur competition which brought great waves of small bank failures from coast to coast of the United States and in Britain in the 1820s. It is quite unreasonable to expect too quickly the emergence of a large group of solid and respectable African merchants. To become a modern trader is not only a question

[49] Not universally. M. Houphouet-Boigny, asked why there were no Development Corporations and Marketing Boards in the Ivory Coast, replied: 'We have a liberal economy: we don't believe in that sort of thing.' *West Africa*, 19 August, 1961.

[50] M. Gelfand, *Northern Rhodesia in the Time of the Charter* (Oxford, Blackwell, 1961).

of learning some techniques or double-entry book-keeping. It involves a certain twist in the social pattern of living and its institutions. It is interesting to watch these adaptations actually happening. In Nigeria, to take only one example, the needs of middle-class traders led, among other factors, to the formation of the Reformed Ogboni Society, thus partially transforming an old tribal 'secret society' into a superior group of credit-worthy businessmen,[51] and there are adaptations going on in the shape of *esusu* societies with an obviously commercial purpose.[52] The wholesale criticisms of 'Africans' as lacking in honesty, in forethought, in diligence, in commercial acumen are completely beside the point in such a period. It is a safe prediction that some African peoples—including some in East and Central Africa—will prove themselves to be excellent merchants. The story of the wood-carving industry developed from one Kamba village in Kenya is a pointer. Walter Elkan,[53] in a fascinating article, has described the growth of this industry, which he estimated to produce between £150,000 and £250,000 of carvings in 1958, with a very large export to the United States, and to be capable of handling orders for as many as 10,000 articles in a single contract. Moreover, to make a big merchant there needs to be a big market; the expansion of purchasing power, particularly in the agricultural economy, will no doubt give their chance to many potentially successful African traders who have not yet got their heads clear from the ruck of small, part-time competitors. It would be the greatest mistake to assume that there are inherent qualities of character in 'West Africans' (which is itself a geographical term covering a huge variety of peoples), or even in Yoruba or Ibo, which make them inevitably better traders than 'East Africans'. The accidents of history and geography and the form and date of European contact mentioned at the start of this chapter did indeed help to produce the conditions in which trading abilities could develop in West Africa and they have developed ahead of East African and Rhodesian peoples. But when the right conditions come in

[51] See F. Morton-Williams, op. cit.

[52] See Clement N. Isong, 'Modernization of an Esusu Credit Society' (N.I.S.E.R. Conference, 1960). An *esusu* society collects monthly contributions from members, which are paid out to a single member, in rotation. It is a minor method of 'capital formation'.

[53] W. Elkan, 'The East African Trade in Woodcarvings', *Africa*, vol. xxviii, no. 4, 1958.

East and Central Africa, it will be very surprising if some at least of the East African peoples, whose existing culture happens to be malleable, do not develop equal skills and energy.

Unless there are an exceptional number of adverse factors, it seems certain that the African market will expand, so large is the felt but ineffective demand and so hopeful are some at least of the development plans already started. It is to be hoped that this increase will lead to increased inter-territorial [54] trade in Africa. Language and administrative divisions, have, of course, had a balkanizing effect. African nationalism could easily emphasize rather than reduce these difficulties, despite the efforts of Dr. Nkrumah, Mr. Nyerere and other leaders. It is sad that the 'Brazzaville' powers of ex-A.E.F. and ex-A.O.F. have found it easier, up to date, to agree upon liberalization of trade than to implement it—at least one of their conferences was followed by the immediate introduction of a customs tariff by more than one member.

But it would be wrong to stress existing divisions too much. African traders are very mobile, and African frontiers are made for smuggling. It is, indeed, quite astonishing what obstacles to existing and mutually beneficial trade are put up, and overcome. Garlick [55] has analysed the great volume and importance of trade with French territories carried on from Kumasi. But it is carried on by traders who risk having all their money confiscated, on both sides of the border, and who run the gauntlet of police and customs year in and year out, paying quite heavily in *douceurs* and unofficial dues even when they avoid a major loss. Part of the difficulty arises from exchange controls applied by the sterling and franc areas, but these could be overcome if the local governments concerned were sufficiently determined. This is but one instance, though a glaring one, of difficulties which arise in many areas; a great deal of time and manpower is devoted to preventing smuggling which might be better used in opening up the channels along which trade is inclined to flow. Officialdom is the worst enemy of trade anywhere in the world. It is likely to be particularly dangerous in Africa where minor officials are (through no

[54] It should now be called international.
[55] P. C. Garlick, 'The French Trade wtih Kumasi' and 'The French Trade de Nouveau', *Economic Bulletin* (Economic Society of Ghana), June 1958 and February 1959. A very rough estimate of the French trade in textiles is given at £2 million in the 13 weeks of the season.

fault of their own) necessarily not highly educated, not easily familiar with commercial documents, and faced by a variety of languages. At least for the time being, the fewer of them the better.

That trade will be progressively 'Africanized' is inevitable: the cry for protection against the alien competitor is as old as trade itself:

A delegation of the Port Harcourt Bakers' Union left Port Harcourt this morning on a tour of Aba, Onitsha and Enugu to ask all Nigerian bakers to join in their protest against a proposal by an alien firm to establish a bakery in Port Harcourt and Lagos.[56]

In the major field of produce-buying in West Africa most of the large expatriate firms have been progressively reducing their operations and simultaneously Africanizing their staff—many of the new licensed buyers are, in fact, men trained by these companies. But a trading network involves fairly large fixed capital, and it will take time and a sympathetic attitude from African governments to continue this process without unnecessary loss of efficiency; for the time being the training given by the companies at their own expense is a major asset to African business.

In East Africa the problem is far more difficult. Leading Asians in Kampala, in Nairobi and in Tanganyika all expressed the same general opinion. First, that Asians would gradually lose much small retail trade to Africans. There would certainly be hardship, because many Asians had not the education to alter their ways, and many of them would have to return to a lower standard of living in India. Three hopeful courses remained open; first, to enter secondary industry, where Asian skills would still have an advantage over African; second, to move back from retail towards wholesale trade, using African distributors and stockists; third, to improve and increase Asian education. On this last issue Asians look anxiously for more government help. They have contributed heavily to their own schools, and the Ismailis in particular have spread their funds to assist the African as well as the Asian community.[57] The prospect of desegregation alarms them, not on racial grounds, but because they fear that the immense pressure for African secondary-school places will cut down the places for

[56] East Nigerian Information Service, 15 November, 1960.
[57] E.g., the Aga Khan Hospital in Nairobi is available to both Africans and Asians. The Asian community in Dar-es-Salaam has also contributed very generously to the new Adult Education College.

Asians in a completely integrated system, such as is proposed in Tanganyika. It is impossible to tell whether, as Africans take over more of government in East Africa, strong discrimination against Asians in trade will be shown. If it is, it will damage East African economies far more than is at present appreciated. It is hard to overstate the service which has been performed by the Asian community in East Africa in providing, for a generation, the commercial substructure on which any modern economy must rely; and none of the East African territories has as yet a fraction of the trained African manpower to fill this place efficiently. If things go well and there is a rapid economic expansion, there will be room for far more African traders alongside the existing Asians. 'We must endeavour to increase African purchasing power, particularly in agriculture, at the fastest possible rate' was a judgement from a prominent Asian in the Lake Province, and it was a wise one.

How far free enterprise in commerce will be allowed to continue in some African countries is a question which leads into a dangerous field of prophecy. On the one hand, centralizing and socialist philosophies have a very great attraction, perhaps the greater because Africa is short of the higher commercial skills and is inclined to believe that government enterprise can be a substitute for them. There is an extra temptation to believe this because so many of the best educated have been attracted to government service. It is no doubt due in part to the 'white-collar' emphasis of colonial educational systems and in part to the prestige of 'government' and the professions as against commerce. It may be, however, that State action is more likely to be directed towards the larger, more spectacular and more easily controlled field of major industry than to attempt to grapple with the elusive and protean flow of commercial life. Moreover, in West Africa there is an African vested interest in free commercial enterprise, and in many areas a women's interest,[58] which is politically significant and not likely to be forgotten by African politicians. Widespread development of many forms of co-operation, linked to statutory Boards, is perhaps the most likely solution, and one not inappropriate to African

[58] Women traders have frequently made their interests felt most effectively in West Africa—for example, in a demand by the Ibadan Market Women's Association for their members to get direct supplies from the factory instead of through the large trading firms.

needs and abilities at the present time. It is in the more technical fields of servicing machinery of all types, of the use of modern chemicals, the handling of international finance and shipping, and in special forms of production and distribution that there is likely to a be field for expatriate skills; and this is a field which should expand steadily.

CHAPTER VIII

THE GROWTH OF INDUSTRY

I. THE PRESENT PATTERN OF INDUSTRIALIZATION

Up to 1939 the economies of Tropical Africa relied primarily on subsistence agriculture, the export of agricultural produce and the export of minerals, particularly from the Rhodesian and Katanga Copperbelt and the mines of Ghana; there was, in proportion, very little secondary industry, and budgets were supported primarily by import-export taxation. There were some large towns with their minor trades and industries, and a certain level of commercial development in the West. Since 1945 there has come, with surprising speed, a more dispersed and general growth of manufacturing industry. This is an exciting period, and many high hopes of industrialization have been expressed. But in looking at the speed of progress, it is as well not to overestimate its real volume. The figures in Table IV of employment in manufacturing industry, and the national income figures for the countries concerned, show clearly enough that they are still agricultural economies. Nevertheless, the growth of manufacturing industry is of real significance for the future.

It is in the post-war period that there comes the great leap forward in government revenues and expenditure (see Table II, p. 51), and a steady, though less spectacular, rise in national income; for example, the Economist Intelligence Unit calculated the rise in Nigerian national income at better than 4 per cent per annum for the years 1950–7,[1] and in Uganda gross capital formation was estimated to be between £18 million and £22 million per annum over the whole decade.[2] This rise is not to be attributed to the growth of secondary industry; it would be far more true to say that the growth of industry is due to the rise of income. It was due mainly to the 'pay-off' of a long period of gradual agricultural advance, a long period of building roads, of steady administration and the growth of education. It reflects the unspectacular spread

[1] Economist Intelligence Unit, *Opportunities for Investment in Eastern Nigeria* (Enugu, Eastern Nigerian Government, 1960).
[2] C. Ehrlich (communication).

of the cash economy and trading activity, an increased investment from overseas, and at certain periods the high prices for African crops, partly connected with the Korean War and with the recovery of the European economies from the after-effects of the Second World War. African countries, with conservative finance, had been quietly gathering strength; and they were ready to respond to the more ambitious budgeting which was to come with the phase of 'colonial development' and the new energies generated by the hope or the achievement of national independence. Certainly, here and there major new resources were found and developed, notably the oil field of the Niger Delta, and the diamond deposits in Tanganyika. But many of the projects much in the news are still in the investment stage. The main cause of the rise in revenue has been the proceeds of agricultural advance—cotton, coffee, and sisal in East Africa, groundnuts, palm produce, and cocoa in the West. The main exceptions are in Northern Rhodesia, still dominated by the fortunes of copper, and in the Congo with an economy dominated by the minerals of the Katanga and elsewhere and by European plantations. It is purchasing power in African hands which is making the development of secondary industry worth while.

The general sequence of development is remarkably similar throughout the whole area, granted that the East African and the French-speaking savannah economies are less rich and started later. There is first the period of mining enterprise and produce trade—the two easiest ways of development when Africa was first opened up. There is then a period of developing communications and establishing sources of power, with a simultaneous growth of cash crops—East Africa needed both the railway and European agriculture to get started. There is then an opportunity for small processing industries, for the growth of trade and a more widespread cash economy, and for the growth of towns. The local production of building materials then becomes more hopeful, and industries such as cement appear on the horizon. The growth of communications, cash crops and consumer power next leads to the possibility of establishing industries previously impracticable for lack both of access and market. New forms of extraction for cement, glass, clay and special minerals grow up, and there is a further major investment in power (such as the Jinja or Tana River or Kariba hydro-electric schemes). Then some consumer industries can really get going—partly in more durable goods, and more particularly in food, drink, tobacco, textiles, and miscellaneous materials. To look at lists of industries established in country after country, East or West, is to find the same items repeated—cement, roofing materials, metal windows, sawmills, furniture, paint; textiles and shoes; tyres or tyre-retreading, service and repair of vehicles; flour mills, oil mills, coffee mills, sugar mills; ginneries, rubber factories, sacks and containers; tobacco factories, biscuit factories, confectionery, bakeries, breweries and soft drinks. Alongside this growth of secondary industry looms the next and even heavier stage of development investment—the Volta River and the French aluminium schemes, large new plantations, such as the £4 million rubber plantations near Calabar, the Ilorin sugar scheme, the major Niger dam project above Jebba, the Rufiji River development planned for Tanganyika, plans for the establishment of oil refineries (Abidjan, Monrovia, Accra, Port Harcourt, Mombasa, Dar-es-Salaam are all announced), and the further improvement of ports (Tema in Ghana, the dredging of the Escravos Bar to open up the Niger, the enlargement of Port Harcourt and Mombasa). A good deal of money is spent on airports, and even railway extensions may be paying, for example, in Nigeria and Uganda; Africa is one of the few countries in the world where railway development is still economic. It is worth noting the difference between investment in production—new agriculture or extractive or secondary industry—and investment which relies upon the future expansion of production as well as making it possible; for some of this expenditure on infrastructure may be based on an over-estimate of the future rate of economic growth—a tendency to project the present leap forward into continuing growth at the same rate. There are reasons to regard these projections at least with caution.

Before looking in a little more detail at industrial growth, it is worth noting that 'heavy' industry, other than mining, is largely lacking. There are proposals for small steel-rolling mills at Jinja, using scrap, and near Enugu; the Eastern Nigerian Government is determined to combine the coal and iron ore resources there, although the ore is of moderate quality (42 per cent metal content) and there is difficulty in coking the coal. There are major coal resources, estimated at 248 million tons, near the Ruhuhu River in South West Tanganyika and also in this area there is iron ore of 49 per cent metal content at Liganga,[3] but both are relatively inaccessible. There is also iron ore in Northern Nigeria, near Lokoja, and coal probably of better quality than the Enugu mines. Russian survey teams have been looking at Northern Ghana for the possibility of a steel industry, and there are the useful iron deposits of Sierra Leone and Liberia already being exploited. But in general it will be many years before steel and the engineering and constructional industries based on it will have a chance of expansion, nor are the engineering skills yet available among Africans. It may well be that aluminium is likely to play a far greater part as the African basic metal; the prophets of aluminium foresee great possible expansion not only in building and household use but in the internal combustion engine; and the fortunate combination of bauxite and hydro-electric power in West Africa may be more significant than the attempt to develop iron and steel.

There are also doubts about any heavy chemical industry, not so much for lack of raw materials (the surveys of Africa are in many cases still very incomplete) but owing to the economies of production and the size of the market. The economies of the present scale of European chemical engineering are so great that they more than counterbalance shipping costs for any African market likely to appear within a decade. There are nevertheless some fertilizer plants or projects, notably the production of superphosphates in Senegal and the planned production at Tororo, Uganda.

Thus, in very broad terms, the future development in Tropical Africa would seem to rely on the development of agriculture and valuable metals, to increase purchasing power; the growth of secondary industry to process agricultural and some mineral output and thus to reduce heavily the import of food, clothing and consumer goods; and the reinvestment of profits and foreign exchange so gained in imports which require massive steel or chemical resources and a heavy use of technological manpower. Further development, much less foreseeable, may make heavy use of aluminium and the new materials and processes which will inevitably appear within a decade.

[3] Report of the World Bank Mission.

2. PROGRESS IN DIFFERENT COUNTRIES

The total numbers of Africans in wage employment is shown in Table IV. Naturally, individual areas have their special problems. East Africa has had to work hard for its economic development—neither the easy palm crops nor the early development of river and creek trade was there to help. Of the three territories, Kenya would certainly look the most lively, were it not for political uncertainty. Bearing in mind the African population figures (Kenya: 6,171,000; Uganda: 6,429,000; Tanganyika: 8,942,000), the following table of Africans in wage employment is of interest :

Table VII
INDUSTRIAL DISTRIBUTION OF ALL REPORTED AFRICAN EMPLOYEES, 1959

	All African Employees	Agriculture	Mining and Quarrying	Manufacturing	Commerce	Transport	Construction
KENYA	537,399	249,400	5,197	46,107(a)	23,028	11,173(d)	16,059(e)
UGANDA	224,260	49,500	5,136	29,035(b)	9,918	9,677	15,344(e)
TANGANYIKA	433,268	220,200	9,560	19,737(c)	12,572	8,940	11,148(e)

Notes:
(a) Manufacturing and repairs 44,206, and electricity and water 1,901.
(b) Manufacturing (misc.) plus food manufacturing, cotton ginning, coffee curing.
(c) Excludes, as do the Kenya and Uganda figures, Public Services. The figure includes electricity supply but excludes much factory employment on agricultural processing. The figure for African employment in factories in Tanganyika is 71,914, including 28,297 on sisal processing, 4,756 on cotton ginning, &c.
(d) Excludes the High Commission service of East African Railways and Harbours.
(e) Private Sector only in all cases.

NOTE.—The low figures for agricultural employment in Uganda are explained by the use of migrant labour, largely employed by Africans and not included in the figures.

To these figures must be added 23,000 European and 37,000 Asian employees in Kenya; 5,000 European and 10,000 Asian employees in Uganda, and 10,000 European and 20,000 Asian employees in Tanganyika.[5] The figures show that, if anything, Kenya has the largest industrial sector, and its figure of 9 per cent of all employees in manufacturing industries is, for example, higher than the 7 per cent claimed for Ghana. Kenya has benefited

[4] East African Statistical Department, *Quarterly Economic and Statistical Bulletin*, March 1960. It is sad that these figures are not drawn up on the same basis, despite a common statistical service.

[5] To nearest thousand. Ibid., except for Tanganyika, which are from *Statistical Abstract*, 1960, of the Tanganyika Unit of the E. A. Statistical Department. The figures are for *all* occupations.

from the customs union of the three territories and because Mombasa serves the railway for both Kenya and Uganda. It has also unquestionably benefited from the concentration of European enterprise and possibly from the more invigorating climate.

The Kenya list of industries is not, however, especially impressive—it contains the usual selection of shoes, tobacco, biscuits, flour-milling, cement, tyres and tubes, rubber, aluminium utensils, Kraft paper, breweries; but it is hard put to it for new industries of large size, save for the oil refinery now planned for Mombasa. There are prospects of a rayon factory with Japanese technical aid and some Japanese capital. The real potentiality of Kenya lies in the exciting growth of African agriculture and the possibility of further development of land now in European ownership, some of which is under-capitalized, particularly as regards water supply. It is here, unfortunately, that political uncertainty creates such great risks. It is not merely that European agriculture provides four-fifths of Kenya's agricultural exports, a proportion which will fall as African agriculture progresses; it is that a major collapse of European enterprise in Kenya would have violent repercussions on the whole economy, particularly as it would inevitably affect the Asian trading sector as well. Moreover, some of the gains in African cash crops might very easily be lost, for they have been stimulated by a good deal of counselling from European administrators and agricultural officers. It was wholly unfortunate that the dependence of Kenya on European enterprise at one time seemed to be delaying the rate of African constitutional advance, so that even a leader of Mr. Mboya's intelligence has been goaded into saying [6] that Kenya could get on without European enterprise; only a modification of African attitudes to European farming can remedy this situation. This is not a question of a respite for a year or two. Kenya European farmers must be able to see further ahead if they are to continue to put money and development into their farms. In fact a large-scale loss of European farmers and administrators would inevitably so cut back African purchasing power and overseas confidence in Kenya that the development of industry and of the whole economy would suffer

[6] *The Times* of 3 June 1961, where Mr. Mboya is quoted as saying: 'This country can go on without the European and its development would be much faster.' To do justice to Mr. Mboya, he has more often and more seriously said the opposite.

a very serious blow. Already political expediency is leading to small-scale African settlement on land previously held by Europeans, and it is far from certain that, by any objective standard, this is the right type of development in the areas concerned. Nevertheless, there is a sense of energy and vitality in Kenya, and a growth of agricultural efficiency, purchasing power, initiative and education among many African groups which could result in a surprising rate of progress if, as is certainly possible, relations between the races now take a major turn for the better, and if inter-tribal difficulties—now more threatening—are overcome.

Tanganyika offers a certain contrast to this situation. The political atmosphere in 1961 was as good as could be hoped; and it is for different reasons, discussed in Chapter X, that there is danger of losing European technical and administrative help. African agriculture is improving in some areas, and there is the expected list of industrial developments, including a project for an oil refinery on the coast and a tyre factory at Arusha. The territory is more fortunate than Kenya on the mineral side, with exports of £4·5 million of diamonds and £1·1 million of gold. The real problems, on which the future of secondary industry depends, lie in the size and comparatively sparse population of the central area of the country and the inaccessibility of the South West, with the consequent difficulties of communication and development. The existing proposal for sugar development on the Kilombero River, as part of the wider development of the whole Rufiji River basin, will go some way to help, but slowly. If it is assumed that the Co-operatives of Kilimanjaro, Bukoba and elsewhere go ahead, and that there is development at Arusha and in the Mbeya and Tukuyu areas of the West, other future progress will turn on the pastoral improvement [7] of the central areas and development of the isolated West and South. This will take time, and the prospects for Tanganyika, good in the long run, are perhaps more distant than for the other territories.

Perhaps Uganda provides the most interesting case of the three

[7] The World Bank Mission pointed out that almost a third of the whole land area, with a 15 per cent or greater probability of receiving less than twenty inches of rain, was unsuited to arable cultivation, but a large part of this is suitable for pasture. Animal populations (7.4 m. cattle, 2·8 m. sheep) are poorly managed and contribute too little to the economy. There is the possibility, in association with a major policy of water supply, to develop the pastoral industry very considerably (Report, pp. 141–173).

territories. Thanks largely to the development of cotton and coffee and the high prices of these products until 1953, the Uganda economy shared the forward surge after the last war. High hopes for industrialization were centred on the Jinja hydro-electric plant. But although in the early 1950s government revenue and money incomes expanded fast, the fall in crop prices, political uncertainty and the boycott of Asian and some European traders combined to make the second half of the decade disappointng, with a deficit on recurrent government expenditure and difficulty in financing a further capital development programme. Although about £50 million had been spent by government on development between 1950 and 1959, the monetary sector of the Gross Domestic Product, after rising from £51·8 million in 1950 to £92 million in 1957, actually fell back slightly in 1958 and 1959.[8] Few major industrial projects have been attracted, although the textiles factory at Jinja, Tororo Cement and the Kilembe copper mine (with an export of £2·8 million in 1959) have been encouraging achievements, and there are projects for saw-milling and a steel-scrap mill at Jinja which will add to the total. The difficulty appears to lie in the fact that, in Buganda particularly, a fairly comfortable halfway house in development has been found by the African growers. Africans can earn a small cash income from very moderate effort and efficiency in small-scale cotton or coffee growing and the incentive to alter a fairly comfortable way of life, with an easy plantain crop as a staple food and imported migrant labour for the cash crop, has not been high enough. Many economists have attributed this failure of the rural economy to develop any dynamism to the policy of government and Marketing Boards in siphoning off such a large proportion of the proceeds of coffee and cotton and spending the funds so acquired mainly on social services and fairly long-term investments. The facts in Uganda are worth a little closer consideration because of their implications for many other African countries. The paternalist philosophy of the colonial government in this field has already been noted in Chapter VII; here we are concerned purely with its economic results.

The facts have been clearly described in a Paper by David Walker and Cyril Ehrlich.[9] In the decade 1948 to 1957 about

[8] C. Ehrlich (communication).
[9] D. Walker and C. Ehrlich, 'Stabilization and Development Policy in Uganda: An Appraisal.' (*Kuklos*, vol. XʔI, 1959, fasc. 3).

£160 million was paid to African peasant growers of coffee and cotton, while the Marketing Boards accumulated an extra £40 million and export taxes about £50 million. In the two years 1951 and 1952, when prices were highest, growers received £29·1 million, the Marketing Boards gained £27 million and export taxes £15·5 million out of the total proceeds of sale of £79·5 million.[10] The export taxes were, of course, used in government expenditure; more surprisingly, most of the Marketing Board surpluses went the same way. In 1952 the Cotton Price Assistance Fund was closed at £20 million and excesses over this were paid to a new African Development Fund; something over £17 million were eventually so transferred. Of this Fund no less than 60 per cent was spent on education and a further 12 per cent on medical and other social services; 16 per cent only was spent on agriculture, including agricultural education. Moreover, about £7·5 million was later borrowed, free of interest, from the Cotton and Coffee Price Assistance Funds in aid of government development expenditure.

Thus three points stand out clearly. First, the growers over the ten-year period forfeited £90 million in taxes and Marketing Board surpluses; second, government expenditure was able to rise far above its ordinary revenue receipts; third, government used the money mainly for investment in social services and long-term expenditure on infrastructure. Quite apart from the danger of inflating government expenditure—which is always very hard to reduce later—Walker and Ehrlich conclude that the combination of such heavy taxation with an investment programme which had few short-term productive effects resulted in a failure to develop any real life and initiative in the peasant economy.

Taxation and marketing policies prevented African farmers from building up their personal capital and, therefore, developing, improving and even transforming their farms . . . It is also extremely probable that extra income and spending power would have stimulated other forms of 'grass roots' economic development. It seems to us that the growth of African traders and small scale 'backyard' industry would have been encouraged and that this form of economic development, firmly rooted in the way of life of the people, might have made a contribution to the development of the country of much greater significance than the sort of development which took place

[10] The difference represents costs of marketing.

with the help of government funds and sponsorship . . . The whole system of export taxation and Marketing Board surpluses has been one of the factors which hindered the development of entrepreneurial sense and has led the African farmer to think of the government as being the sole determinant of prices.

One fact which strongly supports this view is that, despite the great opportunity offered to Uganda in the early part of the period, even by 1959 the production of cotton had never equalled production in 1938. 'The country is still basically as dependent on a couple of export crops as it was ten years ago; without the stimulus of high export earnings the country seems to have little or no internal dynamism.'

The story of this decade in Uganda must be compared with the record of large Marketing Board surpluses in, for example, Ghana, where there is no lack of dynamism;[11] and with the general argument of economists, discussed in Chapter IV, that development of a modern sector must rely on capital raised from the development of the agricultural economy. Three comments suggest themselves. First, that investment and a real enrichment of the farming economy must *precede* heavy taxation—the incentive to farmers must be large enough to make them energetic and eager to expand, and the increase in their incomes be big enough to create demand for the products of secondary industry—the modern sector for which the capital is being raised. Second, that a good proportion of capital raised must continue to flow back either into agriculture or into short-term productive investment; and third, that a lucky period of high prices does not of itself mean an agrarian revolution. Nevertheless, even Ghana may have overshot the mark in government expenditure based on cocoa surpluses, and the same danger could arise for Nigeria, particularly in view of the immense expenditure on education which is envisaged. Other African economies could easily become frozen at a halfway stage in development, by premature or excessive taxation of a cash-crop agriculture before the money economy had developed an impetus in rural areas and before any major reform in methods or land tenure. This danger is the greater because of the threatened loss of many expatriate agricultural staff in the next few years, since they have played so large a part in the reform of farming

[11] Although Peter Bauer, for example, has argued that the West African policy has also reduced the possible dynamism of the rural economy there.

systems. It might be, of course, that the Ganda farmers are un-enterprising compared with the Kikuyu or Ibo, but it would be rash to assume this when they have not been allowed to taste anything like the full reward of such enterprise as they have shown in the past.

Certainly at present purchasing power and demand in Uganda do not seem to be strong enough to attract secondary industry. Businesses which need a larger market are more likely, politics permitting, to choose Kenya as a base and sell to the whole of East Africa. With a political system in Buganda which is conservative, and which has been far from sympathetic to any all-Uganda nationalist democratic upsurge, there is not from the African side any concerted push for economic development which might have led to more imaginative plans; nor has the Asian community, harried by the boycott and uncertain of its future, been able to take any initiative. The announcement of a World Bank Loan of £3,000,000 for electricity extension does not in itself add great hopes. It is not lack of electric power but lack of a real will to develop which has been lacking. A clarification of the political situation and new and far more vigorous African leadership will have to appear if the Uganda economy is to get moving again. This does not imply that the longer-term prospects are bad. The mere fact that there is considerable private African ownership of land, and sometimes in large blocks, gives an opening to agricultural transformation which is harder to achieve in some other territories. The difficulty of European investment involving occupation of land has been ingeniously circumvented by the Uganda Company.[12] There are also possibilities of American investment, particularly when the Report of the World Bank Mission is completed.

Northern Rhodesia, in contrast to East Africa, presents a picture of a single major industry, copper-mining, backed by a largely undeveloped agriculture; and a commercial system which has never really penetrated far from the European areas on the line

---

[12] Land laws virtually exclude new acquisition of land by non-Africans. The Commonwealth Development Finance Co. Ltd. have given a £500,000 twenty-year loan to East African Estates Ltd., an African subsidiary of the Uganda Company, for tea production, the loan being guaranteed by the Uganda Company. Some of the Asian sugar planters are also endeavouring to increase the throughput of their factories by encouraging African farmers to grow sugar on their own land and sell it to the factory.

of rail. Even there, much of the large European earnings in the mines is spent on holidays in South Africa, Southern Rhodesia or Europe, on the education of children outside the territory, and on imported cars and consumer goods; some is saved to buy land, usually in Southern Rhodesia or South Africa, on retirement. Thus expenditure on locally produced goods and services is heavily reduced. African earnings, now considerable, do provide an additional market in the mining towns; but many European entrepreneurs prefer to take advantage of the lower African wage levels in Salisbury and Bulawayo and rail their goods to the North rather than compete with the mines for higher-priced labour in the Copperbelt itself. It seems probable that the concentration of economic and political power in the line of rail area has in fact directed attention to the mines and the European life around them to the detriment of the huge agricultural areas both East and West, despite the efforts of the colonial administration in recent years to redress the balance and despite some major financial contributions from the mines towards agricultural development. Although maize growing has improved in the Tonga area, and there are possibilities of a much improved meat industry in Barotseland, there is no area in the territory which is really showing the buoyant rural expansion to be seen in some other countries, either through Co-operatives, European farming or plantations. The large settlement scheme at Mungwi in the North East (see Chapter VI) is subject to a major doubt as to the market for crops as well as the long and difficult communications, and the same difficulty of access applies to the West and North West. It is encouraging that application for United Nations aid has now been made for a major survey of the whole Kafue basin; but the survey itself will take some years. African political advance is also certainly discouraging European enterprise outside the mining companies and this fear of political change will certainly be strong at least until an African majority is achieved in the Legislative Council.

This is not to say that nothing is happening in secondary industry. There are a number of textile firms, a sugar refinery, cement works, minor engineering and repair shops, and a building industry based on the demand from mine salaries. The Northern Rhodesian Industrial Development Corporation, with capital up to £2 million, is at present mainly concerned in reconnaissance and survey for possible development of such materials as gypsum, felspar and malachite, beeswax, industrial clays and other minerals. At the strategic level about £30 million is the target for the Development Plan, and a Committee on Rural Development has recently reported.

While, therefore, the present opportunities for secondary industry are probably best found by a more determined attempt to serve the growing African demand in the Copperbelt, as Africans achieve both higher wages and higher positions in the mines, the major expansion of the rural economy is not yet in sight. There are serious tribal difficulties as between the traditional rulers of Barotseland and the present nationalist leadership, and a tribal background to rivalry between Mr. Kaunda and Mr. Nkumbula; political difficulties at the time of writing have resulted in attacks of sabotage and violence; there is certainly some way to go before any African 'nation', with a will and energy of its own, can crystallize. An even more vigorous and imaginative agricultural programme, combined with better communications with the North East and North West, will be needed before the territory can begin to generate sizeable purchasing power outside the line of rail.

The future of the Federation is bound to affect the economic prospects of Northern Rhodesia.[13] It is not only African opinion which, at present, is critical of the Federal Government. Many Europeans have no love for it, on three grounds. First, although the establishment of the Federation undoubtedly gave a lift to the economy in the first years, in access to credit and increased investment, some responsible Europeans feel that more recently Northern Rhodesia has been a loser, and that a larger capital development programme could have been mounted if the Territory had been on its own. Second, there is a good deal of jealousy of Salisbury—a feeling not unlike the attitude of Edinburgh to London—a dislike of decisions taken a long way away and a suspicion that affairs are regulated to suit Southern Rhodesia. Third, many liberals and many businessmen feel that the sooner Northern Rhodesian Europeans come to terms with African nationalism— and some feel that Mr. Kaunda could be as statesmanlike as Mr. Nyerere—the sooner the economy will be able to make a fresh start. In consequence, the vigorous interventions of Sir Roy

[13] For official analysis, see the Monckton Report, and for a critique, see Hazelwood and Henderson, *The Economics of Federation* (London, Blackwell, 1960).

Welensky as leader of the United Federal Party, and particularly the effects of his pressure in London to revise the constitutional settlement of 1961 in favour of the U.F.P., have been deeply resented. The inevitable consequence, in disorders and African bitterness, have not made things easier in the North for either the Government, the settlers or the mining companies. If the future is to be in somewhat closer collaboration between liberal Europeans and moderate African leadership (which is the best which can be hoped for) a very considerable relaxation of the Federal tie is to be expected.

It is not very profitable to speculate on the future development of the Congo until some political stability is assured. Far less damage has been done to the industrial economy than might be assumed. Up to June 1961 the Katanga mines were reporting slight increases in almost every aspect of output, and the Chairman of Unilever was able to report in April 1961 [14] that Marsavac (the margarine company) had achieved 90 per cent of normal turnover in Léopoldville, that Sedec, a much larger trading company, was making profits, though in local currency, and that even the plantations, though beset by transport difficulties, had produced £7 million worth of produce in the year. The United Nations report of 1961 was also moderately encouraging. There may, however, be much more lasting damage to plantations in some areas where the owners or managers left. [15] What has been overlooked, in the general criticism of Belgium and in the sensational press reports (no doubt true) of savagery in some parts of a country as big as Western Europe, is the very considerable cadre of well-trained artisans and clerks in the main urban and industrial centres. The Congo needs foreign technicians and graduates for all its purposes; but it has below that level a platform of education and training far more solid than it has been fashionable to mention. With its developed minerals and plantations it could within a decade reappear as the economic giant of Tropical Africa, provided that political stability and technical personnel can be found again. In those circumstances, the gradual modernization of peasant agriculture and ways of life would present the greatest challenge.

[14] *The Times*, 28 April 1961.
[15] Though in some areas Congolese were continuing to maintain the plantations without any European management.

Nigeria and Ghana provide the best examples of economies in which secondary industry has been able to go ahead on the basis of a rich and expanding agriculture and a lively commerce. The list of industries started or planned is, for each country, the standard one, only more comprehensive and more international in source of capital and technical advice. In the two southern Regions of Nigeria there is a constant growth of small African workshops and processing industries, but the market is also big enough for some major foreign firms to put down new plant, usually in some form of partnership with the appropriate regional government. In some cases it is only on the assumption that virtually the whole present market will be covered by a single plant that the proper economies of scale can be achieved. Already, in some fields, self-sufficiency is within sight. About 450,000 tons of cement will come from the two main cement works (Nkalagu, Eastern Nigeria and Ewekoro, Western Nigeria) against a present import of 530,000 tons, and with the four new textile factories planned in addition to the plant at Kaduna, the existing market for simple textiles should be filled. New tyre and bicycle factories, both in Eastern Nigeria, will also aim at a total coverage of the market. To give some idea of scale and variety, it may be worth while to list some of the major industrial projects in the two southern Regions.

Eastern Nigeria [16]

o Oilfield and refinery. Current investment about £70 m. Refinery £12 m.

Tyre factory (£2 m.).

Bicycle factory (£600,000), about 100,000 bicycles per annum.

Textile printing factory (£2 m.).

Steel rolling mill, Enugu.

o Cement works (200,000 tons).

Industrial estate, Port Harcourt (£1 m.).

Aluminium rolling mill.

o Metal windows and doors.

Escravos Bar dredging—£6 m. contract for completion 1964.

Glass project (up to £2 m.).

Shoe factory.

Wire nails factory.

o Tobacco factory.

[16] These lists and figures come from press announcements, usually in *West Africa*, and from Government Reports on Development Plans.

Enlargement of wharves, quays, warehouses, Port Harcourt (£2 m. plus).

° = already in operation.

Western Nigeria

Cement works (£4½ m.).
Mattress factory (£70,000).
Biscuit factory.
Metal-windows assembly plant (£110,000).
Aluminium factory (£165,000).
Textile factory (£1¾ m.).
Rubber factory.
Asbestos cement (£600,000).
Plastic-shoe factory (£100,000).
Tyre factory.

These projects are additional to an existing investment of about £9,890,000 in a variety of industries in the Western Region,[17] in which investments in building and water supplies, ship repair and boat building, timber, river transport, tobacco and rubber processing all run at or near the £1 million mark.

It is necessary, to keep a sense of proportion, to recollect that this industrial growth still represents a small part of national income. The Economist Intelligence Unit [18] reckoned that as recently as 1956–7 manufacturing industry accounted for less than 2 per cent of Nigeria's Gross National Product (it would certainly be higher today), and that the numbers in all forms of wage and salary employment in the Eastern Region only topped 100,000 in 1959. There is every reason to think that an increase in industrialization will continue in the southern Regions for some time and also that there will be an increase in the North. Indeed, a great deal of money is being put into development—about £339 million in the development programmes of the whole Federation in the 1956–62 period, of which £264 million will have come from internal resources.[19] The critical question will come when the results of agricultural investment begin to show, and it is here that the economic wisdom of devoting £4·9 million out of a £13·8 million agricultural development programme in the Western

[17] *Western Region Development Plan 1960–65*, Appendix IV. It is emphasized that these capital figures are of an order of magnitude rather than accurate.

[18] Economist Intelligence Unit, op. cit.   [19] Ibid.

Region [20] to the Farm Settlement schemes comes in question.

Development in the North is naturally more difficult on the industrial side, and most of the major plans are rightly concerned with agriculture. But the size of the market in the Kano region, with between 3 million and 4 million people in a small area, is not to be despised. Kano already has a range of small industries —oil-milling, textiles, enamelware, soap, mirrors, floor covering, household aluminium, tannery, &c.—and there will be room for more if rural incomes rise. Current schemes for other parts of the North include cement, for which three sites were under survey in 1961; a fibre factory near Jemma, three textile factories and the establishment of two tin smelters at Jos, one of which is now in operation. But as late as 1959 there were only 10,000 workers employed in manufacturing industry in the North, with its population of 19 million. This figure speaks for itself.

Many of the conditions of Northern Nigeria apply with equal force to the French-speaking savannah, from Lake Chad round to Mali and Senegal. All are exporters of migrant labour, all are dependent on dry-land agriculture—indeed the French areas are in general not as blest either in fertility or climate as Nigeria. Their political relations, which might be expected to be close, as between Muslim peoples with many similarities of environment, are strained both by the economic need for attachment to the forest zone and the coast and by the purely political cleavages between 'Left' and 'Right', which have part of their origin in the continued dependence of poor countries on French aid. Some further consideration of the economic and political future of these countries will follow in Chapter XI.

The story of industrial growth in Ghana is similar to that in Nigeria, but set in a different atmosphere and moving at a faster rate. By 1960 the Ghana budget, including development expenditure, topped £100 million for the first time, and its current revenue expenditure at over £60 million is more than three times the Tanganyika budget from a smaller population. But the type of expenditure and development is a little different from that of Nigeria.

There is first the very large sum to be devoted to the Volta River

---

[20] *Western Region Development Plan 1960–65*, Appendix IX. There is a similarly large allocation for settlement in the Eastern Region (see above, Chapter VI).

scheme, which will certainly involve the Government in over £50 million. There has also been the creation of a new harbour at Tema with a major industrial layout around it. There is a £14·3 million loan from Russia in prospect for the Bui Dam. Apart from these large projects Ghana has put down a great deal of money on buying ships (a contract for £9 million was signed with Dutch and German firms in January 1960), £5 million to buy gold mines, and an even larger expenditure on aircraft.[21] It is perhaps significant that President Nkrumah, speaking of this air expansion, said :

It will be an earnest of our determination to eradicate the separatism resulting from artificial and irrational territorial boundaries determined by the imperialists and colonialists.[22]

It is clear that much of this expenditure, combined with that on armed forces and Embassies, is partly in a 'prestige' category, to impress upon fellow-Africans that Africa can be modern and think big. Although this has caused a good deal of criticism in other African countries, it has also unquestionably contributed to their ambitions and, in a sense, to African self-respect. These, however, are mainly political issues for later discussion.

In the development of industry, the Ghana record is a mixed one. There are some welcome foreign investments, such as the Oil Refinery (£8 million) to be established by an Italian firm, or the investment programme of the United Africa Company running to £3,200,000 in May 1960 (motor assembly, plywood, cold stores, soap, brewery); and there are a number of smaller projects or achievements, including aluminium products, a tractor assembly plant and the standard run of bottling and biscuit factories; oil-milling at Nzima, fruit-processing at Nsawam, paints and varnishes and other small manufactures. On the agricultural side, in addition to continued heavy investment in cocoa, there is a proposal for a £3½ million sugar plantation and a survey of the pos-

[21] The figures in 1961 for the air fleet were :

2 Britannias at £3 m.	6 Ilyushin 18	8 Karibous
2 Boeing 707 at £4 m.	4 Dakotas	14 Beavers
3 V.C. 10s at £7 m.	2 Herons	12 Chipmunks
3 Viscounts at £1½ m.		and 14 other aircraft

(*West Africa*, 11 February 1961).   [22] Ibid.

sibilities of irrigated crops in the lower Volta Plain. Against these hopeful projects must be set a number of smaller industrial ventures, dating from the early enthusiasm for industrialization through the Industrial Development Corporation, which have made losses or come to grief. There has also been some heavy capital expenditure on office buildings in Accra.

Taking the programme as a whole, it would seem that a great deal is to be asked of Ghana agriculture over the next ten years, before any large returns can come from the Volta scheme. The existing programme has been largely financed by cocoa, and cocoa will have to go on carrying the load. The industries established will to some degree reduce imports, and the shipping investment may prove sound. But commitments on the air fleet, diplomatic representation and armed forces, and the heavy costs of Tema will fall with a dead weight on the economy for some years ahead. Foreseeable development funds of about £150 million are fully committed, and there seems likely to be an awkward period of 'sitting it out' until the long-term projects begin to show a real dividend. Ghana's policy will probably move towards a new emphasis on agriculture and an attempt to maintain industrial headway by attracting foreign capital investment rather than using internal resources which are certainly at full stretch.[23]

Without attempting any analysis of the economies in French-speaking Tropical Africa, it is clear that they face grave difficulties unless France is still prepared to give, and they to accept, very large investment and aid. In the post-war years France spent more lavishly than any colonial power in Tropical Africa, and the results are visible not only in the fine buildings of Dakar and Abidjan but in much fixed capital of roads, bridges and harbours, and in much direct or indirect budgetary subsidy—for example, by paying the salaries of French colonial civil servants from Paris. In consequence, these countries find themselves independent but equipped, in some areas, with better resources, both physical and administrative, than their own internally generated income can support. Some of the units of government are based on very small populations—750,000 in the Congo Republic, 400,000 in Gabon.

[23] Since this paragraph was written, the 1961 Ghana budget has been published, with its further taxation on cocoa and emphasis on forced savings throughout the economy. It looks as if the period of stringency is starting very soon indeed.

Some cover very large areas with extremely sparse populations and resources.

	Area (sq. miles)	Population	Density per sq. m.
British West Africa [24]	496,485	39,178,000	76
French West Africa	1,799,159	16,375,000	9

There will have to be a major re-thinking of the economies of French West Africa, and it may be that this need will gradually come to dominate the shifting pattern of pacts and understandings which at present have more political than economic motives behind them.

3. INTERNATIONAL AID AND INVESTMENT

It would need another book to describe, country by country, the multifarious forms of international aid or investment in Tropical Africa, by way of gift, credit, loan, the provision of expert personnel, training facilities and so on. Proposals are at present changing so fast that any estimate of the future could be no more than guesswork. It is certainly important not to overestimate the importance of direct aid in sheer monetary terms, and it will already be clear that by far the greatest proportion of African development programmes are being met from internal resources and by repayable loans and credits. An issue of which all African finance ministers are very conscious is the mounting total not only of interest charges but of recurrent expenditure generated by investment. For example, in education, even a free gift of buildings for a teacher-training college can be expensive to accept as the salary and maintenance bills roll in for payment each year. Perhaps the most useful forms of external aid could be listed under five headings:

(a) outright gifts which do not involve recurrent expenditure and which lead to economic growth—these are bound to be relatively small;

(b) long-term, low-interest loans for major installations, such as ports and dams; 'soft' loans repayable in local currency may be especially valuable;

(c) technical surveys of many kinds which may be expensive and may carry recommendations that are negative : aid will take the

[24] Steel, op. cit.

form of seconding and paying experts (with this can be coupled
aid to fundamental research on tropical problems);
(d) provision of training personnel to accelerate the growth of qualified African manpower in many fields and extensive offers of
training facilities in metropolitan countries;
(e) aid to tide over emergencies which are bound to arise and which
might unduly cripple young economies in their growing stages.

There would be a clear danger in including in such a list massive
aid to a social service such as education, despite its importance in
the long term; the financing of social services must depend upon
genuine economic growth and willingness to accept taxation. Any
country should have a clear-eyed view of its future recurrent
budget and this can be distorted by tempting offers of university
buildings or technical colleges. The establishment of a system of
social security and education on lines which do not forget the
African traditions of self-help, and on a scale which African
economies can support over the next fifteen years, requires extremely honest thinking. There is also need, increasingly recognized, for co-ordination of at least some of the sources of aid—
the U.N. agencies, aid from single governments (e.g. U.S.A.,
Russia), group aid from the Commonwealth or the European
Economic Community. The danger at present is probably not that
Africa will get too little aid, from one source or another, but that
injection of money will produce distortions in African economies
or a burden of interest and recurrent expenditure which will have
to be painfully corrected in a few years.

Direct commercial investment by foreign firms or governments
in Africa is another matter. The last three years have shown a
mounting interest in African investment from Holland, West
Germany, Switzerland, Italy, Jugoslavia and Israel, apart from
increasing trade relations, technical missions and credits from
Russia, Poland, Czechoslovakia, Hungary and East Germany, and
lively signs of interest from China—all of which no doubt has a
certain political motive. Some of the projects or established enterprises in Tropical Africa mentioned in the Press [25] over the last
two years give a notion of this increasingly international feeling
of West African industry in particular, though the dominance of
British and French enterprise in the countries which they previously administered must not be forgotten:

[25] Mainly from *West Africa* and *African Trade and Development*.

Israel: £13 m. projects in West Africa (Guinea diamonds, Monrovia hotel, Nigeria water supplies, and Ethiopian roads); £30 m. construction programme guaranteed to Israeli companies in West Nigeria; wire-nails factory for Eastern Nigeria; constant exchange of visits, some Ghana enterprises, and Nigerian farm settlements on Israeli models.

West Germany: African trade, £170 m. in 1958; £150 m. invested in Africa up to 1959. Foundation for Developing Countries voted £130 m. in Bundestag 17.9.60. Low-cost housing (capital £3½ m.) in Ghana; printing works at Tema; foundation of German-Africa Institutes and increased academic research programmes and increasing programme of technical training for Africans.

Holland: Trade with Africa exceeded £150 m. for the first time in 1959. Participation of £3½ m. in Komenda (Ghana) sugar scheme; participation of £2½ m. in Kilombero River (Tanganyika) sugar scheme and Marambu Estate (Usumbara Mountains, Tanganyika). Hydrology missions in Niger Delta. Paint and varnish factory (Ghana). Participation in Investment Company of Nigeria, and in fibre factory, North Nigeria.

Italy: AGIP oil refinery (£8 m.), Ghana; IMPRESIT First Volta contract of £16 m. Steel rolling mill, Enugu. Contract (£9 m.) for Onitsha Bridge (Nigeria); £4 m. IMPRESIT contract for roads in North and West Nigeria. (The Kariba dam contractors were Italian.)

Switzerland: Participation in Investment Company of Nigeria. Swiss/Italian textile factory, Ikeja, Lagos.

'Iron Curtain' and Russia: 50 Soviet engineers to rebuild Conakry-Kankan railway. Russian credit to Ghana of £14·3 m. for Bui Dam and other purposes. Russian credit to Somalia of £14 m. Russian steel experts in North Ghana, surveying for rolling mill. £2½ m. Hungarian and £5 m. Polish credits to Ghana. Credits to Guinea. Increasing numbers of students in Iron Curtain universities.

China: 33 Chinese technicians for Ghana enamelware factory. Large-scale programme of invitations to African leaders. Formation of China-Africa Society. Export of rice to Guinea.

Japan: Kenya Rayon Company. Trade and Industrial Missions in most West African countries.

Although this is far from a complete list of activities and will be constantly enlarged, it is clear that for any one country it is only a very small investment at present—a trial run by various enterprises. By far the biggest projects are in the field of major

construction; and the growth of trade with the countries mentioned is more important than the establishment of factories in
Africa. The U.S.A. private entrepreneur is a notable absentee
from most of Tropical Africa, though there are signs of interest
from the Chase Manhattan Bank and the Bank of America, and
the American aluminium investment in the Volta scheme is of
major importance.

The establishment in Tropical Africa of firms from many
different countries is wholly to be welcomed. In the first place it
assures competition with firms from the ex-colonial power, which
is bound to be stimulating. Secondly, it adds to the total list and
variety of industrial enterprises, making subsequent industrialization easier. Thirdly, where the firms are straightforward commercial enterprises, their success would be the surest sign that real
economic needs are being met, without the doubts which always
surround aid or subsidization. Finally, all the newly independent
States naturally wish to get to know the international commercial
world, after a long period in which their contacts were confined
mainly to the commerce of the colonial power. No doubt they will
have varying experiences. It certainly ill behoves the British or
French, who still occupy so dominating a position in the field, to
complain about the still trivial sections of African economies which
are directed towards the Eastern bloc; their main task is to prove
as efficient as any competitor.

4. AFRICAN POLICY—PUBLIC CONTROL AND PRIVATE ENTERPRISE

Two main reasons have inclined the independent countries
towards a high degree of public enterprise or public control of
enterprise. Because most African countries have scarcely any
large African entrepreneurs, the development of private enterprise
appears to mean development of foreign enterprise, and this at
once raises the fear of 'neo-colonialism'. To Western ears this is
apt to sound like hostile jargon carried over from colonial days
or borrowed from Russia. But there are more serious reasons in
African minds. A high degree of dependence upon world trade
would be a sign of progress, not of serfdom. But there are good
reasons not to be too closely tied to one partner, both to avoid
sharing his possible misfortunes, and to avoid the kind of political
pressures which might be exerted. Britain, France and America

are all open to attack owing to their desire to sustain their strategic military position in the world by bases in Africa—Suez is not easily forgotten and the Kenya base is a subject which may become more and more difficult. France has continued to insist on Sahara atom-bomb tests in addition to her troubles over Bizerta and other bases. America on a world scale has partly destroyed the credit she might have gained from her real generosity by openly expecting the recipients to keep to the West in the cold war—it is hard to expect American taxpayers to adopt any other attitude. Yet it would be difficult for an African government to make an effective protest—such as the freezing of assets—against a major Power upon which it was economically wholly dependent. It is unrealistic to suppose that aid can be altogether divorced from political interest, and it is better either to accept this openly or to channel aid through the United Nations, as many Africans would prefer.

Apart from the strategic implications, Africans would also argue, not without reason, that economic dependence on a single power is likely to distort the type and direction of trade into forms which suit the European rather than the African economy. While both these arguments point mainly to a diversification of the external sources of trade and enterprise, they also encourage government control, since it is largely by government-to-government arrangements that new trade partners are found, particularly if the new partner is an iron-curtain country with no 'private' enterprise.

Secondly, many of the leaders of the anti-colonial struggle were socialists, for obvious reasons—they believed in the equation of capitalism and imperialism which is perhaps the best known part of Marxist-Leninist doctrine. There is no doubt of the socialist enthusiasm of many of the younger educated Africans, although it is not to be expected among the Emirs or the traditional kingdoms. It is a socialism more concerned with ideas of central planning than with narrowing the gap between rich and poor, one which lacks much of the moral and egalitarian fervour of the English socialists though equally inspired by a kind of rationalist idealism.

Even Nigeria and Ghana, which can be taken as both educationally and commercially most advanced among the independent countries, lack any large group of African industrial entrepreneurs; they lack not only the technical knowledge but also the managerial experience. Dr. Nkrumah put this issue clearly in

speaking to the 'West African Committee' in London in 1961 :
'If Ghanaian enterprise is to be developed, it can only be through
co-operative and similar bodies, since experience has shown that
private Ghanaian businessmen cannot or will not work on a
sufficient scale to compete with overseas firms.'[26] M. Mamadou
Dia, Prime Minister of Senegal, made a speech at about the same
time, expressing almost exactly the same viewpoint. The question
of scale is important. There are, of course, African entrepreneurs
in many fields—a good example would be the African founder of
a firm doing tyre-retreading and production of foam rubber in
Nigeria, who built up his own business and has sent his sons to
Europe for technical training; or the owner of the 'Kool Kats'
night-club in Lagos who also runs a very large dock-labour force;
or some of the large building contractors in Lagos or Ibadan, who
do a very substantial business.[27] But even the bigger men would
not have the technical knowledge or the capital or the staff to
establish a major modern factory—say, a chemical factory—on
their own. The faster technical advance proceeds in the outside
world, and the greater the capital-intensity of modern production
methods, the more difficult is it for the African industrialist to
appear.

The immediate solution to this difficulty, adopted by both
colonial and independent governments, has been the creation of a
large number of Boards, usually in the form of public corporations, to stimulate or to undertake major industrial functions.
There will normally be an Industrial Development Corporation,
possibly an Agricultural Development Corporation; Boards for
major Public Utilities, Marketing Boards and possibly a Board for
credit and loans. In addition, production as well as marketing of
particular commodities may be controlled by a commodity
Board. These organizations, with political appointments on the
Board and civil servants seconded to the management, do effect
a genuine African control of very wide fields of economic life. The

[26] *West Africa*, 18 March 1961.
[27] For example, one such contractor in Ibadan issued a statement of turnover on the fifteenth anniversary of his firm's establishment showing work to
the value of £152,000 (1946–52), £400,000 (1952–4), £2,000,000 (1955–60).
This is a wholly African firm with an African Chairman and African General
Manager, both trained in the Public Works Department (*Daily Express*
(Nigeria), 17 Feburary 1961).

dangers inherent in them are, of course, clear enough. It is too easy to believe that a good civil servant, probably with a degree, will be able to make good business decisions or control the business decisions of others. But experience in other countries, and indeed under the colonial régime, does not confirm this. Moreover, it may be one thing to superimpose public corporations on a developed free-enterprise economy and quite another to get the process of development started by them. In present-day Africa there are especial dangers in this economic centralization, since it offers too many and tempting opportunities for a 'spoils' system in all its various forms. Political and family patronage, monopoly and a bureaucratic philosophy are the evident dangers.

Moreover, the creation of these central economic agencies, directly or indirectly controlled by the State, does not completely solve the difficulty. In the early days an Industrial Development Corporation with a capital of one or two millions could do quite a lot to finance and even run a certain number of small industries. But after a time, the capital needed for major growth becomes altogether too great, particularly if the I.D.C. is inclined to retain its more successful enterprises rather than sell them. This is a natural tendency, partly to offset losses from failures and partly for lack of willing and competent buyers and of a market for securities. In consequence, while the earlier policy, between 1955 and 1960, was for government to seek a controlling share of new enterprises, the current position is that a share of from 20 per cent to 40 per cent of capital invested is all that is convenient. In typical instances now in West Africa foreign enterprise may contribute about 65 per cent of capital, the Government 20 per cent, and one of the long-established trading firms may contribute 15 per cent and the 'know-how' of local conditions for the establishment of a new venture. This arrangement, usually combined with tax-incentives for pioneer industries, and with government assurances as to repatriation of profits and employment of foreign technicians, has proved sufficiently attractive to bring in the secondary industry already described. It is not a complete solution from the African standpoint, since both financial and managerial control remain in foreign hands. But it does mean that some Africans, as nominees, are gaining experience in the board-room and that it would be difficult for companies to pursue policies opposed to the

Government's interest.[28] Further, companies are often requested, in return for concessions on tax or staff, to undertake to train African replacement for foreign staff. Israel, with great tact, has undertaken to train in Israel two Africans for every one Israeli employed in their African ventures.

The present mixed economies in Africa are thus likely to move in one of two directions. There could be a movement towards a completely State-run economy, somewhat on the Eastern model. Alternatively, governments could continue and expand a policy of attracting expatriate enterprise with a strong emphasis on 'Africanization' of its management, as well as encouraging, and even protecting, African entrepreneurs in those sections of the economy for which they have already the aptitudes and skill needed. The final object of such a policy would be to create a substantial block of free enterprise with largely African management. Which of these two directions will in fact be taken is one of the major question-marks of the present time. In purely economic terms, there is little doubt that a continued stimulation of foreign enterprise in the larger and most technical industries and of African enterprise in the smaller ones would lead to maximum economic progress. This argument rests in part on educational grounds. In the period between 1917 and 1935 Russia experienced appalling difficulties in establishing a wholly State-run economy in isolation from the rest of the world; and Russia even at that stage had considerable resources of educated men and technicians—it was already far further advanced in an industrial revolution than the countries of Africa today. Certainly, conditions for Africa are now more favourable in other ways; African governments would receive help and advice from one part or another of the outer world even in a fully Communist experiment, and the existence of a prototype would help to avoid known mistakes made in Russia's early pioneering years and in the Chinese experiments. But if it once became clear that there was no lasting future for either the existing foreign enterprises in Africa or for new ones, so that African economies became wholly dependent on African direction, whether through the State, or through organizations similar to the Israeli Histadruth, or through some adaptation of industrial Co-operatives, the burden

[28] See the *Report of the Advisory Committee on Aids to African Businessmen*, in Chapter VII.

thrown upon African governments, in trying to run the entire economy with their limited resources of trained men, would be quite unreasonably heavy. Nor is it possible to solve this difficulty by massive employment of foreign experts. The expert must either respect his employer or in effect dominate him; no one of real ability will continue to serve long if his advice is constantly over-ruled by incompetent people. It is certainly possible that in a fairly compact and highly integrated state such as Ghana a combination of both producer and consumer Co-operatives and a series of State Boards could take over the whole economy and finally make it work, although not without extreme difficulty for many years. In larger units, such as Nigeria or the Congo, or in countries with smaller educational resources, it is hard to see how this could be achieved.

However, it is necessary to look squarely at the alternative course of continuing to encourage foreign enterprise on terms which it is willing to accept. This would imply that, at the end of a decade, a very high proportion of a country's industry would be under the ultimate control of foreign firms, however many Africans are employed as managers. The local government might indeed hold a minority of shares; and a certain proportion of equity capital might be held by African nationals—several British companies in West Africa have recently offered share issues to Africans, and with success. But in the last resort major companies in the West will either wish to retain control, even if management is almost completely nationalized, or to sell. If they decide to sell, the same problems of finding capital and top management will arise.

How far could African governments tolerate such a position? In terms of extreme political nationalism it may be awkward, despite the control which a sovereign government can exert over all activities within its borders. But if rapid economic development and strength is also a national aim, it may be worth while to accept a fairly high degree of foreign ownership. And, in the world of the 1960s, extremely mixed ultimate control is becoming a far more commonly accepted pattern. American, British and European shareholdings are becoming increasingly mixed up, and the Common Market is likely to result in complex patterns of international financial structure. There are already projects in Africa in which an African government is partnered by two or even three different foreign sources of capital; and to follow this pattern is more likely to bring Africa smoothly into the modern world of business than to insist on the restrictions of capital and skill which a proud national self-sufficiency might suggest. In the field of agricultural development there is indeed room for purely African co-operative endeavour; but where the developed technologies and heavy capital structure of major industry are at issue, it is neither nationalism, nor partnership with a single power, but a more international type of structure which is likely to bring Africa into the orbit of development in the modern sense; this is the pattern being followed in the Volta Scheme. These considerations may well have an increasing appeal in Africa, as they have had in India, once the first self-consciousness of Independence has worn off a little and the threat of 'domination' by Western private enterprise, which *is* private and takes its own risks, is realistically weighed against the disadvantages of alienating it permanently and relying on governmental aid from the East. This is an issue which can better be considered in a general political context.

These are more distant perspectives. In the more immediate future there is little doubt that the Development Corporations perform a useful catalytic function, in finding opportunities for industry, in contacting foreign investors, in pledging some local capital as an earnest of goodwill, and in stimulating local African enterprise, both by credit and technical advice. Nyhart[29] has pointed out that there is some confusion between helping forward a programme of modern industry, which often involves highly technical plant and management, and helping African entrepreneurs, which may mean a much more humble provision of credit or management advice to craft or small processing industries which Africans have themselves undertaken, often in the agricultural sphere. Some interesting work has been done by the I.D.C.s in this field, and occasionally by foreign companies. As one example, the Uganda Company have helped to launch a number of small African concerns, acting as management agents for an African Board. Although there have been abuses in the management agency system, notably in India, it is one which could have useful training applications, perhaps especially in East Africa where African business knowledge has still far to go. The danger

[29] J. D. Nyhart, The Uganda Development Corporation and the Promotion of Entrepreneurship (E.A.I.S.R. Conference, 1959).

of government help to small men lies in the bureaucratic tendencies, particularly of modern governments, well described by a Uganda Development Corporation official quoted by Nyhart :[30]

The bureaucratic and administrative complications of starting a business are enough to intimidate a knowledgeable, enthusiastic and educated European, let alone the local African. The forms to be filled in, the licences to be applied for and obtained, the inspection of premises, the meeting of complicated specifications, the application for certificates, the labour regulations, the land regulations, &c.—all these are a really formidable display of obstacles for the most enterprising man to tackle.

These obstacles not only inhibit the aspiring entrepreneur; they offer great opportunities for minor graft—every form and licence can easily cost a 'dash' to an official. At the humbler levels of industry—and some kinds of industrial growth must have a humble start—it is almost better for government to keep out altogether than to put up this dangerous row of hurdles as the price of assistance or even permission. Moreover, the all-pervasive national party, or the monopoly Co-operative, can become just as overbearing in their handling of the newcomer whose energy is so badly needed. If there are leopards in the jungle of free competition, there are also extensive quagmires in the open plain of centralized planning.

It is certainly not for Europeans to be superior or critical of the solutions adopted by African governments. They are facing, in particularly difficult circumstances and without either a highly educated public opinion or sufficient trained men, a problem which has not been solved in the West. How to find and maintain the delicate balance between social control and individual initiative is a question not fully answered by America, Russia or Western Europe, however great their claims may be. It is partly a question of values and partly of timing, since different stages of an economy are reflected in different social problems and controls. Those African countries which are willing to give considerable freedom to private enterprise can certainly not be blamed for retaining, through some statutory body, a degree of political control. What is perhaps important is to prevent these government mechanisms from stifling initiative, whether indigenous or foreign, and to avoid too high a concentration of political and economic power in a

[30] Op. cit.

very small party group. The diversification of opportunity and
energy is specially needed in this period of rapid growth.

The attitude of foreign firms in Africa during this period while
African governments are forming a philosophy is important for
their survival. The first necessity, and one which is often difficult
for firms long-established under the colonial régime, is a full
recognition of the new African sovereignty. The business of a
government is to govern, and African governments have no intention of abdicating from this position. To become, or attempt
to become, either a power behind the throne or a kingdom within
a kingdom is a most dangerous error which will attract strong
hostility from every quarter. Indeed, any form of ostentation or
conspicuous expenditure is likely to incur jealousy and criticism.
The reputation of a good but not extravagant employer, competitive and technically skilled, is the desirable one. Secondly,
the foreign firm has no status in political matters; if the foreign
policy of an African government is not what it might wish, this is
a penalty of enterprise in a foreign field. There have been, particularly in Ghana, signs that Western businessmen are far too
quick to expect the Ghanaian Government to conform to Western
and capitalist policies, although Ghana is avowedly and indeed
proudly neutralist and socialist in aim. The existence of expatriate
Chambers of Commerce or pressure groups of any kind is also
extremely dangerous. To imply that expatriates have separate
interests from the whole business community, that they have
peculiar rights, or that they secretly co-ordinate their policies in
some sense 'against' the local government, is to court disaster.

Thirdly, there is the danger of social separatism. It is indeed
difficult for enterprises far out in the bush, which must produce
their own housing, recreation, medical services and even education, to avoid the high wire fence, physical or psychological,
around the concession. But within the fence standards creep up
inexorably towards the full European affluence, exclusiveness
grows, and jealousy outside begins. The situation grows, if anything, worse when a small minority of Africans are included in
the European managerial levels and therefore in the circle of
housing, club and social expenditure typical of the foreign group.
If in fact the enterprise, and particularly its housing and other
environmental services, had been planned on the basis that within
ten years 75 to 80 per cent of the management would be African

(even if the present level is nearer 10 per cent), the shape it has taken might have been very different. Neither the appointment of an African director nor the existence of African shareholders will disguise the social and environmental exclusiveness which has been the pattern in the past and remains sometimes all too evidently the pattern today.

In addition, the offer of air passages to expatriate staff for home leave, sometimes as often as once a year, means that local leave is much reduced or abolished. In consequence, staff learn less of the country in which they work, do not bother to learn the language, and are never committed to Africa in the way which was once true. Living and social conditions, with the aid of swimming pools, air-conditioning, Company clubs and Company housing estates, are made as like as possible to home conditions. Most men in any case are lazy in making an effort to explore and take part in a strange civilization; this policy makes it all the easier for them to create a superior European suburbia in the middle of Africa. This has long been the case in the Copperbelt, where many Europeans are extraordinarily ignorant of the surrounding country and peoples and seldom venture beyond the tarmac and the golf-course; but it is also apt to grow up wherever there is a sizeable group of European technicians and managers. The tendency for more comfort and social life to separate the administrator from Africans ('nous avons perdu nos blancs') has already been mentioned in Chapter III; it is even more marked in expatriate industry today, and less necessary; for conditions in Africa are far better, both in health and comfort, and there is the beginning of an educated African society with whom social contact is eminently possible and desirable. In many parts of Africa the staff of the British Council seemed to have made the most genuinely friendly contacts with Africans. This may be partly because they have a library and a definite cultural contribution. But it is also partly due to more modest salaries and entertainment allowances. Africans, except at the very top levels, cannot afford European-type entertainment in public restaurants, and have difficulty in entertaining in their home. Better social understanding means that expatriates should rely less on expensive parties and more on a more modest sharing of genuine interests. African society, the African countryside, the problems of the new African States surely provide a wide enough field for Europeans who are prepared to be interested in the people among whom they are working.

Social exclusiveness has also often been combined with a slightly patronizing 'wisdom'—the wisdom of 'long administrative experience'. David Apter has pointed out, in a most stimulating article,[31] the preference which African leaders have, and are likely to have, for the scientist and technologist rather than the Arts man, the man of 'high culture'. The stereotype of the technologist is of a man interested in his technique, and in the contribution to human wealth (he might say 'happiness') which it can make; a man who is content to come and do his job, take his salary, train his successor, and go away again. The stereotype of the Arts man is one who is a little too conscious of '2,000 years of civilization', a little too concerned to criticize things social and political in a foreign country, a little too apt to clothe his skill in administration in an air of mystery which makes it inaccessible. Whatever administrative skill may be, educated Africans are determined to master it in a very few years, or to get on, as best they may, without it. They are certainly not prepared to wait, in a subordinate position, for the number of years some Europeans think necessary before occupying the posts of command. Moreover, senior African civil servants are usually Arts men, and naturally find it easier to acknowledge the special training of a technologist than of men who have had the same education as themselves. Just how quickly and how efficiently African management can come to play a full part in the more industrialized societies of the future will be discussed in later chapters.

The future development of industry, as outlined here, may therefore be expected to lie in three main types. There should be a growth from below of ordinary African enterprise in a variety of fairly small industries, based on agriculture and crafts, and in such fields as transport and contracting. Secondly, major industries of high technical content and requiring large markets to achieve the economies of scale, may well be mainly foreign for a decade or more. In these it is probable that shareholdings will be mixed, not only to include African governments but some African subscribers. Governments are likely to prefer a fairly wide variety

[31] David Apter, 'The New Nations and the Scientific Revolution', *Bulletin of the Atomic Scientists*, vol. XVII, no. 2, February 1961. This article is quoted more extensively in Chapter XI.

of nationalities in this sector, and may consciously seek an element from the East as well as from the West. They will certainly want to use this sector for the training of African managers in the full context of private enterprise ; to fill in gaps in the economy which demand special skills ; and to economize in their own capital investment, much needed for other purposes. Finally, there is likely to be not only a public sector, such as Public Utilities, but in at least some countries a field of socialist or co-operative experiment, giving an opportunity to try out wholly African leadership and new organizational forms which may seem suited to the particular traditions and needs of the country concerned.

CHAPTER IX

AFRICAN LABOUR AND THE AFRICAN MANAGER

I. BETWEEN TWO WORLDS

The early history of African entry into the productive system developed by Europeans is characterized by one dominant fact: that there was never a real fusion between the outlook and assumptions of the employer and those of his African employees. At the personal level, there was little meetings of minds; at the cultural level, there was little dove-tailing of institutions. Economically, culturally and emotionally Africans were not identified with organized employment of the Western type; the great majority of those who experienced it were never more than a quarter or a half involved, held by a thread so tenuous and so frequently broken that the real grip which a good industrial organization can have on its members could never get a hold. It was not economically all-important to the Africans who entered it; it was not, as it is for so many in Europe, one main centre of their social life, or the place where roots were put down; its atmosphere and regimen were alien and often repugnant. It was not, as it is for many Europeans, a means of expressing personality through skill. Although this situation is changing now, it is the essential background of the past. Two principal factors give rise to it. First, the relation of population to land and the pattern of traditional rural life. Secondly, the extreme differences between European and African culture and values.

Africans have always had plenty of land. Often it is of poor quality, or capable of yielding only poorly under the traditional techniques and the available power which Africans could apply to it. But there has generally been plenty of it. The average density in West Africa where population is greatest, has been calculated at 13·3 per square kilometre; in areas near the coast it rises to between 20 and 50 and in some parts of Nigeria to 100. In East Africa, the figures are generally lower, from 3 per square kilometre in Tanganyika to 10 in Kenya and 23 in Uganda, although there are patches of high density (Kikuyuland : 160, and the edges of Lake Victoria, Rwanda-Burundi, and the borders of Lake Nyasa : up to 80).[1] In Central Africa the figures are amazingly low—2 per square kilometre in French Equatorial Africa; 3 in Northern Rhodesia, 5 in the Congo. These figures compare with 300 in England and Wales, 111 in India and 22 in the United States.

In general, the land is available to the whole community; there has been no system of inheritance of land by a single heir. It has been the property of a tribe, and in the use of a family or lineage, and every member has a right to use it. In consequence, the landless labourer, who helped to man the European Industrial Revolution, did not exist in Africa, and could scarcely be created. For a man who has land has a means of living, and a source of security. Moreover, even if the African had wanted to cash his land holding and take paid employment, perhaps for a better standard of life, he could not usually sell it. He could only leave it, to be allocated to another. Why abandon, for nothing, the only final security, for the hazards of alien employment?[2] Africa has sometimes been described as 'under-populated', a word which only carries meaning as a relation between population and workable resources. In fact, population was in rough balance with skills and resources, so that there was no free surplus of labour to man new enterprises which Europeans with new skills were able to develop.

When tax in money was imposed by Europeans, many Africans were forced into employment, and often into migration. They went because they had to go, and came back when they could. The fact that forced labour is basically unwilling labour was never fully weighed by those who found Africans so 'lazy' or so hard to inspire. True, when the money economy began to spread more widely, when the desire for possessions which only money could buy overlaid the sheer need to pay tax, it might be said that labour went 'willingly' to work. There is indeed some evidence, even in early days, that the escape from tribal disciplines and family obligations was at least a factor weighing against the unpleasantness of going. Professor W. E. Moore[3] has said :

[1] Figures from I.L.O. *African Labour Survey*, supra. Population growth in the last five years, which has been fairly rapid, would increase all these figures.

[2] Elkan has particularly stressed this point.

[3] W. E. Moore, *Industrialization and Labor* (Cornell University Press, 1951). This is an invaluable study, comparing findings from all over the world,

The picture of primitive or peasant societies as completely integrated, and unchanging because they have achieved a perfect balance of social and natural forces, is grossly overdrawn. There is no culture that is completely integrated, even in the absence of new alternatives. It follows that new patterns of economic activity, if not attractive in themselves, may at least offer escape from the uncomfortable controls of the old social order.

But this is a negative motive, a choice of evils, and there is ample evidence that industrial employment for the migrant was regarded as an unpleasant experience, as indeed was to be expected. The new factory workers in England's nineteenth century found the discipline of factory life and the urban environment almost insupportable, and the novels of Dickens or Mrs. Gaskell are full of nostalgic sympathy for the countryman in town. How much more violent was the change for Africans going to serve alien masters in an alien environment, or for any primitive people. Firth [4] has remarked that it was impossible to recruit the Tikopia of Polynesia for work in other areas because of their acute nostalgia. The sense of security is deeply felt :

Perhaps the most pervasive attitude of withdrawal from the industrial pattern or of only limited, temporary and reluctant adherence to it arises from loss of traditional forms that give security. It is typical especially of the first impact of new economic patterns that they threaten or disrupt previous social relationships, while not immediately supplying new security devices in their place.

Typically, Africans have returned, after a period of migratory labour, to the tribal society, and this is good evidence that, despite

on which I have relied very heavily. I have only added the results of some more recent work, which almost invariably confirms Prof. Moore's findings, and here I am particularly indebted to Miss Merran McCulloch's *Survey of Factors Affecting Productivity in British African Territories*, prepared in 1955 for the Inter-African Labour Institute Conference at Beira, and for additional help, mentioned in the Introduction, from her and from Dr. and Mrs. W. Elkan. I have also relied on the I.L.O. *African Labour Survey* (1958), the First African Regional Labour Conference (I.L.O., 1960). *The Social Implications of Urbanization and Industrialization in Africa South of the Sahara* (I.A.I. for UNESCO, 1956), the 'Sixth Inter-African Labour Conference', C.C.T.A./C.S.A., Abidjan, 1961, and some papers for the C.C.T.A./C.S.A. Study of Productivity and Absenteeism, of which final reports were not yet published at the time of writing.

[4] Raymond Firth, *We, the Tikopia: a Sociological Study of Kinship in Primitive Polynesia* (London, George Allen & Unwin, 1936), quoted in Moore, op. cit.

its 'disciplines' and 'restraints', it was where their heart lay. In the town, living in a 'bedspace', paying for insufficient food from low wages which they also endeavoured to save, surrounded by strangers and working for aliens, Africans were sojourners in a land not their own. Perhaps the impersonality of both the work situation and the social situation chilled them particularly—the move from a village of 35 huts to a compound on the Copperbelt with 1,000; the move from working your land with family and age-mates to the work bench among strangers.

Certainly, as Professor Moore says, it is the first experience which is the worst; and the visit to some place of employment gradually became an institution in many African societies, so that it might become not only the recognized way of earning bride-wealth, and an adventure for young men, but almost equivalent to an initiation. Watson [5] has described how firmly the custom for young men to go to the Copperbelt or to the Tanganyika sisal estates to earn money has been built into the social pattern of the Mambwe in Northern Rhodesia. Living on the plateau between Lake Nyasa and Lake Tanganyika, this tribe was on one of the highways of Arab, and later missionary, penetration. They early became used to working for Arabs and then Europeans, and later both men and women found prestige and excitement in visiting the town life of the Europeans. It is clear, however, that they pre-ferred local to more distant employment, if possible; and that the customs of kinship and respect for the chief were retained because in them resided the real future security—rights to land. They are, as Watson puts it, 'peasants raiding the cash economy for goods'; after the age of about 45 the men settled down at home to take up again the full obligations and satisfactions of tribal society. In the same way it has been noted of the Tonga in Northern Rhodesia that their support of the old tribal system is quite conscious and purposeful:

Consequently, when Tonga migrants eventually retire to their village, they do not fall back upon the security of a tribal system which *happens* to have continued during their absence; the migrants themselves, during their absence, have been contributing actively

[5] W. Watson, *Tribal Cohesion in a Money Economy* (Manchester Univer-sity Press for Rhodes-Livingstone Institute, 1958). A review of some similar situations is contained in the Foreword by Max Gluckman. See also Southall (ed.), *Social Change in Modern Africa*, supra.

and consciously to its continuance, because they know that they may have to rely on it when they are no longer usefully employed in their urban habitat.[6]

Elkan[7] has pointed out, however, that this should not be taken as an altogether happy cultural mutation; for where the necessity to go did not arise, there was no such migration; and the study of migration to the Cameroons plantations confirms that it was not from the crowded areas but from the 'under-populated' and poorest areas that the great volume of migrants came—from necessity, not choice.[8]

Nor is the substitution of a money-earning absence for the older ways of finding bride-wealth innocuous to the home culture:

From the stage when some member of the family seeks employment for the sole purpose of paying tax to the stage when complete detribalization occurs, two intermediate stages commonly occur. In the first instance, the familial economy is sufficiently disrupted so that the ordinary mode of supplying enough cattle for the bride-price (*lobola*) through the obligations of the father and gifts or loans from other kinsmen no longer operates. The young man may then seek work not only to *buy* cattle in order to complete the marriage agreement. This is already a radical and disruptive step. Its logical successor is the complete commutation of the necessary cattle-price into its monetary equivalent, thereby removing the whole arrangement from its functional context in the village economy, the customs and rituals of marriage and kinship and the symbols of familial cohesion.[9]

Here Professor Moore is pointing to the main argument of Malinowski in *The Dynamics of Culture Change*—that a cultural institution can only be replaced effectively by one which carries out the same purposes, and that the attempt to have the best of both worlds—to have Africans in both the modern and the traditional culture—inevitably weakens both. The degree of disruption of the tribal society depends partly on the actual form of their husbandry and social arrangement.[10] While among the Mambwe

[6] J. van Velsen in Southall (ed.), *Social Change in Modern Africa*.
[7] W. Elkan, 'Migrant Labour in Africa: an Economist's Approach', *The American Economic Review*, vol. XLIX, no. 2, May 1959.
[8] Ardener and Warmington, op. cit.   [9] Moore, op. cit.
[10] Where, as among the Bemba, the husbandry demands men for tree-lopping, the effects of migration are worse. Watson and Gluckman (ibid.) tentatively suggest that matrilineal societies where the men in a village have come

this damage was not great, it is admitted that marriage became less stable and that the economy broke down if more than a certain proportion of men were absent from a village. In any case, the 'raiding' of the cash-economy implies very little identification of the African worker with his industrial job.

Unfortunately, European policy in the early days, having made an inroad for its own purposes into the African way of life, was content to foster this half-in half-out arrangement. Like most early industry, it was unable to face the full implications of providing a secure and lasting way of life for African labour around the new enterprises; early Europeans would scarcely have known how to set about such a task, dealing with a people so immensely different in outlook and social needs.[11] Besides, the tendency to racial segregation, indeed the impossibility of real social contact at the beginning, precluded the idea of an integrated town round an integrated industrial enterprise. In consequence, the ability of Africans to return to their village and become lost again in their own social world, however poor, seemed a happy dispensation, provided that new recruits would replace them. As late as 1960 a Southern Rhodesian employer was saying of the 'primitive African' who labours on the mines that 'he is fed, housed, hospitalized and to a certain extent amused by his employers and his pay is to him little more than pocket money. When he goes on leave he slips back again quickly into the tribal pattern of the Reserves.' Many Europeans, especially in South Africa and the Rhodesias, were haunted by fear of a breakdown of the rural economy or of the Africans' wish to stay in it, followed by a tidal wave of unemployable men and women flooding towards the towns. Once again, Belgian policy in the Congo became an intelligent exception to the general pattern—in recent years there was

from different villages and are therefore not closely related, are more apt to break down, whereas in patrilinear villages the men co-operate more closely and take on each other's obligations when some are absent. When, as in the Copperbelt, an increasing number of women go to towns, though without settling permanently, they tend to lose the agricultural skills needed in village life and find the return very difficult.

[11] It is interesting that a deliberate attempt by the *Office du Niger* to provide a replica of their cultural environment for the Mossi settlers on the Niger project was a failure. The buildings were placed in a way which repeated the customary pattern, but it was not a lineage but strangers who inhabited them. See P. H. Hammond, 'Economic Change and Mossi Acculturation', in *Continuity and Change in African Cultures, supra.*

positive encouragement, almost compulsion, for the worker coming to industry to bring his family and settle properly in the town.

Gradually, this situation has been modified in several ways. In the West, where there were real African townsmen, the transition from trading or craft work to industry could be fairly easy and did not imply long-distance migration. Yoruba men, who have so greatly handed over the retail-trading function to women, and who may be living some way from their family land, find themselves in the position of breadwinners and take fairly easily to paid employment.[12] Secondly, after the first push of hut tax, the pull of desire for money, for westernization, for city lights, for emancipation in many forms grows yearly stronger and spreads more widely. The European workman does not go to work for the eager love of it, but because it will bring him money to buy what he needs and desires; and this is a sufficiently positive motive on which the employer can build morale. It is becoming more widespread among Africans. Thirdly, the growth of education began, from earliest times, to produce a class who wanted permanent employment in clerical or higher levels of the Western sector, who had no intention of sinking back into purely African rural life, and were prepared to settle at their new employment. For long enough, this made no contribution to the supply of workmen, and employers were irritated by a superfluity of would-be clerks and a shortage of regular labour. But the growth of primary schooling and the slowly improving opportunities for Africans in factories and other industrial work is gradually producing a class of stable labour, with primary education, who are at least three-quarters inside the industrial system, with a weaker, though still important, link with the old culture.

A migrant labour force does, of course, suit the peculiar needs of economies in their early main stage of laying down a capital structure. The 'navigators' (navvies) of Britain's canal and railway boom were largely migrants from Ireland, working and moving through the English 'bush' as the tunnels and cuttings were made. Now the Kariba Dam, the Volta Dam, the Bornu railway extension, new mines and installations in mounting number are planned or already achieved in Africa. Often these works are far from any

[12] See particularly studies by Alison Izzett, D. McCall and Aidan Southall in *Social Change in Modern Africa*, supra.

town and inevitably the labour force is at a high peak during construction, small or even negligible when the turbines are running and the irrigation channels made. At its peak, in December 1958, the Kariba labour force consisted of :[13]

Africans:	S. Rhodesia	.	.	.	1,000
	N. Rhodesia	.	.	.	1,070
	Nyasaland	.	.	.	1,480
	Portuguese E. Africa		.		2,530
	Others	.	.	.	520
Europeans:	.	.	.	.	1,490
					8,090

It is hard to know how this force could have been quickly gathered if there had not been already a pattern of migratory labour. Similarly, the estimated labour need for the Kouilou Dam (Congo-Brazzaville) is about 8,000, and the possibility of needing migrant labour from other countries, as well as rural recruitment and the use of urban unemployed from Brazzaville, has already been considered.[14] However deplorable in some respects the migratory system may be, there are situations in Africa, and will be for some years, where a controlled use of it will be economically helpful, without worsening the already established situation. Moreover, where a certain industrial labour force is already established, these projects may usefully absorb temporary unemployment—the Bornu railway helped to absorb labour from the closed Enugu coal pits, and much of the labour for the Escravos Bar came from unemployed from Lagos.[15]

Thus, in summary, the African possession of enough land for subsistence, and the close attachment of their whole culture to it, and the European need of labour resulted in this 'wasteful and inefficient'[16] system of labour migration. It is wasteful from the expenditure of time and energy in long journeyings; it is inefficient partly because labour is not effectively attached to the indus-

[13] Sixth Inter-African Labour Conference (C.C.T.A./C.S.A.), 1961, Paper from Federation of Rhodesia and Nyasaland, Item III. The Paper presented by France to this Conference presents in short form many of the social problems of labour supply for large projects.

[14] Ibid., Paper from the République du Congo.

[15] Ibid., Papers from Nigeria.   [16] Moore, op. cit.

trial enterprise, and partly because the rural economy, despite the remittances from migrant workers, may be seriously weakened,[17] while the culture in which it is embedded is eroded away. The social effects, particularly on marriage and children, are likely to be evil. In general, from 5 to 10 per cent of migrants take a wife with them. The remainder find comfort with prostitutes, or in 'temporary marriages' of one form or another. When children are born of these unions there may be competition by the parents to keep them (they are sometimes spirited away by one parent or the other to the home lineage) or rejected. Jean Rouch[18] paints a vivid picture of these children in the Ivory Coast:

Those who have reached adulthood form a sort of intermediary class concerning itself with petty trading and semi-skilled occupations, bad taxi-drivers, non-specialized fitters, semi-literate clerks and shop assistants. Rejected by all, they have formed themselves into separate groups, finding compensation in creating voluntary societies where loneliness, despair and dreams are shared.

The extent of these migrations today is perhaps not widely realized save by specialists. The Sixth Inter-African Labour Conference (Abidjan, 1961) has recorded some of the main figures of organized migration, such as the movement in 1958 of 75,000 migrants from Mozambique and 102,000 from Angola to South Africa. In 1951 there were estimated (I.L.O.) to be 650,000 alien workers in South Africa, of whom two-thirds were migrants. Of the 12 to 13 million adult males in Southern, East and Central Africa, it is estimated that 5 million are absent from their tribal homes, engaged on wage labour.[19] While the movements to South Africa and the Rhodesias are mainly towards European enterprise, with the mines dominating, the West African movements are more focused on agricultural employment—cocoa, coffee and groundnut harvesting. In the latest study (C.C.T.A. Conference, Niamey, 1961) of just over 100,000 migrants moving in 1959 into Ghana and the Ivory Coast about 50 per cent were going to agricultural jobs, 20 per cent for trading, though it is interesting that 65 per

[17] But see Watson, op. cit.
[18] J. Rouch, 'Second Generation Migrants in the Ivory Coast' in *Social Change in Modern Africa*, supra.
[19] First African Regional Labour Conference, I.L.O., supra (Report of the Director-General).

cent were moving to a 'town' as against 35 per cent to 'bush'.[20]
They were men travelling without their family—52 per cent
single and 85 per cent of the married men travelling without their
wives. The great majority come for less than a year, though they
may make repeated journeys.

Again, no less than 250,000 migrants have been checked leaving the Sokoto province of North Nigeria, of whom three-quarters
originated in the province. At least 50,000 migrants, usually called
navetanes, enter Senegal for the groundnut harvest. In East Africa,
about 100,000 enter Uganda by the South West route alone from
Rwanda-Burundi and Tanganyika—201,000 were found to be
using transit camps in Uganda in 1955 and 224,000 in Tanganyika.[21]

A great part of the map of Tropical Africa is thus deeply lined
by these massive movements, yearly renewed, from the dry lands
of the West to the coastal forest, from the poor lands of the centre
South to the mines, or North and East to the plantations and farms
of Uganda and of the Tanganyika coast. These are only the movements which cross boundaries; to them must be added the internal
ebb and flow.

Thus the employer in Tropical Africa has, more often than not,
employed either migrants or men with only one foot in their place
of work. The result in labour turnover and inefficiency was bound
to be bad for this reason alone.

But additionally, the industrial system itself is almost wholly
alien, and contrasted in its assumptions, to that of traditional cultures. The Western system is characterized by Moore[22] as 'impersonal, momentary, functionally specific relations'. 'It is typical of
the industrial way of life that in a large measure the participant's
position in the system and his daily contacts with other persons are
related to what he does rather than to who he is.' Over against
this system, which is not concerned with whether a man is old or
young, married or single, an Emir's son or a slave, but classifies
him as a fitter, a foreman, a Grade III carpenter or a sweeper, is
the African system which is status-centred and in which rights and

[20] These towns are not primarily Abidjan (16 per cent of migrants against
82 per cent into East and S.E. Ivory Coast) or Accra (15 per cent, against
62 per cent going to the Kumasi area). They are the smaller country towns,
from which labourers may then disperse into the bush.

[21] I.L.O. *African Labour Survey.*   [22] Op. cit.

obligations attach to social position and age and land. This is, in its African context, the old distinction between status and contract laid down by Maine. The quite different attitude to economic functions has been described in Chapter V. Nor have Africans imbibed from childhood the Protestant gospel of work. Miller and Form [23] point out that in Western society the cultural expectations about work—'You must work hard'; 'You must learn to accept responsibility'; 'You must learn the value of money', &c., are 'indoctrinated' into the child by the family and other institutions. 'The child hears his father and mother and his older brothers and sisters appraise the conduct of outsiders in the terms of these standards. The school reiterates and emphasizes them. The Church gives its moral sanction to them.' In contrast, Africans worked to perform their social obligations, and to eat and perhaps to earn prestige; they might get credit for being hard workers in some cultures, but in others (as Dr. Richards has observed) they did not. They were scarcely likely, in the early days, to fathom the European attitude or to respond to adjurations about the 'dignity of labour'—particularly from Europeans whose status was partly defined by their complete superiority to manual work.[24]

2. EARLY EUROPEAN VIEWS

The opinions of African labour first formed by Europeans were natural enough, and they would be only of historic interest but for their persistence, as well-established maxims, among many of the 'old Africa hands' and for the attribution of African failings to genetic (usually called 'racial') factors. The African workman seemed 'lazy'; this in European terms really meant that he was unused to *continuous* hard work. Africans work remarkably hard at their own agriculture; but in spasms of activity. The continuity of work, both through the day and through the year, is a strain; many Africans feel that they need a 'rest' after a few weeks of steady work. The records of daily farm work which have been collected show how often family and tribal obligations, funerals,

[23] D. C. Miller and W. H. Form, *Industrial Sociology: an Introduction to the Sociology of Work Relations* (New York, Harper and Bros., 1951), quoted by Merran McCulloch, op. cit.
[24] 'A sense of the dignity of labour seems to decline with increased educational facilities.' (Report of Provincial Commissioner, Central Province, Kenya, 1948, quoted by Merran McCulloch, op. cit.)

or festivities, interrupted the working week, as the many Saints Days did in medieval Europe.

Africans seemed ignorant and clumsy—Elkan [25] points out that many of them had never gone up or down stairs, turned on a light switch, handled a European broom. They even seemed complacent about their own views and standards and abilities—R. H. Tawney's remark is often quoted, that 'The denunciations of "luxury, pride and sloth" of the English wage-earners of the seventeenth and eighteenth Centuries, are, indeed, almost identical with those directed against the African native today.' [26] He needed constant supervision—because his heart was not in his work. He did not even seem to respond to 'ordinary' economic incentives—this was a simple-minded view, typical of the older generation of industrialists in Europe, who were wholly concerned with monetary incentives. Moreover, he was puzzlingly inconsistent in response—Elkan [27] points out that migrant labour is usually in a hurry to earn money, and will work overtime or respond to attendance bonuses; whereas local labour may value a short day (to get home to the farm) and may well find a more profitable occupation than the factory wage, such as selling his own produce, on a certain day of the week. Thus responses may well be different; they are puzzling only if generalizations about 'the African' are made about very different people in very different circumstances.

The result of these earlier and often persistent judgements on African labour, and of the use of migrants, was that it did not seem worth while to take any trouble in either the selection or training of labour. Men were chosen from applicants at the gate because they looked strong or better dressed; even in 1960 an expatriate official of a very modern textile factory in Nigeria informed us that choice was based on 'the ones who have small hands'. Nor was any real effort to train considered worth while, in view of the high labour turnover. Supervision, often carried out by European artisans of much skill but little understanding, was based on simple precepts of 'treating the African as a child' or by using Asians, Arabs or Somalis for supervision, often races

[25] W. Elkan, *An African Labour Force* (East African Studies no. 7, E.A.I.S.R., 1956).
[26] R. H. Tawney, *Religion and the Rise of Capitalism* (London, Penguin Books, 1942).
[27] W. Elkan, *Migrants and Proletarians* (London, Oxford University Press, 1960).

acutely disliked by the workmen, who found themselves the lowest tier of a racial pyramid of African, Asian, European. In a study of dockworkers and others in Tanganyika, Friedland [28] observed that: 'In East Africa the distance between superior and subordinate is so great that supervisors often have no clue as to what their subordinates are thinking', and this difficulty is increased by very imperfect understanding of languages as between African and European. Arthur Lewis [29] observed that most comments on African labour by supervisors were still 'on the level of whisky-and-soda conversation', and Northcot [30] drew particular attention to the strange generalizations of 'men who knew their Africa'. A view held particularly strongly and widely by Europeans was that raw African labour from the bush was much preferable to the more educated men; this was especially noticeable in the Copperbelt in 1959 and 1960, where an element of maintaining racial superiority by white miners, themselves not too well educated, was involved; but in general it was a simple observation that Africans with some education were unwilling to do hard manual work, as well as a typical preference for simple countrymen against 'smart alecks' from the town. It is always easier to handle people who do not ask questions.

It goes without saying that these attitudes, which naturally tended to produce the results which they assumed, led to the greatest inefficiency, though there were of course many exceptions. In the worst cases, without selection, without adequate training, with alien, impatient and often contemptuous supervision, without his heart in the job and often with acute dislike of the whole social situation, the African worker was not likely to perform well. Constant disparagement, as many studies have shown, is one of the strongest disincentives to any labour force, European or African. It was not, therefore, that the European's observation was wrong. It was mainly that his understanding of the reasons for poor performance was wholly inadequate, and because his policies tended to perpetuate the very evils he deplored. In a sense, the Europeans were bound to be the prisoners of their own Western assumptions about the nature of industry and of motivation.

[28] W. H. Friedland, Rhodes-Livingstone Institute Conference, 1960.
[29] W. A. Lewis, op. cit., quoted by Merran McCulloch.
[30] C. H. Northcot, *African Labour Efficiency Survey*, 1947 (Colonial Research Publication no. 3, H.M.S.O., 1949).

Above all, the widespread conviction that 'Africans' or 'Bantu' as a 'race' were less endowed either with intelligence or industrial aptitude, or both, had the most depressive results, not only on African performance, but on European inclination to experiment with training and selection. Perhaps the Belgian management of labour in Katanga provided the best large-scale exception to the general rule.

3. AFRICAN ABILITY—THE MODERN ASSESSMENT

The foregoing sections have sought to establish two main points : first, the real reasons for the partial and ineffective entry of Africans into industry, based mainly on their continued attachment to land and partly on their cultural difference; second, the natural European reaction to this situation. However, particularly since 1945, there has been a major revision of European thinking. There is, of course, a large overlap between the older ideas and the new. There were highly intelligent European managers before the war; and there are today plenty who still repeat the old slogans.

Several factors have contributed to this new approach. In the first place, there has been a revolution in the Western philosophy of management. It was after the war that the work of Elton Mayo, Mary Parker Follett, Chester Barnard, Wight Bakke and a dozen others really began to affect the leaders in Western industry. The new ideas are relevant here in two especially out of many aspects. A sociological approach emphasized the complexity of motivation and of the satisfactions of industrial work—there was a move away from the *simpliste* view of monetary incentives. This approach also studied group relations inside industry and the concepts of morale. Of particular interest, to take one example, was Wight Bakke's [31] concept of the fusion which must take place between the private motives and purposes of the individual entering industry and the corporate purpose of the firm to achieve production. It is this fusion which alone can lead to a point where the worker identifies himself, at least in part, with the firm, and is pleased by its success or worried by its difficulties. In the African context, the lessons of this revolution in 'personnel management' [32] implied a

[31] E. Wight Bakke, *The Fusion Process* (Newhaven, Yale Labour and Management Centre, 1953).

[32] Which was of course carried into all the detailed fields—recruitment, selection, training, incentive schemes, management succession, &c.

careful look at the African sociological background and at the possibilities of achieving 'fusion'.

Thus, as more industry has grown up in Africa, new European managers with new ideas have entered the field. Meanwhile, Africans themselves have become more acclimatized to industry, their performance has improved, and the possibilities of infinitely better performance, under intelligent selection, training and management, have begun to show themselves, so that it is now evidently worth while for management to take some trouble. Further, the gradual rise in African wages is beginning, or will soon begin, to force employers into a far more careful utilization of their labour resources. A large number of experiences and experiments have contributed to a new outlook. Northcot's [33] work in Kenya contained such sentences as 'the picture shows that most Africans in employment work systematically and well. In their occupations they show a capacity for training and have acquired a satisfactory degree of skill.' The investigation sponsored by Dunlop and carried out by the University of Natal [34] showed the importance of selection. The Carpenter Report in Kenya [35] shed a great deal of light on African wages and incentives. Individual firms, such as the Bata Shoe Company, Shell, the United Africa Company, British American Tobacco and others began to experiment with new training and management methods, with highly favourable results; one factory manager stated as his considered opinion that the quality of Kikuyu labour was higher than that he had personally managed in the West Indies, and in South Eastern Europe.

Finally, a flood of academic work, partly in classical anthropology and partly in the applied field of industry (such as the work of Elkan or the Sofers at Jinja), supplemented by the I.L.O., UNESCO, C.C.T.A./C.S.A. and other international agencies, began to affect industrial management and enter into the currency of thought. It was significant that the conference of managers and trade unionists from all over the British Commonwealth and Empire convened by H.R.H. The Duke of Edinburgh in 1956 had as its subject 'The Human Problems of Industrial Commun-

[33] Op. cit.

[34] *The African Factory Worker. A Sample Study of the Life and Labour of the Urban African Worker* (London, Oxford University Press, 1950).

[35] African Wages Committee (Carpenter Report), (Nairobi, Government Printer, 1954).

ities', and that the Background Papers to the Conference [36] included contributions from Raymond Firth, J. C. Mitchell, W. A. Lewis, C. A. Mace, W. Elkan, D. W. Harding, F. Fraser Darling and E. B. Worthington, all notable for academic work in the social and natural sciences in relation to the transition from traditional to modern societies. This work is well known to specialists and far too voluminous to review here. Its general effect has been to apply some rather more refined sociological thinking to African conditions, and especially to break down futile generalizations about 'the African' into a study of the particular cultural and educational background of a particular labour force in a particular country at a particular stage in the process of acculturation.

Thirdly, the new approach has been aided by a frontal attack by biologists and social-psychologists on the whole concept of 'innate' or 'racial' or genetic characteristics of 'Africans'. As early as 1951 Moore [37] stated categorically that the belief that different ethnic or 'racial' groups differed in capacity to assimilate industrial skills owing to differences in hereditary biological constitution 'is supported by no anthropological evidence and may be dismissed as having no scientific standing'. Herskovitz [38] is equally clear:

Scientific enquiry has established beyond serious dispute that whatever may be the nature of inborn differences of a psychological order associated with differences in physical type, the range of ability in any human group is such that no item of behaviour invented in any society is beyond the capacity of any other to learn it, granted adequate opportunity and motivation.

Biesheuvel [39] concluded in 1943, on the basis of extensive tests and research:

If the observed African I.Q. were therefore corrected for the adverse influences to which both the growth and development of African intelligence are subjected, the estimated mean African I.Q. would come to approximately 100, which is the normal mean European I.Q.

It is not necessary to waste more space on the cruder aspects of the old theory of racial inferiority. But it is important to state

[36] H.R.H. The Duke of Edinburgh's Study Conference on the Human Problems of Industrial Communities within the Commonwealth and Empire, vol. II, Background Papers. (London, Oxford University Press, 1957.)
[37] Op. cit.
[38] M. J. Herskovitz in Grove Haines (Ed.), *Africa Today*, supra.
[39] S. Biesheuvel, *African Intelligence* (Johannesburg, South African Institute of Race Relations, 1943).

briefly some of the reasons (apart from racial prejudice, which still keeps the theory alive in some minds) why it should ever have obtained any credence among educated men. To suppose that 'Africans', if the immense differences in physical type between the major groups are taken into account, could possibly share some identical genetic inaptitude is clearly fantastic, though even this has been believed. The real difficulty has arisen mainly from the results of applying I.Q. tests to African and European children and comparing the results. In repeated instances of careful and scientifically controlled testing, the Africans have shown significantly and consistently lower figures, and this has naturally given some support to the old theory. But it is now widely established that this effect has two main causes. First, that it is not possible to establish a 'culture-free' test—that is, a test which does not handicap members of one culture if it is conceived and applied in terms of another.[40] Second, that it is impossible to make accurate allowances for the retarding effects of bad environment, from conception onwards, on the I.Q. as we measure it. These two points are both covered by Biesheuvel's statement. Further, it is becoming more clear that we have no watertight definition of 'intelligence' or of what constituents of it we do or do not measure in an I.Q. test. For example, Dr. Philip Vernon [41] has said :

First, we would do better to admit that first we do not know whether there are differences in Intelligence 'A' and are unlikely to be able to find out; and secondly, it is really Intelligence 'B' which interests us, and this is best regarded as the level of development of those intellectual capacities which a particular culture favours.

The same emphasis on cultural environment comes from Mannoni :[42]

In any case, the measurement of natural intelligence is not very useful in itself, since experience tends to show that there are psychological obstacles, deriving from the social environment, which hinder the development of Intelligence . . . Apart from obvious cases of mental deficiency, the idea of inborn intellectual aptitudes, which has never any very clear meaning, proves to have none at all in group psychology, for we have no means of gauging latent capacities save

[40] See Nadel et al. in Bartlett (Ed.), The Study of Society (London, Kegan Paul, Trench and Trubner, 1939).
[41] P. Vernon, in Man, Race and Darwin (London, Oxford University Press, for Institute of Race Relations, 1960).   [42] Op. cit.

through observing manifest abilities, and these depend, at least for their development, on the social environment.

The conclusion is clear. While there will be a range of intelligence as between individuals, which may have a genetic basis, there is no means of proving, and every reason to think unlikely, any genetic inferiority as between one substantial ethnic group and another, still less between 'Africans' and 'Europeans'. What we must recognize are differences in the development of 'intelligence' (a word which needs definition in each specific use) due to environment and culture; in so far as there are wide differences between the early environment and pervading culture of Europeans and Africans, in particular circumstances, these will show in possibly quite generalized differences of behaviour, and give the appearance of being, in common language, 'racial characteristics'.

It is now necessary to reverse the emphasis, and observe that these environmental and cultural differences may go deep. There is, for example, much-quoted evidence that some Africans find difficulty in understanding three-dimensional representation, possibly from never having been used to the European conventions of perspective; clearly, if this is true, it would affect methods of training and instruction. Some psychologists would suggest differences in qualities of understanding and judgement. For example, Professor Maistriaux,[43] who is wholly free of the older theory—he states categorically that 'there is no qualitative difference between the intelligence of black and white men'—is inclined to believe that the absence of certain stimuli *('incitations fonctionelles')* in an African childhood may lead to a weakness in the power to manipulate complex ideas in which several relationships are involved; he suggests, as a hypothesis, that some African groups (i.e. those with a particular cultural background) may be more often *'particularisants'* than *'généralisants'*.

Maistriaux also points out the lack of richness of association which a word from the European world will have in African minds. European education is conceived for children 'who have profited from innumerable occasions of training and instruction which the mere passage *('jeu')* of daily modern-type life necessarily throws in their path', while African children, of the same age and

[43] R. Maistriaux, *L'intelligence et le caractère* (Paris, Presses Universitaires de France, 1959), and *L'intelligence noir et son destin* (Problèmes d'Afrique Centrale, Brussels, n.d.).

in the same class of the same school may have missed this. Further, he observes that where knowledge is learned by heart without full understanding, it may be fatally lost if a doubt creeps in—as happens to us in spelling mistakes. This may well help to explain the extraordinary 'lapses' in behaviour often noticed among African labour—the occasions when something done correctly for two years is suddenly done wrongly; withdrawal of attention into a private world, or sometimes a kind of Blue Beard curiosity to see what happens if the forbidden door is opened or the emergency lever pulled, may also explain other instances.[14] It may also explain why Africans, in the view of many expatriate managers, can apply their knowledge *to the context in which they learned it*, but find great difficulty in applying it to new situations to which it is equally relevant. This work of Professor Maistriaux is quoted only to show that the employer may well be faced with real difficulties, culturally caused, about which expert advice may be needed. But once the notion of genetic (and therefore ineradicable) difference is finally killed, the prospect is one of the greatest hope. For cultural and educational differences are rapidly narrowing in Africa, and we are therefore entitled to believe in an equally rapid disappearance of their side effects.

Thus the way is now fully open to apply to labour management in Africa the most sensitive and intelligent programmes of the best personnel practice in Europe. This means above all that there are no easy rules and shibboleths. Managing Welsh miners, Coventry car-workers and Yorkshire weavers requires very different styles. Managing was very different in the 1932 slump from managing in the 1960 boom; even managing, at the same time and place, miners and tobacco-workers in Nottingham is not the same. If these differences appear within a small country with a single over-all culture, with regard to its regional and occupational sub-cultures, how much more do they apply with regard to the far

[14] Elizabeth Hoyt confirms this view:

'The African as an employee . . . has small choice but to accept, without adequate understanding, the conditions imposed on him from without. He has little idea of the value of conforming to a schedule, of the importance of organization in effort and development in skill, and of the cost of tools and their need of care. He can be disciplined in these respects . . . but ordinarily he sees no reason in this discipline; hence his "forgetfulness", his lapses, and his failures at crucial points.' E. Hoyt, 'Economic Sense and the East African: Impressions of a Visiting American Economist', Africa, vol. XXII, no. 2, April, 1952.

greater differences between African groups, and in a situation changing so fast. The importation of detailed European practices, the reliance on labour studies carried out in Africa indeed, but 1,500 miles away among different peoples in a different context— these are not intelligent procedures. But if there are no detailed rules, there are the general methods of approach. There is the obligation to know accurately the social background of the working force, their motives and values; to select rationally; to train supervisors; to give to the worker some idea of what he is making and for what purpose; to keep contact and to consult; to praise and blame, and in fair proportion; to avoid the anomalies and injustices which do far more damage than rough conditions or low pay. These and other principles have been tested with every labour force in the world.

Apart from such principles, so often neglected in Africa owing to a racial theory or to the laziness which a large supply of cheap labour encourages in so many managements, there is a more serious difficulty mentioned at the outset of this chapter. It is the problem of attaching the African more closely to industrial work. Good management, good conditions and good pay will go some way—and will go farther as the proportion of Africans who really care about losing a well-paid job increases, as it must among those who have effectively settled in towns. But they do not solve the problem of men with one foot in the land and one in the factory. In certain areas, where individual freehold land tenure on indivisible units of land is growing, and in the major towns, a land-free labour force will slowly grow. In some areas it may be possible to arrange small gardens for the work force, so that the family can settle and the minor crops be grown without migration—anything is better than bachelor labour lines or the impersonal married quarters where wives have nothing to do. But the major issue of large-scale seasonal and industrial migration has to be tackled at both ends—in building a worth-while social environment for the worker in industry, to stabilize him and his family; and in accelerated rural development which will make farming a more modern and a more commercial whole-time occupation and will put a maximum number of industries and services into the rural areas to provide alternative careers.

Employers in Tropical Africa are now much concerned with

their own local problems of stabilization and the conditions of labour. The situation differs greatly between factories established in the largest towns, and enterprises, whether of plantation or processing or mining, which are out in the country and have to house their labour force. In towns, the physical health of the worker is a problem. He may well be lodging in extremely poor and overcrowded circumstances, and buying too little food at what may seem to him high prices; he may also be walking or bicycling a long way to work, or paying quite high bus fares from a distant suburb, as from the new estates outside Lagos. Employers who provide food have in general found the African increasingly anxious to have money instead, and this is a tendency typical of the early stages of Trade Unionism. It is probable that a purely optional canteen is the best solution, with prices which should not be so heavily subsidized that a demand to be paid the subsidy in the form of wages will arise. In West Africa, mammies with a vested interest in feeding the workers can make things very difficult for an employer who cuts their trade. It is indeed remarkable that, with so much against him, the African worker is not a persistent absentee; yet the final summary of the C.C.T.A. enquiry concluded that absenteeism was 'not a serious problem'; the common rates were between 2·5 and 4 per cent with the highest figures 4·6 per cent (Dakar) and 4·4 per cent (Kano). While some employers are concerned at the drop in physical fitness associated with leave to the rural areas, it is probable, in most parts of Tropical Africa, that the gradually increasing rural standards will give him at least as much food at home as in the town, though with fewer European items in it.

Some employers are already giving, or considering, a pension scheme (African industrial workers in the Belgian Congo had it years ago on a universal compulsory basis) and schemes for a 'National Provident Fund' are just coming into force in Nigeria. There is no doubt that the question of providing a reasonably balanced social security system for at least urban Africans will have to be faced in the next few years (this is a major issue which will be discussed in Chapter XII); mere reliance on the extended family without additional support is not only putting African adults under great strain but is causing hardship, particularly to urban children. The records of the Sekondi-Takoradi Social Survey,[45] the Accra Survey,[46] and the work of Miss Alison Izzett [47] in Lagos reveal the terrible conditions under which some children and adolescents grow up in West African towns and the high incidence of virtual abandonment—abandoned children can be picked up by Welfare Department staff in Lagos almost every night of the year. Employers have a strong interest in coming forward with help to municipal and housing authorities in urban areas, with the long-term object of providing an environment for workers living in their own (not Company) housing which would be tolerable and stabilizing; and the same applies to cheap and efficient urban transport.

In rural surroundings the whole problem is easier. It is interesting that at the Samreboi Timber enterprise of U.A.C. (Ghana) 50 per cent of workers at the sawmill and 70 per cent of those in the forest units took up the offer of a garden to cultivate for maize and vegetables. Even where men have land not far away this may be worth while—a tannery outside Nairobi attributed a low turnover (less than 5 per cent per annum) to the provision of a *shamba* attached to each house and irrigated from the tannery effluent. The creation of real villages, instead of labour lines called villages, can be helped by this, since wives, social life, minor traders and services will come in and create a community in place of a camp of migrant labour. This is a complex problem which can only be solved in the light of particular local circumstances. Men (and women) may be quite unused to the type of local agriculture and diet near their industrial work; it is usual for migrants to want Company housing to be arranged in tribal groups (as was the case at the Jinja dam) and to need tribal friends and associations: on the other hand, on the Cameroons plantations [48] and near Calabar there appears to be a willingness and even a preference for tribal mixture. The Kampala Survey suggests that tribal grouping is preferred in the early stages, but that as men get more self-confident they wish to break through purely tribal links. Certainly

---

[45] Busia, *A Social Survey of Sekondi-Takoradi*, supra.

[46] Acquah, op. cit.

[47] See Reports of the Department of Social Welfare, Lagos.

[48] 'Men were asked in our surveys whether they would prefer to live in camps or work in gangs with men only of their own tribes, so far as might be practicable. About 80 per cent of those questioned rejected the idea. Part of the novelty and interest of plantation work is the contact with men of other areas. . . .' E. Ardener, in Southall (Ed.) *Social Change in Modern Africa*.

some are consciously entering a wider, modern world, and know in any case (more clearly than Europeans) that a mock tribal village[49] is not and cannot be remotely like a real tribal village, since both the familial and economic basis of it is so different. There may well be a need for temporary and tribal camps for new-comers and also a more mixed township, of which the aim would be to create a lively, inter-tribal social existence, with many modern elements (such as football or 'high life'), but on an African level and without excessive European nursemaiding. As Max Gluckman has observed,[50] obsession by both employers and anthropologists with 'tribal life' has tended to obscure the fact that Africans in the industrial or urban context are *primarily* workers and townsmen, not 'tribesmen in town'; this will become increasingly true; but they are still Africans, with their own tastes.

Despite the many difficulties and inefficiencies of the entry of African labour into industrial life, the modern picture of well managed enterprises in Tropical Africa is often highly encouraging. There are plants which record an output of 90 per cent of European productivity from recently trained African labour; high dexterity in textile manufacture; low absenteeism rates fairly generally; labour turnover which may be high in the first year almost universally but remarkably low later—the number of long-service men in some enterprises in Africa would stand any European comparison. The C.C.T.A. enquiry remarked, in the general conclusions:[51]

Both absenteeism and labour-turnover rates prove to be much lower in urban areas than was commonly supposed when the research was first decided. This is truer of absenteeism than turnover; both rates could however be used to support the view that the rapid increase in urban populations, far outstripping the employment opportunities at the unskilled level, has created a social situation and climate in which retention of a job becomes more and more necessary.

This is a most significant finding, offering as it does to management a so much greater opportunity to grip and hold a permanent labour force. A recent investigation by an American Fulbright

[49] See above, Hammond, 'Mossi Acculturation'.
[50] In Southall (Ed.), *Social Change in Modern Africa*.
[51] Sixth Inter-African Labour Conference, Paper: Labour VI (61), 35.

scholar [52] of the productivity of African labour in sixty-three enterprises in Nigeria concludes that there are no inherent disabilities,
that willingness to work 'considerably exceeds that of labourers in
developed economies' and that bad results are normally the reflection of insufficient training or poor management. Although even
the best employers would not accept such a sweeping judgement,
is it not without significance.

There are still blind spots in management—in one modern
factory Muslims were being pulled off their knees at the time of
prayer, until it occurred to management to institute a rest pause
at the appropriate time. But where management is intelligent in
selection training and personnel policy, and where the work force
is not mainly migrant, the picture is one of rapidly increasing
efficiency.

4. INDUSTRIAL RELATIONS

The growth of 'two nations' in the industrial revolution of
Europe led to a need for special machinery to negotiate between
what they came to be—the 'two sides of industry'. European
Trade Unions were slow growing and had many aberrations and
much internal debate before they found a form and policy which
allows at least a militant coexistence with employers. In Africa
there were two, often three, nations, separated by race as well as
culture and economic power, and the need for some means of
communication and negotiation in industry, across a much wider
gap, was and still is undeniable. In all the British, French and
Belgian territories the metropolitan form—Trade Unions—was
introduced, with the added complication of Catholic and Socialist
Unions duplicating in Africa their rivalry in French-speaking
Europe. It was not always the employers in Africa who favoured
this course: the Labour Government in Britain after the last war
was an active evangelist of Trade Unionism in Africa, and it became official policy of colonial administration to foster and train
it. To a very large degree, Trade Unionism came into Africa from
above—from the encouragement of government, of some employers and of a handful of ambitious Africans.

There is some debate about popular African reception of this
entirely new institution. Warmington's study of the Cameroons
Development Corporation Union [53] suggested, as might have been

[52] Peter Kilby, *Economic Journal*, June 1961.
[53] Warmington, op. cit.

expected, that African workers tended at first to choose a white and fairly senior official as their representative, because he would naturally be able to deal best with the white employer. Further, to some extent Africans would naturally expect an employer to act as a chief—that is, one who would listen to and remedy the complaints of his group, if suitably approached and placated. The analogy with chiefs is too simple—not all Africans have chiefs, or the same kind of chief; but the attitudes expressed were none the less natural and widespread. As Unions became more common and effective, there is evidence that Africans paid their subscription in order to conform—and to fulfill accepted social obligations is a strong imperative in most African societies—and no doubt to avoid an element of intimidation in some cases. They expected primarily to get increased wages from their contribution, and were apt to be violently disappointed if they did not. It is interesting and very significant, that African workers on the Copperbelt quickly realized that the early attempts of employers to handle industrial relations through tribal elders in the work force was inappropriate—this is another case where Africans quite clearly realized that in the Western context tribal systems were out of place.

The first and ever-continuing difficulty lay in the quality of African Trade Union leadership. In the colonial period leadership of a Union was one method of carrying on the struggle against Europeans, and it produced such leaders as Mr. Mboya in Kenya, M. Sékou Touré in Guinea, Mr. Siaka Stevens in Sierra Leone. But below these leaders there has been a constant upsurge of smaller men, trying to get a foot on the ladder of power by the industrial approach; in most cases they were not well fitted for their job, either by training or personality. Further, many of them, with more moderate and more mercenary ambitions, found it easy to gain certain privileges, such as travelling expenses, on the members' subscriptions, even if they did not decamp with the whole of Union funds. Finally, as employers have so often complained, the only way by which the leaders could retain enthusiasm was by violent strike action and pay demands. The formation of a new Union was a particularly dangerous moment, since it was apt to lead to an immediate strike, even if there was no current dispute with employers.

Both sides of industry have complained bitterly about this situation. Many groups of workers have paid up their money to a new visiting organizer, only to lose it; employers complain that it is the well-meaning and liberal employer, who recognizes a Union, who is immediately attacked; those who have chased the Union leader off the compound have sometimes had a peaceful life. Not a few employers, and good ones, have resolutely refused to recognize Unions and have dealt with their labour quite satisfactorily by joint consultation. Company Unions have been widespread, and often efficient; but where there are two or more employers in the same business an industrial Union will be formed sooner or later, and will then fall into the general pattern.

Perhaps the fundamental difficulty has been not so much the alien character of the Trade Union in the traditional context but the fact that the movement came from above and was never lived and suffered by the bulk of the membership. The cohesion and discipline of European Unions is not simply due to a suitable form of organization or to education. It is primarily due to many decades in which members learned, at great personal risk and with great suffering, the necessity for unity and loyalty, the necessity for sacrifice, and the limits of possible achievement. The British Trade Union member is held by the memory of battles, victories and defeats of long ago and by an emotional link with his Union which is of enormous strength. Not so the African member.

Despite these troubles, patient effort by Labour Departments and some employers, the gradual appearance of better leadership and the better understanding of the industrial situation has led in many countries to the growth of many quite solid and competent Unions. Nigeria, with about 280,000 members in the movement, can point to such achievement. The African Mineworkers' Union on the Copperbelt, the Railway Unions in East Africa and a few more are major groupings which are unlikely to fall apart. The capacity for communication (perhaps a better word than organization) in Africa should never be underestimated; employers in the 'Otraco' transport strike on the Congo, or in some strikes controlled by Mr. Mboya in Kenya, received a rude shock when their prophecies of feeble response or indiscipline turned out to be entirely wrong. Some—though not enough—training of Union leaders is now going on in Africa, both at the I.C.F.T.U.[54] College in Kampala, through the efforts of the I.L.O. Field Office in Lagos, through Labour Departments and through a few major employers.

In 1960 and 1961 there has also been a change of policy towards the 'check-off' (deduction of Union dues from wages by the employer). It was previously resisted on the grounds that it could lead to easier and better exploitation of membership by dishonest or extravagant leaders; there is no need to look far for extravagance in the hiring (or buying) of cars and the claiming of travelling expenses.[55] But the counter-argument, that unless a Union has regular funds it will never become efficient, or will spend its time in spectacular strikes to maintain interest, has now begun to prevail. A clause has now gone into Nigerian labour legislation allowing check-off with an effort to retain an element of government supervision. It runs as follows:[56]

If the Minister is satisfied that a reasonable proportion of all contributions of a worker paid to a Trade Union in accordance with sub-section (1) will be devoted to schemes which in the opinion of the Minister are of benefit to the worker, the Minister may by order approve the Trade Union for the purpose of sub-section (1).

This change, which now seems likely to spread widely over Africa, will certainly strengthen the Trade Unions; but employers are still justifiably nervous of the uses to which the very considerable sums involved may be put; as one employer remarked, the thought of £200,000 in the hands of a single Union with inexperienced leadership, and in an explosive political situation, is a little frightening.

The approach or achievement of Independence has already brought new and even larger issues to light. The whole African Trade Union movement has been rent by a battle between the exponents of an All-African Trade Union Federation, neutralist and not affiliated to any international body, and the followers of I.C.F.T.U. affiliation. Mr. Tettegah, leading the forces of Ghana,

[54] International Confederation of Free Trade Unions, headquarters in Brussels.
[55] One leader had recently claimed £60 for a two-day stay at a plant which we visited, where he had been accommodated free of charge in the Company Rest House.
[56] Federation of Nigeria, *Official Gazette*, no. 70, vol. 47.

Guinea, Morocco and some others, including half of a divided Nigerian movement, declared 'total war' (in his own words) at Casablanca in June 1961, against the I.C.F.T.U. contingent, of which Mr. Mboya has been the principal leader. The I.C.F.T.U., unfortunately in the throes of an internal Anglo-American war, and widely felt to be the Western 'Cold-War' instrument against the Eastern W.F.T.U.,[57] is in no shape to fight this battle, and it will be surprising if its influence survives effectively in certain African countries. On the other hand, there are major non-Communist elements in all the African T.U. movements, including both the Christian (or 'Croyants' in Muslim countries) groups and many branches of the main French-speaking *Union Générale de Travailleurs d'Afrique Noire (U.G.T.A.N.)* originally mainly inspired by M. Sékou Touré and other nationalist leaders. The future of the East African Unions will depend much on the final solution in Kenya, including particularly the attitude of Mr. Mboya. There is thus a general likelihood that the A.A.T.U.F. will be neutralist in fact as well as in name, though much divided internally and with a strong left-wing element. Influences from Cairo and the Arab world are not, at the time of writing, at all pro-Russian.

But while this battle has damaged some African Trade Unions severely—and provoked, particularly in Nigeria and East Africa, some savage comments on 'the intrigues of Ghana imperialism'— it is perhaps less important than the future attitude of sovereign African governments to their own Trade Union movement. The drive for production, and for national monolithic unity under Party guidance, is unsympathetic to the hold-up in production and the embarrassment of two strong and warring factions which a strike of African workers against, say, a government-backed Development Corporation or major hydro-electric project would cause. Mr. Nyerere in Tanganyika intervened, though tactfully, to halt a strike at the diamond mines in 1961; Ghana has voraciously swallowed the Trade Union movement into the Party system—it was recently described by Mr. Tettegah as 'the industrial wing of the C.P.P.'; President Sékou Touré seems likely to take much the same line in Guinea. At present the future in East and Central Africa is uncertain; Nigeria, with a strong Labour Department and no monolithic system, may retain an independent

[57] World Federation of Trade Unions.

XIII. Layout of African housing on the Copperbelt, Nchanga, Northern Rhodesia

[*Photograph by Nchanga Consolidated Copper Mines Ltd.*]

movement; and the French territories, where they avoid a totalitarian approach, may allow the Unions reasonable scope. Whether these countries are willing to retain a strong, non-governmental institution, a 'secondary power' within the community rather than an organ of either the State or the Party, will be one of the significant indicators of future political philosophy in Africa.

Indeed, at this point an even deeper issue is raised; for the future of Trade Unions is bound up with the whole social form which the growing industrialization of Africa is to take. In Europe, as Marxists teach, industry grew within societies already strongly divided into social classes, and increased this division. But it is arising in Africa *before* any long history of class-division and bitter struggle between employers and workers; any struggle has been more between Europeans, the major employers, and Africans, the workers, with the emphasis on nationalism rather than class. M. Sékou Touré has rejected outright the Marxist theory of industrial relations for this very reason, and it is one of the chief distinctions he makes between his own political philosophy and that of the Communists. A question arises—and one of deep interest to the Western world—whether in Africa it may be possible to organize, without direct imitation of the Communist system, a social form of industry which does not create the profound horizontal cleavage between employers and labour which grew up in the pioneer period of the Industrial Revolution.

When it is considered how profound are the effects of the factory system as we know it on the whole social and political life of the West, there could scarcely be a more important issue for the whole future of African culture and the 'African personality' (if such is to exist as a reality rather than as a myth) than such experiments in productive organization which might produce a variant. Simone Weil,[58] asked to prepare for General de Gaulle a Paper on the regeneration of France after the last war, replied in *The Need for Roots* with a direct and fundamental attack on the whole social system incorporated in and radiating from the factory, and on the whole set of motives upon which both employers and Trade Unions relied. This is not, as Mlle. Weil pointed out, a question of private enterprise versus State control. It is a question of the human organization of the productive process, the

[58] Simone Weil, *The Need for Roots* (*L'Enracinement*). Translated by A. F. Wills (London, Routledge and Kegan Paul, 1952).

relations and motives within it, the methods of control and consent to control. In Africa, before the institutions of industry take rigid forms in the old Western pattern of conflict, there is need for vision and experiment and every possible use of the springs of co-operation and social unity. Some African societies have shown themselves quite able to evolve, from within their traditional pattern, new occupational and social structures—for example, the cotton growers in Uganda and cocoa farmers in Ghana.

It is worth emphasizing how great are the differences in the modern African context from that in which Unions first grew. It is not only that 'classes' have not in the past existed in the Western sense, but that there is to this day a far closer link between rich and poor through the extended family and through tribal linkages. In most African societies there is no precedent for the type of organization embodied in the modern Trade Union, though there is certainly precedent for craft guilds. It might be argued that, although industry is alien to Africa, it is certainly coming, and its corollary of Trade Unionism is bound to follow; but this would be to assume that industry can only take one form. In fact, modern industry has greater flexibility. Today, highly automatic plant reduces the need to concentrate huge numbers of employees; a determined use of electric power can assist the decentralization of production; more thoughtful personnel policies can reduce the frictions of the working situation. There are also precedents for different forms of productive organization, such as 'outwork', and much greater flexibility in systems of payment. Experiments in the leadership of groups, and in the setting of work targets to be achieved in a tempo which the group itself decided, could prove fruitful. Such changes in the methods of management and organization might well involve different institutions for representing grievances or negotiating conditions. Professor Moore[59] hints broadly at this:

> The factory system is on such hazardous grounds in any undeveloped economy that, if it is deemed wise to expand it at all, there is some basis for experimenting with many modes of organization and appeals to workers' motives. *It is possible that the adaptability of the factory system itself has not been adequately explored,* (My italics.)

Far more thought could now be given in Africa to experiment in

[59] Op. cit.

relationships between producers which might avoid some at least of the animosities of the Western system and reflect better the social instincts developed by African traditions. It may well be that forms of Joint Consultation, and even a variant of the American system of plant bargaining, would prove effective. There has been, after all, a long African tradition of communal co-operation at work. It is to be hoped, as Professor Moore [60] has observed, that 'where traditions of co-operation between employer and employed already exist, it may not be necessary to disrupt them, only to face the problem of their establishment all over again'.

5. AFRICAN MANAGERS

There are two main reasons why African governments or politicians are anxious for a much increased Africanization of management, both in private companies and public Boards. The first is to secure increased political control; here the demand is for competent men to serve on public corporations and Development Boards. For the early period this is primarily a watchdog function which a well educated man could hope to do without technical training until the African engineers and other specialists, who need both training and long experience, can come up from below into the top executive posts. The second reason is simply to gain experience, so that more Africans will be useful in the general field of industry and development. From below there is also a strong push from Africans who want a better share of the jobs, whether from a Trade Union, such as the African Mineworkers' Union on the Copperbelt, or at higher levels, where the demand is likely to be raised through political parties by young Africans who can combine personal ambition with a nationalist programme.

In many respects, firms employing expatriate staff are also anxious to 'Africanize'. It will cost up to £5,000 to find, bring to Africa, house and pay an expatriate for a year, and he may not be doing a very senior job. Moreover, foreign firms are well aware of the quite proper political pressure to employ Africans, though more difficult issues arise when Europeans or Asians who have settled in Africa are competing for work. Apart from this special problem, there is no real disagreement in principle; the difficulties lie in the supply of candidates for management, the rate of their advancement and their salary level.

[60] Ibid.

Before the possibility of Independence became real and pressing, and before the new hopes of industrialization and development, training in Tropical Africa was mainly concerned with supplying the needs of government and the Public Utilities, and the largest industrial schemes were to be found in the Railway and Harbour enterprises, electricity supply, Post Office and Public Works. In addition, most countries had a set of Trade Schools for the training of artisans, with a strong emphasis on the building trades and often with a rural bias. Alongside this government work, individual firms had their own training schemes, mainly for operatives and the supply of first-line supervision. In East Africa the Asians supplied a considerable group of artisans mainly by family apprenticeship. It was to be expected that the two major areas of heavy industry—the Katanga and the Rhodesian Copperbelt—would be far more advanced, and this was true in Katanga, where the level of craft training was easily the highest in the whole of Tropical Africa. Unfortunately, pressure from the European Mineworkers' Union and the general political atmosphere in Northern Rhodesia [61] put a virtually total block on full craft apprenticeship for Africans, although operative training, including that of some process workers, crane-drivers, &c., has been of very high quality. Southern Rhodesia up to 1960 was even more backward, without a single public institution where Africans could reach fully skilled status in an industrial trade. The Federation will thus find itself behind almost every territory in Tropical Africa in the supply of fully trained African craftsmen and technicians.

On the commercial and clerical side, training was mainly by learning on the job and various in-service schemes, supplemented by the Banks and some larger trading companies by more formal programmes and a trickle of students sent to overseas courses. Naturally, in West Africa, with the earlier development of education and emphasis on a trading economy, the commercial side was further advanced; the more manual crafts and techniques

[61] The Technical Foundation in the Copperbelt was effectively for Europeans only, as were the Company apprenticeship schemes; and the Unions, by demanding the (expatriate) rate for the job if Africans were to be employed, made it virtually impossible for Africans, even from Hodgson Technical College, to find an employer willing to apprentice them. In Southern Rhodesia the foundation of a Technical College for Africans has begun to remedy a situation in which, as late as 1960, it was impossible for an African to gain fully qualified status as, for example, a fitter, electrician, tinsmith, &c., &c. 'Masons and carpenters only' appeared to be the rule.

were, however, until recently mainly concentrated in building and transport, without a strong growth of the skills associated with manufacturing industry.

The independence of some countries and a policy of industrialization have already begun to change this general situation—even in the Rhodesias there are signs of hesitant and carefully circumscribed advance. The first impact has been to multiply the demand for administrative officers in every branch of the central and provincial administration, and thus intensify government competition for graduates. But there has been and will be an increasing realization of the excess of literary over technical education, and a general strengthening of the technical schools and colleges which will slowly begin to produce results. Further, as many of the expatriate firms move a little away from trade and towards industry, their apprenticeship schemes take on a more technical character. This will help to remedy one of the most dangerous gaps in African industry—between the manager and the first-line supervisor, a gap which is now filled by expatriate technicians for lack of qualified Africans.

More detailed consideration of the needs of technical and managerial manpower and of the output of the educational system will be given in the next chapter. Looking at the present situation in extremely broad terms, it can be said that in West Africa the employment of African artisans and first-line supervisors has reached a high level—for example, all the supervisors of the Nigerian Tobacco factory in Ibadan are African, as are the staff maintaining very complex cigarette-making machines; on the training side, both U.A.C. and Nigerian Railways have over 600 apprentices in their respective training schools (the East African Railways have done equally well). As an example of their quality we were impressed to see the steel frame of a very large plywood factory in Ghana which had been erected in six weeks by African artisans and labour under the supervision of a single European. In East Africa, the predominance of Asian artisans continues, but Africans are making respectable headway. In the Federation, for reasons considered below, the position is still sombre, though there are growing signs of light in the North. At the technician level there is weakness over the whole area.

At the 'management' level, progress in both East and West Africa is fairly rapid, though the West is naturally ahead. Figures varying from 15 to 25 per cent are given for Africanization of managers in some of the expatriate trading firms in the West, with higher figures in some cases. Branches of the Banks have, here and there, an African manager, and substantial training schemes are going ahead. In some particular cases, large undertakings are assuming a really African character—for example, the Ghana Electricity undertaking, which employs only two or three expatriates, or the Enugu Coal Industry, which appointed an African general manager with full technical qualifications in 1961, and which has for long enough been almost wholly Africanized at and level of deputies, overmen and under-managers.[62]

In general, as might be expected, it is the office staffs, the Personnel Departments and the middle commercial posts which are most quickly Africanized, while the production, engineering and other technical and higher executive posts are still mainly in expatriate hands. In East Africa progress is much more recent, and largely in the form of African supervision, and the engagement of graduate or near-graduate management trainees who are finding posts in the trading companies, the oil and tobacco firms, and on some of the larger plantations. It is interesting to find that, for example, the Bata Shoe organization has many African shop managers getting up to £1,000 per annum in East Africa, in charge of shops with a turnover of £75,000 per annum.

It is important not to overestimate the numbers involved in the Africanization problem, even though the question of quality is all-important. Thus, to take a few fairly large organizations, the employment figures were in 1961 as follows :

Shoe Factory (East Africa)	950 Africans, 38 Europeans, 7 Asians.
Timber Mill (Ghana)	2,200 total employment. 78 managers, of whom 11 African.
Textile Factory (East Africa)	1,500 Africans, 30 Europeans, 42 out of 69 shopfloor supervisors were African.
Plantation (E. Nigeria)	843 total employment. 2 Europeans.

From the point of view of efficiency, these small European staffs have been and still are absolutely vital; but from the point

[62] Three out of thirty overmen were European in 1960. All but one of the under-managers were Nigerian.

of view of the training problem—in countries where industry is in any case as yet so small a part of the national economies—the size is not overwhelming. The figures are, of course, heavier in highly technical industries, such as the railways, where the numbers employed in East African Railways in June 1960 were 1,583 Europeans, 3,768 Asians, and 8,076 Africans in superscale and graded scales, and a further 27,932 Africans in the lowest ranks.[63]

Industry and Commerce have two main methods of finding local managers. They can promote long-service employees; or they can take in management trainees from a younger group of better educated Africans. In general, the older employee has proved the more reliable; but he has a lower 'ceiling' than the young man, not so much for lack of education, which may have been offset by experience, but from the habitual pattern of relationships with Europeans formed many years ago. It is easy to break a first-rate head clerk by promotion into higher management. There are, however, special difficulties in the handling of the younger trainee with higher potential. As the first graduates began to appear from African universities, or returned from training overseas (much earlier in the West than in Central or East Africa—but the same issues arose), they were much sought after. Government secured a very high proportion, partly by bonding the students to enter or return to government employment, partly by the attraction and prestige of government service. For example, we were informed that in 1958 out of eighty graduates leaving Makerere College all but ten went into Government service. The attraction of government has been partly security, partly the expectation of a car and other privileges, partly the hope of rapid promotion 'after Independence' when the Europeans leave or dwindle in numbers. There has been, however, a noticeable preference for headquarters rather than provincial administration, where much hard work, heavy responsibility, and a high degree of initiative are needed. By contrast, the large expatriate companies could indeed offer slightly higher rates than government, but a more exacting test of efficiency which might mean losing the job. There have been some signs, more recently, and particularly in Nigeria and Ghana, of a swing away from the Civil Service. The official posts are filling up; 'you need influence to get on'; promotion prospects

[63] East African Railways and Harbours, Establishment Division. To these figures should be added 745 Asians and 6,053 Africans on Wages Staff.

are getting quickly less attractive, since the top posts are uniformly held by young men with decades of service ahead of them. This has resulted in a swing of preference back towards industry. The commonest preference rating before this last change would have been, for an African graduate : 1. further and higher education overseas; 2. government; 3. large companies; 4. teaching (if all else failed); and there would be some vacillation between government and industry, according to country and circumstance.

The difficulty in attracting good quality staff had obvious results. African graduates with so many opportunities expected much from their employer, and were certainly unwilling to undertake long periods of additional training, particularly if it involved some experience of manual work. In many cases employers were apt to cling, with singular lack of imagination, to time-honoured principles about putting management trainees 'through the mill', with the result that they lost their recruits; out of twenty-one boys from Munali school in Northern Rhodesia (regarded as the premier African school, with a VIth Form) recruited into one mining company, eighteen had left within two years, having been sent underground to handle pick and shovel for the good of their managerial souls. Europeans in Africa are all too ready to draw derogatory conclusions about the character of educated Africans from such events (which have been all too common), instead of recognizing that a man with qualifications which less than one in 100,000 of his fellows possess, in a situation where twenty employers are willing to take him on, is a man who is likely to know his own opportunities. The very real possibility of becoming a senior civil servant, or even a Minister, in a matter of six or seven years weigh heavily against the prospect of hard work in a coppermine, with little prestige, with the hope of becoming an Assistant African Personnel Officer in about the same period.

This situation moves gradually up the educational scale as education increases. At one time a completed primary education was a passport to many jobs; then Cambridge Overseas School Certificate; finally a degree. As the ranks fill up, industry will find its task of recruitment easier, and the discipline which can be imposed more strict—though not, it is to be hoped, unintelligent. In the meantime, there is also particular difficulty in recruitment at middle levels; for the African who has got his School Certificate will move heaven and earth to get into some kind of degree-giving college, be it only the humblest of 2,000 such colleges in the United States. The Eastern Region of Nigeria, having decided to recruit an 'executive' grade in the Civil Service with School Certificate as entry, found it impossible in 1959 to attract recruits: those who had got so far were determined to go further. In the same way, the Nigerian Colleges of Arts, Science and Technology were subjected to great pressure to run degree courses, on pain of poor or insufficient recruitment if they refused.

Before dealing with the difficulties of training African managers, something must be said concerning a major organizational difficulty—wage structures originally and unavoidably sharply divided between European and African (and, in East Africa, Asian) rates. The same difficulty in the Civil Service, resulting in an expatriate salary level in very poor countries, has already been mentioned; it has been modified a little by separation of the basic salary from the expatriate inducement allowance, although there are intractable difficulties where, as in Kenya for example, locally born and engaged Europeans have been employed in considerable numbers. But in industry the structures are more complex, and the engagement of Africans at managerial levels before the posts below them have been Africanized has led to many strange situations. Most companies are struggling towards 'the rate for the job', with an expatriate allowance shown separately where necessary; East African Railways and Harbours, for example, have been slowly struggling to a 'colour-blind' wage structure through many delicate negotiations. On the other hand, there are still jobs in Africa for which the European rate is double or more than double the African rate, as was the case in at least one Ghana mining company employing both European and African shift-bosses, with no attempt to separate basic pay from inducement allowance. A great deal of fumbling has characterized this issue, which (for once) is a straightforward one. There can be no justification for racial differences in basic pay; if a man is capable of doing the job efficiently, he is worth its pay; and the levels of pay should be set so as to produce a defensible gradation of rates for Africans in an African economy from the bottom to the top of the scale. If Europeans or others have to be imported to do any job as a temporary measure (however long 'temporary' may be) this is an additional cost to be shown separately.

The real difficulty arises in the 'settler' territories, where many

Europeans do not regard themselves as expatriates and could not honestly be paid inducement rates, and where the less gifted are fitted only to do jobs which can now be done by Africans, although expecting a far higher standard of life. The long-term choices are equally clear. These choices are either to maintain a system of 'apartheid' for as long as possible; for local Europeans to accept work for the rate at which a full complement of properly qualified Africans could be engaged; or for them to emigrate to another country where conditions are more favourable. However much these choices are muffled in evasions and temporization, they are unavoidable in any country in which African education in all fields is pursued at the rates now common in Tropical Africa.

Many Europeans will find it intolerable to accept what will become the competitive rate for the job, especially if it involves working alongside or even under Africans; and there is unquestionably a danger of losing too many of them before enough Africans are ready to take their place. Nevertheless, it is impossible to maintain a double and purely racial standard in an integrated society, and the alternative to integration is 'apartheid'. It follows that a single wage and salary structure, with inducements only for those genuinely and necessarily recruited abroad, can be the only answer. For the time being this structure will, on purely economic grounds, have to contain rates high enough to attract local and qualified Europeans into work for which not enough Africans are at present available (since the employer must pay to all men in the same grade the marginal cost of the last man he needs), but it should be lower than the cost of attracting men with no higher qualifications on expensive 'expatriate' contracts from overseas.[64] As more Africans become qualified for particular work, either the economy will be rich enough to sustain the old 'European' rates (though without inducement allowances) or competition and economic stringency will force a reduction. High rates for a few managers might not seem to matter much economically. But as these posts are Africanized, a huge gap appears between African managers and African workmen or supervisors;

[64] To spell this out economically: suppose twenty jobs *must* be filled and ten, but only ten, Africans are available with proper qualifications, who would accept a £1,000 a year. But local and qualified Europeans will not accept less than £1,500. Then the rate for the job must be £1,500, since the alternative would be to import expatriates at £2,000. The employer can only avoid this conclusion by adopting frankly racial scales.

so that the whole wage level, from the labourer upwards, comes into question.

It is, of course, useless to blink at the political pressures to avoid the logic of the situation in settler territories. While the future of Southern Rhodesia is still wholly uncertain, Kenya and Northern Rhodesia seem clearly destined to have African majority governments which will presumably tolerate expatriate inducement pay but not a double, racially based, standard for locally engaged staff, and which will accelerate technical training for Africans in occupations at present partially or wholly occupied by Europeans or Asians. The difficulty of this solution in Kenya should not be great in the industrial sector; but the copper companies in Rhodesia, which have been for so long imprisoned by political and Trade Union pressures in an indefensible wage structure, will have some stern decisions to make which have been perhaps too long evaded. A start has been made in constructing a 'colour-blind' wage structure in the mines, but there is still a very long way to go.

It is essential to add that the word 'qualified', as applied to any management or supervisory job, does not mean simply that the necessary technical tests have been passed. It means qualified to manage, in terms of character, reliability, initiative, judgement and power to control and lead staff. It is around these intangibles that much of the difficulty, and much opportunity for racial argument, has been found, particularly in settler countries. Even where European and African staff are organizationally integrated, racial attitudes may make it practically impossible for Africans to lead effectively, not from their own fault but because their leadership is unacceptable to Europeans. One of the best integrated training schemes, run by Shell-B.P. in Port Harcourt, included discussion groups in which Europeans discussed in full with Africans the difficulties which they found in getting on with them, followed by an equally frank critique of the European by his African colleague. Although this might appear a clumsy or even embarrassing technique, it is in fact positively therapeutic, on the evidence of both sides.

Evidence of the quality of African management is surprisingly uniform, wherever an intelligent effort has been made in recruitment and placement. There is a general emphasis on the peculiar difficulties which the young educated African faces. In the first place, he can be extremely lonely, posted to an executive job outside his home area, where he may find not a single other African of his own status or education and a small, tightly-knit expatriate group with whom his relations may be at best friendly but uneasy; this will apply as much to the Branch Manager of a firm or Personnel Manager of an isolated plant as to a young District Officer in a remote rural area. His wife may not be educated as he is, and the social pattern of the area may be one in which it is hard for him to fit. This is naturally most acute in East and Central Africa, but similar problems can arise, for example, in Muslim areas of West Africa for educated African Christians.

Secondly, the successful African is often under great pressure from his family, not only for money but for patronage, and here he clashes with the European objections to 'nepotism', although this frequently operates among Europeans on the 'old boy' basis rather than through direct family links. He is also constantly offered bribes, of one kind or another; but in general there is little complaint on this score against the manager in a good firm. Firms find far more of this difficulty in the temptation to bribe small officials in order to get business done, or occasionally to bribe much bigger political figures where large contracts are involved. It is the constant drain from the family which not only subjects the African on a good salary to temptation, but greatly reduces his power to live equally with Europeans on the same rates of pay; for he will not have a half or a quarter of the 'spending money' for drinks and entertainment which his European colleague can afford.

Thirdly, African managers are very apt to be unsettled and impatient. They see friends who have caught the tide of fortune sitting on the Boards of Corporations; becoming Ambassadors to Washington; becoming party bosses with large cars and expense accounts; becoming rich contractors with money to splash about; and they wonder anxiously whether the prospect of a long haul of patient management experience, with perhaps a senior post by the age of forty-five, is the right choice for a graduate of twenty-seven with such a tempting world at his feet. As one experienced European remarked: 'If you promote too fast, you break them; if you promote too slow, you lose them.'

Finally, the depth of educational background and richness of association is a real problem, and one more difficult to solve. Many Africans with degrees have never lived in a world in which, as

Maistriaux said, the daily play of events is teaching him the standards and judgements of people which characterize a Western industrialized society. His father was not a manager or an engineer; he has no uncle in the City. He may well have come from a simple home, a Mission school, through the political (but not industrial) hothouse of an African university, straight into an industrial firm, with somewhat vague ideas of the uses of a cheque book and none at all about 'business practice', European-style, into which he is flung. In direct comparison with a young European graduate, of the same age and qualifications, he runs in blinkers down the path of just that knowledge which he has been taught, where the European, with no more special knowledge (any business in England will tell you how hopelessly 'green' the young English graduate is) none the less has a vague view of the surrounding country which he has absorbed unconsciously in his own society; and it is this view of other possibilities which makes him capable of initiative and constructive innovation, if he has the ability in him.

All these difficulties—the emotional strain of family and social life, loneliness, a narrow background of European (though not of African) life—will be cured by time, by the increase in the numbers of the educated, by the spread of the business economy, by the relaxation of European exclusiveness. As long as they are not attributed to an ineradicable 'African character', they can be intelligently handled in training and management. They underline heavily the advantages of foreign travel and experience which Africans are rightly so anxious to have, and which visibly increase their self-confidence in handling the European world.

Management Training, in the sense of formal courses, is now on the increase in Tropical Africa. There are residential training centres in West Africa operated by private companies;[65] there is a probability of a Nigerian Centre of Management and Administration in Lagos, for which Ford Foundation advice has been given; there is the College of Administration in Achimota (Ghana); there are courses in some universities [66] and technical

[65] In particular, John Holt, The United Africa Company, Shell-B.P. and Barclay's D.C.O.
[66] There is a Mobil Fellow of Business Administration in Legon University, Ghana, doing admirable work, and some courses, arranged jointly with industry in Ibadan, in Salisbury, in Makerere and at the Royal Technical College, Nairobi.

colleges; there is an extremely valuable Selection Unit under the Department of Labour in Kenya; and there are, of course, the many residential centres in Britain maintained by firms who bring back African employees for training, as well as the substantial number of technical and commercial students from Africa in institutions all over Europe and the United States, both on public scholarships and on their own initiative. While it is of overriding importance that a man should be technically master of his job (which will add both to his self-confidence and to his accept-ability), the main value of these more general courses lies in another direction. It will be to narrow the gap between all the unspoken assumptions of a Western industrial society and the emotional and associational equipment of Africans, who have but recently and fleetingly encountered it.

Most assessments of African managers have come from their European employers, and little detailed work has been done on the reaction of Africans themselves to their job in an expatriate firm. It is useless to rely on impressions gained by fleeting contacts, however vivid they may seem. I am therefore extremely grateful to Dr. C. Kumalo of Makerere College, who, as a trained sociolo-gist, designed and carried out for this Study a small piece of research, by questionnaire and interview, with twenty-seven African managers employed by a variety of firms in and around Kampala, Uganda.[67] The full analysis of results may be published later; only a few outstanding points are mentioned here.

On the whole, the African comments on the management of their firms was reassuring. Most seemed to have found the training given reasonably suitable; to feel that they were reasonably in-formed about policy at their level, normally consulted when issues affecting their work arose, given adequate responsibility, with reasonable prospects of promotion and fairly assessed. Asked to rank the possibilities of promotion as between government (Civil Service), government enterprise (such as the Development Cor-

[67] The sample included Personnel Manager, accountants, administrative assistants, sales service supervisors, Public Relations assistants, Supervisors of Stores and similar posts. All had at least 12 years of education and 12 had a university education; 8 had some post-secondary education, though not in a university, and 7 had nothing after school. The majority (18) had been 3 or more years with their present employer (the longest, 8 years); all but 8 had had some previous employment, in most cases three or more previous jobs; 14 were under 30 years of age, 8 were between 30 and 39 and 5 were 40 or over.

poration) and large or small private enterprise, the entire sample of twenty-seven put government first (eighteen first choices for Civil Service and nine for government enterprise) with large private enterprise as an almost unanimous third choice.

With regard to their standing in the firm, most of these managers felt that they were as well or better equipped by education and training (not experience) compared with their Asian and European colleagues at the same job-level—fifteen thought that they were better or much better equipped than Asians and sixteen said the same about Europeans. But over half thought that they owed their job in the firm to political expediency, or to a European belief that African managers would be able to mediate Company policy to other Africans (workers or consumers) better than Europeans.

Informal relations with Europeans were described by eleven managers as 'cordial and genuine', eleven as 'cordial and patronizing', five as 'indifferent'; but relations with Asians were mainly felt to be either 'genuine' (eight) or 'indifferent' (fourteen). To the questions 'Who would you rather have—(a) as a colleague, (b) as an immediate superior', twenty-one put an African as first choice as colleague and six a European, and fourteen chose an African for immediate superior against thirteen who chose a European. Only three gave even second choice to an Asian in either position. In view of the important rôle which Asian technicians and engineers play in East Africa, this is a gloomy result, though it is possibly influenced by the ill-feeling aroused by the Asian boycott, which has not spread to Kenya or Tanganyika.

There are, of course, severe limitations to opinion surveys of this kind. But this inquiry, carried out by a South African from the independent standing of a university, should have as great a validity as the method and the limited sample allows.

The prospects for both increased numbers and higher quality of African management in both East and West Africa (it is too soon to speak of the Rhodesias) are unquestionably good, if they are considered solely in terms of continued training by experienced and sympathetic expatriate firms. But little has been said of the world in which the job will be done. A great deal depends first on the willingness and secondly on the ability of the leadership of the independent African societies to establish a standard of administrative and industrial probity in which alone any real degree of efficiency can be achieved. Thoroughly corrupt societies exist and can continue to exist, after a certain fashion; it has even been remarked that corruption has been one substantial method of capital accumulation in poor societies. But such societies are self-limiting, not only in the industrial but in the political field. For the intrigue and uncertainty which are bound to accompany secret dealings, wherever they originate, creep as surely into politics as into industry, and politics are bound to be even more closely tied to industry in Africa than they are in the West. In both cases, the results are delay, high costs and the inability to make long-term investment, the freezing of both an economy and a society half-way along the road. It is both too easy and too soon to say that this mediocrity is bound to fall on Africa as it has on other countries where corruption is rife. Because, as is so often stated, corruption was endemic in the petty trading economies of the West, or the extended family system involved selection by kinship rather than merit, it does not follow that these characteristics of the old society need be carried forward into the very different circumstances of the new. Only African leadership can resolve this doubt; and if it is to be resolved at all, it will have to be tackled in the political as well as the commercial field. If there is one danger of the single-party system, for all its obvious attractions to the new African leaders, it is that here if anywhere, by the overwhelming testimony of history in every age and country, is the breeding place of corrupt influences which can spread poison through the whole bloodstream of society.

XVa. Literacy class, Nigeria

XVb. Without comment

XVIa. Turkana women in Northern Kenya with voting cards in the cleft stick traditionally used for carrying important messages

XVIb. Legislative Assembly building, Bamako, Mali

[*Photograph by R. J. Harrison Chu*

CHAPTER X

EDUCATION AND MANPOWER

The new African nations are determined to create a modern type of government and economy without delay. Much therefore depends on how greatly they are handicapped, and in what respects, by their present levels of Western education. It is important to separate the requirements for running a modern society from the claim for independence. Africans have often and rightly pointed out that most European nations achieved sovereignty long before they had general education. Indeed, a map of Europe as late as 1800 would not have shown in any single country the level of primary schooling which exists in Southern Nigeria or Ghana today; in England the Industrial Revolution had been largely achieved before the great growth of State schools in the early 1870s. The issue is not the ability of Africans to govern themselves in the old ways, but to create a modern State; not merely to take part in it, but to direct it. The parallel with nineteenth century Europe must be used with caution; for despite the widespread illiteracy, there was a ruling group and a 'middle class' in Europe with long traditions of political and administrative experience; there had been universities for many centuries, and there were a host of institutions in the community—the Bar, the systems of county administration, the Churches, the merchant houses and many more—which gave a basis for growth.

The demands of a modern system can be very roughly divided into the technological, the commercial and the administrative. The requirements of technology admit of no argument; an electric power station must have an electrical engineer. Certainly, much can be achieved by fairly simple techniques—wooden bridges, laterite roads, one-storey buildings will serve many of Africa's present purposes. The Western assumption that everything must be done by the very latest technology reflects an economic system and a level of wages where mechanization pays. But this assumption is false in the present circumstances of Africa; China has already adopted a different solution for her society which is rich in manpower but short both of capital and of technical education.

Nevertheless, over a wide field there is no substitute for technical training.

On the administrative side very simple systems will work provided that the government is not attempting to plan and direct the economy. But this is just the task which African governments are setting for themselves. The civil servant who is authorizing expenditure of some millions of pounds on an agricultural settlement scheme or a new harbour must be able to marshal a great number of figures and arguments, and he must have below him a system for collecting and collating the necessary information, both in his own office and in the field. Much could go wrong with African economic progress if those who direct it are not well equipped both to get the facts and to use them selectively. In the middle levels of society the administrative and commercial blend a good deal; the handling of local government contracts and public utilities, and even the running of a Co-operative Union, does need a knowledge of how to draw up or read a specification; how to budget for next year; to distinguish between capital and recurrent expenditure; to allow for depreciation and maintenance. Further, a modern system of industry and commerce rests more than might be supposed on certain quite simple technical services —for example, a telephone system which works efficiently.

Thus it is useless to suppose that the type of society which African governments wish to create can be run without a small group of highly qualified men at the top and a very substantial middle sector capable of keeping administrative and commercial life going. But we should be cautious, particularly in the administrative field, of judging by Western standards. 'Administrative experience', in the mind of a European civil servant, is in part a knowledge of how the European system works—what the public will accept, what colleagues must be consulted, what experts are available, what happened on the last occasion, how to handle the Minister. In a transitional period, where Europeans are training Africans, they naturally train to their own conventions and standards and are apt to see many shortcomings. But as an African administration feels its feet, there may well be—no doubt there are already—different conventions just as valid and perhaps more easily established. Knowing the ropes is not the whole art of administration—certain very definite qualities of character and intellect are needed as well; but it is an important part which

Africans will quickly master in their own style. As to the arts of the politician, Africans have long practised them. In short, experience and practical wisdom are words too big to measure by educational qualifications (as the best of British Trade Union leadership has shown) and this thought must qualify the use of formal categories of education in this chapter.

One further caution is needed. The quality and success of a society does not depend only on the technical and administrative skill with which it is run. It depends on that wider definition of education which includes not merely competence but character in the widest sense. Education itself will be judged by the opportunities it gives for the growth and variety of personal qualities and by the standards it sets for community life. Much of the early part of this chapter must treat education as though it were merely vocational training; but the wider issues cannot ultimately be shirked.

I. THE GROWTH OF EDUCATION

Once again, it was only in 1900 that Europeans began to make really extensive contact with the main populations of the interior. In consequence, Africa remains, despite the devotion of the missionaries and the more recent energy of governments, the most backward in overall averages of education of any major area of the world. The maps, reproduced by courtesy of UNESCO[1], on pages 240 and 241, show that in primary education Tropical Africa in 1957–8 compared reasonably, though not well, with the selected Latin American and South-East Asian countries; but in secondary education only Ghana and Lagos achieve their level of over 10 per cent. out of the population of secondary age.

The way in which education grew has some importance for our purpose. Starting almost wholly through Christian missionaries (save in areas dominated by Islam), the schools were well scattered in the bush; often their original site was chosen because a local chief was friendly. Naturally, their first aim was to teach reading and writing and to train catechists who could help to spread the

[1] Maps 1 and 2 are reproduced from the working paper prepared for UNESCO for the Conference of African States on the Development of Education in Africa, Addis Ababa, 1961. The Figures are based on Table 1 of the working papers and the appropriate footnotes from Table 1 are transferred on to the Figures. The Figures portray the situation in 1957–8 for the majority of countries.

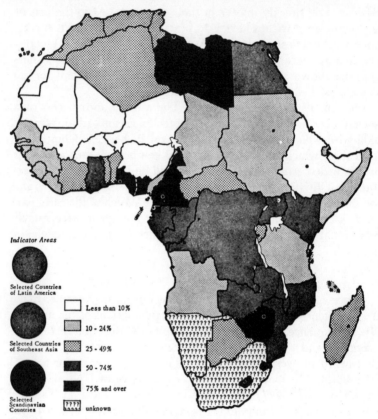

Indicator Areas

Selected Countries
of Latin America

Selected Countries
of Southeast Asia

Selected
Scandinavian
Countries

Less than 10%

10 - 24%

25 - 49%

50 - 74%

75% and over

unknown

Source:

Statistics taken by the Unesco Statistical Division from official publications and
replies to questionnaires.

MAP 1

Ratio of primary-school enrolment to the school-age population
5–14 years old, adjusted for the duration of primary school,
latest year available.

Notes:

1. The figure for South West Africa is the latest official estimate 1956, and
   includes secondary education.
2. Figures for the Union of South Africa include general secondary education.
3. Figures for Southern Rhodesia include African education only.
4. Figures for Rwanda-Burundi include public and aided schools only.
5. Figures for former British Somaliland include public schools only.
6. The majority of the figures cover the years 1957/8.

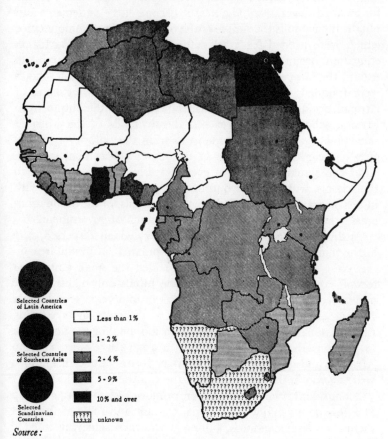

Selected Countries of Latin America

Selected Countries of Southeast Asia

Selected Scandinavian Countries

	Less than 1%
	1 - 2 %
	2 - 4 %
	5 - 9 %
	10 % and over
????	unknown

Source:

Statistics taken by the Unesco Statistical Division from official publications and replies to questionnaires.

MAP 2

Ratio of secondary-school enrolment to the school-age population 15–19 years old, adjusted for the duration of secondary school, latest year available.

Notes:

1. Figures for Niger for 1956/7
2. Notes 2 to 6 inclusive to Map 1 also apply.

Gospel. Some Mission stations, partly because they were a refuge for escaped slaves or tribal outcasts, became large settlements and taught their pupils the simple crafts of building and maintenance which were needed for a self-sufficient community. As Mission education began to flourish, the main target was naturally to extend the Gospel teaching, and so more and more bush schools were founded, while at the central stations a growing band of African priests and teachers was trained. When the output from Mission schools began to exceed the demands of the Missions themselves, governments came in to train the boys—very rarely girls—as clerks and artisans in the many government services. Thus the system grew, with ever-increasing government aid to the schools, with a major output of Christian teachers, and with in-service training and later some trade schools for the occupations outside teaching, mainly within some branch of government.

At this stage primary schooling was very widely dispersed, save in the mainly Muslim and sparsely populated savannah areas in the West where Koranic schools provided the small amount of formal education. But it touched the pupils only lightly; huge numbers drifted away after two or three or four years, semi-literate at best, and there was still widespread difficulty in persuading African parents to send their children to school or to allow them to stay on. In Southern Rhodesia in 1956 there were 112,000 African children in the lowest primary form, 34,000 in the fifth year, 13,700 in the sixth, 6,045 in the eighth.[2]

Alongside this large but uneven primary system there grew up at a few points major educational centres, and some of these set themselves high standards, aiming at and then achieving entry to a metropolitan university for their best students. Fourah Bay in Sierra Leone, Achimota in Ghana, Katsina in Nigeria—these became household names; and Central and East Africa were to have their peaks—the great Mission centres of Southern Rhodesia; Munali at Lusaka; Makerere and Budo in Uganda; the Alliance High School in Nairobi. These centres set a standard of excellence which brought Africans for the first time to the doorway of the international society of educated men.

The second stage—and this sequence was repeated in every country—corresponds to a sudden and widespread change of attitude among the African peoples. Suddenly, education became

[2] Southern Rhodesia Government education statistics.

prestige, became the key to a job, the heart-felt ambition. Children began to flood to the schools. The schools were inadequate, the teachers far too few; an immense and costly programme of more building and more teacher training, for the primary level, was forced upon governments. This was almost an emergency; and on top of it, in recent years, have been piled the political decisions of some countries to have universal primary education.

At the moment when this wave of extra children hit the schools, there were still few secondary schools in proportion to the first intake at primary level. This situation was at first masked by the enormous wastage rate during the primary course. But not only did more children now enter : they began to come earlier, to stay longer, to clamour for places in the higher primary or middle schools, and then to demand secondary education. This emergency, falling upon a system which already had a broad base and very narrow apex, and forcing it to broaden the base still further, has caused a critical shortage of secondary education throughout the area. Nor is it easy to expand. For full secondary teaching demands graduates or near-graduates, of which in any country there were few among Africans, and in East and Central Africa virtually none. A swift expansion of the numbers of secondary teachers, with the buildings and equipment they would need, became and still is the overwhelming task in African education, and one impossible to achieve very fast. Certainly, Great Britain, faced ever since the last war with bitter complaints from teachers and parents at the size of classes and the shortage of teachers at home, was in no position to help on a really major scale in Africa; nor was it easy to create African universities or higher colleges for training any faster because of the very weakness in secondary education and the increasing calls of African governments and the new industries for the products of even the existing schools.

One result of this situation has been to create, in all territories, the problem of the primary school-leaver—the boys with eight years of mainly literary education, too young for adult work, unable to find a secondary school place, unwilling to revert to a peasant life, endlessly filling application forms for clerical work, a socially and politically inflammable group of dissatisfied young people. It is a desperate race against time and primary education to find ways of absorbing this group into the rural economy, apart from the small number that industry and commerce, on their present scale in Africa, can employ and train. In relation to this problem the lag in education for girls, although of immense social importance, is less pressing.

There was a difference of emphasis in both French and Belgian practice. In the Belgian Congo, the same, and even more remarkable, expansion of primary education (70 per cent. or more) was achieved, and there was the same training of a small *élite* in the Missions. The main effort was to train a large number of Congolese in artisan and clerical work, so that they could take a useful place in a growing commercial and industrial civilization. In this the Belgians were, by general agreement, outstandingly successful. The *élite* were trained almost exclusively for the Church, for teaching and for the junior agricultural and medical services of government. None were sent to Belgium until the very last moment of Belgian rule, but the establishment of two universities in the Congo since 1956 was a significant step towards a new policy. A fairly rapid expansion of secondary education between 1955 and 1960 was just starting to produce a small flow of Africans capable of manning the middle levels of the Civil Service. The distinguishing features of the Congo situation were two— the high level of artisan and clerical training and employment, and the absence of an educated *élite* save in the Church, teaching and some junior technical services.

France, on the other hand, wished to create an educated group of Africans deeply touched by French culture, and in a great measure succeeded. Standards of the *Lycées*, high in France, were high in Africa too; and comparatively large numbers of Africans from the main towns went to France, and for long periods. In Dakar or Abidjan or Brazzaville no one could fail to remark on the high level of African sophistication. Mass literacy, however, was never an object of French policy. As Lord Hailey [3] remarks : 'They have never failed to be mindful of what Renan described as the crime of creating a volume of popular instruction without a serious supply of higher education'. Moreover, France was faced with great difficulties in the Muslim savannah areas. The Figure on page 240 shows clearly enough the great sweep of territory, from Dakar round to Brazzaville, in which primary enrolment does not reach 10 per cent. In consequence, it is not necessary to

[3] Hailey, op. cit.

travel many miles from the main cities even in Senegal before the basic illiteracy begins to show.[4]

There is thus a rough gradation—French areas with a highly polished top layer, comparable only to the older educated families of Freetown, Accra and Lagos, but a low level of general literacy; British areas with much higher primary education but less sparkle at the top; the Belgian Congo, considering its immense extent, remarkably well developed at the base and lower-middle layers but almost wholly lacking at the top.

There is little need to emphasize the different dates of growth—today there are thousands of graduate Africans in Ghana, just over thirty in Nyasaland, perhaps 130 in Tanganyika. Unfortunately, politics do not wait upon education and the late starters are just as determined on self-government, graduates or no. Yet these vast differences in human equipment are bound to create a special problem of their own. Tables VIII and IX (opposite) give some key figures for the countries mainly covered by this book, and reveal again the points of weakness—secondary and technical education. One vital stage of education barely exists—the stage between the level of School Certificate and the entrance to university. The number of African VIth Forms in the whole of Nyasaland, Northern and Southern Rhodesia and the three East African territories put together did not reach ten in 1960.

Before looking at the implications of these figures in terms of trained manpower, a word must be said on the quality and the policy of African education. It has been fiercely criticized, especially by Europeans,[5] as too academic, and too closely modelled on the metropolitan systems of England or France. For the past, this criticism is a little unreal. Without simple literacy, there can be no teachers; without teachers there could have been no education. The first generation of literates in any country will go to literate jobs; the early schools in England produced clerks for the counting house, not shepherds or coal-miners. Even if the missionaries had been trained both in education and as technical instructors for the conditions of African agriculture (mostly, they were not; nor were the conditions fully understood), how could their pupils have

[4] 23 per cent. of primary-school age population enrolled (UNESCO).

[5] But also more recently by Africans. Mr. Tai Solarin, founder of a notable Nigerian school, is one of the most lively and outspoken critics—see his booklet *Towards Nigeria's Moral Self-Government* (privately published, Ibadan University Press, 1959).

changed the agricultural practices of tribes who long resisted the power and persuasion of governments to change their ways? That the detail was too English or French cannot be denied—English botany, the wives of Henry VIII, Napoleon's Marshals had little relevance to Africa. Yet perhaps this very fact brought Africa more quickly towards her destiny of sharing in the civilization of the outer world. If the gradualists and the functionalists had had their way, we might have found an Africa yet more balkanized into a hundred languages, separated from the European centres of learning, practising a slightly improved version of their own culture and technology, a far more alien continent in a modern world whose influences were bound to break in more and more insistently. Nor is literary education to be despised : it is the entry to the heritage of political and religious experience of mankind. If today the *Ashanti Pioneer* [6] can speak and think of freedom, it is perhaps partly because Wilkes and Cobbett and George Fox live in the minds of its editors, because Francis Place, the Chartists, Tom Paine and even Rousseau are not unknown names but living symbols of what courageous men have done; and symbols of a particular relevance which African tradition could not supply. Buddha or Confucius, the Samurai or Dr. Sun Yat Sen might have served Africa's purpose as well; but some point of entry, from East or West, was needed, and it was not to be found through carpentry or contour ploughing.

For better or worse, this is past history. Certainly, on the credit side, this education gave entry to Africans, not in special segregated classes but on mixed and equal terms, to the universities of the West, to its great institutions and to its literature. In some sense the standards of the Inns of Court, or of the Sorbonne, or of the great teaching hospitals are alive in Africa, as are the words of Shakespeare and the New Testament. But clearly today there is need for review. Access to the world of learning, in science as well as in the arts, is long established; there is an easy come and go. Now indeed there is time and necessity for greater selectivity, for

[6] Above the door of the Aburi Press in Kumasi, where the *Ashanti Pioneer* is published, appears the following inscription : 'Cross-roads of civilization; refuge of all the arts against the ravages of time; armoury of fearless truth against whispering rumour; incessant trumpet of trade; from this house words may fly abroad—not to perish as waves of sound but fixed in time; not corrupted by the hurrying hand but fortified in proof. Friend, on entering this house you stand on sacred ground : THIS IS A PRINTING HOUSE.'

an education better suited to agricultural countries and to the social tasks of Africa. Moreover, now it is more possible to define the type of economy, the needful distribution of manpower, the special tasks and weak points in each country. Suddenly, within the last five years, education is becoming directional—part of a social policy for growing countries—and manpower surveys and commissions are the order of the day. Perhaps within ten years voices will be raised to push the pendulum back, and to remind the planners that education is something more than a huge manpower factory turning out the estimated needs of pharmacists and radio engineers.

2. MANPOWER AND TRAINING FOR THE PUBLIC SERVICE

It is the natural ambition of African governments to Africanize the principal cadres of three main sectors—the Civil Service, the professions and industry. Of these three, the Civil Service has the highest priority, and the professions the lowest. If expatriate lawyers, doctors or architects can make a living in Africa, without cost to the government, they are in general welcome, since they release Africans with similar training for government work and they give a service which is neither a monopoly nor politically dangerous. A supply of expatriate school and university teachers is equally welcome, provided that at certain key points there is African surveillance. Something more will have to be said of university life in Africa, because dangerous social and political issues are involved. Nationalist governments are determined both that universities should conform to higher manpower policy and that they should not become enclaves of political criticism, the more dangerous for the intellectual ability of the critics and their easy access to public opinion in the international world. In industry the desire for African control is rather higher, both for prestige reasons and because of the possible danger of having too many of the commanding heights of the economy in expatriate hands. However, even industry can to some degree be controlled by the Civil Service, and some of it can be guided or forced into co-operative or other forms which make African access and control easier. Thus, politically, the key point lies in the Civil Service.

The Civil Service can be divided for this purpose into four main sectors—the top administrative posts in central government; the

Provincial Administration; the technical services; and the middle and lower ranks. As to the last, there is little urgency. It will in any case fill up most easily, and if expatriates are prepared to serve in subordinate positions for a time, there is a saving in African manpower. The same is partly true of the technical services, such as agriculture, civil engineering and the government medical services. It is in the administration, central and provincial, that the real urgency is felt by Africans. They have been well aware of the power wielded by a Permanent Secretary in a key post. In the Provincial Administration, the long record of European Provincial and District Commissioners has been characterized in two ways— by their evident power (to most Africans they were 'government'), and by their continual pressure on local people to change their ways. They were also, at certain periods, the chief agents for controlling the local party leaders who were conducting the anti-colonial 'cold war'. It is clear that an African government will have many reasons for wanting to have Africans at District level. How these will fit into a new African political administration of the Districts and Provinces is another matter.[7]

The three types of appointment which Africans would therefore most wish to fill are the top Civil Service posts, the District Administration and certain controlling points in major industrial and commercial life—the Marketing Boards, Central Banks, major development projects. These are, of course, just the posts most difficult to fill, since at the centre experience is the chief qualification and in the Districts there is a burden of direct personal responsibility for a great range of decisions made in close contact with the people, which it is very difficult for a young African graduate to face; for in his home area there are too many relatives; elsewhere, people, customs and even language are strange.[8]

There are difficulties in showing the comparative degree of Africanization of the public service[9] as between different countries, partly because of different nomenclature and partly because different countries divide their statistics in different ways. But Table X (opposite) gives a rough picture of the position in 1960-1. There are really three groups among the countries

[7] See Chapter XI.

[8] A Muganda Officer in one of the outer provinces of Uganda is virtually expatriate—food, language, custom are all strange.

[9] See also K. Younger, *The Public Service in New States* (London, Oxford University Press, 1960).

covered in this book. Northern Rhodesia has just begun the
Africanization of senior staff. Figures in July 1961 showed four
Africans in Division I, eighteen in Division II (including twelve
District Assistants), ten Assistant Inspectors of Police (Grade I),
and thirty-one Masters in the Unified African Teaching Service.
(Nyasaland, with a total of thirty-three African graduates in the
country and the possibility of about 120 by 1970, is even worse
placed.) The Belgian Congo in January 1960 had two Africans
in senior posts (M. Bolikango and M. Sita) and about 600 in
'Category 4', including a large number of agricultural and medical
technicians. A special problem in the Congo will be to find French-
speaking administrators if the objection to the return of experienced and often devoted Belgians is maintained. The second group,
where much more headway has been made, with from 16 to 25
per cent of Africans in senior posts, includes all East Africa, with
Uganda in the lead, and Northern Nigeria. Finally, Ghana,
Western Nigeria and Eastern Nigeria are within sight of full
Africanization, with only a few senior and professional posts to
fill. The Western Nigerian Government replaced all expatriate
Permanent Secretaries and heads of professional divisions with
Nigerians at Independence (1 October 1960), and there are few
white faces to be seen in the new government buildings in Ibadan;
although Eastern Nigeria has also moved fast, it has been with
much greater difficulty—only the Chief Secretary and two Permanent Secretaries were Africans in January 1960, though there
were ten Africans of Permanent Secretary rank by October of
that year, and there are still a number of senior expatriates in all
Ministries in 1961. Moreover, numbers are not everything. The
author of the Ford Foundation Report to the Eastern Nigerian
Government [10] remarked in April 1960 :

The administration is not only young; it is quite inexperienced in
Government. The average member of the Administrative Class
(again I am using the median) entered the Public Service in the
summer of 1956—roughly three and a half years ago. Only thirteen
officers in the entire Administration have been in Government as long
as ten years.

The median age of the Administrative Class was then thirty-

[10] J. D. Kingsley, *Staff Development in the Eastern Region*, April 1960 (by
courtesy of the Eastern Nigerian Government).

three and of Permanent Secretaries and Principal Assistant Secretaries, largely expatriate, only thirty-eight.

In the intermediate group, Northern Nigeria is an interesting example. With many men of high ability and education in the top ranks, it is far thinner further down, as the figures in columns 2 and 3 in Table X show. This is mainly due to the backwardness of primary education in the past,[11] now being energetically tackled. The Northern Nigerian Government is not publishing more recent figures, which would no doubt show an increase in Northern appointments. It is also faced by the need to contribute to the Federal Civil Service in Lagos. In the remaining East African countries of this group, Asians at present play as large a part as Africans, and they have been especially useful at the executive and technical levels. Their percentage is bound to drop fairly steeply in a few years, not through discrimination but because they are so heavily outnumbered by Africans, of whom there will quickly be the same or greater numbers (though not the same proportion) in the higher educational levels.

The staffing of the Provincial Administration, virtually complete in the advanced group of countries, and moving rapidly in Northern Nigeria,[12] is proving more difficult in East Africa. Tanganyika, which will be independent on 9 December 1961, has made great efforts; 119 out of 396 Administrative Officers [13] were African in July 1961, and of these eleven had already been posted as District Commissioners and seven more were 'Designate'—i.e. taking over a District. The aim is to have at least half of the fifty-eight Districts in the hands of African District Commissioners by the end of 1961. Uganda, with twenty-four Administrative Officers and cadets and nineteen Assistant Administrative Officers, is beginning to move ahead; and Kenya, despite the special tensions there, has also much accelerated its progress. Here again, numbers can be deceptive. These young officers have been serving under experienced expatriate officers of the colonial government; an entirely different weight will fall upon them, probably in a new system of administration, as the number of expatriates dwindles

[11] The original agreement with the Emirs excluded Christian Missions.

[12] Two of the Residents were African by February 1961, and a fairly high proportion of the more junior staff.

[13] The titles 'District Officer' and 'Assistant District Officer' have been dropped and both are combined in 'Administrative Officer' (Grade III and IV).

and as local government is reshaped by an African government in the future.[14]

There is, however, a slightly more junior group of staff in all the East African countries in which, over the years since the last war, really solid progress has been made in training Africans. This is in the training of extension staff for agricultural and medical services (as well as teaching), for the police, for co-operative officers, for local government officials. An attempt to calculate total numbers of such men in Kenya (January 1959) resulted in an estimate of 15,000 Africans [15] with a small proportion of Asians) in the field who had completed primary education and undergone a further two years' vocational training, and about 2,000 who had completed School Certificate and a further period of two years or more of training. There were then, for example, in addition to teachers, 1,680 junior medical staff in the field and 500 under training; 216 medical staff with School Certificate and 138 under training. On the agricultural side there were about 700 Agricultural Instructors and Assistants in the field and 164 under training, and twenty-six African Assistant Agricultural Officers with Makerere diplomas.[16] In addition to these there is the considerable number of junior officers trained at the Jeanes School in Kenya and Nsamizi College, Uganda, and the output of Departmental Training schemes, covering (in addition to Agriculture, Medical Services and Police) Public Works, Community Development, Co-operation, Survey, Forestry, Game, Housing and Town Planning, Water and other services. A similar effort is being made in Northern Rhodesia, both departmentally, at Chalimbana College (primarily local government officers and chiefs) and in a number of special training colleges. Once outside the capital cities of East Africa, or Lusaka and the Copperbelt, the impression of countries run by Europeans is very much changed. Although Southern Rhodesia is not here discussed in detail, the training of junior African agricultural staff (over 1,000 Demonstrators and 120 Superintendent Demonstrators in the field in 1959 after a four-year course at three different colleges) and to a lesser extent

[14] Some discussion of the future of local government will be found in Chapter XI.

[15] This includes teachers.

[16] G. and L. Hunter, *Adult Education in the Federation of Rhodesia and Nyasaland and Kenya, 1959* (Report to the Beit and Dulverton Trusts).

medical staff, must be recorded; it is the brightest spot in the whole training provision for Africans in that country.[17]

Before attempting to assess the effect of this shortage of trained manpower, some estimate of future supply may be helpful. Tables VIII and IX (facing page 244) attempt some comparisons of the output of the educational systems at secondary level and in higher education respectively. There is no need to labour the differences between the advanced countries of West Africa and the state of affairs in East and Central Africa. If Nyasaland had to rely solely on the output of VIth Forms in the country, the number of graduates resulting were calculated as :[18]

1966	4	1969	8
1967	5	1970	11
1968	6	1971	12

These figures would have to be multiplied by about twenty-five to reach the expected output from local universities for Kenya or Uganda.[19] Northern Nigeria is in roughly the same position as East Africa, with an expectation of about 100 graduates a year up to 1965.

It is of interest to compare the table for secondary with that for higher education since it shows up the great gap between total secondary and VIth Form enrolments. If only a better proportion of those entering secondary education reached School Certificate standard, and more of those at School Certificate level went on to VIth Forms, the possible supply of graduates would be vastly increased. The school system for about the first ten years of education is big enough for this particular purpose; it is from year ten to year fourteen that the weakness lies. This leads to the weakness in the supply of secondary-school teachers. East and Central Africa, with still a small load, have managed to keep qualifications high—for government secondary schools in Kenya, Uganda, Tanganyika and Northern Rhodesia the figures for trained

[17] G. and L. Hunter, op. cit.
[18] *Report of the Localization Committee, Nyasaland Protectorate, 1960* (The Adu Committee).
[19] As Kenya and Uganda have each about three times the Nyasaland population, the ratio is about one to eight in proportion to population. But the size of a government service does not rise proportionately to population, so that even this is not very comforting.

teachers are 100, 88, 100 and 100 per cent. respectively. But with
the vast expansion of education in Nigeria, some alarming
figures appear. The Ashby Commission found that out of 4,378
secondary teachers on the rolls in 1958, 3,470 were not graduates
and 1,082 were not certificated. Figures for trained teachers in
Ghana grammar schools were running at about 30 per cent. in
1960.[20] It is for this reason that all over the tropical area the need
at present is not so much for more places in overseas universities
but for *more expatriate secondary teachers.* It is useless to offer
more university places to countries where every student who can
reach the necessary standard is already assured of a university
place, and this is roughly true of the whole of East and Central
Africa and Northern Nigeria. In Nigeria as a whole, the Ashby
Commission recommended the import of 6,500 expatriate secondary 'teacher-years' between 1962 and 1968 at a cost of about £16
million.

This is not to underestimate the importance of overseas
graduate training. In East and Central Africa it is at present
rather more important than local output, and this will continue
to be true if secondary education goes on expanding faster than
local university provision. Asians here make a very important
contribution.[21] It must be emphasized that the figures of overseas
students, particularly in West Africa, cover only those known to
be abroad on scholarship. Any statistics of total numbers abroad,
in all countries and on private funds, are either unobtainable or
worthless. While there are, for example, just over 1,000 Nigerian
scholarship students in the United Kingdom in 1961, the Nigerian
High Commission estimate that there are from 14,000 to 15,000
Nigerians currently studying here. There are thought to be well
over 2,000 Ghanaians in the United Kingdom, although the
official scholarship list shows only 1,315 in this country.

A full study of the situation in French-speaking territories would
demand a separate book. But it is of interest to note the levels of

[20] C.T.E. (See Table VIII).
[21] It is interesting how well, in Tanganyika for example, African and Asian
overseas students are balanced by subject; out of 514 Asians, 335 were studying engineering, accounts or medicine, nursing and pharmacy, while out of
the 465 Africans, 248 were studying arts and social science, agriculture and
veterinary, education and science; only in medicine were the figures high in
both cases. Tanganyika Government, *List of Students Studying Outside the
Territory, 1960–1.*

enrolment in the University of Dakar, 1960–1, from French-speaking Africa :

Enrolment of Students—Université de Dakar, 1960–1 [22]

France							431
Mauritanie							17
Haute-Volta							33
Sénégal							434
Niger							16
Côte d'Ivoire							6
Soudan							89
Dahomey							211
Autres Pays d'Outre-mer							18
Étrangers y compris Guinée, Togo, Cameroun							143

Totale générale   1,398

Note 1: The low number from Côte d'Ivoire is due to the establishment of the Centre d'Études Supérieures in Abidjan. In 1958–9 181 Côte d'Ivoiriens were enrolled at Dakar.

Note 2: There were also 1,696 'auditeurs' in the various University Institutes of the University of Dakar.

These figures, to which must be added the considerable number of African students on higher courses in France,[23] must be read against a background of about 23 per cent. literacy in, for example, Senegal, and probably not much over 10 per cent. in the savannah countries. The Centre d'Études Supérieures in Brazzaville is just reaching university level, and the similar Centre in Abidjan (Côte d'Ivoire) began degree courses in 1960. The tendency to fill the highest posts with Africans before the intermediate grades are Africanized will be marked in French-speaking territories, and perhaps a lesser cause of difficulty because Frenchmen have always moved more easily among Africans and are prepared to accept intermediate positions more readily.

In summary, it is clear that in the advanced West African countries, Africanization of the Civil Service is not a question of numbers but of quality and training. If the Ashby proposals in Nigeria and the plans of Ghana are fulfilled, these two countries

[22] University of Dakar Statistics.
[23] Some figures for Senegal are given in Table X.

will be equipped with qualified African manpower by 1965 for most of their main purposes and for all by 1970. By contrast, it is clear that the intermediate group in East Africa cannot hope to find from their own nationals more than about 1,000 African graduates each by 1965, counting both home and overseas university places, a figure which is tied down by the number and quality of secondary schools. Nor could an expansion on the Ashby scale, even if it could be financed, make much difference by that time. Since Tanganyika already has internal self-government, and the other two territories may achieve it in 1962, they are bound to rely on expatriates (some possibly African) for several years to fill more than half of the 4,000 or more senior posts involved in each country. This is true even if every graduate African went into public service (which they will not) and without allowance for graduate teachers. The situation in Central Africa is, of course, far less advanced. What are the implications of this situation and what can be done in the immediate future to meet it?

Clearly, direct training for administration can be increased, and plans are laid in all three East African territories to do this. The College at Nsamizi (Uganda) is already being expanded fast; there are plans for a College of Administration in Kenya;[24] and in Tanganyika Mzumbe Training Centre will be training about fifty Assistant District Officers per year (six-month course) or possibly even more. A comparable task of high quality is being carried out by the Institute of Administration in Zaria, Northern Nigeria. All the departmental training schemes can be increased, new colleges and centres can be established. But however much money and effort is spent, the critical issue remains the output of secondary schools. There is no way of turning primary schoolboys into graduates, or even near-graduates, in five years. What the training schools can do is a very marked up-grading of experienced ex-primary Africans for the middle ranks. I believe that the insistence on high educational qualifications for some administrative work must be modified. A three-year agricultural course given to a boy of fifteen with eight years of primary education behind him will produce an invaluable citizen who can have immense influence on the economy and even the administration of his country after a few years of practical experience in his post; and this goes for a large range of work which does not require a de-

[24] Not final at the time of writing.

veloped scientific training. It is illogical to complain of lack of experience in one context and to fail to use it to the very fullest degree in another.

As to the higher posts, there is some possibility of accelerated promotion; to take one example, the Uganda Government is considering a compensation scheme for expatriate civil servants for loss of promotion prospects, under a system where almost all promotions would be given to Africans with any reasonable quali-fication, even if on experience and merit the post should have gone to an expatriate. In any case, intensive in-service training, and the creation of supernumerary posts alongside Europeans, are to be used as they have been in West Africa. Some carefully controlled relaxation of academic qualifications for the senior service will also no doubt take place, as the Adu Committee advised for Nyasaland.

Nevertheless, nothing which can be done with even a show of reason can alter the dependence of East and Central Africa and Northern Nigeria on expatriate civil servants, whoever they may be, for some years to come, as to well over half the present service up to 1965 and perhaps a quarter for some time longer. The very first implication is that a relaxation of European/African tension in Kenya is now desperately urgent; and that the sense of injustice felt by the Colonial Civil Service in East Africa, which had reached a bitter intensity in 1960-1, must be removed. The alter-native, which would be recruitment of new expatriate officers from non-British sources, could virtually destroy morale and effici-ency, not because Americans or Russians are inefficient but be-cause a public service relies on local experience and above all on the morale of the service as a whole.

Even if East Africa can slowly conquer the problem of numbers and initial training, the problem of experience remains, as it does in the West. Young and inexperienced officers, with enthusiasm, can do wonders if they are led by wise and devoted seniors; with-out this backbone, the outlook would be bleak indeed. The present practical outlook is that the upper ranges of the service, African or European, East or West, will be heavily overburdened. There has been a desperate difficulty in East Nigeria in developing an executive grade which is of any use to the administrative officers —they have to do the real work themselves. In East Africa, expatriates, if they are willing to stay, will have a gigantic task of training young African officers.

As a temporary measure, if politics and prejudices do not weigh too heavily, it might be that in East Africa, when African majority government becomes a fact, the wish of an African Minister to have at least one senior African by his side could be met, for example in Kenya, by using a dozen of the most experienced and able Africans at the level of Permanent Secretary. Alongside and immediately below there must be a considerable layer of experienced expatriate staff; and below that a swelling army of secondary-educated junior African staff in every service, including the graduate cadets, who must win their way to higher posts by merit and performance. There are probably also many men now between thirty-five and forty-five years of age who have served their Departments well in agricultural or medical services, community development or local government, who could help to man responsible posts at a time when experience and ability should count far more than either the grade or the education a man took twenty years ago when opportunities were few. Finally, if East Africa is also to have a Federal Government, or some adaptation of the High Commission, there will be an additional and heavy demand on African manpower. The Ramage Report shows how little progress has been made in Africanizing High Commission senior staff up to date.[25]

3. MANPOWER FOR INDUSTRY AND COMMERCE

In 1960 a survey of high-level manpower needs was carried out both in Nigeria, by Professor Harbison with the Ashby Commission, and in Ghana by the Ghana Government and E. D. Hollander for the Ford Foundation. Remembering that Ghana has only between one-fifth and one-sixth of the total population of Nigeria, it is interesting to look at some of the gross estimates of existing manpower and needs given in these two surveys (p. 258).

The Ghana survey included also an estimate of about 29,700 skilled workers (of whom 900 were craft foremen) in 1960. The nearest similar estimate for Nigeria has been put at around 50,000 by consultants. It is clear from these figures that, per head of population, Ghana is far ahead in the supply of men actually

[25] Sir Richard Ramage, *Report on the Localization of the Civil Service, etc.* (East Africa High Commission, March 1961).

	Administrative and Professional		Sub-Professional Technical and Supervisory		Secondary Teachers (Graduates)	
	Existing 1960	Required 1970 Nigeria 1965 Ghana	Existing 1960	Required 1970 Nigeria 1965 Ghana	Existing 1960	Required 1970 Nigeria 1965 Ghana
NIGERIA	13,67ʋ	28,875	11,075 (excluding teachers)	37,275 (excluding teachers)	1,700	7,000
GHANA	5,900	8,300	4,500 (plus 12,900 primary teachers)	7,000 (plus 19,250 primary teachers)	700	2,200

employed (the figures include expatriates) and by 1965 will be, again in proportion to population, ahead of Nigeria's targets for 1970, except perhaps in the sub-professional and technical levels. But in some ways this comparison should be handled carefully. Technical and industrial manpower is needed for the technical and industrial sector of the economy. Very little is needed at present for the twenty million population of Northern Nigeria, much of which is almost self-administering (there are no police-men in enormous sections of the North) and more than self-supporting, but wholly agricultural. A comparison between Ghana and Western Nigeria, where the population is nearly the same, would come out very much less adversely to Nigeria. The critical fact here is that Nigeria as a whole has a much smaller 'modern sector' *per head of population* than Ghana, but that sector is probably as well manned

Both surveys emphasize heavily the two outstanding problems which the whole history of education and training in Africa has thrown up. First, there is the lack of technical education for modern trades; the real shortages are not in carpenters and masons but in all the electrical trades—radio, refrigeration, telephone, &c. To this point must be added the shortage of trained supervision. Of 900 foremen in Ghana,[26] one-third are expatriate, and the total is inadequate for the skilled, let alone the total, labour force. Secondly, there is the critical shortage of trained secondary teach-ers, for which both Ghana and Nigeria will have to rely heavily on overseas help. Shortages of doctors, engineers of all types and graduate scientists are inevitable; but they are not so short, in relation to the modern sector, as the technicians who should be

[26] These are foremen 'with managerial functions', not just headmen or gangers.

there to support them, and whom the domestic educational system ought to be producing; for this reason much higher multipliers have been used in estimating for 1970 for this group than for graduates; and the ratio would be higher still but for the shortage of graduate secondary teachers.

There are no comparable manpower estimates for East Africa. At the top managerial, administrative and professional level it is obvious that East Africa is still far behind in 1960. But at the lower levels and for the future a great deal more caution is needed in making judgements. If we take from Table VIII (facing page 244) for four countries with comparable population, the figures for enrolment in the last six years of secondary grammar school, the results are somewhat surprising :

Kenya (pop. 6,551,000) .. .. 15,177 (African and Asian)
Uganda (pop. 6,499,000) .. 34,154 (all races)
W. Nigeria (pop. 6,929,000) .. 22,374 (plus 64,209 in secondary modern schools)
Ghana (pop. 6,690,000) .. .. 11,874 (56,696 in last two forms of middle school, school years 9 and 10)

Further, the figures in the same Table for full-time enrolment in trade and technical schools, allowing for differences in classification, are not at all far apart,[27] though the low West Nigerian figures gives a false impression. The extensive training by Departments for the extension services, and by the railways and public utilities, is almost certainly as far advanced in East as in West Africa—there is need for more accurate figures of the total output of craft and technical training from all sources. It is more than likely that, if the research could be done, East Africa would be found to have, for its population, as good an output of craft and minor technical and administrative skill as West Africa. There is a great pressure on vacancies—6,000 applications for 300 places in 1959 at the Kabete (Kenya) Trade School is one example among many. More than one industrialist remarked to us that, in manufacturing industry, East African workers responded better to training because they were not already indifferently trained, and that the output of trained craftsmen by the public institutions was of a higher quality than in some West African countries.

Historically, this situation is quite normal. The grammar school *élite* in West Africa was created long before East Africa was born;

[27] Uganda 4,040; Ghana 2,522; Kenya 1,288; W. Nigeria 432 (see Table VIII, facing page 244).

but technical education was not. While the colonial governments in the East were concentrating on bringing both Africans and Asians steadily upwards through lower grades in all fields, West Africa was striding ahead at the top level, but not so fast lower down. This was particularly true in the technical field, which did not carry either the same prestige or prospects as white-collar work. The Principal of a Gold Coast Craft School has recorded the following remarks : ' "How many carpenters or masons own motor cars?" I was asked. "None. But look at the number of them owned by people who started at the bottom and became clerks".'[28] There followed the immense increase in primary education in the West which has sadly diluted the standards of teachers, both in primary and secondary education, and left little room for teachers on vocational subjects. In consequence, for the modern sector East Africa is not nearly so far behind as is so often thought. There is, certainly, a higher output of the training schemes of expatriate industry in West Africa, both from its extra age on the commercial side and its more rapid growth on the industrial side since 1950. But the manufacturer going to East Africa, with its smaller industrial sector, might well find as good material for all his lower ranks—there is no point in having more industrially trained men than industry to employ them.

Even at the higher and graduate levels, the future position is not wholly discouraging. The total domestic output from Ghana's higher education is estimated at 1,932 for 1961–5, while that for Uganda is at 764, Kenya at 624 (Table IX, facing page 244). This is a substantial, but not a killing, difference; the advantage of Ghana is that she has behind her the accumulated higher output of the past, and a much higher number of students abroad.

It would seem, therefore, from this brief analysis—and far more detailed research is needed in this field—that while Nigeria and Ghana will provide a fair share of the management and professional grades, East Africa will have to rely on expatriates for the higher positions in both for much longer. On the other hand, the lower echelons in East Africa may well be as good as their West African counterparts, partly because teaching has been less diluted, partly from Asian skills, partly because both Africans and Asians have been, in recent years, in far closer contact with

[28] J. A. Hamilton and P. E. Williams, *Training for Industrialization in the Gold Coast* (Duke of Edinburgh's Conference Report, vol. II).

Europeans who inevitably set the standard for European-type enterprise and administration. In French-speaking territories, African participation in industry and commerce at a high level is very much smaller. The African *élite* of Dakar, Abidjan and Brazzaville have chosen the public service and the professions almost exclusively, and have been content to leave the industrial sector very largely to the French.

4. OVERSEAS AID

Certain conclusions can be drawn as to the rôle of developed countries in helping Africa to achieve her ambitions.

First, the provision of graduate secondary-school teachers would be of the highest value for the whole area—far higher, in present circumstances, than the provision of more university places. University teachers for the new universities of both East and West will also be needed, but relatively easily provided without government intervention.

Secondly, staff for highly efficient supervisory training is badly needed. It may well be that subventions to the existing training schemes of expatriate firms, to enable them to train 50 per cent beyond their own needs, would be the most efficient method. Supervision by poor-quality Europeans or untrained Africans has been a major weakness. The same can be said of the training for technicians; before higher management can be effective, there must be a corps of men at lower levels who know their job, not sketchily, but really well; who can not only do it, but can improvise, maintain, repair. This is a straight task of thorough training with good equipment and—more important—first-rate instructors.[29]

Thirdly, there is the issue of 'management training', now much under discussion. There is little doubt that management training in formal courses can be done, and with effect, provided that it is conceived and executed by staff who know exactly what they are about—and these are very rare. It is not a substitute for experience, but a form of catalyst which enables a manager to interpret and use experience. I would myself look with extreme suspicion at any 'Harvard Business Schools' in Africa unless they were

[29] Many people have emphasized how important it is that European instructors should first have a thorough knowledge of African conditions and of the kind of men they are to teach. See, for example, Hamilton and Williams, op. cit.

staffed by men professional in the field of management education; in any other case, they would be a dangerous illusion, turning out men with paper qualifications and little or no idea of the real function of management. Otherwise, experience in industries still with experienced expatriate management will remain vital. There is, however, a strong case for bringing African managers to industrialized countries. It is not mainly a question of the speed and style of industrial life, nor of self-confidence, nor of picking up ideas, though all are important. It is a question of broadening the whole mental horizon for men who have seen too little of the context and atmosphere of the institutions of industry and commerce into which they have lately moved. Lower techniques and crafts can and should be taught in Africa; but when the policy level or the technological level is reached, the case at least for seeing the fully-developed system at work is overwhelmingly strong.

In training for the public service the best contribution which Britain and France can give is to make it possible, by their political policies and by their personal handling of staff, for their own nationals to remain as trainers in their posts for as long as they are needed, and even to renew them with younger men where they are requested. Colleges of Administration will be invaluable, although again the design of the syllabus and method is a highly professional task. But nothing can be a substitute for learning in-post under an experienced and sympathetic chief. Old tensions, prestige, personal considerations of career, sheer weariness after years of tension may result in a heavy loss of expatriate staffs in East Africa. But there are young men in England, and in East Africa, who would still feel it a worth-while job to serve these developing countries, who are more free of the associations and perhaps the bitterness of the past, who could do priceless service if Africa is willing to accept them. Whether nationally, or under international auspices, the offer of a career to men who want it in such countries as East Africa is still surely worth consideration. A determined attempt is needed to overcome the difficulties of pension, continuous employment and security which are bound to arise.[30]

[30] An extremely limited scheme for the provision of Operational and Executive Officers (OPEX) was started by the United Nations in November 1958. Only twenty-five posts were budgeted for in the first scheme. Although there is hope of enlargement, this service is not likely to be more than a useful but very small source of special skills. See particularly Younger, op. cit.

Perhaps, too, there has been too much emphasis on the gradu-ate. It is not only degrees which are wanted in Africa but contact and interchange between the wealth of professional associations in developed countries and the loneliness of technicians and pro-fessional men in Africa. It is through hospitals, editors, staff associ-ations, the Inns of Court, the great industrial associations, the associations of headmasters and teachers, the women's organ-izations, the professional journals, the institutes of professionals in a score of fields, through the action of a modern highly differen-tiated community opening its doors and its heart to Africa that so much help and encouragement can be given.

5. THE WIDER ISSUES

From this descent into the valley of practical problems and numbers it is time to climb again to a broader view over these societies which have had so short a time of modern growth. There are two standpoints: from one, to see more widely the practical problems, of competence, of wise use of manpower and resources; from the other, to look at the human quality of these growing nations, the space in which the individual spirit can develop and flourish and the political and spiritual traditions of a civilization be nurtured and confirmed.

At the more practical level, no one can fail to admire the courage and energy of Nigeria in accepting the £100 million plan of the Ashby Commission, the determination in Ghana to brush aside caution and difficulties and to produce a modern nation in fifteen years. But a time has come at least to ask if the targets are rightly set. The cost—and the recurring cost—of Nigeria's pro-grammes is enormous for the size of her economy; no nation before has devoted so much to social expenditure before the main forward surge of the economy. Denmark in the nineteenth century created the Folk High Schools, often quoted as one foundation of her future progress. But these were not massive institutions, archi-tect-designed in modern materials, but simple—simple in diet, in buildings, in staff. There is, after all, a real chance that the figures 4 or 5 per cent economic growth will not be maintained; that there must at least be a pause for a few years after this first ex-ploitation of possibilities which were long in building. Varied and exciting as are the new industrial projects, they are really few and small in relation to nations who have still a long way to travel into the modern world. While the dams and power stations are being built, and before they give their real reward, there may be financial hard times, and that during the peak of educational effort.

However much foreign capital is lent or invested, the real 'take-off' in Africa can only come when Africans themselves see opportunities, can raise money and found enterprises, can start from their own initiative the mounting hum of self-supporting and self-accelerating economic energy. There is still some way to go before that time. Present growth has perhaps had a hot-house forcing, and it will have to harden off in the colder open air of world prices and competition.

There is, too, a danger that present planning is aimed too much at the top levels. For political reasons, African governments have felt it important to supply the high managerial cadres. But once honour is satisfied, there should be a second look at the emphasis on graduates. Not half, probably not one-quarter, of the top executives of ten thousand British companies ever saw a university; many never saw a secondary school. They rose the hard way, through apprenticeship and long years of night school, and hard competitive responsibility through years of slump and boom; and the centre layers of all Western industry are filled with just such men. Without them, no graduate at the top can make things work. This centre layer has yet to grow in Africa, and it will take time. There is a danger of creating a group of 'managers' who give orders to men below them which they do not really understand and could not execute. The same may well be true in public administration; a toughening of the middle layer is badly needed.

While a period of consolidation of quality goes ahead, there will be time, too, to turn the emphasis of primary and some secondary education more towards the modern agriculture on which African economies must still rest. Again and again the glamour of industrialization turns policy aside from this, its main task. Husbandry, in all its forms, can today be as modern and technical, as worth the skill of teacher and pupil to pursue, as any other work. Now that the pressure to aim the schools towards academic and London-based examinations is less strong in the great bulk of schools, there is both time and need to create what could become one of the best agriculturally educated continents.

At the highest level of education there is also a question of policy and standards. Impressed both by the American Land

Colleges designed to meet the needs of agricultural States in the U.S.A. and by the larger intake and more practical bent of part of the American university system, Dr. Azikiwe and some other Nigerian leaders felt that the new University of Nigeria at Nsukka might follow more the American than the British pattern, producing for the new Nigeria young men with practical knowledge in agriculture, commerce and many other applied subjects—trained less as scholars than as citizens. Progress on the physical level at Nsukka was indeed remarkable to see, although there were signs of haste in the planning. The fact that in 1961 the University seemed rather uneasily poised between conflicting American and British educational theories is no doubt temporary. Clearly, there is a case in developing countries for a strong 'applied' slant to university life. Without entering this argument, it is surely safe to say that, whatever the policy and faculties, the standards of teaching and performance should be equally high. It is of great importance to Africa that universities there, however practical their bent, should not slip into second-rate standards, accepting boys at School Certificate level and turning them out unable to meet squarely the agricultural scientists or economists or statisticians of other countries. A reputation once lost is hard to regain. There is a tremendous field for natural scientists, for men who really know the behaviour of soils, fertilizers, trees, animals and crops in tropical conditions. Contact with the best that the developed world can produce—whether from Europe, Russia, China or America—is essential if the Nigerian graduate of Nsukka is to hold his head up in scientific or technological company. There may well be a case for colleges with simpler aims and a School Certificate intake—indeed, they are certainly needed. But it is important not to confuse technical institutes with universities, or the latter will suffer.

This leads to the human, political and moral ideals which are to be enshrined in African education and their relevance to the future of African societies. The old African system of tribal education impressed upon boys and girls the standards and patterns of behaviour which would be expected of them in adult society. It did so by subjecting them to the solemn, even frightening, and unforgettable experience of pre-initiation training and the final climax of initiation. By bringing to bear simultaneously the psychological forces associated with religion, sexual maturity and the man's combative instinct (in many cases a test of courage and endurance was involved), it must have made an enormous impact on adolescents.[31] Its whole aim was to strike deep into their minds and hearts the traditions of the community, the wisdom of the elders and the continuity with ancestors; in some ways it was comparable to the methods of ancient Sparta. It is indeed strange that Western education in Africa has made so little attempt to rival the psychological force of the old system. As Hailey points out, the new education could not follow the old form : 'The African child will be introduced to a world of thought, of achievement and of conduct which lies outside the experience of his parents. This . . . is bound to make a break in his life, however much the educationist may wish to respect indigenous tradition.'[32] But if the schools have different things to teach, they still have to make an impact on character and values. Courage and the combative instinct may be in part trained by games, though less impressively; sexual instruction is almost wholly shirked; and even if the preparation for religious confirmation does make a considerable emotional impact, it is far less related to modern community life, which is so deeply secularized.

Yet the need for a firm foundation was never greater. African society is in a turmoil of moral and social doubt; it is between Christianity, Islam and the higher forms of African traditional religions, and assailed, as are our own societies, by agnostic or Marxist views of the world. On the social side, it is between the traditional culture of family obligation and the Western pattern of individualism in self-development and self-expression. Standards of sexual morality and social obligation are so confused that they can scarcely be said to exist in the westernized sectors of society. If this is an issue for religious leadership to face, it is also a fundamental problem for the schools. Without these standards, education cannot exist;[33] it becomes instruction, and instruction

---

[31] For an autobiographical account, possibly a little idealized, of an African child's education and initiation, see *I was a Savage*, by Prince Modupe (London, Museum Press, 1958). The period of education in the uses and dangers of every plant and animal, and the lonely expedition into the forest to kill a leopard with bow and arrow, are especially interesting. For an anthropologist's account of a girl's training and initiation, with its emphasis on the duties of marriage, see *Chisungu*, by Dr. A. I. Richards (London, Faber and Faber, 1956).

[32] Hailey, op. cit, pp. 1134–5.

[33] This issue is discussed more fully in Chapter XII.

not backed by qualities of character is a rotten plank which will
not carry the loads of growing industrial and political life. As
the schools slowly become integrated with the life of adult society,
so that the gap between children and tribal parents begins to
shrink, a new tradition of building character and social values
suited to the new African society may be created, if there is the
will and vision to insist on it.

At the higher level there is a particular danger that the humanities—philosophy, politics, history, among them—will be brushed
aside in favour of more practically directed studies. As David
Apter has so skilfully shown,[34] there is an association between
socialism and technology in the developing countries which goes
very deep, and is apt to be hostile to, or at least impatient with,
the 'high cultures' based on the humanities :

For the areas now becoming independent of colonial rule, the relationship between science and society is much closer to the Marxist
position than any other. The leaders of new nations share an urgent
and understandable desire to make a gigantic leap across time, to by-
pass slower and more 'natural' processes of economic and scientific
growth and place science at the service of an immediate technology
—a technology of improved agriculture, of industrial expansion, of
health and sanitation and of startling new methods in education and
training.

Again :

To a Sukarno, a Nkrumah or a Houphouet-Boigny, the higher
moralities defended by the literary intellectuals appear spurious. The
task of building nations has its own imperatives in the form of changing public wants and images. The formation of ideologies which will
help establish a corporate discipline, transform the countryside and
abolish temples, demands slogans rather than thoughts, and rally-
ing cries rather than ideas. The intellectuals are thus robbed of their
functions, or are barely tolerated.

And :

High cultures always oppose rationalistic egalitarianism; it is those
who have absorbed high culture, either at home or abroad, who
shrink from the full consequences of social change. The conflict
mirrors the antithetical aims of preserving individual liberty and
values and the complete and rational overhauling of institutions.

[34] Apter, 'New Nations and the Scientific Revolution', supra.

No wonder there has been tension between Legon and Accra, between Ibadan town and gown. Apter describes, almost to the point of caricature, the possible conflict of these British foundations with African leadership :

Founded during the last stages of colonial rule, they are exotic hot-house plants, modelled after the Universities of Paris or Cambridge or Oxford, with all the real and fancied privilege and protocol awarded to the student in Europe and England. They are outposts of Western traditionalism, designed to carry on the culture of literary intellectuals first and only then the more pragmatic sciences, pure or applied. It is no wonder that they remain centres of political opposition, antagonistic to the effects of social engineering and contemptuous of science and of the politicians whose friendship they do not want.

But his caricature was, in some African eyes, not too far from the mark. The *Ghanaian Times*,[35] some months after Apter wrote these words, greeted the reform of Legon as follows :

Since its inception in 1948, the University College of Ghana has been a den of academic reaction. The content of university teaching in Legon has been moulded to suit the needs of London University, which is a stronghold of bourgeois education.

Students of economics in our University College are taught nothing about Ghana's or Africa's economic history, nor is any guidance to be found about Ghana's or Africa's rapid and balanced economic development. The teaching of African history is falsified to suit the needs of British imperialism.

The classics are extolled.

Karl Marx, the founder of scientific socialism, and his philosophy of historical and dialectical materialism are ignored. . . .

Africa's New Man has to be fashioned in our institutions of higher education, and we are certain that with Osagyefo at the helm, with a new recruitment policy in being, wedded to positive neutralism, and priority given to the teaching of science and applied science, the University of Accra and the University of Science and Technology, Kumasi, will soon prove their worth as within the vanguard of the world's institutions of higher learning. Bravo to Osagyefo! Long Live the New Ghana! Long Live the African Liberation Movement!

The whole conception of 'manpower planning' inclines all too easily towards this view. Having estimated manpower needs, the

[35] *Ghanaian Times* Editorial, 6 June 1961.

next step is to direct the whole educational system towards fulfilling them and to imbue the teachers, consciously or not, with the idea that they are shock troops in the national economic effort rather than men trying to bring out the varied personal qualities of children, and to fit them for life in the community. Institutions or individuals who are contributing to this or that Five-Year Plan are favoured : those who are not are starved of support. This is one of the most dangerous elements of Statism—dangerous, that is, if the width and variety and freedom of the human spirit is valued as a contribution, not merely to an economy but to a civilization. For it is not, in fact, the scientist (who is surely a civilized man) who comes in at the door when the humanities go out of the window; it is the technologist, the practitioner, the man who is concerned with what is useful and efficient. John Stuart Mill [36] saw clearly enough the arguments that would be used :

We know how easily the uselessness of almost every branch of knowledge may be proved, to the complete satisfaction of those who do not possess it. How many not altogether stupid men think the scientific study of languages useless, think ancient literature useless; all erudition useless; logic and metaphysics useless; poetry and the fine arts idle and frivolous; political economy purely mischievous? Even history has been pronounced useless and mischievous by able men. Nothing but that acquaintance with external nature, empirically acquired, which serves directly for the production of objects necessary for existence or agreeable to the senses, would get its utility recognized if people had the least encouragement to disbelieve it.

The whole of de Tocqueville's [37] amazingly prophetic analysis of democracy emphasizes first the tendency to centralization—of which more later—and second the tendency to value the useful, the material, over the other qualities which make up a human rather than a sub-human world :

But while man takes delight in this honest and lawful pursuit of his well-being, it is to be apprehended that he may in the end lose the use of his sublimest faculties; and that while he is busied in improving all around him, he may at length degrade himself. Here and here only does the peril lie.

[36] J. S. Mill, *Essay on Liberty.*
[37] Count Alexis de Tocqueville, *Democracy in America.*

The case for valuing the poet, the philosopher, the historian, the
artist no less than the scientist, even in the revolutionary conditions of Africa today, has never been more eloquently and un-
compromisingly stated than by Sir Richard Livingstone :[38]

> The final goal of education is not the capacity to earn one's bread
> or to live in a community, though these are included in it, but the
> making of human beings. Body, character and, in the widest sense,
> reason, make the man. A body undeveloped, a character weak or
> debased, a mind unaware of the universe which we inhabit or of the
> achievements and ideals of mankind, proclaim the failure of educa-
> tion and walk the world as a standing reproach of it.
>
> It follows that education, for all men and women, for the artisan
> and labourer as well as for the 'educated classes' must find ample
> room for a liberal, cultural element. If its aim is to make men and
> citizens as well as breadwinners, to develop what Shakespeare calls
> beings of infinite capacity, and to help them to live intelligently in the
> world which they inhabit, then handicraft, technical skill, physical
> training belong to such an education, if the body is to achieve its
> perfection, and hand and eye to develop their powers; but so also
> does science, if we are to understand something of the physical
> universe; and so do literature, history and, in an untechnical sense,
> philosophy. . . . If a man is incapable of these studies, he is not, in
> the Shakespearean sense, a man. And if the majority of the elec-
> torate is incapable of them, we must either abandon democracy or
> resign ourselves to be governed by an electorate which can never
> know what a state should be. Ancient tradition and political instinct
> may preserve such a democracy from disaster, but not only will its
> stability be precarious but its political and spiritual life will be poor.
> The bad film and the betting news will be its relaxation; the bad
> press its literature; passion, prejudice, the catchword and the slogan,
> will be its masters.

It is on this note that I would like to return to the opening of
this chapter. Education, in its full sense, has other cares than the
economic. Manpower planning is not only necessary but highly
desirable, provided that it is confined to encouraging the right
proportion of different vocational studies *within a wide general
education*. To abstract from the whole Western system just those
elements designed to produce engineers or geophysicists (rather
than the whole, which is designed to produce citizens and men)

[38] Sir Richard Livingstone, 'The Future in Education', in *Report of the
Proceedings of the British Association for the Advancement of Science*, 1936.

could be to fall into a grave mistake. For what is in issue in Africa is the growth of new nations, new societies of men, not merely the construction of new economies. Growth, which education must nurture, may be slower than construction, for it includes more complex factors, and a wider, apparently less purposeful, range. But for this very reason it retains an internal balance which makes for stability. It would be unwise to assume that merely by planning and massive expenditure on a technological education any African country can turn itself in two decades into the reality, rather than the façade, of a developed modern society. The real growth must have time to spread its roots deep and wide in the life of the community, aided by an education which fully replaces the old tribal training as a preparation for modern citizenship. Even the economic structure will stand or fall by reference to the political wisdom and social stability of the new societies now being born. It is to these subjects that the last part of this book will be devoted.

CHAPTER XI

THE CREATION OF A POLITICAL SYSTEM

The political map of Tropical Africa owes its shape to a multi-tude of strange factors—sometimes to a river, sometimes to the rivalries of Missions or explorers or European Powers, sometimes to a tribal boundary or the result of a battle—usually to a com-bination of all these and other reasons, both ancient and modern. This is a normal state of affairs in large areas of the world, and especially in Europe. There have been fashions in frontier-making. Sometimes the emphasis has been on an ethnic or linguistic or religious group as the natural foundation for a nation; sometimes on defensible boundaries; sometimes on a balance of economic resources, a river system or access to the sea. Seldom do the ideal administrative, economic, ethnic and strategic boundaries co-incide; and in any case they would change through time, with changes in the techniques of communication, of production or of war : the countries of Europe are at present engaged in yet another attempt to find a compromise between nationhood, econ-omic strength and self-defence. These conflicting criteria make it impossible to define what boundaries a nation *ought* to have; and in fact a nation (as against a political entity on a map) comes to exist when a large group of people feel themselves to be one; and its existence is rapidly re-inforced if the group can maintain its unity over a number of years.

Thus in one vital sense nationhood is a matter of feeling. It might be said that many choices of how to form nations are open to the peoples of Africa. But, living within history, no people have a clean start. There have been, in modern times, two major points around which a sense of nationhood has started to grow—the unities of major peoples, such as the Yoruba, five million strong; and the unities created by colonial rule. Nothing could be more absurd than the constant accusation that European colonialism balkanized Africa. In almost every area it created far larger entities than had existed within historic times, save for some of the Muslim empires of the South West Sahara. Moreover, it did not only create entities—and the Muslim empires could not rightly have been called nations—but in latter years the idea of nationhood was actively instilled by the colonial governments and taken up by African leadership. However accidental the boundaries, which occasionally split a previous tribal unity, colonial rule established an administrative state around which a political system and a sense of nationhood could grow. President Senghor, in a full discussion of 'African Socialism', significantly entitled his two main sections 'The Will to Nationhood' and 'The Road to Nationhood'.[1] Thus in effect the choices open to African leaders are to build upon the older sentiments of tribalism; or upon the unities established by European governments; or upon some larger unity, which must be projected into the minds and hearts of their peoples, until the sense of nationhood begins to grow around it.

The entities created by colonial rule are very various; sometimes a whole country has been a patchwork of small tribes; sometimes, as in Northern Nigeria or Uganda, a whole kingdom or confederacy has been included in a mixed bundle of far smaller groups and allowed by indirect rule to retain much of its historical and political unity. At first sight it might seem that an African government can none the less take over the existing State and march straight on in the process of making it a nation : the very gradualness of African entry into both Parliaments and the Civil Service encourages this sense of continuity, for Africans themselves subconsciously accepted the colonial boundaries as national. But this is to forget the difference between administration and politics. The sanction and authority of colonial rule lay in London or Paris, Brussels or Lisbon; the authority of the government went back to a metropolitan country willing and able to enforce it.[2] The quite new task of African leaders is to legitimize a political system, to establish authority and sovereignty in a constitution which shall be unquestioned even if governments within it change. True, most African governments have been legitimized in theory by elections; but the unity of the State and the sense of nationhood are alike

[1] L. S. Senghor, *African Socialism, Report to the Constitutive Congress of the Party of African Federation* (New York, American Society of African Culture, 1959).

[2] A colonial civil servant can follow policy—what is felt to be best for the country; an African politician must also follow politics—what his constituents will support. Much of the alarm of the Colonial Service at the vote-catching statements of African politicians sprang from this difference.

precarious and young. At any moment some powerful group can challenge the bluff of 'Kenya' or 'Nigeria', demanding a separate or an extended boundary. Thus, at Independence, large and simple questions are at issue : What shall be the new nation? Who shall run it? How shall it be run? Where shall its boundaries lie? The difficulty is greater because the unities created among Africans by opposition to foreign rule lose their validity when they lose their opponent. A unity for the independent nation, strong enough to hold diversity of interests within an unquestioned frame, has still to be created in many countries. The surge of enthusiasm on which a new independent State is launched will die away within less than a decade; while it is there, something must be built which will be strong enough to survive the blows from the outer world and the rending divergences of interest within, divergences which every vigorous society must assuredly produce.

I. POLITICS IN THE COLONIAL SITUATION

The rise of African politicians and of African political power was briefly sketched in Chapter III. But simple generalizations, so attractive to make, are hard to sustain. Since it is probable that the similarities between countries in the first flush of independence may lessen as time and development go on, it is worth looking more closely at some individual situations.

As suggested in Chapter III, the first real political leaders in West Africa were perhaps much the same sort of people as those in East Africa a generation or more later. They were men with some education, ex-teachers, lawyers or journalists, able to live without government employment and to appeal to their people under the disapproving eye both of the government and of the more conservative chiefs. But the time for Independence was still far ahead, and these men often became respected members of a constitutional Opposition. They became more senior and responsible until, after the last war, there was in Lagos and Accra and Freetown, and in Dakar and Abidjan, quite a large group of highly educated, much Europeanized men, some in professions, some in the public service, some traditional rulers, who were playing their part in gradual constitutional advance in the Legislative and local Councils and in the promotion to senior public posts. After the war the mass movements of Nkrumah or Azikiwe, skilled in party organization, with popular support and with far more radical programmes and political methods, swept past the older group into power. In Ghana, the C.P.P. included most of the 'have-nots'; the Nigerian parties carried a good section of the 'establishment' with them. Something similar, though more intellectually radical, happened in French-speaking territories such as Mali, Guinea and the Ivory Coast in the days when M. Houphouet-Boigny was of the extreme left. Ghana is the outstanding example of the mass nationalist party with a large but subdued intellectual and traditional opposition—from the University, the Civil Service, displaced moderate leaders and chiefs rendered powerless by the Party machine.

In contrast, in Kenya, Tanganyika, Nyasaland and Northern Rhodesia, the first effective leaders (excluding Jomo Kenyatta as a special case) appeared after the last war and made straight to create the mass party. Mr. Nyerere, a teacher, only finally plunged into politics with TANU in 1955. Neither he nor Dr. Banda, nor Mr. Kaunda and Mr. Nkumbula in Northern Rhodesia, had any older intellectual forces either to supersede or gather to their side. Thus, though the East and Central African parties may run into trouble from traditional chiefs, they have not also to contend with a highly educated older *élite*, save in Uganda. With this major proviso, there was much in common in methods of political action between this group of mass parties—Ghana (C.P.P.), Nigeria (N.C.N.C.), Northern Rhodesia (UNIP), Nyasaland (Congress) and in the French-speaking area, Guinea (P.D.G.) and Mali (U.S. and R.D.A.); Tanganyika (TANU) and possibly the Kenya parties, if they unite under Mr. Kenyatta, should be joined to this group, though there are tribal jealousies in Kenya which may yet change the scene.

In contrast, Western Nigeria, and perhaps Senegal,[3] wear a more upper-middle-class and bourgeois look. The Action Group in Western Nigeria mobilized the big traders and many Obas to its support and has a solid and loyal Civil Service behind it,[4] so that it seems in some ways the most weighty and well-found

---

[3] And even the Ivory Coast under the revised régime of M. Houphouet-Boigny.

[4] The University at Ibadan is more doubtful, partly owing to influence from the rival party from Eastern Nigeria (the University has been described by some Western politicians as 'a nest of Ibos') and partly to some Yoruba and Edo opposition to the Action Group.

bourgeois party in the whole area, not even needing a personality-cult to sustain it. The N.C.N.C., although based in Eastern Nigeria, provides a strong democratic Opposition in the West, relying on old divisions there and on the more radical elements. In Senegal, it is a middle group of intellectuals and functionaries, heavily dependent financially on France, and well organized to bring in the vote from the bush, which is in power; though there is a good deal of impatient but as yet ineffective sniping from more revolutionary spirits, impatient at lagging behind as the last member of the French Community outside the excitements of *progressiste* African politics.

The third main type of political development is that of Northern Nigeria and of Uganda, where the scene is as yet uncertain. The régime of the Emirs has come through to Independence much reformed and somewhat modernized; there are some tensions between the Emirs and the Northern Government, but in combination they remain firmly in control, as the 1961 election again proved. The prestige of a conquering group, the enormous possibilities of patronage, the many ways in which life can be made difficult for political opponents, and the pride of the North in dominating the new Federal Nigeria have together made it difficult for any large opposition party to get a hold. This is true despite the efforts of the two main Southern parties, tribal opposition in the non-Muslim countries of the Middle Belt, and the stirrings of radicalism among the young educated 'Mallams'.[5] In Uganda, the local patriotism of the kingdoms of Buganda, Toro, Bunyoro and Ankole have equally made it difficult for the young progressives. Yet it became clear that Uganda as a whole would not gain independence except through a national parliamentary system based on national political parties; and after many abortive attempts the two present parties were finally able to gain mass support, despite efforts by the kingdom of Buganda to re-establish itself as a separate independent State in its old political form. One essential difference between Uganda and Northern Nigeria was that the Emirs still felt themselves to be part of a single system, and were therefore able to co-operate in creating a political party which would satisfy democratic forms although still under their control. In contrast, the kingdoms of Uganda were rivals, with no common policy. Further, there was, and still

[5] 'Mallam', a title given to those educated in Koranic studies.

is, in some of the Uganda kingdoms a real local nationalism at all
levels of society, operating in favour of the old régimes; this made
it more difficult to start all-Uganda parties and supported the
ruling groups in a belief that they could avoid the necessity of
national democracy. In Northern Nigeria such patriotisms at
tribal level were likely to be hostile to the régime, and it was
necessary to create a patriotism of 'the North' to override them.

These three groupings—the modernist mass parties, the bourgeois parties and the reforming aristocrats, have been classified
by David Apter and Carl Rosberg [6] as the 'mobilization system',
the 'consociational system' and the 'modernizing autocracy'. But
while form, as such, is of some interest and importance, it hides
fairly wide differences in real content. As I shall hope to show,
the mass party may be formed for different reasons and rest on
different foundations in different countries. It may be simpler to
think in terms of a social revolution in Africa pointed towards the
emergence of what is most naturally—though still inaccurately—
described as a bourgeois-bureaucratic society; one, that is, in
which the trader and contractor, the manager, the lawyer, the
civil servant, some modernizing chiefs, the professions and university staffs, the controlling interests in large Co-operatives and the
more wealthy farmers will in fact hold power and influence
policy, keeping the necessary links with the general mass of an
enfranchised population through a party system suited to the
country concerned. This group may tolerate or support a single
mass party and even a dictatorial leader if they are valuable in
maintaining national unity and energy, and will be content or
even anxious to be called 'socialist', in so far as this implies centralized economic planning and co-operative forms in agricultural
production and marketing. But it might not tolerate political
leadership, whether from the right or the left, which frustrated
its interests too violently or too long.

Perhaps the peculiar difficulties facing African political leaders
in the colonial period can best be illustrated from Central and
East Africa, where the issues are still contemporary. In these

[6] D. E. Apter and C. G. Rosberg, in *The Political Economy of Contem-
porary Africa* (National Institute of Social and Behavioural Science, Sym-
posia Studies Series No. 1, George Washington University, December 1959).
I am, of course, deeply indebted to T. Hodgkin's *Nationalism in Colonial
Africa*, supra, and to James Coleman's *Nigeria: Background to Nationalism*
(University of California Press, 1958).

territories, where secondary and university education is both recent and fairly scarce, the educated nationalist leader has been in an anxious position. With his qualifications a career in public service or teaching was usually wide open to him. But government service, teaching and even employment in a large expatriate company all ban politics.[7] The nationalist politician must find a means to live which yet keeps his hands free. He must, in the early stages, avoid the wrath of the District Commissioner who may well classify him as a dangerous agitator, and he may also have to elude or convert a chief who may feel his traditional authority threatened by young democrats. He must create enthusiasm without unleashing violence, and he must play a game of forcing bluff with the colonial government to extract constitutional concessions, although his forces are perilously ramshackle, impatient, fickle if a more plausible rival appears, and desperately hard to control without either massive funds or good communications. Too close an association with Europeans, from whom he might get support, may ruin his reputation without gaining him advantages—Mr. Chileshe in Northern Rhodesia had his business broken by the nationalists and was then ejected from the liberal, multi-racial Central Africa Party for being too extreme; more than one United Federal Party African member had his house stoned. He must recruit lieutenants who do not discredit him, and as he looks for support among educated Africans he will find the majority of them unable to act because they hold official posts.[8] Yet every African teacher, every young civil servant, every manager, every Native Authority clerk or treasurer, every young educated District Councillor is a nationalist, in Nairobi as in Dar-es-Salaam or Lusaka, in the country towns and in the bush; but they must wait until it is possible to show their allegiance. Mean-

[7] It has been, I think most unfortunately, a policy of most of these companies to forbid political activity to employees in East and Central Africa, in contrast to West Africa, where some companies, though not all, have allowed it.

[8] The Study Groups in Tanganyika and Northern Rhodesia both agreed that, apart from the top leadership, politicians in TANU and UNIP were not of the *élite*; or, in reverse, that the *élite*—civil servants, senior teachers, managers and most of those with a relatively high assured income, European dress, Christian religion, a superior house and (sometimes) an educated wife—kept out of open political activity. The situation in Kenya, with a number of graduate African political leaders and some lawyers, doctors and civil servants, is nearer to the early situations on the West Coast, with politicians leading the *élite* in Nairobi; but in the Districts the local politicians would be of lower social prestige than the more educated Africans in the area.

while the Party must move on, with its orators, its mass meetings and, unfortunately, its hangers-on and opportunists, without their open help. Quite a few of the organizers of TANU were men who had lost official jobs; local secretaries of the Kenya African parties were not always men of substance or among the African *élite* of their area; UNIP in Northern Rhodesia is desperately short of well-qualified lieutenants. This situation will help to explain why a leader with few educated lieutenants and a mass of semi-literate or illiterate supporters is at first so suspect to colonial administrators and yet, within a moment of time, capable of appearing as the responsible leader of all the best and best-educated African opinion in his country.

The political issue in 'settler' countries is, of course, exceptionally tense and complex. Between the African nationalist and the straightforward believers in European leadership the issue is simple—a battle, in which the Governments in London and Paris and Brussels have recently aided the African cause, with its inevitable sequel of African majority rule. Far more complex is the relationship of African leaders with European liberals and multi-racial parties in their own countries. There is, in Tanganyika, an example of racial tolerance under the leadership of Mr. Nyerere which is the best model in East and Central Africa of what can be achieved. It is simply a position in which Europeans and Asians are assured, while the Government's word holds, of equal rights with all other citizens, under a rule of law, with opportunity to farm or to trade, or to stand in elections if they wish and can find support. This situation is not perfect from the non-African point of view—there have been some wild speeches from local TANU firebrands, Asians here and there have had reason to be nervous, the quality of the administration, under rapid Africanization, will inevitably suffer for some time. Moreover, European settlers were so few that in fact Tanganyika has always been a country dominated by the Colonial Office rather than by settlers, and racial tensions were for that reason much less acute. None the less, the present situation reflects the greatest credit on all races and above all on Mr. Nyerere.

But 'multi-racialism' in Kenya or Central Africa has had a different ring. It has always in fact concealed an assumption that Europeans would continue to play a part in *politics* (for few would deny their rôle as specialists, civil servants, entrepreneurs) wholly disproportionate to their numbers. As late as 1959, Sir John Moffat was saying in the same speech: [9]

It is necessary for us to stop deceiving ourselves. The ultimate result of development in the Federation is that Africans will outnumber all other races on the Voters' Rolls and thus be in control. This will happen all over Africa, including the Union of South Africa.

and

It appears likely that the swing of power from European to African will take place in Nyasaland within a year. In Northern Rhodesia it may take fifteen or twenty years.

In some ways the constitutional tactics of the Colonial Office appeared to lend support to this multiracialist dream. In the necessary progress from a Communal to a Common Roll, the first stages have in many countries contained a mixture, some seats being reserved for Asians, Europeans, Arabs or Africans and some being on a Common Roll. But since a simple Common Roll, in face of African nationalism, clearly and openly involves either an African victory or an obvious tailoring of African franchise to prevent it, complex mechanisms by which Africans must get European votes, or vice versa, were invented in differing forms at certain stages in Tanganyika, Kenya and Northern Rhodesia. This mechanism was presumably designed first to ensure a continued and liberal European representation in a Legislative Council and, secondly, to ensure the election of moderate Africans. It was also a time-gaining mechanism, to give Africans experience of limited responsibility and Europeans time to adjust to the future. Thus its appearance of multiracialism, if that implies disproportionate European representation, was not its main or lasting purpose.

It is not surprising that Europeans in the Rhodesias and Kenya should have supposed that, granted a measure of African advancement, a share of political control quite disproportionate to mere numbers would still be reserved to them. This was the last shred of their original expectation, undoubtedly shared by most responsible people and by the British and French Governments up to

[9] Sir John Moffat, speech in Study Conference, 'Rhodesia: the Development of a Multiracial State' (Lusaka, United Northern Rhodesia Association, 1959).

1939, that most of the colonial territories in Africa would remain dependent for an indefinably long time—in fact, until such time as African and European 'standards' had become virtually indistinguishable. Thus as late as 1960 the Election Manifesto of the Kenya Coalition, led by Sir Ferdinand Cavendish-Bentinck, contained as one major aim of policy 'To prevent any lowering of the standards of Western Civilization'.[10] The relevance of Independence in West African countries such as Ghana or Nigeria, so much more advanced and with an economy not actually created (as were those of Central and East Africa) by Europeans, seemed to be small. The deplorable Belgian abandonment of the Congo before any reliable African political system had been founded seemed, particularly in Kenya with its strong tribalism, a plain warning of the risks Whitehall was taking. Nor have Africans, or the metropolitan governments, given full weight to the intense local patriotism of settlers. Among the best of them, it has not been prejudice or superiority to the Africans which has created the deep anxiety and bitterness which the Europeans have felt; it has been a love for the country of their adoption into which their lives have been committed, and a passionate wish to go on tending, in security, the homes they have built and the fields which they have made to flourish. In case this should seem a purely British notion, it is worth quoting a few comments from the Congo.[11]

The settlers repeatedly showed their bitterness at the indifference with which their opinions were treated. Some groups insisted strongly that without them the Congo could never have been what it is today. Declarations of attachment to 'la patrie congolaise' have become more and more frequent. For many of our compatriots in Africa, the Congo has the same significance as the home country once had for them. Some have gone as far as to demand autonomy, even secession.

And again :

It has become so much a question only of the rights of the natives (*autochtones*) that in the end the Belgians who have established themselves in the Congo with their families are altogether forgotten.

[10] *Now and the Future* (Nairobi, Policy Statement of the Kenya Coalition, 1961).
[11] Record and discussion of dominant opinions of Congolese, Government and Settlers in a Symposium organized by the *Institut Belge de Science Politique* and published as *L'avenir politique du Congo Belge* (Brussels, 1960) (translated).

It is, of course, absurd to claim that European settlers built these countries for the Africans. Their motives were mainly self-regarding and claims for gratitude are misplaced, although they are sometimes made. But too few people in metropolitan countries realize the risk and hardship of the early days, the determination needed to conquer wild nature, and the superb achievement which some of the Kenya farms, or the mines of the Copperbelt, really represent.

It was perhaps inevitable that the gradual change of political opinion and power in democratic metropolitan countries should be reflected in their colonial policies. The deep discrepancy between the 'trustee' assumptions of modern European governments and the 'daughter-state' assumptions of colonists of an earlier age was bound to come to the surface in a conflict more agonizing for its sincerity on both sides, a conflict which has already issued in tragedy in the Congo and Algeria. Even in a country so well integrated as Great Britain, these changes have strained relations acutely. In Belgium the profound internal dissension, cultural, religious and political, had fatal results on its colony into which such a remarkable effort of enterprise and devotion had been poured.[12]

From the African point of view, this might seem to be a domestic matter of good faith and conscience between Europeans : if settlers are misled by their own governments, their own governments should compensate them. The implications of Sir John Moffat's statements—that Nyasaland, backward but with no European settlement, would have self-government at once while Northern Rhodesia, far richer and rather better educated, must wait fifteen to twenty years, could have only one meaning in African ears—that the presence of settlers delays independence. Africans are naturally not prepared to accept such an argument. To the European demands for good government—i.e. the European-type government of a daughter-cell—the Africans oppose a demand for self-government for a huge African majority. They

[12] For some account of the reflection of metropolitan politics on the Congo administration, see G. Brausch, *Belgian Administration in the Congo* (London, Oxford University Press for Institute of Race Relations, 1961), written by an experienced colonial Belgian administrator. A correspondent wrote in the summer of 1961 that the two premier Institutes of Sociology in Belgium were still fighting each other in the Congo and in Belgium 'with the tenacity of Chicago gangs'.

are therefore extremely wary of the bait of multiracialism where it implies continued minority rule. Yet they are equally conscious of the need to co-operate with Europeans in the economic and technical field in the interests of the economy and of their whole people, and may be personally quite willing to do so. Thus their policy will include a resolute demand for nothing less than majority government, a rejection of multiracialist political parties; and an offer of co-operation outside politics. This is a situation which Europeans have been slow to understand. They have interpreted African intransigence about political power to mean a total rejection of Europeans, a mere racialism, and have persisted to the last moment with multiracialist political parties, long after any political action by Europeans has become futile and confusing. An acceptance by both sides that a multiracial state is one in which all citizens, irrespective of colour, can play a full part on equal terms, but without minority rule, is desperately needed if East and Central Africa is to develop its real potential.

2. AFTER INDEPENDENCE—THE PROBLEM OF POWER

Before turning to the entirely new problems facing African leaders after Independence, it may be interesting to look at the actual African members of the Parliaments and Legislative Councils, the men who are the first legislators of these new societies.[13] The Tables on pages 284-5 give at least some simple information as to age, education and occupation for seven countries, including all the four Houses of Assembly in Nigeria. The figures given for the Members' connexion, if any, with a chiefly family must be taken with great caution. There are many kinds of chief; the extended family means that 'connexion' is a very wide term indeed; and it does not always follow that membership of a chiefly family was decisive or even always of great importance in securing election. But perhaps the negative answers—the large number of Members who did not claim any such connexion—is of some interest. The main inferences from these Tables are obvious—the

[13] These details were collected for this book by Dr. P. Whitaker for Uganda, Mr. C. Hayes for Kenya, Mr. J. A. K. Leslie and Mr. A. Nihill for Tanganyika, Mme. de Lusignan for Congo (Brazzaville), Mr. E. Twumasi for Ghana and the four Nigerian Governments, and Mr. M. Crowder for Senegal. The figures were reduced to tabular form by Miss V. Taylor. I am deeply grateful to all of them for carrying out a task needing much patience and tact.

Table XI
AGE DISTRIBUTION

	20–29	30–39	40–49	50–59	60+	Unknown
NIGERIA—						
(1) FEDERAL HOUSE OF REPRESENTATIVES						
Ministers & Junior Ministers (40)	2	14	21	1	1	1
Other Northern Members (146)	28	64	39	14	—	1
Other Eastern Members (61)	2	40	19	—	—	—
Other Western Members (56)	—	25	20	10	—	1
Lagos (1)	—	—	1	—	—	—
TOTAL (304)	32	143	100	25	1	3
(2) EASTERN HOUSE OF ASSEMBLY	1	23	39	14	2	7
(3) WESTERN HOUSE OF ASSEMBLY	6	54	42	16	3	—
(4) NORTHERN HOUSE OF ASSEMBLY	14	47	38	29	6	1
GHANA NATIONAL ASSEMBLY	5	41	45	8	4	6
KENYA LEGISLATIVE COUNCIL	4	25	8	4	—	—
TANGANYIKA NATIONAL ASSEMBLY	12	23	3	—	—	10
UGANDA LEGISLATIVE COUNCIL	7	29	12	4	—	—
SENEGAL NATIONAL ASSEMBLY	—	20	36	15	7	1
MALI NATIONAL ASSEMBLY	2	20	34	13	2	7
REPUBLIQUE DU CONGO NATIONAL ASSEMBLY	7	31	18	2	—	—
	90	456	375	130	25	35

General Note. In all four tables, a sample of 52 out of 77 African Members is given for Uganda, and 135 out of 170 for Northern Nigeria.

Table XII
EDUCATION

	Primary	Secondary	Teacher Training	Higher Technical or Professional	Graduate	Unknown
NIGERIA—						
FEDERAL	126	24	70	34	49	1
EAST	22 + 3 (a)	6	23	13	17	—
WEST	36	16 + 2(b)	26	12	28	1
NORTH	85 + 15 (c)	6	22	7	—	—
GHANA	43	8	32	13	13	—
KENYA	—	11	11	5	13	1
TANGANYIKA	3	16	1 (d)	8	5	15
UGANDA	2	14	19	8	9	—
SENEGAL (Ministers only)	—	1	6	2	8	—
REPUBLIQUE DU CONGO	46	6	3	3	—	—
	381	110	213	105	142	18

Notes:

    (a) 3 took a 'commercial course', probably after primary.

    (b) 2 took a 'commercial qualification', probably after secondary.

    (c) Arabic or Koranic studies.

    (d) Presumably several informants failed to recall this, since in Table XIII (Occupations) 11 are given as 'Teachers'. But some may come among the group of 'unknowns', and some are graduates.

Table XIII
PREVIOUS OCCUPATION

	Teacher	Trader Business-man	Lawyer	Civil (c) Servant	Pro- (a) fessions	Farming Fishing	Village or Local Chief	Clerical & Co-operative	Miscel-(b) laneous
NIGERIA—									
FEDERAL	98	44	23	87	20	8	1	15	5
EAST	34	17	5	9	13	4	1	1	2
WEST	43	34	14	7	6	4	—	6	7
NORTH	26	16	—	76	3	2	7	—	2
GHANA	38	24	9	22	7	6	—	—	3
KENYA	19	4	2	5	3	4	—	—	4
TANGANYIKA	11	7	—	7	1	1	3	6	12
UGANDA	21	6	5	8	2	—	—	6	4
SENEGAL	21	9	12	23	5	—	—	5	4
MALI	22	8	1	9	13	—	—	20	4
REPUBLIQUE du CONGO	18	9	—	—	6	3	—	13	9
	351	178	71	253	79	32	12	72	56

Notes:

(a) 'Professions' include medical, journalist, engineer, Church, veterinary.

(b) Miscellaneous includes craftsmen, foremen, a few Trade Unionists, a political organizer, and some 'unknown'.

(c) 'Civil Servant' includes staff of Native Authorities, but 'Scribe' is included under 'Clerical'

Table XIV
CHIEFLY CONNEXION

	Yes	No	Unknown
NIGERIA—			
FEDERAL	116	186	3
EAST	18	65	3
WEST	39	81	1
NORTH	83	46	6
GHANA	30	78	1
KENYA	4	34	3
TANGANYIKA	13	29	6
UGANDA	—	—	—
SENEGAL	—	—	—
REPUBLIQUE DU CONGO	19	38	1
	322	557	24

preponderance of the 30–39 age group; the large numbers of teachers, civil servants, lawyers and businessmen, and the very low representation of farmers; the quite considerable group with only primary education. The effect of patronage in Northern Nigeria is indicated not only by the large number connected with ruling families but by the 'civil servants', mainly on the staff of the Native Authorities largely controlled by the Emirs; by contrast, the Ibo-dominated Eastern Nigerian House shows relatively few men of 'chiefly' connexion (and most of them 'honorary chiefs') from a society which traditionally was not organized under chiefs. The fairly large number of men from chiefly families in Ghana is largely due to the Northern membership, where the sons or heirs of traditional chiefs in many cases joined the C.P.P. in order to retain influence.

Tribal origins were also recorded, but the information is somewhat too detailed to record here, and it follows a necessary pattern if it is assumed that a fellow-tribesman is likely to be elected in a particular tribal area. Since constituencies are geographical, the distribution would thus be bound to follow tribal distribution and population density. From the well-known facts it is clear that Western Nigeria must have a large Yoruba group (90 out of 121 members), East Nigeria a large Ibo group (58 out of 86). In North Nigeria 89 out of 135 were recorded as Hausa or Fulani. In Ghana 55 out of 109 were recorded as Akan. In Senegal, Wolof (26) and Toucouleur (11) account for just under half of the whole Chamber; in the République du Congo, the 'downstream' tribes (Bacongo, Balali, Bassounde, Bateke) dominate. By contrast, in East Africa, where tribal groups are smaller, the Tanganyika figures show well over twenty tribal groups, while the highest figure for any group is four (Sukuma); in Kenya, the highest figures are Luo (five) and Kikuyu (four); in Uganda, the Baganda rise to 14 out of the 52 in the sample. Thus as far as the supreme legislative body is concerned, assuming geographical constituencies, none of the East African territories can be dominated by a single tribal group, whereas the opposite is true of much of West Africa.

As a new African government first assumes power, there seems to be much in its favour. There is enthusiasm, there are congratulations and good wishes from the world; many promotions to make, ambassadorships to be filled, national development plans to occupy energies and give a sense of progress and achievement. Above all, it is an African government, it is 'ours'.

But there is a debit side. Naturally, the age-old frustrations of being governed were turned against the colonial power over years of agitation and electioneering. 'The anti-colonial struggle had aroused much expectation of greater freedom from restraint which is not compatible with the other goals of the nationalist movement.'[14] Nervous expatriates had often quoted the wilder expectations of the uneducated ('We shall print more bank notes'; 'The Bank will be nationalized and forced to give us loans') and as caricature these stories are not important. But there is a more serious side. In rural areas there could be great impatience with continuing agricultural reform;[15] and in the modern sector much expectation of a quick inheritance of the opportunities and profits of expatriate trade. And there are other reversals. The Trade Unions, once a weapon of anti-colonialism, may seem to be sabotaging the national effort. Expatriate capital, once described in blood-thirsty terms, is now to be welcomed. Tribal ceremony, once described as 'bush', may be valued as traditional. Independence brings its own confusions.

More important is a vacuum in social policy, though there may be plenty of administrative plans. Parties coming to power in the anti-colonial phase usually beat their rivals by better organization and publicity or by tribal appeal rather than by detailed policies. It was, as Africans admitted, impossible to discover any real policy differences between the Action Group and the N.C.N.C. in the Nigeria of 1961, and much the same could be said of the two parties in Northern Rhodesia, in Kenya and in Uganda. This is a difficulty not widely perceived as yet in Africa; it will become acute as there begins to be a differentiation of interests under the façade of national unity or a social problem which arouses a strong conflict. What does quickly strike the new government is that they are now the object of criticism in place of the colonial administration, and they often find it hard to bear.

Also troublesome to the national leadership is the widespread

[14] E. Wallerstein in *The Political Economy of Contemporary Africa*, supra.
[15] A. I. Richards: 'It is a striking fact how often modern political parties ... are said by the villagers to favour a return to the old ways and to a world in which there are no latrines to be dug and no anti-erosion ridges to be made' (*East African Chiefs*, supra).

jubilation of self-seekers in the party ranks. Power means at last the reward for much work and energy, it means jobs and privileges and possibly cash for services rendered. The imposition of a standard of conduct and discipline is a trying task for a victorious party.

These are mainly secondary matters. The great issues, taking a different form in different countries, are tribalism; the conflict between traditional and modern—the old authority and the new democratic forms; the whole control and status of land; the whole system of local administration; and, ultimately, the moral standards and social norms which are to be established in society. To tackle problems of this scale and depth will mean that the authority of government itself has to be deeply entrenched and legitimized; that a sense of national unity overriding sectional interests has to be built. So much, indeed, African governments clearly foresee. But in the very process of achieving these ends, frictions and antagonisms are bound to be caused. At least by Western ways of thinking, the new governments should be making provision for change of government without revolution or dismemberment. To put it differently, government should foresee the gradual differentiation of interests within a community and be prepared with a constitutional system capable of containing them.

By far the best known reaction to these problems in Africa, and the only one which is capable of analysis as a coherent whole, is the system most clearly expressed in Ghana, with its variants in Guinea and Mali and affinities in many other States. It is based on the *parti unique* and its leader; 'socialism'; 'democracy'; anti-imperialism.

Socialism in West Africa has certain definite meanings at the leadership level—Dr. Nkrumah, M. Senghor, M. Sékou Touré are men well read in political philosophy. It has also a vague popular appeal,[16] particularly since leaders under Marxist influence equated the battle against imperialism with one against capitalism, and much oratory in press, radio and public meetings has published the equation abroad. The serious content includes above all the devotion to central planning of the use of resources, both human and material, for the common good. The West

[16] E.g. 'In plain language, a "socialist state" is a state in which every citizen is free, contented and happy.' 'Ghana's Road to Socialism', in *Labour*, Official Journal of the Ghana T.U.C., vol. 1, no. 6, December 1960.

African press, both English and French, and the speeches of
leaders hammer home again and again this planning theme, often
opposed to the selfishness of the profit motive. Planning, in African circumstances, does in fact mean not only State control but
a great deal of State enterprise, particularly in the field of industry,
finance and marketing. The major private enterprise sector, being
mainly expatriate, is *hors concours* to some extent, and the attitude to the (mainly small) African private entrepreneur is uncertain, though contractors and traders still flourish. Guinea has
repented of an attempt to handle all distribution through the
State, and there was nervousness in Ghana in 1961 about the
reaction of traders and mammies to the rumoured plans for State
Consumer Co-operatives. It would seem that in practice a mixed
economy will be allowed, with State enterprise at the key points
and in major undertakings. It is more the size and importance of
their enterprises and, of course, the fact that they are foreign
rather than their profit-making which makes expatriate firms the
target of nationalization rumours and it applies, naturally enough,
more to the long-established than to the foreigners newly tempted
into the country.

There is, however, little or no emphasis on the moral aspects
of socialism, the gap between rich and poor. In Tropical Africa
as a whole exactly the reverse process is at present in full swing;
the salaries and perquisites of the ruling group and of the whole
professional and educated class are at or near the old expatriate
level, the profits of contractors and politicians are often enormous,
while very large sections of the economy remain at the old levels.
Despite constant inquiry, we could find little evidence of 'socialist'
thinking in this moral sense, save among a few of the younger
intellectuals in Lagos and Accra, mainly in salaried or professional jobs, who were becoming anxious about the gap between
the Chevrolet society and the bicycle society.[17]

The second main element in the African idea of socialism is in
fact linked to the conceptions of the single Party. Perhaps M.
Sékou Touré has explained most articulately this conception.[18]

[17] Mr. Nyerere's decision to ask all Tanganyikan Ministers to accept a cut
of £1,000 a year in salary is a notable exception to the general rule.
[18] For an analysis of his philosophy in terms of political science, see E.
Wallerstein, 'Political Theory in an African Context', Third Annual Meeting,
African Studies Association, Hartford, September 1960. He draws mainly on
M. Sékou Touré's own publication, *L'action politique du P.D.G.*

He has made it clear that it is not wholly Marxist, since he specifically rejects the class struggle as irrelevant to Africa. The Party is
a party of all classes; it is 'supreme over all other institutions
existing in the country', particularly in terms of political philosophy. It is not a party of the *élite*, the vanguard, the intellectuals,
but of the whole of society. Indeed, to be in advance of the people
is a fault which intellectuals must correct in themselves. It is a
parallel but superior structure to the administration, and has
rights even in the judicial field. 'Magistrates are reminded that
the political party will interest itself in everything without reserve. Everything which is political is part of its domain.'[19] It is
democratic because its policies should result from a constant up-
ward movement of discussion and suggestion from the popular
level, and through many branches of society such as youth,
women's movements or Trade Unions, to the centre. Many paral-
lels can readily be drawn from Ghana, where the main Party
newspapers carry the banner 'The Party is Supreme'. The extreme
form of the doctrine can be quoted from Mr. Tettegah's T.U.C.
paper, *Labour*:[20]

In Ghana, the Party is both triumphant and supreme. The Party's
supremacy is unquestionable. Its decisions of democratic centralism
are binding on every individual no matter what. All instructions go
out from the Central Committee to ministers, to constituencies and
wards, to the workers in the Trades Union Congress and farmers
under the United Ghana Farmers' Council and Co-operatives who
form the main stream of the Party, to schools and to homes.
Nothing is less important for the Party, nothing is too small to
escape its house-to-house attention. Not even the little steward boy
who got tired of waiting seven hours to take part in a 'spontaneous'
demonstration for a visiting dignitary.

Some Ghanaians would regard this—particularly the statement
that the Party gives instructions to Ministers—as an exaggerated
statement from a group anxious to establish the supremacy of the
Party and its great organs of the T.U.C. and the Farmers' Council
as superior to the Cabinet. But since the Cabinet and the Central
Committee interlock, since both are ruled by the President, and
since words are not used very accurately in the Ghana Party press,
this is a fruitless inquiry; what in fact matter are the ever-shifting
personal relationships and groupings within the leadership. And,

[19] Wallerstein, op. cit.   [20] *Labour*, vol. 2, no. 7, January 1961.

whatever rivalries there may be, in fact the Party wields a devastating power throughout Ghana. Villages in the Party's bad books get no road repairs (this is apt to happen in Nigeria too); university lecturers guard their tongue, even foreign visitors may find themselves expelled if they offend.

It is not necessary to elaborate on the 'leader' cult, which has been carried to its furthest lengths in Ghana, save perhaps to recall the observation of Mannoni,[21] that when colonial paternalism is withdrawn local leadership assumes immense emotional significance as an alternative.

The final element of the recipe—anti-imperialism—is a substitute enemy to replace the colonial government, and of course fits well with socialism and with the Pan-African ideal.

It is not difficult to see the reasons for this composite formula and its effectiveness. Times of crisis and times of violent social change have always made liberal politics difficult and dictatorship easy. Cromwell had many of the same troubles from his followers as Dr. Nkrumah, and the mind runs back to the Athenian demagogues and Aristotle's *Politics* and to other great revolutions—in France, in Russia, in the Turkey of Mustapha Kemal. I remember seeing on one African desk the life of Kemal, the life of Napoleon, the works of Clausewitz, Lenin's *Imperialism* and a copy of Rousseau—a somewhat strange company, but with some significance. What emerges is the deeply-felt insecurity of the leadership in a country which has only felt nationhood for a matter of months or a few years and which is ruled, not by a distant and mysterious Great Power, but by its own people. When Ghana gained its Independence, political divisions almost verging on civil war still existed.

For a period of well over two years before Independence Ghana politics had taken a very violent and bitter turn; the National Liberation Movement, with its headquarters in Ashanti, had, over some parts of the country, effectively challenged the Government Party, the C.P.P., and had almost denied them freedom of speech. There was bloodshed; Dr. Nkrumah himself had been unable to visit parts of the country; the Independence celebrations were virtually confined to the capital city, and, even as they proceeded, there was an armed uprising in Togoland.[22]

[21] Mannoni, op. cit.
[22] David Williams in *The Africa of 1961* (London, Royal African Society, 1961).

The imprinting of unity takes precedence over every other need; even Mr. Nyerere took the view in 1961 that Tanganyika could not afford an opposition for a time; it would arise eventually when policy differences within TANU and within the community had crystallized, *within the assumption of national unity*, to make it both desirable and safe.

Western attitudes to this African solution are apt to fly to extremes. At the one end is the whitewashing attitude of those who ignore the real elements of dictatorship. Chief Awolowo of Western Nigeria gave them a sharp rebuke : [23]

There is a new-fangled theory now being propounded with erudition and gusto in the countries of the so-called Western democracies. The proponents of this theory hold the view that it is inappropriate and hardly fair to expect a newly emergent African nation to practise democracy as it is known and practised in the countries of Western Europe and the United States of America. Every mortal blow that is struck by an independent African nation at the vitals of democracy is rationalized by these theorists as the African's peculiar method of adapting democratic usages to his barbaric and primitive environment. The denial of fundamental human rights, the destruction of the rule of law, and the suppression of opposition have been brilliantly and felicitously rationalized. The outrageous declaration by an African leader that a one-party system is in accord with the democratic way of life has been ably defended by these spokesmen of the Western democracies.

His words would be echoed by many highly educated and democratic men in Ghana, who are striving in their way to retain or regain individual liberties, who are deeply concerned about Ghana's dictatorial reputation in the world, and who feel betrayed when foreigners—and particularly the British—whitewash the régime.

The opposite attitude is one of panic—to which expatriate businessmen have been too addicted—or hostile criticism, of which there has been much in the British press. In fact, few if any foreigners know the real relationships within the Ghana leadership, still less the President's mind. He has openly described himself as a Marxist-Socialist, and as a non-denominational Christian; he has a tremendous hold over the Party and over Ghana; he has a mind quite capable of flexibility; and he has not

[23] Chief O. Awolowo, *Awo* (Cambridge University Press, 1960).

passed any point of no return either domestically or internationally. To prophesy whether he and Ghana, or M. Sékou Touré and Guinea, or M. Modibo Keita and Mali will move this way or that is to make guesses for which neither history nor the facts of today provide sure indications. The reasons for the present policy of national unity controlled by a monolithic party are clear enough; the derogation from individual freedom is clear, and to be deplored; the shrill tone of the press is unfortunate—though, as one Ghanaian observed, well within the West African tradition. For the future, it is by deeds rather than words or rumours or theories that judgement must be made. At the present moment no one could honestly say that the extreme one-party systems enshrine any of the really important elements of democracy as it has come to be understood in the West;[24] this is too important an issue to evade.

It is vain to look for an alternative political theory in Tropical Africa, though practice is often widely different. The two southern regions of Nigeria, though dominated by largely tribal parties, have retained far more of the Western parliamentary air; the North is still an aristocracy. Most of the French-speaking territories are governed by a small group of intellectuals backed by a massive party majority. Neither in Northern Rhodesia nor in Uganda is any pattern of the future yet clear, though Mr. Kaunda would no doubt like to move to a solution based on TANU's precedent. In Tanganyika, TANU is indeed a monolithic party, and the opposition probably tolerated only because it is too weak to count. There are ambitious and impatient young men within TANU, but the tone has been set by Mr. Nyerere, and at present it is a moderate and liberal tone. Unlike Dr. Nkrumah, Mr. Nyerere has contrived to win to his side virtually all the intellectuals and many important chiefs, and his parliamentary team is a good mixture of all the most important African elements—the intellectuals, the chiefs, the Co-operatives and the businessmen. It will take time before government is so established that it is

[24] Perhaps the most vigorous onslaught on centralism is that of F. A. Hayek in *The Road to Serfdom* (London, Routledge, 1944), but see also the writings of Berdyaev and many others. Hayek quotes Peter Drucker's remark in *The End of Economic Man* (London, Heinemann, 1939): 'The less freedom there is, the more there is talk of "the new freedom". Yet this new freedom is a mere word which covers the exact contradiction of all that Europe ever meant by freedom.'

294 THE NEW SOCIETIES OF TROPICAL AFRICA

beyond attack; and the weakness of the present situation is solely that too much depends on the central lynch-pin, the Prime Minister himself. On the whole, Tanganyika seems to be moving fairly smoothly towards a bourgeois intellectual society, in which real and varied interests can be combined by negotiation and compromise and the existence of a single party and leader is less destructive of free discussion than in some other areas.

The possibilities in Kenya are still not yet fully disclosed. It is, to say the least, uncertain whether Mr. Kenyatta can unite Kenya Africans behind a single nationalist party. Not only tribal jealousies but individual personalities are strong; and it may be that a coalition, in which the main areas and tribal groups of Kenya are carefully balanced at ministerial level, will be the first and strongest form of African government which the country's divisions and personalities allow. Although there is good economic sense in the proposed East African Federation, it may well be that limited co-operation through a successor to the East African High Commission is as much as African resources of trained men can at present manage. The figures in Chapter X have shown the heavy demands for Africanizing the public services in all three States; to attempt to add a federal government, with both legislators and civil servants, on top of the three territorial governments would be an excessive strain. It is certainly quite possible that the main leaders in Kenya, Tanganyika, Northern Rhodesia and Nyasaland will announce some form of political co-operation, since Federal Rhodesian policies at present are forcing Africans in Northern Rhodesia to look to the East rather than to Salisbury for any sympathy and support. Such international interests might divert attention from internal rivalries in Kenya and give wider scope for leaders who are jostling each other on the smaller Kenyan stage. Nevertheless, the first task is to create a real sense of nationhood out of the very varied elements in Kenya; and in this Kenya European settlers, with their strong patriotism, could greatly help if the new government proves willing to win their support. It is from the basis of a stable unity that any of the three territories is most likely to be able to contribute to federal co-operation. Although Kenya is not rich in mineral resources, and agricultural development is still patchy, it could be the dark horse of East Africa. Both European administration and European settlers have set standards of performance which are becoming part of African standards. Arabs and Asians have also contributed much, and there is a vitality in this close contact of races which, if it does not issue negatively in conflict, must mean positive progress. There is still a chance that Kenya could show what can be achieved when African majority government is combined with continued European enterprise on the land as well as in commerce and industry. If this should happen, the implications for Southern Rhodesia, the other country where such a partnership is theoretically possible, would be very significant.

It is in Uganda that the current political horizon is most gloomy and overcast. Undoubtedly, Buganda and the smaller kingdoms are in a very uncertain position. Should a really colourful democratic leader arise from either of the two democratic national parties, with a strong party organization and an inspiring programme of united nationhood, the Kabaka's government could find itself undermined and isolated. But at present there is little sign of real strength in the democratic parties, nor of real statesmanship among the traditional rulers. Bunyoro will certainly fight hard for the return of conquered provinces from Buganda; and none of the other provinces have shown, from their present ruling elements, any lively enthusiasm for national unity. It is probably true that local patriotism is still the strongest political force in Uganda; while that remains so, the prospects for energetic government and for economic development remain bleak. Without strong leadership, degeneration into separatist movements, and even sporadic outbreaks of civil disturbance would not be far away.

In West Africa probably the three biggest issues are the future of Northern Nigeria and the political thinking within Islam; the future of Ghana; and the possible reunion of some of the French-speaking territories, which is mentioned later in this chapter.

If the Northern rulers in Nigeria can give enough scope to their younger and better-educated men, and relax some of the authoritarian aspects of the régime, they may well have a long expectation of control. The danger is that, irritated by the 'subversive' activities from the two southern parties and by discontent in the Middle Belt, and with a growing realization that there is no British government to inhibit them, the Emirs might feel more moved to re-establish or at least re-emphasize the Empire of Sokoto, deal forcibly with opposition, and create an almost impassable boundary between their own kingdom and the other Regions. A reaction of this type would bode ill for the Federal Government, dominated by Northern members. Thomas Hodgkin [25] has pointed out the powerful reforming movements inside Islam, which are both modernist in politics and social policy and stricter in Islamic belief; but these reforming movements have made little impact in Nigeria. Although some of the French-speaking Muslim territories, such as Mali, are counted among the most modernist, socialist and progressive, there are certain similarities of feeling and tradition among the powerful Muslim groups of the savannah country which might take a political form if the tensions with the sophisticated, democratic and in many ways subversive philosophy of the coastal towns and forest peoples became too intrusive. Economically, the marriage between savannah, forest and the towns, ports and factories of the Coast is of high importance; politically it will suffer many strains. The high quality of many Northern Nigerian statesmen, both at Kaduna and in the Federal Government, and the universal respect for Sir Abubakar are encouraging signs that more moderate and progressive policies will prevail.

The situation in Ghana hangs upon quite different factors. It is already clear that the next five or six years will be a period in which heavy economic sacrifice may have to be demanded, especially from the farmers. There is certainly a smouldering opposition to the régime in Ashanti and among many intellectuals and displaced chiefs; and there are some acute tensions among the C.P.P. leadership. But even if the President cannot bring home many resounding successes in the next year or two, his personal prestige and the support of so many officials who depend upon him are at present unassailable. It would be a mistake to assume that the critics are all whole-hearted. While the loss of democratic freedom is deeply felt by some of the best elements in Ghana, pride in her achievements, excitement at her prospects, the lack of any real alternative, and in some cases either fear of dismissal or hope of promotion makes any single-minded opposition unlikely. It may be that there will have to be a 'New Economic Policy', in which the farmers have some concessions; a purge, or several purges, of

[25] T. Hodgkin in a series of articles in *West Africa*, 22 September, 10 November, 1956. The Tijaniyya movement, led by Sheikh Ibrahima Nyas, of Kaolack, Senegal, has some strong contacts in Kano.

the Party leadership; a good deal of begging for credit from Iron Curtain countries and a foreign policy which pays for it, at least in strong words. But the dynamism of Ghana is far from exhausted, the Party grip is strong, the President himself flexible and a necessary symbol of national pride. There is every reason to think that this combination can carry the régime through the rough waters which probably lie ahead.

Even where the political situation seems clear, prophecy is exceptionally dangerous in Tropical Africa, since we are dealing with societies which have yet to find their political balance, in which the internal differentiation of economic interests is not yet disclosed, and in which the real social issues have not yet been faced. This is true even in Ghana, the most politically evolved, since the Party is not solving issues but postponing them by keeping public opinion in a constant state of effervescence around the symbol of the Leader and the Pan-African ideal. But a few general issues can be identified.

First, there are differences in where power rests. In Kenya and Tanganyika, and probably in Northern Rhodesia, where no one tribe dominates, where the commercial and industrial sector is largely in Asian and European hands, the leadership, mainly of the intellectual type, will have to rely upon dispersed support from the more powerful tribal groups through their chiefs and councils and from the Co-operatives—in Northern Rhodesia the African mineworkers would take the place of the Co-operatives. This points towards a more collaborative system held together by a single party machine. In contrast, the leadership in the southern regions of Nigeria and Ghana has a much larger commercial and managerial element, and its danger lies in neglecting the political force which the new young unemployed may exercise. These young school-leavers whose predicament has already been mentioned will soon have a vote, and all over Africa, but especially in the West, they will be troublesome. Ghana, with some opposition from at least three quarters (chiefs, farmers and intellectuals) is more dangerously placed than Nigeria, where the Western Government rests on broad traditional support and the Eastern gives full opening for Ibo competitive energy; danger there lies more in the minority tribes. It would appear that in the main French-speaking areas the highly sophisticated leadership in Abidjan and Dakar, and probably in Brazzaville, will retain mass support with the aid of French and Common Market funds to subsidize agricultural advance, while Guinea and Mali rely primarily on the mobilization of national enthusiasm through extremely active party cells right down to village level.

Second, it could be said that all governments face the problem of 'tribalism' and of building a nation. But in fact the various countries are very differently placed in this issue, and these differences create quite separate problems. In some areas, such as Eastern and Western Nigeria, it is the government itself which is tribally dominant, and difficulties spring from this fact. In Kenya and Tanganyika the question is one of managing coalitions involving six or eight major but not dominant groups. In Uganda, tension could take two forms—the arrangement of some confederation of the kingdoms, with a series of minority problems from the peripheral tribes; or a social struggle in which all-Uganda democratic parties in fact supplant the effective power of the traditional kingdoms and operate through the familiar party mechanism. In Ghana it is not so much tribalism as such but the possibility of economic tensions, into which tribal issues might be brought for support, which are threatening. In all areas, and especially those in which national unity and 'democratic centralism' is most heavily stressed, the process of creating the feeling of nationhood is bound to conflict temporarily with that of creating large 'unions' of states. It already seems clear that the smaller nationalism will have to come first, as the Nigerian Prime Minister has so often stressed, and that collaboration is likely to replace union as the key to inter-African relations.

Third, all governments have to face the need to maintain and accelerate the modernizing economic movement in the rural areas. In some areas this may mean facing critical issues of land tenure; in some areas (for example, Eastern Nigeria) the extreme reluctance to alienate land may have to be modified if European investment in mining or plantation is to be continued. In all areas some system of local administration suited to the new political circumstances will have to be evolved and strengthened. This is a complex issue which needs separate discussion.

3. LOCAL GOVERNMENT

The attention of the world is apt to focus on Lagos, Accra or Nairobi, where governments sit and speeches are made; little is

said of the government of the great mass of the African population, in the smaller towns, in forest villages and out on the open
plain. In colonial times there was the structure of Provincial and
District Commissioners, and below them some variety of indirect
rule through chiefs and councils. This structure was itself varied
and complicated. Colonial governments took some time to discover
that a great many African societies did not possess chiefs, or that
chiefs were not sole administrators. For long enough the Masai
'laibons' were believed to be chiefs, though in fact they had primarily magic-religious rather than political functions; societies
organized by age-sets or segmentary lineages [26] were a high trial
to District Officers ordered to discover a chief and administer
through him. Gradually, however, some kind of local chain of
command was established, often by using Africans in capacities
for which there was little or no sanction within their own cultural
pattern.[27] Dr. Richards well describes two of the main and contrasting difficulties in East Africa : [28]

The problem in the Interlacustrine tribes has been of turning
aristocracies into something more like democracies, and then altering
their whole concept of authority; that in the segmentary societies,
on the other hand, was at first a task of centralizing and amalgamat-
ing tiny discrete units and turning kinship heads and other informal
leaders into executive and often autocratic chiefs. This policy has
been followed more recently by an attempt to introduce our own
concept of democratic control by local councils.

The urge to establish more democratic procedures at the local
level, and also to create an African administrative link between
the village chief and the central government, led to the creation
of a fine miscellany of local Councils and Native Authorities, of
which every possible permutation must have been tried in different
territories and at different times. For example, in Tanganyika as

[26] A large lineage going back many generations may be split into segments
each of which manages some of its affairs—for example, land, although some
functions may still be reserved to the whole lineage.
[27] To give only one example of the difficulties, Fosbrooke mentions a tribe
(the Sonjo) in the Tanganyika Rift Valley where in effect authority rested with
the five 'owners of the water' whose sentence to deprive a tribesman of access
to water amounted to one of exile and probably death. (H. Fosbrooke, 'Tanganyika: The Application of Indirect Rule to Chiefless Societies', in *From
Tribal Rule to Modern Government* (Lusaka, Rhodes-Livingstone Institute,
1959).   [28] Richards, *East African Chiefs.*

late as 1960 a Native Authority could be a chief as Sole Native
Authority; a Chief-in-Council; a chief with a nominated, an indirectly elected or a directly elected Council or a mixture; there
might also be a fully modernized County or District Council,
based on election, with the chief either as active chairman or in-
active president. Similar difficulties arose in West Africa. While
in Western Nigeria the Resident was an immensely powerful
figure up to 1948, a large number of local Councils were then
instituted (many of which had to be suspended) and the Provincial Administration stepped back into an advisory role. In Eastern
Nigeria the first attempt at indirect rule was a failure, and the
Administration was forced to cancel it and install a new system
of elected councils.

Out of the great variety of forms and changes, it is roughly
safe to say that in most British territories, until African self-
government came, the District and Provincial Administration was
responsible for law and order and the channelling of government
orders to the Province, with a corps of agricultural and other
extension services loosely clustered round the Provincial Headquarters in an organization not unlike (though far from identical
with) that adopted in Britain in the Civil Defence regions. A
variety of chiefs would have direct responsibility for Customary
Law and certain other customary functions, usually with provision for appeal or review of legal decisions by the D.C. In some
cases judicial work was being or had been removed from the D.C.
to a Resident Magistrate in a Judicial Service. Thirdly, many
local government functions had been delegated to a variety of
local councils, in which chiefs were likely to play a nominated
part, often with executive functions, and to which the D.C. might
act, officially or unofficially, as adviser or supervisor.

The growth of powerful political parties and the establishment
of local M.P.s began to complicate this already complex situation
still further. As in India, before Independence but with internal
Congress Government, District Commissioners in Africa had to
accustom themselves to the political organizers of the party in
power not only making speeches—and naturally anti-colonial
speeches—all over 'their' District, but exercising very considerable
influence there too. It can be imagined that in, say, Tanganyika
the existence of a District Commissioner, a number of chiefs, a
District Council, a District Secretary of the immensely powerful

TANU, and finally a Legislative Council Member for the area could give rise to intricate definitions of powers and responsibilities. A circular issued from the Prime Minister's office in 1960 reminded the public that, since District Commissioners were no longer the representative of an alien power but servants of an African government elected by popular will, they were not to be approached with political complaints which should in future be directed to the Member. Further, the TANU local officials were separately reminded that they were not local rulers but party organizers. District Councils, although they had the inevitable TANU majority, even found it possible to rebuke the local TANU official for interfering in their sovereign jurisdiction; chiefs remained jealously in control of their customary functions.

This one example of the complexities of transition is perhaps enough to illustrate the problem. There would seem to be a tendency to create *political* posts in the Provincial Administration; this has been done, for example, in Eastern Nigeria, where Provincial Commissioners have been appointed from the party in power, with a Provincial Secretary as an advisory official on his staff, and with Provincial Assemblies, the first of which met in Enugu in February 1961. There have been proposals to assign junior Ministers to a provincial responsibility in Tanganyika. Below the provincial level, the tendency is gradually towards all-purpose elected Local Authorities, with jurisdiction on such matters as health, education, roads, sanitation, public works. The exact placing of police—which is clearly important—varies considerably; and the role of the District Officer, although important in practice, is becoming more nebulous and advisory in theory as his specific functions are gradually passed to all-purpose Authorities, a special judiciary, and a local political representative. This will make the D.C.'s job a very difficult one for Africans to assume. The tendency in some areas is also to rob the chief of 'modern' powers but to retain him in his customary role, which will vary widely in different societies. In other areas, by contrast, a regular bureaucracy of 'Civil Service' chiefs has been established. Special studies of East African chiefs [29] have shown the peculiar conflict

[29] Richards, *East African Chiefs*, supra, and Lloyd Fallers, *Bantu Bureaucracy*, supra, Fallers remarks : 'A person's position within the State was liable to distort his position within the lineage and thus disrupt the operation of the lineage in terms of its own rules. And conversely, lineage ties tended to intrude into the State system and to make for instability within it' (pp. 16–17),

of roles and loyalties in the gradual creation of these 'Civil Service' chiefs by the Protectorate Government of Uganda out of men who had lineage roles in the first instance. More comparative study of the policies adopted by independent African governments in this field of local administration would be of great interest.

The political significance of this uncertain situation is considerable. Clearly, in those countries which have adopted the supreme single party as the main tool of government, there is an opportunity to place a party 'Commissar' either overtly in control of a local area or as a political check on the local administration. There was a strong feeling in Ghana, for example, that in some cases a staunch C.P.P. District Officer might have direct access to Party headquarters or even to the President's office in parallel to the hierarchy leading to the appropriate department. Combined with Party domination of locally elected Councils, this system could ensure that neither a local chief nor an obstructive civil servant could stand in the way of Party policy. In the countries which are endeavouring to create a democratic local government less tied to the central party machine, the main difficulty has been in the quality of staff and in the difficulty which officials may have in standing up to powerful Councils bent on corrupt practice. Much thought is being given in West Africa to the creation of a permanent, transferable local government service, adequately paid and properly protected; but this is both a costly task and one hampered by the difficulty of attracting good candidates. Moreover, in many areas—for example, Western Nigeria—the local chief is an extremely important person; it was much easier for even a junior expatriate officer with the weight of the colonial government behind him to take him to task, courteously and even jokingly, than for a junior African official with little family standing. Between Africans there is naturally a tendency for the older prestige ratings to reappear, even if they had long slumbered beneath the bureaucratic ratings of the colonial system.

Some important issues arise from this transition from a colonial administration to an African political system at the local level.

and: 'Soga society does not consist of one group wholly committed to civil service, i.e. universalism, and another group wholly committed to kinship and clientship, i.e. particularism; it consists rather of individuals trying to follow both patterns' (p. 246).

First, African governments will have to make up their minds how far at least the customary functions of the chief, where there is a chief, or of the lineage heads, age-sets, or other social regulators, are compatible with the systems of politics which they want to erect. There is complete confusion in Tropical Africa on this issue, though less in French-speaking areas, where direct French administration appears at present to be being adopted by Africans, subject to the party influence.

Secondly, there was a real tendency for British indirect rule, however democratic in intent, to decrease rather than increase the democratic element in African life. Fallers [30] remarks:

> One of the early consequences of British administration [in Uganda] was to remove this check [removal of a bad ruler by princely revolt] by guaranteeing the chiefs' and rulers' positions. The task of controlling the exercise of authority thus fell on the administrative officers.

This observation could be paralleled in many other parts of Africa where in effect government recognition of the chief stopped up the safety valve by which popular discontent with his performance could remove him—'a chief is a chief by his people'. Further, the system froze the old institution just when it should have been changing:

> The difficulty in Nigeria was that the exponents of indirect rule, in their zeal to prevent the destruction of indigenous institutions, inadvertently prevented them from evolving at their normal tempo and so aided in their eventual stultification . . . The very group (i.e. the middle class) which might have aided the transition from the old to the new in tribal society was restrained by an administrative theory which sought to preserve intact the institutions of tribal rule.[31]

It may be that, in a purely African situation, some of the genuinely democratic systems of African local government could be revived, though in new forms. And it is wise to be careful of this word 'democracy':

> It is important to distinguish between democracy, used in the sense of what people at the moment want, and democracy as a system of control of government processes by the majority of the people.[32]

[30] Op. cit., p. 247.   [31] Cowan, op. cit., pp. 23, 29.
[32] Richards, *East African Chiefs*. 'What people want' may be their own traditional chiefs.

These thoughts are a comment on the 'democratic centralism'[33] of the monolithic parties. If in fact there is to be a way for African public opinion to express itself, an outlet for a deep African tradition of discussion and democratic control of immediate local government, the philosophy of democracy, which at present in Africa is so centred on universal adult suffrage in national elections, will have to widen once again to include all those other aspects of the democratic ideal which are not expressed always on ballot papers but in the liberties and balances of everyday life in the village, in the tribe or even in the traditional quarters of West African towns.[34]

Another major change, which will be hard to measure, is the loss of the expatriate District Officer. It is in many ways easier for an expatriate, adequately paid, a member of a disciplined service with high standards, with the prestige of a major European power behind him, to give impartial rule. It is easy to sentimentalize the record of District Administration, which was often intensely irritating both to the young educated nationalist and to the traditional chief, faced by instructions which might misunderstand his position or outrage traditional ways. But the greatest impact of European rule over the great mass of African populations, the impression which will be left among the millions rather than the hundreds, was the impact of the District Officer, the man who came to the village, on foot or in his Land Rover, with authority and usually with a patient justice. Perhaps it is safer to quote from another country. Philip Mason[35] ('Philip Woodruff') has recalled how in India, many years after the old régime had passed, a Christian preacher in a village meeting was speaking of

[33] 'Our trade unionism is exclusively Ghanaian in character and centralized. Our centralism is centralism based on democracy and our democracy is democracy under centralized guidance' (*Labour*, vol. 1, no. 5, November 1960).

[34] In Yoruba towns, a quarter would contain a group of lineages, with one dominant. The Council was formed by senior representatives of each quarter, the chief or Oba being the head of the ruling lineage. Representatives were elected by lineage meetings, including minor chiefs from minor lineages. In addition *elegbe* chiefs (with a role in calling out groups for communal work or defence) were included. The Native Authority system, by excluding both minor and *elegbe* chiefs, was less democratic and weakened the link between government and people. See P. C. Lloyd, 'Some Modern Changes in the Government of Yoruba Towns' (Ibadan, W.A.I.S.E.R. Conference, Sociology Section, 1953). For the traditional Nupe system in Bida, see Nadel, *A Black Byzantium*, supra.

[35] Philip Woodruff, *The Men Who Ruled India*, supra.

Jesus, 'who went round among the people doing good' : and how an old man, who had not caught the context, murmured : 'Ah, yes! Lely Sahib', naming the District Officer of his young days. Foreign rule, even if it were of angelic quality, must pass because it denies the responsibility of men to mature and rule themselves; even in a sovereign nation the day has passed when, for example, Lord Palmerston could deny the right of men to govern themselves but concede 'the right to be well governed and under good laws'. When simple people are hard pressed for food and shelter, ravaged by war or slavery or disease or famine, in a culture which cannot deliver them from their afflictions, the foreigner who brings peace and the famine-relief lorry, justice and health, will for a brief time be rightly called the father of his people. With self-government, something may seem to be lost—not only the comfort of dependence, but sometimes impartial justice and even real concern. What is gained is a certain intimacy of understanding and the challenge to become adult; 'a feeling of responsibility is essential to the attainment of an independent personality'.[36] There may be difficult times during this period of achieving psychological independence.

This, then, is in part a matter of timing and of the quality of the new African system—of how much the villager is going to miss 'dependence', of how much he will welcome a chance to slip back into old ways, of how well the local leaders carry out their task. Because time has been short and Africa so large, there may well be many places where rage and frustration break out, old jealousies revive, old customs come back. In some countries, it seems as if the formal systems of local government are weakening, partly owing to rapid changes in personnel as African officers take over from Europeans, and that it is the Party, through its local machine, which really runs and vitalizes local affairs, often causing some resentment. In the colonial era, it often seemed that the focus of trouble was in the towns, where politics ran high, and the focus of progress in the country. It would be well to consider whether this may not now be reversed; that while the new Ministers rule confidently in the capital city, trouble may begin to stir far out in the bush. There is, through the extended family, a unique link in Africa between the Minister and his village cousin,

[36] Mannoni, op. cit.

and this may help; but it would be unwise to forget how great a change is happening and how deeply it may be felt.

4. THE RELATIONS BETWEEN AFRICAN STATES

Until Nigeria emerged as an independent nation, all eyes were turned to Ghana; until East Africa emerges too, the balance of relations in Tropical Africa is uncertain. Whatever may be said of Ghanaian leadership, it has been courageous, a beacon fire lighting up the Western sky. It established, with amazing speed, the fact that Independence is real; and it has given to the new African nations self-confidence and pride. That one small African nation could speak out fearlessly to the Great Powers; could pour out its resources, on its own responsibility, in great projects of development; could step outside an expected conformity in the 'Cold War' and shake Russia or China by the hand; could throw into the African imagination ideas of unity, of African identity, of a continent great enough to play a part in the grand issues, and not only in the provincial skirmishes of the world—this is Dr. Nkrumah's achievement. It is a great one, however much jealousies in Africa or the self-interest of NATO may now look askance at it; it brings forward by many years the adult responsibility of Africa which the outer world must recognize; it shortens equally what could have been a period of 'inferiority', a dangerous trait in nations. To a lesser degree, the stand of Guinea has played the same part for the old French areas of Africa.

Yet if there has been psychological value in Ghana's stand, the practical issues of relationships between African States are all to settle. Their first task is to become nations. As Coleridge once said: 'The cosmopolitism which does not spring out of, and blossom upon, the deep-rooted stem of nationality or patriotism is a spurious or rotten growth.' [37] Ghana herself is far down the road of nationhood; perhaps Senegal, Guinea and Ethiopia are the only others in the tropical belt so convinced of nationality; it is often said—and significantly—that the independence of Senegal started, not with the treaty with France, but on the night when the Mali Federation was broken up. 'Sénégalaises, Sénégalais,' cried M. Senghor, 'la patrie est en danger.' Nigeria is moving along the path. Sierra Leone and Liberia have their own tradition;

[37] S. T. Coleridge, 'Table Talk', from Coleridge, *Select Poetry and Prose* (London, The Nonesuch Press, 1933).

among many of the French-speaking territories and in the Congo there is still far to go. In East and Central Africa, probably Tanganyika has at present the greatest African sense of unity; how far the passionate sense of 'Kenya', felt by Europeans, is real in African minds is still unsure.

In theory, larger unities and federations might be easier to make before the national boundaries and patriotism have crystallized. But in fact Coleridge is more probably right. A divided Uganda or Kenya, a Nigeria with internal conflicts not assuredly subject to nationhood, would be unstable members of any larger grouping. It may be that in East Africa a Confederation, in a form loose enough to allow its parts to establish their own national pride, yet with the advantages of a common market and common services, is the most hopeful framework. It is one, too, which some areas of French-speaking West Africa could achieve if they wished. Unfortunately, it must be recorded that the national pride of new countries, however small they may be, is at present operating against even the use of common services. So far from using Lovanium, across the river, the République du Congo must establish its own university, and it is doubtful if its three French-speaking fellow-republics will consent to use even that. So also Abidjan is setting up its own university in rivalry with Dakar. Many regional organizations have been broken up; self-sufficiency, however insufficient, is the order of the day, regardless of the cost.

I have already suggested that the odds against any total unions on a large scale are at present very high. The birth of a State establishes Ministers, Ambassadors, a public service, a seat at the United Nations, free access to the outer world, a personality which, new-found, will not be readily surrendered. Further, the so-called neutralism of Ghana and the 'Casablanca Powers'[38] has become divisive. To the more conservative States it has an unwelcome ring both in public style of speech and in domestic and foreign policy. Northern Nigeria would not wish to be associated with it, nor Ethiopia, nor many others. African leaders in East and Central Africa in 1961 were becoming increasingly loth to accept leadership from Ghana. The divisions have been emphasized in the Trade Union world to the point of bitter warfare; there have

[38] Ghana, Guinea, Mali, Morocco, F.L.N. (Algeria) and United Arab Republic.

been unhappy moments in the relations of Ghana and Togo, Mali and Senegal, the Ivory Coast and Upper Volta; and there is, in 1961, a sense of Africa divided by parties of the 'left', the *progressistes*, and parties often labelled by their African brothers as feudal, European stooges, or in other unflattering terms. There seems to be a real danger that African leaders will not be able to resist political agitation within each other's boundaries (encouraged by some elements in the outside world, including Cairo),[39] in fighting out the issues between 'left' and 'right' in Africa's social revolution. It is, indeed, more likely to be the pressure of economics which will pull together certain groups.[40] While there may be some larger political associations, their reality for some time is not likely to go past the paper-thin Ghana-Guinea Union.

If, in five to ten years' time, Tropical Africa contains a stable unified Nigeria, some loose Federations in the French-speaking areas and in East and Central Africa,[41] and a Congo climbing fast back to its proper weight in African affairs, this would be a degree of unity immensely creditable to African statesmanship and as much as African administrators and communications could easily sustain. It is certain at present that some boundaries or affiliations are still fluid, particularly in Central Africa (the whole area of the Eastern Congo, Rwanda-Burundi, Northern Rhodesia, Nyasaland, Tanganyika) and among some of the smaller countries of the West Coast. It is clear that some units are barely viable in economic isolation, such as those of the old French Equatorial

[39] It is of interest that in July 1961 Mr. Nyerere banned political meetings of the Opposition party, partly on grounds of their interference in Zanzibar politics, much influenced from Cairo.

[40] It is noticeable that neither Mali nor Guinea has finally severed its economic links with France, and both have been glad of French help in recent months.

[41] I have not intended to include Southern Rhodesia in this pattern. Prophecy is nowhere likely to be more confounded than in Africa. On the evidence of common sense, it is indeed hard to conceive how either Northern Rhodesia or Nyasaland can remain in the present Central African Federation. The attraction of common services, the relative poverty of East Africa as a partner in place of the higher income of Southern Rhodesia, enormous concessions from Salisbury and massive external aid might yet achieve the result which still appears to be the considered policy of the British Government based on the Monckton Report. Very much turns on which way the Copper revenues of Northern Rhodesia go—to the East or to the South.

Africa.[42] From Europe attention has mostly been given to 'Independence', to the colonial situation and its resolution. In Africa, within a short time, it is upon the internal political and social revolution and upon building stronger economies that the great issues and deep feelings will run.

5. RELATIONS WITH THE OUTER WORLD

If the chances of immediate African unity are small, Dr. Nkrumah has still had good reason to cry for it. For the small nations enter an international jungle far more dangerous than the African bush. There is one safe place—the United Nations, where numbers of votes count and where the anxieties of mankind are easily turned against the deadly quarrel between East and West. Much good work can be done there, in forwarding African interests, in blunting the edge of the 'Cold War', and in strengthening the work of United Nations agencies. But the United Nations is apt to encourage illusions, and to expose small nations to pressures which are not genuinely concerned with their interests. Ultimate power remains nuclear power, and those who have it can still ignore the votes they do not welcome.

Even if all the nations of the world were to take a decision which would not correspond with the interests of the Soviet Union and threatened its security, the Soviet Union would not recognize such a decision and would maintain its rights by force. And we have the means to do this.[43]

Without going to ultimates, power lies also in large developed economies. It is perhaps unfortunate that the East-West rivalry and the forum of the United Nations have drawn so much world attention to Africa and encouraged her leaders to attempt so large a part in world affairs. For in fact—and this must be remembered in all that follows—most of the African States are small, relatively weak economically, and unable to deflect the main stream of world trade or policies. They may well be devoting too much time and energy to international interventions which bring them little

[42] Populations are. Gabon, 417,000; République du Congo, 780,000; Central African Republic, 161,000; Chad, 2,600,000. Others below 3 million are Togo, 1,100,000; Dahomey, 1,725,000; Niger, 2,490,000.
[43] Mr. Kruschev at a luncheon in honour of Dr. Nkrumah in Moscow on 11 July 1961—*The Times*, 14 July 1961.

real benefit. The building of stronger economies and closer unity is a first task.

The 'neutralism' of African States is easily defended by facts and figures. If there are 3,000 Ghanaian students in the West, neutralism could fairly claim 3,000 in the East; if 90 per cent of trade is with the West, the loss of 40 per cent would not mean that Africa has 'gone Communist'. These are hard facts for Western powers to swallow; but on paper they are fair. The days of the easy monopoly, the subconscious sense of proprietorship, are gone. The days of competition, not only from the Communist world but from Israel or Japan are here. So much is clear and many Western governments and businessmen have yet to accept it. It is natural and right that independent governments should spread their wings, and should see if there are not bargains to be had, friends to be made, a style of life to study in areas of the world to which colonial powers have more or less firmly barred the way. But there remains, at the last, the question of commitment. African States have allowed themselves great liberties of speech and action :

U.S. Imperialism, The Greatest Threat to World Peace. The colonialists in Africa have only been able to continue their criminal exploitation of the African people, notably in the Congo, because of the support given them in loans, arms, radio, support and influence in the United Nations organization by the aggressive monopolistic circles of the United States of America ... U.S. imperialism is the worst enemy of the African People. All true nationalist forces must regard the struggle against racialism, religious oppression and humiliation of the black people as being closely allied with the economic battle against American monopolies and foreign capitalists in the NATO countries ... In order to raise the standard of living of the peoples in Africa, U.S. capitalism must be destroyed in all its forms. (*Ghana Evening News*, 23 December 1960).

America's aims are irreconcilable with the interests of African nations ... To abduct Africa, the moguls of American business pretend to be its friends and benefactors. But no mask can conceal their fangs. American imperialism is the worst enemy of the peoples of Africa. (*Ghanaian Times*, 10 and 11 January 1961).

This is strong talk from the Government press of a Commonwealth country anxious for American support for the Volta River Dam and dedicated to 'neutralism'. Western observers, who fail to find equal and opposite remarks about the Chinese conquest of Tibet or the Soviet rockets, may be forgiven for wondering what 'neutral' means. Perhaps, indeed, the West has never made it clear enough that the 'Cold War' is not a war against the Russian nation. It is against a systematic distortion of the truth about events all over the world, combined with censorship to exclude alternative versions, for the purpose of Communist policy; against the use of situations, such as that in the Congo, not to save suffering or restore order but to further Communist interests; and against the effort to inflame rather than to calm animosities, whatever may be the result. When the Tunisian Government, understandably impatient with France, openly launched an attack on Bizerta, this was described, and by some African countries, as French aggression; 700 Tunisians died in the resulting battle. What is distressing in the 'neutralism' of some African countries is that they have adopted the diplomacy which is *parti pris* and violent when neutralism could have been of value strengthening those forces in the world which are concerned with the truth, with conciliation, and with the interests of the humble, the inarticulate and misled. The world is weary of violent language; African States do not improve their reputation by using it.

Although Ghana is not Tropical Africa, nor even West Africa; although the gusto of West African journalism is in part a daily entertainment for writer and reader which must be taken as such, still there is no doubt that Western capitalism is a popular target for all the progressive African parties. The reasons are not hard to find. First, there is the natural persistence of opposition to the colonial powers, and among these the U.S.A. is vaguely included for a variety of reasons. Despite her anti-colonialism, which has so often gravely embarrassed the British and French, the U.S. Government has unfortunately earned the reputation of wanting allies (and sometimes strange ones) more than friends, particularly by her military aid programmes. In consequence, America has been seen as the most bellicose 'Cold War' leader, in the closest alliance with the colonial powers; and colonialism, imperialism, capitalism are almost interchangeable words in the vocabulary of the Left. Moreover, the American Negro problem is unhelpful to her reputation. But in a wider sense the Western programme of free enterprise, decentralized democracy and personal liberty has no great attraction for African countries, particularly if it involves signing the pledge against Communism. There is as yet no really powerful African entrepreneur class to practise or value free enterprise; decentralized democracy is extremely hard to explain, being of long growth and deeply interwoven with the general culture of the West in many different aspects. It certainly has no attraction whatever to the planners who lead some African governments. Personal liberty in its Western sense is barely within the conception of the mass of African people, however well their rulers may understand it. In contrast, the Russian and Chinese programmes have many attractions. Russia virtually invented anti-colonialism; Russia has no 'colonies' and her subject states in Europe are little known and well camouflaged. Russia, with a huge agricultural population and much illiteracy in 1917, is believed to have caught up the West in forty years. Russia believes in science, technology and planning; and China shares most of these attractions.

This is not merely a matter of propaganda; the West would surely be wise to recognize that Africans, within their assumptions, have much real sense on their side. If they want to 'catch up' quickly—and it is hard to avoid humiliation otherwise—and if they want to unify and inspire their peoples, then planning, the central Party and State enterprise make sense, and the sacrifices of freedom and dispersed initiative (of which Dr. Nkrumah is certainly well aware) may seem worth while. Liberal democracy, as practised in Britain and America, implies a deep unanimity on the essential national image, so that democratic argument can play as fiercely as may be round the lesser differences without endangering the unity of the whole; deep cleavages always endanger it. African nations have not yet built this unity, and the new society which they are creating is so unlike the old that the strength of old traditions is hard to bring to its support. Again, neither Britain, France, Germany nor the United States has in fact had the living experience of Russia and China in social and economic construction, in twentieth century conditions, with a huge semi-literate population. Eastern experience, successes and failures, are bound to seem more relevant and useful to Africa. Finally, there is a deep *malaise* within the Western world about the values of the affluent society which it has produced; and this is contrasted with the smiling self-confidence of a Kruschev, whatever mutterings there may be below him. The peoples of East Germany or Hungary would have a different tale to tell, but they do not go to Africa. In some ways the democratic European neutrals, such as the Scandinavian countries, with their developed agriculture, or Switzerland with its industrial wealth built upon so small a population, would put the Western case best in Africa.

For all these reasons, the possibility is that for a decade at least many African countries will, at least overtly, lean far to the East; and that the West (particularly while the Portuguese colonies and Rhodesia remain under European rule) will have to suffer, as gracefully as it may, much violent attack. Africa needs a whipping boy, and we are cast for the part. But we should not read into this, · even in Ghana, a deep and lasting hostility. On the contrary, the fund of goodwill and friendship from individual Africans, influential in their country, is great and firmly based. They would ask us to distinguish between the loud words of the orators and Press and the real deeds of trade, interchange of men and ideas in every professional and cultural field, modern traditions of thought and speech and social action which are so deeply Western, whether drawn from Britain or from France. It is far more by this professional, cultural and personal friendship, which welcomes Africans into the great company of English- or French-speaking civilizations throughout the world, that we can help. To be impatient, to take offence, to seek to force the African hand either in military alliance or in political alignment will be futile. For better or for worse, Western Europe has had fifty years or more to show its quality to Africa; we must now be content to let that record work, as we did for India, and to allow the African nations to take a good look round the world and to sample other traditions and other performances. With every year that passes after Independence their judgement, on performance and on wider knowledge, will become more objective.

In the meantime, the left-wing African leaders have many horses to drive—anti-colonialism, Pan-Africanism, neutralism (and they are well aware that Russia is in the 'Cold War' too), the Afro-Asian bloc, Arab friendship and Israeli friendship, socialism, the need for private foreign investment. If this is a team of their own choosing it is not an easy one to control. It is futile to record the glaring inconsistencies which have resulted and will no doubt continue. But in the long run, it is not possible for a nation with some self-respect to avoid commitment; it must work out at last where to stand in the great affairs of the world; it must decide to choose friends and treat them as such, even in disagreement; to have principles and stand by them, even at some cost. This time has not yet come for Africa.

It would be a mistake to generalize too widely from the Ghanaian or other extreme statements of the African outlook. Ghana herself is regarded with deep suspicion by many other States; many of them are also very cautious in accepting Russian promises or propaganda at their face value. M. Houphouet-Boigny in the Ivory Coast, still one of the most powerful politicians in French-speaking Africa, and many of his fellow statesmen have managed their Independence without a violent break with France and, with their own French sympathies, could well settle down to a comfortable and subsidized relationship with a nation which they understand and respect.[44] It is more than conceivable that East Africa will have a comparable relation with Britain and that Nigeria is large and strong enough to pursue a genuinely neutralist policy with strong continuing links at the personal and institutional level with the English-speaking world.

Both language and culture have made it difficult for relations between English- and French-speaking Africans to move past the point of purely official friendship, and it may be that a greater unity in Europe will do more to bridge that gap than the efforts of leaders in Africa. At present the Common Market is chiefly in the news. While at first sight some of the English-speaking countries in Africa have been greatly alarmed by Britain's proposed entry (although Dr. Okpara of Eastern Nigeria has been more favourable) in the longer run it may be much welcomed. The economic arguments, recently well expressed by Mr. Soper,[45] would be strongly in favour, provided that African countries were put on an equal footing *vis à vis* the Market. The political arguments should also be put in favour. No doubt some African countries might feel the Market to be a bigger and better instrument of 'neo-colonialism', or a hindrance to their efforts to benefit from inter-European competition for African contracts or influence. But in

[44] Describing the scene at the Independence celebrations at Abidjan, *West Africa's* correspondent remarked : 'Dominating the scene in the background is the vast new flour mill—a Franco-Ivory Coast concern that is about to start producing on the biggest scale in Africa, and is a fitting symbol of the industrial and commercial partnership between France and Ivory Coast which flourishes without anyone raising a protest about "neo-colonialism" ' (*West Africa*, 12 August 1961).

[45] Tom Soper, 'Africa and the Common Market', *The Listener*, 10 August 1961.

the other scale must be weighed the fact that direct relations with France and the franc zone, or Britain and the sterling area, are a real hindrance to economic unions in Africa, as well as arousing 'neo-colonialist' fears. A relation with a more anonymous Europe, particularly if some arrangement was made between the franc and the pound sterling, would suit African aims of larger economic unities far better. Culturally, the two major international languages in Africa still divide African States, over and above the different heritage from very different colonial systems. A far greater collaboration between the members of the French- and English-speaking world in the sphere of culture and technical aid would also be helpful to Africa in her present effort to break down barriers. It would be our own fault if we took too hesitant a view of the possibilities of a richer collaboration with Africa than we have had in the past—upon the single condition that we welcome the progressive elements as warmly as the rest.

For while the more extremist attitudes of Ghana and Guinea may prove to be in a minority, the ideas proclaimed in Accra have a ready echo among the young intellectuals throughout Tropical Africa, not least in Eastern Nigeria. These ideas often seem to suit the African situation—and their support of the forces of social revolution in the more conservative countries can always prove powerful. It will be unfortunate if Ghana and Guinea, by driving ahead too fast or by arrogating leadership to themselves too tactlessly, alienate other countries so far as to divide Tropical Africa into two camps, corresponding roughly to East and West, left and right. Little but continuing instability and recrimination could result. A sober neutrality could play a healthy part in the world, as India has done in recent years. These are issues which Africans themselves must settle; it would certainly be unwise for Western nations to 'adopt' only the conservatives of Africa or to antagonize finally the progressive parties, however aggressive they may be. The social revolution is not yet finished in Africa; it has barely begun.

CHAPTER XII

THE QUALITY OF AFRICAN SOCIETIES

I. INTRODUCTION

In the choice of title and the arrangement of the last chapters of this book, the emphasis has been upon the growth of new societies rather than of new nations. The political task of nation-building is important; but nationalism, although it has been an idol worshipped in the world for the last hundred years, is not enough. What gives its quality to society is the network of relationships and values within which men and women live out their lives and develop their powers. Many single aspects of the scene in Tropical Africa have been discussed. But societies do not live as a simple addition of their economy, education and political system. There comes now the larger question of the quality of African societies as living wholes.

It is tempting to think that this last hundred years has been a passing episode in the longer history of Africa; and particularly so on the West Coast, with its old record of kingdoms and arts and trade. The Yoruba towns were towns in the sixteenth century; some of them retain today the big compounds of the lineage-houses; how deeply has European influence changed them? Kano is an old city, looking both towards the desert and the sown, ruled by a Muslim culture with centuries of tradition behind it. How much has sixty years altered the real quality of its life? As the European rulers leave, these are questions worth asking. But in fact, Europe has not abandoned Africa as the Romans once abandoned Britain, leaving, after an occupation of 400 years, little which lasted but their roads, until far later the Christians and then the Normans brought back their Roman heritage. The stream of Europe's influence in Africa flows on more strongly.

Certainly, in local affairs the European as a person face-to-face with Africans and as the supporting administrator behind a Co-operative, a hospital or a school is becoming more rare. This has been true for some time. Older men in Uganda have remarked how the younger Makerere graduates know less of the white man personally; for the old men were taught in primary school by a white missionary and they dealt constantly with the white District Commissioner. The young men, taught by Africans, moving in a university of Africans, though with European staff, dealing with African District Councillors, may know more of Europe from their books, but less in life. At the airports and in hotels waiting for the ship, the traveller in Africa today will meet a Medical Officer or a Matron, a Headmaster, a District Commissioner, now returning home, leaving his charge in African hands. It is hard to measure what these changes will mean for a country, let alone for a half-continent. Europeans are quick to fear 'deterioration'; but rather, things will be done in a different way, in a different personal and social style, as African society, now on its own, settles down to find a way of life which can be sustained over the years from its own character and resources. All the while the outside influences will flow in; but they will come through African voices to African ears, and they will be transformed a little as they pass on into action.

As the shadow of colonial rules moves on, how deep is the real effect of all that has happened in the last fifty or hundred years, how strongly have older traditions lived on below the surface? There is extreme variety. There are tribes in the bush and on the plains whose old basic culture is still wholly dominant, although the trader will bring European goods; there are villages with a cash crop, still with the old land tenure, but with young men educated, with a lorry or a tractor to be seen; there are cocoa farmers in Ghana or Nigeria, half farmer, half townsman and trader; coffee farmers in Kenya employing labour for a wage, sitting on District Councils; there are the country traders with credit from a bank and two wives at home; Buganda factory workers with a farm as well; taxi-drivers in Brazzaville, with their smart white shoes and well-pressed trousers, and their even smarter girls, living in a modern house in Poto-Poto, drinking a French apéritif in a café; there is the Apapa rush hour at 4.0 p.m. as the factory workers stream away on bicycles, scooters, in old cars, on foot, to the Lagos suburbs; the middle civil servants going home to a new brick house, car, refrigerator and radiogram, models of respectability; there are the Northern Ministers in fine houses outside Kaduna, each with a sentry-box for the Visitor's Book;

there are scholars in the universities; Permanent Secretaries carrying a heavy load of work; there are the Ambassadors, drinking champagne in Bamako at 10.30 a.m., to the scandal of Mali's Muslim society; and there are, once again, the older chiefs and kings before whom counsellors and suppliants must roll on their back in deference. Every country, Britain not excluded, has such contrasts, not always so wide; because they are understood, they scarcely seem remarkable. What is significant is the dominant note, the direction of change, the television set in the Hebrides or in the African village and the strange longings it may bring. The persistence of influence from the outer world is not now due to force or cunning; it is sought eagerly by Africans for the possibilities of a new life which it brings.

There is deep difficulty in finding a standpoint from which to assess the temper of these societies which are at once new and old. It is a temptation to take our own system as a measuring rod, assuming that Africa must move towards it; too often it is not even the real Western society, warts and all, which is so used, but an idealized version, full of grace and virtue.[1] But the real danger is to assume that our institutions, our values and motivations, are the only and necessary accompaniments of a developed economy. Despite some care, no doubt much of this book falls into this assumption, so easy and natural for Europeans to make. But our institutions are the expressions of a society valuing thrift, enterprise, economic advance, the highly individualized personality, a secular egalitarian outlook which has grown up with the scientific revolution and industrialization.

In fact our way of life may be a special phase of history in many different respects. The nuclear family, and especially its extreme form in Britain, which the French or Dutch note with amazement, is certainly exceptional in the societies of the world. 'The fact and the idea of kinship remains for the vast majority of societies the one sheet anchor in a shifting world—the point at which individual and community recognize each other.'[2] With

---

[1] Expatriate managers, for example, are apt to think that all British Trade Unions are responsible, all plumbers efficient, all clerks honest; and to attribute to the 'African' character failings which are as common in Coventry as in Kaduna. The same is true in government. 'All too often there is an inclination, on the part of Western observers, to set for Africa standards of performance and efficiency in democratic bodies which are not even met by the equivalent bodies in Europe or America' (L. Gray Cowan, op. cit.).

[2] Niculescu, op. cit.

the family go the rules of betrothal, the concepts of sexual morality, the whole ideal of the marital relationship and the upbringing of children, and these in turn are sanctioned in religious rules. This is a large realm of life, which may be temporarily unbalanced in the West.

Again, the great upthrusting tree of energy, which we call science and the industrial revolution, rooted so deeply in the soil of European culture, which in two centuries has transformed the West and spread its branches over the whole world, is not likely to spring in the same form elsewhere, where the soil has different elements. Its over-arching canopy alters the climate for late-comers in its shade. Even our own real life and outlook are changing faster than we can clearly see. As the heirs rather than the creators of the modern system, the new generations of Europe, knowing well its value, are far different from the men who made it; perhaps we shall never see their like again. We should certainly be wary of persuading or expecting African societies to adopt the economic virtues of the nineteenth century in a world where some of them no longer apply.

Here lies a vital question. Our system, which made possible the growth of technology, has also been much shaped by it. How far is the technology separable from the values and the social institutions which grew up with it in the West, and is it possible for Africa to borrow the one without the other? It is not only for Africa that this question is asked, but for India and South East Asia, for all the societies with their own tradition who face the twentieth century Western world.[3] 'We need clean drinking water for our people', said Mr. Nyerere,[4] 'and that means that we must have analysts and doctors. Doctors mean universities to train them, and hospitals and scientific equipment, and administrators. Thus we are forced to create your institutions; and because they must be paid for we must enter the world of economic competition; we must make our people want these things so that they will work for what they want. Yet we do not desire either the extreme individualism of your society or the extreme collectivism of Russia.'

[3] Even in the Pacific Islands this question is asked. Those who have worked with the people of Tonga find them deeply impressed by our technology but equally scornful of our social system.
[4] In conversation, 1960, and therefore paraphrased.

It would be easy if industrial knowledge could be taken by itself; but it is the human motive which sustains the industrial system and the motive which can also corrupt—the will to work, and save and risk and compete, the individualism, the emphasis on material equipment, the whole social structure and personal drive which has until now been bound up with the technical achievement. It is as yet unknown whether, starting at this point of time, a new society can separate the two. Certainly, the qualities needed to build a society and an economy in the later twentieth century may be different from those which founded the new system 200 years ago.

Further, it is too easy to assume that there are lasting characteristics of African cultures, different from our own, which can be summoned up to temper or transform the borrowings from the West into a civilization more in tune with the African past, and perhaps more suited to the future. Often enough co-operativeness, the sense of community and common social effort, is quoted as one such trait—'The foundation of democracy in Africa lies in the community principle, expressing itself in the common working of the land.'[5] But it may be—indeed, it seems likely—that these characteristics were developed out of the necessities and the techniques of the old African life, and could die away when those conditions change. Europeans, in the political sphere, relied upon the chiefs, while changing the conditions and beliefs upon which a chief's power rested; and the power began to fade. In the economic or the social fields too we have relied on social custom, the 'community principle', the Wolof co-operative work group in Senegal,[6] *Mwethia*[7] among the Kamba of Kenya, traditions of self-help and community action among the Ibo of Nigeria and a score of other peoples. But as individual land tenure, Trade Unions, wage labour, contractors with earth-moving equipment— the institutions, motives and techniques of the cash-economy and the Western system—spread inwards into Africa and into African

[5] Resolution of the Second Congress of *Présence Africaine*, Rome, April 1959 (translated).

[6] See D. W. Ames, 'Wolof Co-operative Work Groups', in *Continuity and Change in African Cultures*, supra.

[7] A custom by which the whole village group turned out for communal work on the land, extensively used in Kenya in Community Development work for digging irrigation trenches, ridging and contouring, building village improvements, &c.

minds, will this social institution outlast the conditions which created it? Can the motive behind it find other forms of expression?

Here, then, are certain questions—of how deep and lasting are some characteristics of African ways of life and tradition, and how strongly they may re-emerge as the hand of European supervision is withdrawn, or continue as the conditions which created them are changed; which of the institutions and values of the industrial societies are still vital to support technology and economic growth, and which are partly accidental additions from a different culture or relics from a recent but dying past; how far they can be separated; how far there is a will and a need to make this separation. Only the future can answer in full. But to make sure that the questions are rightly put and perhaps to hint at the direction from which answers may come, we must look a little more closely at the evidence which earlier chapters have in part provided. It may be as well to plunge in at a critical point[8]—the quality of economic life in Africa.

2. ECONOMIC LIFE

A good deal has been said of the adaptation of African labour to modern economic life. The evidence is strongly encouraging. With thoughtful training, most African labour will give all that is needed in factory or farm or mine. If much migrancy is wasteful, the tradition of mobility is also helpful. Apart from raw labour, there is already in certain towns a pool of men well used to industrial work. There is a basic structure of education and the will to spend on it; Russia's high valuation, in pay and status, of the educational system will not be lost on Africa. The desire for what money will buy is there, and increasingly the desire for a stable job—the day of the 'target' worker is declining, save in the areas of seasonal migration.

The same encouraging report is true of petty commerce and administration. Quality and experience have still to come, but will

[8] Certainly, Marxists would regard this as *the* critical point—cf. *The Communist Manifesto* (*1848*). When the revolution in control of the means of production comes, says the *Manifesto*, 'All that was solid melts into air; all that was sacred is profaned; and man is at last brought face to face with his real conditions of life and his relations with his kind.' The remainder of this chapter will provide a comment.

come; 'honesty'[9] and reliability will be slower, because of the strains of private life. For these men, workers by day in the new world, are Africans after work in the old. As they come to town or factory or plantation for a job, they come bringing much of the old life and its obligations with them. Stabilization and the slow formation of new conventions in the urban world will take some time yet to make the contrasts between job and home less striking and the conflicts fewer.

This is to speak only of employees; the supply of enterprise and management for an African economy is more doubtful. Certainly, there is competition of the most acute degree in trade and in towns. But the wish and the power to save, to accumulate, to plough back profits are still hard to find, partly from the social drain of the family, partly perhaps from deeper reasons in personality.[10] The emerging leadership in Africa seems at present headed towards administration and politics. There are many who want power, and may be inclined to mulct enterprise to sustain it; and there are many who feel able to administer what they did not, and perhaps could not, create. The decisions of management are of a different order, often hard decisions of profit and economy which need a long view of the enterprise and single-minded determination to serve its needs as an entity in itself; there is something detached and impersonal here which Africans, personal and impulsive, may find uncongenial.

This is dangerous ground, too near to myths of 'African personality' for comfort. Yet a certain lack among Africans of that impersonal calculation, drive and perseverance which characterizes the European manager has been genuinely observed and there is no reason to shy away from any cultural (as against

[9] In quotation marks because 'dishonest' implies a moral condemnation and is too simple. Africans pressed by traditional and sanctioned demands from close kin are perhaps most nearly in the position of an unemployed European who steals food for a sick child. Even then, the parallel is far from exact, for Africans have come from a society which often freely shares possessions, though within conventions of its own, and the absolute character of property, well known to the European who steals, is less felt in Africa. 'Honesty' then means honesty in the European commercial context, not as a fundamental trait of character.

[10] 'It is difficult to see any point at which economic initiative might be found, sufficiently free and untrammelled, to produce the results it has been known to produce in the West and in North America in the past. Probably this is a phenomenon not to be reproduced in the twentieth century.' Niculescu, op. cit.

genetic) theory which can throw even a partial light on it. Is there any convincing theory of 'African personality' which could indicate its probable mode of action in economic life?

Biesheuvel's [11] thoughtful work gives at least a stimulating hint of where to look. He first eliminates various theories of racial personality differences, particularly those based on the sudden weaning of African children, pointing out that such weaning does not always take place, that psychological evidence of its effect is contradictory, and that there are glaring differences between Bantu tribes (the Pedi, aggressive and anxious, and the Lovedu, peace-loving and conciliatory, are quoted) which makes generalizations of this type valueless.[12] This conclusion was repeated by a C.C.T.A. meeting of specialists in Madagascar, who rejected such generalizations as 'devoid of practical and theoretical value because of the diversity of cultures and sub-cultures on the African continent'. He moves on to recall Riesman's [13] far more general classification of personality types into three—those governed by a strict culture ('tradition-directed'); those governed by a strong inner sense of duty and conscience, implanted in childhood ('inner-directed'); and those governed by an anxiety to please and conform with others and with the fashions of the present outer world ('other-directed'). Clearly, there is much in common between the first and third, the difference being that the 'other-directed' personality is concerned with a much wider world, which contains more choices, not all traditional. Riesman links the 'inner-directed' personality with Renaissance Europe, and here Biesheuvel, quoting the work of R. H. Tawney and of Max Weber[14] on the Puritan association with capitalism, emphasizes

[11] Biesheuvel, *Race, Culture and Personality* and *African Intelligence*, supra.

[12] Biesheuvel does allow of the posibility of a lower 'activity level' in Africans as a characteristic which might have been produced by selection, since high activity in a hot climate might have a selective disadvantage. The theory was suggested by some differences between the alpha frequency (electro-encephalogram) between Africans and Europeans, which is associated with visual perception and, less directly, with activity level. This theory is not proved, and Biesheuvel points out that selection could be reversed where, as in the urban cash-economy, high activity had a selective value.

[13] David Riesman, N. Glazer and Reuel Denny, *The Lonely Crowd* (Yale University Press, 1950).

[14] *The Protestant Ethic and the Spirit of Capitalism* (London, Allen & Unwin, 1930).

the element of inner compulsion which makes the European so insistent on work and its virtues and so dedicated to it. The suggestion is that Africans—and an increasing number of *modern* Europeans—may jump straight to the 'other-directed' personality aimed at social conformity, at 'organization man'. This personality is sanctioned by a diffused anxiety to conform, while the inner drive is sanctioned by moral conscience or 'guilt'.[15]

This possible attitude of personality is illustrated by the studies of African clerks carried out by Rae Sherwood.[16] Her work showed the exceptionally high value which African middle-class office-workers attributed to service to fellow human beings—they rated 'service to the community' and 'pleasant human relations' highest in a rank order of satisfactions at work. This motive of service was confirmed quite independently by Balandier when studying the career preferences of educated Africans in Brazzaville.[17] Biesheuvel concludes first that 'the more deeply Africans are drawn into the essentially Western culture, the more thoroughly do they acquire the personalities functional for that culture' (a conclusion of enormous importance); and, second, that for those near the top of the occupational ladder, 'African personality differs from its Western counterpart in the relative absence of the compulsive work motivation which is characteristic of Western culture and which, without economic necessity, impels it onwards to its remarkable and continuous course of material advancement'. Finally, he draws the striking contrast between some of the attitudes of Négritude as expressed by the well-known poem of Aimée Césaire :

> Hurrah for those who never invented anything;
> Hurrah for those who never explored anything;
> Hurrah for those who never conquered anything; &c.

with the equally extremist *Ulysses* of Tennyson :

> To strive; to seek; to find, and not to yield.

[15] Riesman happily describes the inner drive as a gyroscope, the anxiety to conform as a radar set.
[16] R. Sherwood, 'Motivation Analysis: A Comparison of Job Attitudes among African and American Professional Workers', *Proceedings of the South African Psychological Association*, nos. 7–8, 1956–7, and 'The Bantu Clerk: A Study of Rôle Expectations', *Journal of Social Psychology*, 1958, no. 47, pp. 285–316. [17] Balandier, op. cit.

These most stimulating thoughts put into more theoretical form a view of the probabilities which observation and the opinions of many experienced men, African and European, might be inclined to take. This view is perhaps strengthened by the markedly instructional and passive atmosphere of African education, in which children are seldom encouraged to ask questions, whether at home or in school, but to accept and conform to the dominant attitudes of the 'other' world. While every precaution against racial generalizations is fully justified, it may well be legitimate to speak in general terms of a cultural situation which is bound to affect personality. It has been suggested in earlier chapters of this book that there have been elements in the traditional African situation, however great its diversities, which differed in common from the Western world, particularly differences arising from the subsistence economy and communal organization; and that those differences justified certain generalizations on motive and values. The new suggestion of this chapter is that the cultural situation of the educated African today may well favour a type of personality more suited, not to the enterprising Europe of the nineteenth century, but to the organized Europe of planning and giant combines and social conformity in the twentieth. Such a personality may lack the compulsive initiative and perseverance which still persists in the West as a relic of the first industrial revolution.

It is remarkable how well such a view chimes with the present philosophy of African socialism. Perhaps instinctively African leaders incline towards the State-run economy as against competitive free enterprise, knowing that their peoples have neither the taste nor the capacity for this extreme of individualism and personal dedication to an economic aim.[18] Individual acquisitiveness sorts ill with the obligations of the extended family, although, as Paul Marc Henry has observed,[19] it is growing:

As the traditional system, which was based on co-operation, is undermined by changes in the mode of production and pecuniary rewards for labour on an individual basis, the African is developing a type of individualism which is alien to his traditional culture . . . There is implicit in these values a certain rationalistic and materialistic attitude towards people and nature.

[18] Cf. Dr. Nkrumah's speech quoted on page 183, Chapter VIII.
[19] P. M. Henry in *Africa Today*, supra.

The idea of the 'common good' recently expressed by Mr. Krus-chev in his programme of development towards true Communism, when food and some other basic needs may be free for all in Russia, naturally appeals far more. Nor do Africans realize the background to the developed techniques which the Europeans brought with them. Elizabeth Hoyt noted of second-year Economics students at Makerere that they were 'quite without experience of the long process of effort, sacrifice and discipline by which economic rewards are secured'.[20] We heard of an African who, watching a Boeing 707 taking off from Kano airport, re-marked: 'We could have made those if you had given us our Independence ten years ago.'[21]

It may well be that the pioneering which is still needed in Africa will have to be led mainly by the large foreign companies in which the competitive spirit of the West has been embodied, while the contribution from Africa will lie more in humanizing and social-izing the relationships of economic life. If the old African tradi-tions of communal effort can pass by the century of competition straight into a century of organized co-operation, they could find a new validity suited to the new conditions of the third industrial revolution. We should also perhaps remember how much our technical progress has been stimulated by major wars. Both we and African societies, aiming at peace and co-operation, will have to find an alternative outlet for the instincts of aggression and competition—the instincts of the young Bemba pollarding their trees.

3. SOCIAL LIFE

The same major questions may be put in the social field—how far the social structure can bear the sheer speed and ubiquity of change, how strongly the older African traditions will be main-tained, whence will come the social and moral standards without which the new society cannot stand firmly on its feet.

In face of the usual ogres, Ignorance, Poverty and Disease, there is no reason to despair. Population is indeed growing fast,

[20] Hoyt, op. cit.
[21] Everyone is slightly annoyed when the results of years of effort are taken for granted by the next generation. But Africans see no reason to live through the nineteenth century before they can enter the twentieth. An African, com-plimented on his beautifully cut suit, remarked: 'I don't have to go through all the stages of wearing ill-fitting ones first.'

and there are areas where its growth is serious in relation to resources, as in Rwanda-Burundi and possibly in East Nigeria and
Kikuyuland, where densities up to 1,000 per square mile occur
locally. But compared with India, where development runs a
desperate race against the growth of numbers and land in the
South is pressed beyond all limits, Africa is fortunate. Its food
supplies can be much increased even on existing land, and in
many areas there is land to spare. The battle against disease goes
on at a quickening pace—probably infant mortality and parasitic
infections are now the worst enemies. There is certainly no room
for complacency, but probably the improvement in health will
progress at least as fast as the provision of the necessary extra food.

Poverty is there, but there is scarcely anything to touch the filth
and degradation revealed in English nineteenth century towns;
shelter, warmth and clothing are not costly in the tropics. Hunger
is there when crops fail, or in the hungry season between crops,
but malnutrition (kwashiorkor and other symptoms) is more
serious, and remediable in most areas by variation of crops and
diet. Ignorance is the worst enemy, and it is not only a question of
the schools. It is the ignorance of diet and domestic hygiene, and
the lack of simple needs, such as clean water and storage of food
away from contamination. It is here that community development
and community education have their great part to play. There is
surely needed, at the lowest level, a double system : a school for
literacy from which the secondary schools will be fed; and a school
for life, and for adults as well as children, where the fight against
social ignorance can be waged.

These major battles against poverty, ignorance and disease will
follow a course largely dictated by the rate of economic growth,
which not only deals directly with poverty but supplies the funds
for mass education and for the training of teachers and doctors.
The more difficult issues concern the new structure of social life—
for example, a system of social security for sickness and old age;
the morals and disciplines of society—for example, in marriage;
and ultimately the overriding beliefs and ideals (in effect, the
religion) which sanction and support these disciplines. In Chapter
V I have tried to describe, very briefly, some of the main strains
in the transition from the old culture to the new, and particularly
the kind of situations which can arise in a modern African town.
There is the vitality and competition and search for modernity;

the strain on marriage and the widespread growth of casual sexual relations in concubinage or prostitution; the difficulty of caring properly for children in the town, where food and clothing and shelter and education all demand cash payments; there is the growing emancipation of women. Here the two systems are being lived simultaneously, in tension. There has been the tendency from above to prejudge the issue, by forcing Africans into European-type housing, as there has been in industry by pressing the adoption of European Trade Unions. But there has also been from below the growth of new institutions in the African tradition—the tribal and mutual benefit societies—and an amazingly strong persistence of the old familial and tribal forms and feelings.

Looking at this whole social scene, which is changing so fast, it is on balance the continuing strength and flexibility of African tradition which impresses rather than its decay. As to flexibility, even in rural areas it has not often been a question of tribes obstinately refusing, without good reason, to change ways which preclude economic progress. There are some of these. But, to take one example, the work of Alan Jacobs [22] on the Masai of Kenya and Tanganyika is a warning against hasty judgements. Here is a tribe which has a distinctive social organization of age-sets, and an even more distinctive economy, wholly dependent on cattle, in which to till the soil is regarded as an outrage on mother earth, and even game is not killed for food. The Masai have often been quoted as a group which refuse to modernize. Jacobs would assert, nevertheless, that the Masai are not only willing but anxious to accept modern methods to supplement and improve their way of life, such as small dams and other water control for cattle; to get education, with certain limits; to adopt a more modern system of local government suited to their culture. They have by instinct chosen a way of life which, granted free range, may be best suited to the ecological conditions of their country, and which even has the advantage of conserving game. It is at least possible that they could be integrated into a modern economy as a ranching system, with an associated industry of meat canning and hides. [23]

But it is in the towns, where the westernizing impact is greatest,

[22] Unpublished contribution.
[23] Cf. the recent transfer of control over the Amboseli Game Park to the Masai by the Governor of Kenya—July 1961.

that the strength and flexibility of the extended family and of custom is, in a way, most impressive because most highly tested. New institutions and patterns of behaviour spring up,[24] often European in form and in name; yet their real content remains essentially African.[25] It is not the brick house, radio set and Western dress which really count, but the relationships and values which are lived. Certain parts of the older custom will surely weaken or die, and nowhere is the revolution more noticeable than in the emancipation of women, already far advanced in some West African societies and much encouraged in East and Central Africa by European-organized clubs and societies and by the influence of women's programmes on the radio. Nevertheless, custom can bend and adapt very far without finally breaking.

The example of Mau Mau, in part a reaction against over-rapid westernization, may well be quoted to oppose this emphasis on flexibility. Certainly there is real strain all over Tropical Africa, and where it is severe there is always a danger of a regressive revolt to 'the old ways'. This, because a sign of despair, is always liable to be violent and archaic—a regression, as in Mau Mau, far beyond the old ways. But these reactions, which have sometimes taken the form of religious revival (as in Messianic sects in Nyasaland, or the Kibangui movement in the Congo) have been, in perspective, remarkably few in the light of the pressures exerted; perhaps because the new culture has, in most cases, brought real and valued advantages.

Despite this degree of adaptation, it is often said that the older pattern is bound to be gradually eliminated. The modern cash economy, so the argument runs, is too expensive for the old social security system of sharing from the common pot, using the common land and the quickly-added thatched hut. But this argument really assumes that men are not prepared to tax themselves in cash as heavily as the State can tax them to provide social security. Certainly there are signs of failure to support children or the old. The evidence of child neglect in Sekondi-Takoradi, Accra, Lagos

[24] Cf. David Apter: 'The introduction of secular political forms demands a substitution of new cultural forms, new symbols and artefacts to supplant the old as guides to action' (*The Gold Coast in Transition*, supra).

[25] M. J. Herskovitz in *The Myth of the Negro Past* (New York, Harper, 1941) has pointed out the persistence of essentially African institutions and attitudes, heavily camouflaged in Western forms, even in modern American cities after a far longer period of living actually inside a Western culture.

330 THE NEW SOCIETIES OF TROPICAL AFRICA

and doubtless in other towns, is too important to brush aside. Dr. Busia,[26] writing of the failure of the family system in towns, has said :

> Its collapse or inadequacy for the new situation has meant the weakening or, in some instances, the breakdown of the moral and legal sanctions of the Community. This fact came out repeatedly in discussing the problems of marriage, government, education, juvenile delinquency, unemployment and destitution.

Certainly in the large towns, government will have to supplement the family system, though economic progress and a rise in wage levels could do much. But this is not only a matter of institutions and systems; it is also a question of individual compassion. Africans have often been accused of insensitivity to suffering in others. In the old world of Africa, which still so widely exists, at least three children out of six would probably die in infancy. Hunger, accidents, disease, war, slavery breed a necessary stoicism about suffering; it may be deeply felt but it *must* be quickly forgotten; even laughter is a way of self-protection. Humanitarianism in history has grown where easier conditions have made it possible.

But, in perspective, breakdown is on a small scale. Africans in West Africa have in fact taxed themselves, through tribal societies in the modern economy, to a degree which startles observers from a European Welfare State. While neither the familial system nor the tribal system is probably adequate to give the full range of social security in the large towns, at a level which we, *from far richer societies*, would feel necessary, most of Africa is not, and will not be for years, an urban society; and Africa is, after all, poor. Rural society may well be able to continue its social security arrangements for a long time, and it is unreasonable to expect that, merely through State taxation, poverty can be quickly abolished in the towns. There is no huge reserve of national income ready to give pensions and a free health service to all. Indeed, it is all too easy to condemn 'witch-doctors'. The alternative for many years is to have no doctors at all in many areas. Native doctors, as many observers testify, do give psychological reassurance, often of a most valuable kind. If their physical remedies are sometimes useless or dangerous, their herbalism is also often good. It may well be that the signs of willingness to sustain social security

[26] Busia, *Social Survey of Sekondi-Takoradi*, supra.

from within the community rather than through the State are both economically and morally immensely valuable—we ourselves often bitterly criticize our own impersonal provision for the sick and old.[27] The traditional African system might be capable of considerable persistence if it were fostered and aided at its weak points by the State. Certainly, some West Africans would wish to preserve it. Here is a statement by a young Ghanaian graduate :[28]

Examine the whole Akan people and it will be found that the unfortunate children and the aged are properly cared for by their families. And if this is what our American brothers describe as an impediment to our economic progress and the spread of laziness among the people, all I shall say is that while both our countries face the same problems . . . we differ in our approach. While the Americans are solving their problems through more or less centralized institutions, we are doing so by our decentralized institutions, that is, families.

Although the author is over-optimistic as to the care of families in towns, his analysis and the evaluation are significant.

Certainly, there are difficulties here in the growth of both personal and economic individualism. The way of life of the African lawyer, doctor, civil servant, university professor is to some degree necessarily modelled on his Western counterpart. He does work requiring concentration and some privacy, maintains a social standard which is costly, may be married to an educated woman, is probably Christian or Muslim in belief. Yet he is still socially and emotionally tied to the older pattern; his house may be constantly used by poor relatives, and certainly his purse will contribute heavily to them :

As society develops towards functional complexity and differentiation, we may expect the emergence of several cultural levels; in short, the culture of the class or group will present itself.[29]

The growth of an African wealthy class, with larger modern houses, expensive furniture and cars, is of course already happen-

[27] An African visitor to a splendid orphanage in England is said to have observed, to the consternation of his guide. 'We should be ashamed to allow strangers to care for our children in my country.'
[28] K. A. Akwawuah, *Prelude to Ghana's Industrialisation* (London, Mitre Press, 1959).
[29] T. S. Eliot, *Notes Towards a Definition of Culture* (London, Faber and Faber, 1948).

ing; and there is a professional middle class, whose demand for privacy is especially important, and whose salaries are not big enough for heavy subventions to a large family. But, while there is certainly a strain on this group, there is no reason to assume that 'class' will take on the exclusiveness which it has in some parts of the West. The continuing link between rich and poor, town and country, through the family and tribal systems, is a major social asset, and many African societies may contrive to retain it. Nor is economic individualism bound to develop on a general scale, despite the group of traders and contractors which is springing up; a more co-operative, socialist and managerial pattern, towards which some countries are moving, might keep the private enterprise sector to limited proportions.

Social analysis, particularly when dignified with the name of social science, is always tempted to a determinist view of human affairs, since its business is to detect 'laws', or at least regularities, in social development. It is constantly necessary to remember that no such iron laws exist—only human choices springing from values and beliefs. There is no intrinsic necessity for African societies to follow our own route of development, or for the family system to disintegrate, though there are certainly pressures upon it and signs of weakening. The answer to the future must lie in the nature and strength of the system of beliefs and values. Very large sections of African populations have adopted Christian or Muslim beliefs. But the depth of this conversion, on a large scale, is hard to measure. In both religious groups outward conformity is common and means little; the crowds for Sunday Services at the Cathedrals in Kampala are less impressive as a token of deep belief when compared with some of the standards of private domestic life.[30] The simultaneous belief in magic, the ancestor cult, and one of the higher religions has already been noted in Chapter V. Clearly the danger in this eclecticism is that no single standard is applied when there is any conflict between immediate satisfactions and principle. The fundamental discipline of character upon which a social system should rest demands something far more strict. Christian missionaries in Africa have been

[30] See the semi-autobiographical book, *Drawn in Colour* by Noni Jabavu, for a somewhat acrid comment, by an educated South African woman, on domestic *mores* of some educated Baganda: a book which, even if over-coloured, would not have been written if some cause for it had not been there (London, John Murray, 1960).

apt to concentrate their attack on polygamy, and on ancestor worship (often mistaken for a form of idolatry). But even the polygamous system, and certainly the ancestor cult, had their own disciplines in their own context. The attack upon them is in danger of discrediting the disciplines without substituting a real understanding of the self-imposed disciplines upon which Christianity rests. It is probably significant that Islam, with its clear rules, and the Roman Catholic Church, again with a more emphatic discipline, are both outstripping the Protestants in Africa. Perhaps both will have to be stricter in discipline and essentials, and far more flexible in cultural forms (the rules of marriage included) if they are to grip and hold the mind of Africa. At present it is as much the ethical as the economic element in cultural change which is disruptive in the modern life of the towns. It is by no means impossible that this ethical vacuum will corrupt and degrade the social temper to a point which endangers both political and economic progress. A determined reassertion of traditional values, and a conscious effort to shape both economic and social institutions in ways which would still enable them to work would certainly be preferable to the drift which is now taking place. It is by no means impossible that such a traditionalist movement could be combined with the essentials of Christian belief.[31]

4. POLITICAL LIFE—AUTHORITY

It seems to me to be the worst kind of self-deception to believe that any group can continue a practical and progressive life unless authority in fact resides somewhere and is, wherever it rests, effectively discharged.[32]

Both in the social and the political field this statement by Sir Philip Morris is very relevant to Africa today. Under European influence, there has been a constant move to place authority in a system of election by universal suffrage, both centrally and locally; how far this will prove an effective substitute for older systems of authority remains to be seen. There are considerable differences in the traditional cultures of Africa in the placing of

[31] Mair, op. cit. 'Would it not be possible to disentangle the essential principles [of Christianity] from the application or misapplication of them which European society represents, and to inculcate those principles in a way which would confirm and strengthen rather than disrupt the structure of native life?'

[32] Sir Philip Morris, 'Summing-up' to the Duke of Edinburgh's Conference, Oxford, 1956. Report, vol. I, supra.

authority; it may be in an extension of the kinship system, or in a more hierarchical and directly political structure descending from a king; it is usually directly or indirectly linked with the cult of ancestors. In his study of Bunyoro (Uganda) John Beattie [33] has described how pervasive were the ideas of subordination and superordination in social as well as political life :

> It is remarkable that in Bunyoro this idea of 'ruling' is not restricted to the political sphere . . . ; it pervades the whole field of social relations. Almost all institutionalized social relationships have an inegalitarian, hierarchical aspect; the notion that people occupy different categories, and that these are always unequal, is ubiquitous . . . Such a state of affairs is consistent with the centralized 'feudal' structure of Bunyoro, in which all authority right down to the base of the pyramid, is thought of as being at least ideally derived from and validated by the Mukama [King].

Other African societies have a very different form, so that in some it has been at first difficult even to see where authority lay. But closer knowledge has always revealed its existence, and usually in a form which, in one way or another, is ultimately sanctioned by religion—perhaps it would be better to say by beliefs concerning the guardianship of the group's well-being. While in many societies there was a democratic element, in which chiefs could be removed by popular will expressed in various ways, most societies distinguished perfectly clearly between the man and the post. This has often been openly expressed in the hierarchical societies ('A Chief is like the sun, a sacred thing to illumine'; 'God created a King amongst the people and He gave him power to govern his people by the laws He made');[34] in societies where authority is more dispersed, and particular groups, such as age-sets, have particular functions and privileges, ultimate authority is more likely to reside in the religious system.

It has already been remarked that both missionary and administrative policies have weakened these concepts of authority. Although the Nyoro reverence the Mukama and the system embodied by him today, they also recognize that in fact he has been made subject to the real power, the European government. In many ways, as Beattie says, they regret this. They say that the Europeans have 'spoiled' the country and that the effect of the

[33] John Beattie, *Bunyoro: An African Kingdom* (New York, Holt, Rinehart and Winston, 1960).   [34] Westerman, op. cit.

changes 'has been to lower the standards of morals and social behaviour which prevailed in pre-European times'. Although the older generation in all countries in the world, and in all ages, are apt to deplore the decadence of the times, it is important that change in Bunyoro is not simply felt in the area of political authority—'there is scarcely any aspect of Nyoro social life in which the traditional and the contemporary values are not to some extent at odds with one another'. Strangely enough, policy in the very last years of European rule has probably slightly reinvigorated the old system in many areas. By establishing fairly authoritative local councils, with considerable administrative and financial powers, on a geographical basis which has naturally corresponded to traditional societies, some new power and life has flowed back into tribal groups (even if it has a different formal basis) and a revival rather than a weakening of tribalist feelings develops.

It is extremely doubtful whether universal suffrage will prove a satisfactory substitute for the real authority of the older system. At the national level, which did not exist before, all may be well. Studies of elections in Africa show that at least the mechanics have been remarkably well understood and conducted, often with great enthusiasm.[35] How far the real meaning and purpose of this kind of democracy is understood is a great deal more doubtful. Certainly twenty years ago most Europeans would have been highly sceptical of the wisdom or appropriateness of introducing our own system so rapidly. Dr. Mair,[36] writing in 1934, puts the fundamental issue very well :

Conferred from above on a populace which is not aware of any desire to manage its own affairs [democracy] can never be anything but a mechanical system, to be manipulated by a few individuals for their own ends, while the majority remain indifferent to its proceedings. To offer it, as a means of causing the government to satisfy their wishes, to people who cannot hope to understand the complicated hazards upon which the achievement of that result depends, is only to lead them to disappointment.

After greater experience of universal suffrage in West Africa,

[35] See W. I. Mackenzie and Kenneth E. Robinson, *Five Elections in Africa* (Oxford, at the Clarendon Press, 1960). The enthusiasm of the Ibo at elections, and the overcrowding of polling-booths in hot weather led to a new name for the democratic process—'Universal Suffering' (cf. C. St. J. Woods in *Myth in Modern Africa* (Lusaka, Rhodes-Livingstone Institute, 1960).

[36] Mair, op. cit.

criticism is somewhat modified. Neither European nor American electorates understand all that Dr. Mair would wish, and Africans certainly cannot be expected to do better. With the present levels of illiteracy and lack of modern political experience, they have perhaps done well.

But the real issue is at the more local level, right down to the village. Not only is a conflict between two parties extremely embarrassing, since it may cause painful splits within the kinship system; the persons or council elected are not really clothed with an authority which is felt and meaningful, and no religious or mystical sanction attaches to it. Universal suffrage is a great leveller; by itself, it could only produce a society without structure. This difficulty is overcome in Western societies by the multitude of institutions of the community which have survived from earlier times, and which operate outside the political process of the polling booth. In Africa this differentiation is equally necessary, and may take place in one of two ways. There may be new institutions, of 'modern' type, which will gradually acquire prestige; or the older institutions may find a new vigour alongside, if not in competition with, the new elected bodies. In Northern Nigeria today there is a strange state of co-existence of the prestige and authority of the Emirs and the modern system of local elected authority. In Tanganyika, the Chagga have carried out a peaceful revolution in the Chagga Council by substituting an elected President for a hereditary Paramount Chief. Detailed studies in different types of society in Africa would be needed to establish how far the older authority continues to exert influence, however unofficially, alongside the new.

It is, of course, characteristic of the invasion of industrialized culture that new tasks and responsibilities are introduced into society and that new kinds of people are found to accept them. This creation of a new source of leadership is a valuable sign of growth. But it is not necessary to insist that it should supplant the older authority at breakneck speed. It was only slowly that the new industrial leaders in Britain were accepted into the ruling group, over a period of a hundred years.[37] Meanwhile, perhaps

[37] Sir Ivor Jennings has pointed out that as late as 1865 the landed gentry and ex-Army or Naval officers in England made up 55 per cent of the Conservative Party and 32 per cent of the Liberal Party, although the new industrial middle class had been given the vote in 1832 (Duke of Edinburgh's Conference, Report, vol. II, supra).

more account could be taken of older systems, which could play a valuable part in the differentiation of groups in society despite the uniformity of the suffrage. The Ghana recipe of immediate and resolutely imposed national unity is a severe one which will carry its own troubles later on.

There is, after all, a quite extraordinary richness and variety of political forms in traditional Africa. These manifold systems, ranging from autocracy to near-anarchy, have been a happy hunting ground for scholars but an embarrassment both to colonial administrators and to the new nation-builders. For this reason, they are at present undervalued. Yet they present a range of choice of political forms, often still in full vitality, which would be hard to find elsewhere in the world. Almost all of them incorporate some mechanism for combining order with freedom, some workable plan for embodying a human need in a social system. Some at least of these systems, if only in a single aspect, could surely provide to African leaders a valuable alternative in their search for the best channels for evolutionary change. Moreover, the cost of attempting a general *Gleichgeshaltung* would be high. There are real anxieties in Kenya over the relations between the Kikuyu, the Kalenjin group, the Luo and the Masai; in Eastern Nigeria some of the smaller groups feel stifled by the Ibo; there is a strong wish to reaffirm identity among some groups in the 'Middle Belt' of North Nigeria; there is a strain between Benin and the main Yoruba majority; the Lozi Kingdom in Northern Rhodesia will not easily be contented to be submerged in a single adult-suffrage nationalism; and so on. While these strains are usually referred to as 'tribalism', and deplored, they also reflect the conscious sense of their own system of authority in particular groups, and a certain resistance to the bureaucratic or party authority emanating from central government. To have two Chambers where some of these strains can be expressed; to have a system of local government which can leave room for traditional authority to continue; to allow a certain cultural differentiation might seem both desirable and even prudent. It may be that this will only be possible after a period of centralization, at least in some fields, such as the economic, which establishes the image of the nation and of central power more firmly; but it will not contribute to stability in African societies if this policy attempts to destroy local loyalties rather than add a new dimension to them.

Certainly those who have dealings with Africa from abroad would be prudent to take full account of both the strength and the value of local entities and not to rely wholly on establishing overriding contacts with the central government.

5. CONCLUSION

In the present scene of change which I have tried to describe, it is easy to forget how long a road has been travelled. The new nations today stand on very different ground from the tribal societies which Lander or Livingstone or Burton found only a century ago. There is much to count for the good—freedom from superstitious fear, not yet won but growing as the higher elements of religion spread more widely; abolition of the grosser forms of cruelty—the slave crucified round a cask, the witch wrapped in banana leaves and set on fire. There is a common currency of language and education over huge areas, valid to bring Africans into the conversation of the outer world; national boundaries often wide enough to give the richness and variety of culture which only the larger human groups can achieve today; a legal system able to sustain a contractual society; great economic growth. Finally, there is a set of exciting and dangerous ideas in politics and personal life, tilted perhaps more towards liberty than order, more towards material than spiritual gain, but capable of inspiring energy and hope. This is a record which other and earlier civilizations have taken centuries to achieve; it is no small justification of the original 'Civilizing Mission'.

It is in this last realm of ideas and values that the present choices lie. Three moving forces in particular are powerfully at work throughout Africa—the idea of the free and responsible individual personality; the idea of democratic authority; the idea of economic competitiveness. Matched with them are the institutions which have, in part, expressed them in the West—the nuclear family, universal education, the ballot box, the individual ownership of land and property, the industrial corporation. It must give us pause to think how shattering has been the impact of these ideas upon the three most vital elements of a culture—on Religion, on the Family and on Authority.

T. S. Eliot [38] has perhaps analysed most clearly in our genera-

[38] Eliot, op. cit.

tion the fundamental ways in which a culture rests in the last resort on a religious basis. His conclusions are quite simple :

... any religion, while it lasts, and on its own level, gives an apparent meaning to life, provides the framework of a culture, and protects the mass of humanity from ... despair.

and

I do not believe that the culture of Europe could survive the complete disappearance of the Christian faith and I am convinced of this not merely because I am a Christian myself but as a student of social biology. If Christianity goes, the whole of our culture goes.

Whatever good things have been brought to Africa, certainly the religions which sustained pre-European African culture have been gravely shaken.

If we turn to the concept of authority, the destructive process has gone perhaps even further. Hans Zehrer [39] has given the most detailed and powerful description of the levelling process which has happened to Europe (and with which Europe has infected Africa) in the destruction of the authority of religion, of noble birth, of wealth, of the father, of learning. He notes the assumed security in which the work of destruction is done :

One thing becomes clear : liberty, which destroys authority and levels out the hierarchy, is only made possible and given some security by the old authority. What has been destroyed still exists in the consciousness of those carrying out the destruction. While they are destroying the pillars of the old cupola, they fancy themselves to be still in the shelter of the edifice. The liberty here experienced is the liberty of transition. What is being destroyed itself still gives security to the work of destruction and those who are engaged in it. But when the Level has been reached and the consciousness of the destruction of the old hierarchy dawns, the transitional liberty also begins to weaken, and anxiety mounts.

And he notes one result :

Power becomes the sole visible and accepted value. The Level is the Cradle of Caesarism. In it are born Caesars, who suddenly raise themselves above the tumult of the market-place and offer the masses the spectacle of a brief, bitter struggle until one finally triumphs

[39] Hans Zehrer, *Man in this World* (London, Hodder and Stoughton, 1952).

and, as a blazing star, begins his lonely trajectory across the firmament.[40]

Simone Weil [41] puts the need for order and authority in no less absolute terms. Among the 'needs of the soul' which she lists, order is first.

The first of the soul's needs, the one which touches most nearly its eternal destiny, is order; that is to say, a texture of social relationships such that no one is compelled to violate imperative obligations in order to carry out other ones. It is only where this, in fact, occurs, that external circumstances have any power to inflict spiritual violence on the soul.

The second is hierarchism.

Hierarchism is a vital need of the human soul. It is composed of a certain veneration, a certain devotion towards superiors, considered not as individuals, nor in relation to the powers they exercise, but as symbols. What they symbolize is that realm situated high above all men and whose expression in this world is made up of the obligations owned by each man to his fellow-men. A veritable hierarchy presupposes a consciousness on the part of the superiors of this symbolic function and a realization that it forms the only legitimate object of devotion among their subordinates. The effect of true hierarchism is to bring each one to fit himself morally into the place he occupies.

It will not be difficult to see in the first of these two quotations some of the tensions in African life today and in the second a description, which might have been written by an anthropologist rather than by a French doctor of theology, of the essence of authority as it was seen by perhaps the majority of African tribes.

The attack on the family system is equally radical. Mr. Eliot is again quite decisive.

By far the most important channel of transfusion of culture remains the family; and when family life fails to play its part, we must expect our culture to deteriorate ... In the present age it means little

---

[40] It has been pointed out that the grant of universal suffrage to an inexperienced population was almost bound to result in the emergence of 'Caesars' in search of personal power. As Nicolas Berdyaev pointed out in *Slavery and Freedom* (London, Bles, 1944), it was the temptation of power over the kingdoms of this world which Jesus rejected in the wilderness; and it is the temptation of power now which reduces so much humanity to serfdom.

[41] Weil, *The Need for Roots*, supra.

more than its living members but . . . I have in mind a bond which
embraces a longer period of time than this : a piety towards the dead,
however obscure, and a solicitude for the unborn, however remote.[42]

Against an attack at three such vital points it is indeed doubtful
how far the African tradition can find strength to survive. If the
incoming culture were wholly satisfactory, there might be little
reason for concern. But in fact there is the gravest disquiet in
Europe (and increasingly in America) at some of the characteristics of our system. No one denies the freedoms and emancipation
which it makes possible; no one would wish the conquest of superstition, of tyrannical privilege, and of nature to be undone. But
the freedom and emancipation carry power and temptations and
responsibilities. Few would question that the temptations of
materialism have at least temporarily and in some respects proved
too strong; that the explosive breaking of the family has left a
vacuum; that the attack on superstition has overshot the mark
and gravely injured the spiritual quality of our life. D. H. Lawrence, passionate, naïve and direct, put one question into the
simplest language :

> The wages of work is cash.
> The wages of cash is want more cash.
> The wages of want more cash is vicious competition.
> The wages of vicious competition is—the world we live in.
> The work-cash-want circle is the viciousest circle
> That ever turned men into fiends.[43]

A good deal has been said in this book of the uneconomic
policies of paternalism in Africa, and some were unquestionably
overdone. But underneath there was, I believe, a conscious or
instinctive revulsion by European administrators against the cor-
ruptions lurking in our own system; a realization of certain values
—manliness, dignity, courage, hospitality, piety, reverence—so
often found among people in hard and simple circumstances, in
the desert or the mountains. These virtues are too quickly lost as
easier circumstances, commerce, greed, the relaxation of moral
standards and the loss of religious awe come flooding in with the
cash economy, science and Western ways. There was much that

[42] T. S. Eliot, op. cit. Again the last phrase could easily be taken as a
description of African culture.
[43] D. H. Lawrence, *Pansies* (London, Martin Secker, 1929).

the District Commissioner admired and valued in the cultures which he knew he was destroying.

Europe has immense spiritual resources to fight back against her own diseases once they are recognized—the whole tradition of humane and religious culture from Plato to the present day and a tradition not merely learnt but in many ways built into the formation of personality. But Africa, even though converted to Christianity or Islam, lacks the real depth of this support. The books are there to be read, and the Missions are there to teach; but more than that is needed to make a tradition into a living force. The danger Africa faces is that of complete uprootedness :

Uprootedness is by far the most dangerous malady to which human societies are exposed, for it is a self-propagating one. For people who are really uprooted there remain only two possible sorts of behaviour; either to fall into a spiritual lethargy resembling death, like the majority of the slaves in the days of the Roman Empire; or to hurl themselves into some form of activity necessarily designed to uproot, often by the most violent methods, those who are not yet uprooted, or only partly so.[44]

Thoughtful Africans are aware of these dangers. The whole movement associated with *Négritude, Présence Africaine,* 'the African personality', is a gesture of alarm and protest. M. Senghor has led this attack; M. Sékou Touré has denounced the West for destroying a human culture whose values it did not understand.[45] Père Lebret has sought to give a quality to economic planning which will not recapitulate the 'desperate style of life of the affluent societies'.[46] This is not simply a sentimental nostalgia; as M. Senghor has said, 'it is not a question of resuscitating the past or trying to live *dans le musée Négro-Africain,* but of animating the world of today with the values of the African past'.[47] But there is, none the less, a lack of precision and definition in this ideal, and it is as yet only a movement among a small group of intellectual leaders. Most of the new societies of Africa seem to be

[44] Weil, *The Need for Roots,* supra.
[45] See Chapter I.
[46] Père Lebret, *Développement et Civilisations,* no. 1, March, 1960. 'Mais une fois le nécessaire acquis leur style de vie peut être en définitive plus valable et humain que le style de vie acharné des populations dispendieuses.' He sees the direction of progress as 'la série de passages . . . d'une phase moins humaine à une phase plus humaine'.
[47] L. Senghor, at the 2nd Conference of *Présence Africaine* (translated).

rushing blindfold and eagerly into the very temptations we now deplore.

In fact, both the values and the dangers of the modern world have to be faced. This was put in a series of paradoxes by Sir John Maud at the Duke of Edinburgh's Conference in Oxford :[48]

Industrialization brings us more freedom and more slavery. It brings us more fellowship and more loneliness. It brings us more security and it increases our precariousness. It makes possible a higher level of civilization and it also barbarizes our life as individuals and as societies.

His development of these paradoxes, too long to quote here, brilliantly illustrates this theme. It is an old truth that the higher man climbs in the development of his powers, the deeper the fall he risks. The issue, therefore, is whether African societies can accept what is of value and reject at least some of the temptations; and here particularly the danger is in accepting institutions from Europe wholesale. M. Senghor is aware of this :[49]

Certainly parliamentary democracy and socialism have their virtues—and Trade Unionism, co-operation, the police, compulsory secular education. The problem is not to stop them at the customs barrier. It is to analyse their form and their spirit.

This is a key issue. If the prophets of *Négritude* are accused of vagueness, it is just here that the accusation sticks. It is indeed remarkable that Père Lebret is in Africa, not as a philosopher, but as a practical planner. For it is easier to talk of humanism than to settle down to the hard thinking needed to design, in the concrete, real institutions (factory systems, social security, organs of government) which will give the practical opening for a new style of human relationships. If Africa accepts not only the motives but the institutional forms of the affluent society, she will inevitably accept also the values and style of life, however loudly the intellectuals may complain. As the traveller moves through Africa and sees European-type housing policies, European-model Trade Unions, European-model factories, Probation Officers, Old People's Homes, the scream of commercial advertisement in Press and television, the almost mechanical adoption of suffrage as a

[48] Sir John Maud, 'The Impact of Industrialisation', Duke of Edinburgh's Conference, Report, vol. 1, supra.

[49] L. Senghor, ibid.

substitute for authority, it is indeed hard to believe that the same mixture of good but also of deadly genes is not being introduced into the heredity of African cultures.

Yet the possibility of choice is surely not barred. It is impossible for Africans to master the whole weight of the historical culture of Europe; it is too large for us to handle ourselves; even the well-educated European today is well aware of the width of his ignorance and of the impossibility of knowing all his inheritance. But Africans can learn from our mistakes. Our destination was not known in 1800; it is only now that we can begin to see how each step, natural in its day, led us on from decision to decision, from expedient to expedient, to the strengths and the weaknesses we now show. But now the outcome is here, plain to see, and the lessons can be learned by those who are only starting on this journey.

Moreover, if we go back some centuries, our own culture was built eclectically. For when Europe, after the Dark Ages, came back towards the light, it was with threads of many different colours that the tapestry of modern Europe was woven. A picture by Hieronymus Bosch [50] can show German peasants peering into a medieval thatched hut, in an Italian landscape, illustrating a Virgin Birth in an imagined Palestine, with both Roman and Greek mythology and symbolism. Africa may well find her own economic, social, political and spiritual traditions interwoven with elements from Russia, from China, from Christianity and Islam, and from spiritual perceptions drawn from the deepest levels of African religion. Certainly, it is not likely that the form which Western institutions happen to have at present would best suit Africa. Professor Moore [51] has remarked that our type of factory organization might well need modification for African conditions; Japan in the nineteenth century adopted consciously a different pattern to suit the family structure of her own culture.

And indeed our own pattern may now be overdue for change. Many writers [52] have commented on our failure to analyse the basic assumptions of rights and duties on which our present systems of industrial relations rest. As the analysis proceeds, and as

[50] I am thinking of the Nativity attributed to Bosch in Petworth House, Sussex.
[51] See Chapter XI.
[52] There is a long line of criticism from Mary Parker Follett to Peter Drucker and others. Dr. V. H. Allen has recently renewed the attack in Britain (*The Listener*, July 1961).

the changes in the real structure of industry which have already happened are more fully recognized, there is bound to be change : indeed, it is already happening. Equally in domestic life we may well begin to reverse the movement towards the nuclear family in favour of a larger companionship in which at least three generations play their part. It will be a different family from that of the last century, before the element of domestic tyranny was broken; personality must be freed before it can reassume obligations freely. In moving towards a more socialized industry and a less atomized domestic life, we should be coming nearer to a pattern which it is natural for Africans to choose. There may be no reason for them to overshoot the mark as we did, in the conditions of the next half-century, in which they may not be called upon to carry the burden of invention and enterprise which shaped the Western world.

In setting their course, in the half-conscious choices by which a nation moves, African societies have three cultures to draw upon —the Western, the Communist and their own. In their own lies certainly one treasure which could easily be lost in the haste of progress—the spontaneous relish of life itself, of leisure, human contact, the will relaxed and the senses and spirit open to receive and give. It was this which made Simone Weil [53] ask 'whether even the black man, although the most primitive of all colonized people, had not after all more to teach us than to learn from us'. It is a quality which neither Communism nor the West can supply; its chance of survival is perhaps greatest if some at least of African institutions, even in new forms, live through into the new era.

Outside their own traditions, probably Russia and China at the present time offer the most enticing model for Africans to follow. Their political attractions have been noted. Their modernity is vouched for by Russian triumphs in space-flight. Their uninhibited pursuit of science, so highly valued in Africa, may well seem more attractive than humanist hesitations from Western philosophers; their ideal of the common good more moral than conspicuous consumption. The new African societies, nationalist, socialist, untrammelled by nostalgia for their past, unimpressed (as are our own young generation) by the dire warnings with which the old cultures admonish the young, are likely to find more

[53] Weil, op. cit.

congenial company among the revolutionaries and the adventurers, with the energetic rather than with the wise.

The West, which could still give so much, may for a time seem less attractive, partly because our offering is less self-confident. Indeed, the greatest contribution which Europe can make to Africa today is to regain the nerve to face and conquer her own spiritual doubts. At times, when courage is low, there are moments of nightmare for the intellectual leadership of the West—the nightmare of a human civilization crumbling and stifled under the weight of its own material success, while only the icy mountain of science thrusts up through it towards space. But in the light of day, among the great mass of people who have worked hard for their new opportunities, when the first appetite for consumption is sated, there may well spring up new energies and a response to fresh leadership, if it can be found. The task in Europe is to include the knowledge and freedoms which science gives within a faith and a humanism which is not nostalgic or superstitious, but both fully modern and fully sovereign;[54] to emerge, not merely from materialism, but from a more dangerous agnostic despair (however courageous it may seem) into a philosophy more worthy of her history and achievements. The Europe which sent Livingstone, Cardinal de Vigerie, Sir Harry Johnston, Lugard, Goldie or Mary Kingsley to Africa was sure of its faith, though limited in its knowledge. All the sciences, of nature and of man, which have given us so much deeper an understanding and sympathy for Africa, have also undermined, though temporarily, our own confidence and power of action, until we are in danger of falling under Yeats' gloomy judgement :

> The best lack all conviction; while the worst
> Are full of passionate intensity.

—a judgement which also carries a warning to Africa. Because a new vision is not yet achieved—it would be an achievement far greater than the Russian—Europeans who have their business in Africa should walk there with an open mind, in sympathy with societies which face unsolved problems which are also our own.

By any standards, if much has been gained in Africa, much too has been already lost. The great herds of game have been

---

[54] Such a task is that attempted by Pierre Teilhard de Chardin in *The Phenomenon of Man* (London, Collins, 1959).

uselessly slaughtered; the deep forests ignorantly felled; the dignity of family life gravely injured; reverence for authority and the sense of the numinous behind the sensual world drowned by the clamour of elections and mechanical advance; the violent tone of modern politics has spread; 'passion, prejudice, the catchword and the slogan' have a strong grip. If Nkrumah has helped to win for Africa her political kingdom, a Gandhi is still awaited to point to a spiritual one. But much is left and could be nourished among peoples still so open-hearted, still deeply rooted in the land and in the sanity which it has always offered to those who live close to it. In the immediate future, the prospect is of energy and even violence, a still faster assimilation of Western techniques and Western ways. It will take time, and perhaps revolutions, for the bulk of African people to realize that Independence does not of itself bring individual liberty within the State, and that the long battle to establish rights and disciplines and obligations has still to be fought, against Caesarism in the State and materialism in the heart. No one can foresee the religious or political genius which may spring up from peoples so newly fired with opportunity; in past civilizations, vision has come often from the mountains and deserts and lonely places; wealth from the woods and river valleys; authority from those who have trained themselves to bear it. There is room enough in the great span of Tropical Africa and in the traditions of her many peoples to provide all three.

INDEX OF AUTHORS QUOTED

Achebe, C., *Things Fall Apart* (London, Heinemann, 1958), 31

Acquah, I., *Accra Survey* (London University Press, 1958), 85

Akwawuah, K. A., *Prelude to Ghana's Industrialization* (London, Mitre Press, 1959), 331

Albert, Ethel M., 'Socio-Political Organisation and Receptivity to Change', *South Western Journal of Anthropology*, vol. 16, no. 1, Spring 1960, 72

Allen, V. H., Article in *The Listener* (July 1961), 344

Ames, D. W., 'Wolof Co-operative Work Groups' *Continuity and Change in African Cultures,* ed. Bascom and Herskovitz (University of Chicago Press, 1959), 320

Apter, David, *The Gold Coast in Transition* (Princeton University Press, 1955), 39, 85, 329

——, 'The New Nations and the Scientific Revolution' reprinted, with permission, from the February 1961 *Bulletin of the Atomic Scientists,* 935 East 60th St., Chicago 37; copyright 1961, by the Educational Foundation for Nuclear Science, Inc., Chicago 37, 191, 267

Apter, D. E. and Rosberg, C. G., *The Political Economy of Contemporary Africa* (National Institute of Social and Behavioral Science, Symposia Studies Series No. 1, George Washington University, December 1959), 277

Ardener, E., Ardener, S. and Warmington, W. A., *Plantation and Village in the Cameroons* (London, Oxford University Press, 1960), 74, 113, 120, 197

Ardener, E., in *Social Change in Modern Africa,* ed. Aidan Southall, q.v., 118, 214

Awolowo, Obafemi, *Awo* (Cambridge University Press, 1960), 292

Balandier, G., *Sociologie des Brazzavilles Noires* (Paris, Armand Colin, 1955), 35, 324

Baldwin, K. D. S., *The Niger Agricultural Project* (Oxford, Blackwell, 1957), 104, 121

Banton, M., *West African City* (London, Oxford University Press for International African Institute, 1957), 34, 90

Bartlett, V., (ed.) *The Study of Society* (London, Kegan Paul, Trench and Trubner, 1939), 209

Bascom, W., *Yoruba Urbanism: A Summary* (Summary of a Communication to the Royal Anthropological Institute, June 1958, *Man*, no. 252, December 1958), 132

Bascom, W. and Herskovitz, M. J., *Continuity and Change in African Cultures* (University of Chicago Press, 1959), 88

Bauer, P., *West African Trade* (Cambridge University Press, 1954), 57, 132, 150, 151

——, *Economic Analysis and Policy in Underdeveloped Countries* (Cambridge University Press, 1958), 63

Beattie, John, *Bunyoro: An African Kingdom* (New York, Holt, Rinehart and Winston, 1960), 334

Belgian Administration (Plan Décennal). *Activités indépendantes de la cité indigène de Léopoldville* (1959), 149

Berdyaev, N., *Slavery and Freedom* (London, Bles, 1944), 340

Biesheuvel, S., *Race, Culture and Personality* (Johannesburg, South African Institute of Race Relations, 1959), 78, 323

——, *African Intelligence* (Johannesburg, South African Institute of Race Relations, 1943), 208, 323

Bonham-Carter, V., Article in *The Listener* (April 6, 1961), 25

Bovill, E. W. and Matheson, J. K., *East African Agriculture* (London, Oxford University Press, 1950), 120

Bovill, E. W., *The Golden Trade of the Moors* (London, Oxford University Press, 1958), 129

Brausch, G., *Belgian Administration in the Congo* (London, Oxford University Press for Institute of Race Relations, 1961), 282

Brown, C. V., 'The Supply of Bank Money in Nigeria', II, *The Bankers' Magazine*, December 1960, 137

Burdo, A., *Les arabes dans l'Afrique centrale* (Paris, 1885), 102

Busia, K. A., *The Impact of Industrialization on West Africa* (Nigerian Institute of Social Research Conference, 1960), 68, 71

——, *A Social Survey of Sekondi-Takoradi* (London, Crown Agents, 1950), 85, 214, 330

Cameron, V. L., *Across Africa* (London, Dalby, Isbister, 1877), 6

Caprasse, P., 'Leaders africains en milieu urbain' *CEPSI*, vol. 5, 1959, 42

Coleman, James, *Nigeria: Background to Nationalism* (University of California Press, 1958), 277

Coleridge, S. T., 'Table Talk' from *Select Poetry and Prose* (London, The Nonesuch Press, 1933), 306

Colonial Office, *Survey of Problems in the Mechanisation of Native Agriculture in Tropical African Colonies* (H.M.S.O., 1950), 94, 104

Colson, E., *The Social Organization of the Gwembe Tonga* (Kariba Studies, Manchester University Press for Rhodes-Livingstone Institute, 1960), 72

——, 'Migrant Labour in Africa : an Economist's Approach', *The American Economic Review*, vol. XLIX, no. 2, May 1939, 197

——, *An African Labour Force* (East African Studies No. 7, E.A.I.S.R., 1956), 204

——, *Migrants and Proletarians* (London, Oxford University Press, 1960), 204

E.N.I.S. Bulletin, Enugu, No. E2,200, 18 January 1961, 122

Epstein, A. L. and Mitchell, C., *Politics in an Urban African Community* (Manchester University Press for Rhodes-Livingstone Institute, 1958), 37

Fallers, Lloyd, *Bantu Bureaucracy* (Cambridge, Heffer for East African Institute of Social Research, 1955), 22, 84, 301–2, 303

Fearn, H., *An African Economy* (London, Oxford University Press for East African Institute of Social Research, 1961), 148

L'économie congolaise à la veille de l'indépendance (Brussels, Fédération des Entreprises Congolaises, April 1960), 54

Field, M. J., *Search for Security* (London, Faber and Faber, 1960), 74, 79, 136

Firth, Raymond, 'Work and Community in a Primitive Society', Report of The Duke of Edinburgh's Study Conference, 1956, Report, vol. II (London, Oxford University Press, 1957), 79

——, *Primitive Economics of the New Zealand Maori* (New York, Dutton, 1929), 80

——, *We, the Tikopia: a Sociological Study of Kinship in Primitive Polynesia* (London, Allen and Unwin, 1936), 195

Forde, Daryll, *Habitat, Economy and Society* (London, Methuen, 1934), 19

—— (ed.), *African Worlds* (London, Oxford University Press for International African Institute, 1934), 10, 13

Form, W. H. and Miller, D. C., *Industrial Sociology: an Introduction to the Sociology of Work Relations* (New York, Harper, 1951), 203

Fosbrooke, Henry, 'Tanganyika : the Application of Indirect Rule to Chiefless Societies', *From Tribal Rule to Modern Government* (Lusaka, Rhodes-Livingstone Institute, 1959), 299

Frankel, S. H., 'The Tyranny of Economic Paternalism in Africa,' *Optima* (Supplement) October 1960, 25

——, *The Economic Impact on Underdeveloped Societies* (Oxford, Blackwell, 1952), 25, 105

——, Article in *International Affairs*, October 1960, 61

Fraser Darling, F., *Wild Life in an African Territory* (London, Oxford University Press, 1960), 52, 107

Friedland, W. H., at Rhodes-Livingstone Institute Conference, 1960, 205

GENERAL INDEX

ABA, 156
Abeokuta, 149
Abercorn, 123
Abidjan, 29, 130, 135, 161, 177, 202, 244, 254, 261, 274, 297, 314: University of 307
Absenteeism, 119, 213, 215
Abubakar, Sir, 296
Aburi Press, Kumasi, 246
Accra, Survey of, 85, 214, 329: University of, 268
Achimota College, Ghana, 38–39, 233, 242
Action Group, W. Nigeria, 275, 284
Administrative officers, 247–51
Ado, 84
Adu Committee, 256
Adult Education College, Dar-es-Salaam, 156
Advisory Committee on Aids to African Businessmen, 143–4, 185
Afikpo Ibo people, 88
Africa Development Fund, 167
Africanization, in trade, 143–5, 147–8, 156, 157, 223, 226: in administration, 247–57, 279, 294, 301
African Loan Fund, 145–6
Mineworkers' Union, 217, 223
'personality', 221–3, 342–7
Trade Development Department, 148
Afrikaans, 130
Aga Khan Hospital, Nairobi, 156
'Agitators', 42–43, 278
Agrarian revolution, 98, 109, 116, 124–5, 169
Agricultural Development Corporations, 183
Institutes, 112, 251
Services, 91, 251, 257
Agriculture, development of, 42, 58, 96–100, 104, 106, 187; basis for industrial progress, 56, 59–60, 63–70, 162, 173, 191, 264; in Kenya, 104, 106, 164; loans for, 146–7;

employment in, 163; in Tanganyika, 165; in Uganda, 169; in Ghana, 173, 176–7; in Nigeria, 173–5, 265; in French-speaking areas, 175; technology and, 267 (*see* Husbandry)
Airports, 161, 326: aircraft purchased by Ghana, 176–7
Akan people, 286, 331: Akan Family Clan Societies, 90
Albert, Lake, 8
Algeria, 44–45, 282, 307
All-African Trade Union Federation, 219, 220
Alliance High School, Nairobi, 242
Aluminium, 52, 161, 162, 164, 173, 174, 175, 176, 181
Amboseli Game Park, 328
American Land Colleges, 264–5
Ancestor-cult, 12, 74, 82, 126, 332–4
Angola, 52, 94, 201
Animals, 11, 107, 165, 265: animal husbandry, 68, 93, 95, 97–98, 126
Animism, 35, 73–75
Ankole, Kingdom of, 276, 295
Anti-colonialism (-imperialism), 38, 45, 57, 182, 248, 287, 288, 291, 300, 311–12, 313
Apartheid, 15, 25, 230 (*see* Colour bar)
Apprenticeship, 134, 224, 225, 264
Arabs, 4, 8, 18, 26, 73, 112, 129, 131, 196, 204, 220, 280, 295, 313
Arboriculture, 93
Art, 15, 45
Arusha, 165
Ashanti, 52, 133, 291, 296: Ashanti Wars, 9: *Ashanti Pioneer*, 246
Ashby Commission, 1960, 253, 254–5, 257, 263
Asia, 239–41, 319
Asians, and E. African trade, 26, 131, 132, 134, 142–3, 144–5, 147–8, 149; and Legislative Councils, 40, 280; in Tanganyika, 113, 279, 297; and early African trade, 129;

Fort Lamy, 133
Fort Rosebery, 123
Foundation for Developing Countries, W. Germany, 180
Fourah Bay College, Sierra Leone, 38, 242
Fox, George, 246
Franchises, 40, 41, 44, 280
Freetown, 9, 34, 90, 131, 245, 274
Friendly Societies, 89–91
Front de Libération Nationale, Algeria, 307
Fulani (a) empire, 31, 77; (b) tribe, 286
Funerals, 87
Furniture works, 59, 62, 161

GABON, 177, 309
Game, 3, 14, 94, 98, 107–8, 328, 346–7; Parks, 107, 328; Services, 251
Ganda people, 32, 84, 169 (*see* Buganda)
Gandhi, M. K., 347
Garfield Todd, R. S., 57
Garlick, Peter, 137
Germany, 4, 312; East, 179–80, 312; West, 179–80; Germans, 8, 176
Gezira, 21, 28, 33, 106
Ghana, views on Europeans in, 32; effect of independence, 38; rising political leaders, 39, 275; revenue of, 51; minerals in, 52, 159, 162; development of, 53, 54, 99, 168, 173, 175–7, 180; population and labour in, 55; trade in, 62, 103; religion in, 74; marriage in, 82, 87; town-life in, 85; infant betrothal in, 86; scope for ambition in, 88, 227; agriculture in, 98, 103, 104, 113, 118, 222; doubling of occupations in, 100, 317; 'free' labour in, 111; Co-operatives in, 114–15; settlement schemes for, 121; small businesses in, 136, 140; supply of credit in, 139; commerce in, 141, 182–3; employment in, 163, 227; industry in, 182–3; anti-West 'neutralism' of, 189, 307, 311, 313–14, 315; migrant labour and, 201; Trade Unions in, 219–20; Africanization in, 226, 249, 254–5; European scale of pay in,

229; education in, 237, 239, 242, 245, 253, 259–60, 268; technical training in, 257–8; achievements of, 263, 306; independence and, 281; National Assembly of, 283–4; single party rule in, 288–93, 295, 296–7, 298, 337; State control in, 289; party and local administration, 302; and Togo, 308; Ghanaians, 253, 286, 290, 293, 310, 331
Ghana—Electricity Co., 226; *Evening News*, 310; Farmers' Union, 152; Guarantee Corporation, 146; —Guinea Union, 308
Ghanaian Times, 268, 310
Gold, 52, 119, 129, 165; -work, 129; mines, 176
Gold Coast, 9, 40, 59, 89, 260
Goldie, Sir G., 8
Government service, 34, 36, 157, 227, 242, 244, 261, 278 (*see* Civil Service)
Governor's Advisory Council, 39
Graduates, 172, 252–3, 255, 257, 258–9, 260, 263, 264, 283
Great Britain, 90, 243, 282
Greeks (a) ancient, 4, 13, 31, 266, 291, 342, 344; (b) modern, 130
Gross National Product, Nigeria, 174
Guinea, 39, 52, 62, 152, 180, 217, 220, 254, 288, 289, 293, 298, 306, 307, 308, 315 : Guinea Coast, 3, 7
Gwembe Tonga tribe, 72, 93

HALL, SIR JOHN, 50
Handicrafts, 11, 13, 29, 129, 133, 270, (*see* Crafts)
Harbison, Professor, 257
'Harvard Business Schools', 261
Hausa tribe, 111, 131, 286
Hayes, C., 283
Health, 20, 50, 67, 106, 112, 213, 307, 327, 330 (*see* Public health)
Hire-purchase, 138–9
Histadruth, Israeli, 185
Hodgson Technical College
Holland, 179–80
Hollander, E. D., 257
Holt and Co., John, 133, 134, 233
Houphouet-Boigny, M., 267, 275, 314
Houses of Assembly, Nigeria, 283–4, 286

Livingstone, Dr. David, 8, 9, 49, 338, 346
Livingstone, N. Rhodesia, 72, 77
Loans, 26, 122–3, 136–8, 143, 148 (*see* Credit)
Lobengula, King, 5
Lobola (bride-price), 197
Local Councils, 27, 40, 42, 110, 274, 299, 301, 302, 335
  Development Fund, 146
  Government, 37, 40, 46, 251, 303, 304, 305, 328; Services, 257, 302
Lokoja, 8, 9, 121, 162
London, 43, 137, 171, 172, 183, 273, 279: University of, 268
London and Kano Trading Co., 133
Lovanium University, Congo, 28, 307
Lozi tribe, 32, 94: Kingdom, 337
Luapula tribe, 97: Province, N. Rhodesia, 123
Lucca, Italy, 68
Lugard, Lord Frederick, 8, 32, 346
Luo tribe, 90, 286, 337
Lusaka, 242, 251, 278
Luvale tribe, 94, 97, 123

MACARTNEY MISSION (1793), 5
Mace, C. A., 208
Machakos country, Kenya, 52
Machinery, 59, 60, 61, 104–5, 122, 158
Mackenzie, Bishop, 8
Madagascar, 323
Maiduguri, 133
Maize, 119, 147, 170, 214
Makerere College, Uganda, 102, 108, 227, 233, 234, 242, 251, 317, 326
Malachite, 171
Malagasy, 62; Malagasies, 15
Mali, 45, 55, 175, 275, 284, 288, 293, 296, 298, 307, 308, 318: Federation 306
Malnutrition, 327
Mambwe tribe, 196, 197
Management, Africans and, 115, 144, 191–2, 223–6, 260, 261, 264, 332; European ideas on, 206, 211–12, 216, 222
Mannoni, O., 15, 43
Maramba Estate, 180
Maritain, Jacques, 73
Market Economy, 80
Marketing Boards, 26, 66, 125, 128, 150, 152–3, 166–8, 183, 248

Marriage, 78, 80, 82–83, 85–87, 91, 126, 197, 201, 266, 319, 327–8, 330, 333
Marsavac Co., 172
Marx, Karl, 268; Marxism, 182, 221, 266, 267, 288, 290, 292, 321
Masai tribe, 32, 49, 97, 126, 299, 328, 337
Maseno, 102
Mashona tribe, 32, 126
Mason, Philip, 112, 304
Matabele tribe, 5, 32
Materialism, 269–70, 338, 341, 346
Matrilinear society, 78, 82, 140, 197
Mattress factory, 174
Maude, Sir John, 343
Mau Mau rebellion 33, 115, 329
Mauritania, 254; Mauritanians, 144
Mauritius, 62
Maybury Committee (1955), 147
Mayo, Elton, 206
Mbeya, 165
Mboya, T., 164, 217, 218, 220
Mechanization, 65, 116, 237 (*see* Machinery)
Medical Services, 42, 167, 251–2, 327
Mekhadma, 33
Meru, 65
Messianic sects in Nyasaland, 33, 329
Metal windows factory, 161, 173, 174
Middle Belt, N. Nigeria, 276, 295, 337
Middle class, 34, 35, 83–84, 138, 154, 303, 324, 331–2
Middlemen in business, 26, 118, 147, 149–50, 151, 153–4
Migrant Labour, 24, 66–67, 90, 94, 95, 100, 101, 120, 123, 126, 163, 166, 194, 195–7, 199–204, 214, 321
Mitchell, Sir Philip, 9
Moffat, Sir John, 280, 282
Mokwa, 104–5, 120–1
Mombasa, 90, 161, 164
Monckton Report, 71, 308
Monogamy, 22, 82, 86–87
Monrovia, 161, 180
Morocco, 134, 220, 307
Moscow, 309
Mossi tribe, 198
Mount Kenya, 29
Mount Kilimanjaro, 29, 52, 106, 114, 165
Mozambique, 201

050017